India's Greatest Minds

Mukunda Rao is the author of several insightful philosophical and spiritual works, among which *The Biology of Enlightenment*, *The Buddha* and *Sky-clad: The Extraordinary Life and Times of Akka Mahadevi* are much-read classics. He lives with his wife on a farm outside Bengaluru.

India's Greatest Minds

Spiritual Masters, Philosophers, Reformers

MUKUNDA RAO

First published in 2022 by Hachette India
(Registered name: Hachette Book Publishing India Pvt. Ltd)
An Hachette UK company
www.hachetteindia.com

1

ISBN 978-93-89253-53-5

Hachette Book Publishing India Pvt. Ltd
4th & 5th Floors, Corporate Centre,
Plot No. 94, Sector 44, Gurugram 122003, India

Typeset in Dante MT Std 10.5/13.5
by R. Ajith Kumar, New Delhi

Printed and bound in India
by Manipal Technologies Limited, Manipal

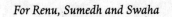

For Renu, Sumedh and Swaha

Contents

Introduction

THE STORY OF HUMAN EXISTENCE HAS NOT ONLY BEEN ONE OF TIRELESS struggle for survival, security and happiness, but also – and perhaps more importantly – one that has involved a relentless search for answers to existential and metaphysical questions such as, 'Who am I?' 'What is the purpose of my existence?' 'Is there life beyond death?' 'What is consciousness?' 'Does God exist?' 'How did life begin?' 'What is the Universe made of?' 'What is Time?' and so on.

Around 2500 years ago, when such philosophical enquiries were being seriously explored in different parts of the world, several schools of thought were already prevalent in the Indian subcontinent, tackling these very questions in varied ways.

A significant number of distinguished Western scholars, philosophers and scientists have quite rightly recognized the contribution of Indian thinkers in the fields of spirituality, philosophy and science. For instance, Mark Twain (1835–1910), the famous American writer, called India 'the cradle of the human race, the birthplace of human speech, mother of history, grandmother of legend, great-grandmother of tradition'. (Twain, 1897)

Max Müller (1823–1900), the German scholar who spent his life studying India and its religions, wrote, 'If I were asked under what sky the human mind has most fully developed some of its choicest gifts, has most deeply pondered over the greatest problems of life, and has found solutions of some of them which well deserve the attention even of those who have studied Plato and Kant, I should point to India.' (Müller, 1883). Henry David Thoreau (1817–62), American thinker and poet, was deeply moved by the wisdom of the Vedas: 'Whenever I have read any part of the Vedas, I have felt that some unearthly and unknown light illuminated me. In the great teaching of the Vedas, there is no touch of sectarianism. It is of all ages, climes and nationalities and is the royal road for the attainment of the Great Knowledge. When I am at it, I feel that I am under the spangled heavens of a summer night.' (Dhawan, 1985). And, Romain Rolland (1866–1944), famous French writer, had no doubt that 'If there is one place on the face of earth where all the dreams of living men have found a home from the very earliest days when man began the dream of existence, it is India.' (Susan Ratcliffe, 2017)

True enough, even before the Buddha came on the scene, the Indian mind was engaged in tackling the hard questions of life through various schools of philosophy, such as Sankhyas, Vaisheshikas, Naiyayikas, Ajivikas, Jainas and so on. During this pivotal period, several significant and far-reaching insights and concepts with regard to the human condition, the nature of reality, mind and experience, and soul or self were proposed. These included Sankhya's notions of prakriti and purusha, Kanada's atomic theory, Patanjali's idea of body as a field of energy, Upanishadic notions of atman and Brahman, Mahavira's principle of ahimsa, Buddha's notion of anatman (no soul) and Nirvana, and so on, which laid the groundwork for the development of Indian philosophy and numerous spiritual traditions and sects.

The richly plural bhakti movement, which spread across India from the seventh to fifteenth century, also had a crucial role in transforming the spiritual and social landscape of India forever. Schools of thought such as Shankara's Advaita, Ramanuja's Vishishtadvaita, Madhva's Dvaita, bhakti traditions such as Shaivism, Vaishnavism, Veerashaivism, among others, made an indelible mark on Indian consciousness and influenced its different spiritualities and societies.

Indian society had also long been riven by caste hierarchy and gender discrimination. Alongside ennobling and liberating spirituality existed the tyrannical and oppressive religious belief systems and practices. In other words, religion was used as the justification for some of the worst social evils, including casteism, untouchability, sati and the oppression of women.

This cruel side of religion went against the free spirit of the spiritual questers, and their faith in the oneness of life and equality of all humans before God. A new, revolutionary spirituality was born, with women and people from the lower castes as its torchbearers. Poet-saints like Akka Mahadevi and Meera Bai fought against the strictures placed on women by walking out of traditional families. Basavanna challenged Brahmanical authority and social order, and endeavoured to create a community of equals in quest of truth. Ravidas, who came from the downtrodden Chamar caste, rejected the authority of the Vedas and envisioned a casteless society, which he called Begumpura Shehr—*Be-gum-pura*, a land without sorrow. In Assam, the poet-saint and social reformer Sankardev rejected the caste system and the need for idol worship, and started a new faith called Ekasarana Dharma, literally, shelter-in-one-religion, that drew people from all castes, as well as tribals and Muslims, into its fold. In Odisha, Mahima Gosain and his follower Bhima Bhoi, who hailed from the Khond tribe, founded a new religion called Mahima Dharma by rejecting caste hierarchy and the need for idols, images, priests and temples, and practised equality between men and women.

The story of India, therefore, is not all about Brahmanical beliefs, debates and disputes about Sanskrit literature, the Upanishads and the Gita, or even the varnashrama dharma, the caste system. It is also the story of rebellion against the caste system, of varna-samkara (inter-mixing of caste), of revolts by Chamars and Mahars, Kurubas and Pulaiyas, Farsis and Ezhavas, of spiritual strivings that were non-Vedic in origin and character and outnumbered Vedic forms. It is the story of mystics like Kabir, Bulleh Shah and Sai Baba of Shirdi, who did not identify with any religion but attempted to bridge the divide between Hinduism and Islam; of Pandita Ramabai, who embraced

Christianity for its promise of equality and became a pioneer in education and emancipation of women in India; of Bede Griffiths and Raimundo Panikkar who synthesized Christian faith with Hindu philosophy to transcend the divide; of women such as Akka Mahadevi and Lalleshwari, who subverted male-controlled spiritual orders and walked beyond even male-female binaries. In short, it is a complex history of an uncompromising quest for truth, reconciliation and transcendence. It is a cry for freedom and an assertion of the dignity of every individual.

This book charts these complex and profound adventures by telling the stories of spiritual questers, sages, saints and thinker-activists who played a vital role in shaping Indian society. It must be noted that though 'India' is used in the title, the thinkers covered here come from all over the Indian subcontinent, including places in Nepal, Tibet, Pakistan and Bangladesh. After all, thinkers such as the Buddha, Guru Nanak, Meera Bai, all the way up to Mahatma Gandhi lived and travelled freely across the subcontinent.

Indeed, from the time of the Upanishadic seers to Buddha, to Basavanna, Kabir and Narayana Guru, an unbroken stream of spirituality has enriched Indian thought and culture. Over centuries, there have been continuous interactions, debates, dialogues, even borrowings among different schools of thought; so much so that one cannot pinpoint and assert any one idea as *the* Indian philosophy. Rather, Indian thought has to be understood in plural terms, and includes not only Hindu, Buddhist, Jain and Sikh but also Christian and Islamic ideas, since, for more than a thousand years now, India has been – however clichéd it may sound – the cradle of many tongues and religions, and of a bewildering variety of sects and religiosities, culture and art and music.

If at all we need to describe the philosophical and cultural heritage of India, we would describe it not so much as an idea but as a character epitomized by anveshan – the quest for truth. Metaphorically speaking, it has been something like the sangam: the confluence of many rivers that swell as thousands of tributaries flow into it from different directions, nurturing the land it passes through.

~

This book is not an exhaustive work on the makers of India. It is only a representative selection, majorly from the spiritual field, of those who were most influential in shaping Indian consciousness which, I reiterate, cannot be captured within a nationalistic, ideological framework. Some people may point out that I have ignored a few important figures. And I myself will admit that not just a few, but a hundred more could find a place here.

For instance, I have considered only Kapila, Kanada and Patanjali out of the six founders of the Hindu philosophical systems; I have included Tilak but not Gokhale, Kanaka Dasa but not Purandara Dasa, E.V. Ramasamy (the only atheist on the list) but none of the modern Shankaracharyas. I have limited my selection to those who have had a substantial influence on Indian consciousness, and who have left behind inspiring legacies and a compelling body of work.

One may ask why individuals such as Jyotirao Phule, Bal Gangadhar Tilak, Ram Manohar Lohia, E.V. Ramasamy and a few others, who were primarily political, have been included in a book that focuses on spiritual thinkers. These individuals feature here as they are thinker-activists who have shaped our social and cultural consciousness, by virtue of which they have become an integral part of the great Indian story. In a sense, they were the modern acharyas who inspired and provoked Indians to revisit the country's religious, cultural and social history with a critical eye, reject religious beliefs and social practices that were inhuman and retrogressive, and strive towards building a society based on compassion, social equality and freedom.

No work is perfect and so it is quite possible that there are overlooked errors and inadvertent omissions, but I sincerely hope that this book gives readers a real taste of Indian thought and acquaints them with the remarkable personalities who lived and travelled around the Indian subcontinent, singing their songs of life and playing a crucial role in the making of what we call India today.

It's incredible how books come to you, take possession of you and then in due course take their birth. This book was suggested to me by Rukmini Chawla Kumar, and I'm thankful to her for giving me the opportunity to work on a book of such great significance to our times. I must say though that, in a way, I am not really the author of the book; rather, I am only its editor, who has put together stories and ideas borrowed from several works on the great luminaries who dwell in these pages. I am immensely grateful and profoundly indebted to the authors of all these works. Without them a book of this magnitude and depth would have been impossible.

India's Greatest Minds

Kapila

(c. 600–700 BCE)

WHAT IS THE ORIGIN OF LIFE AND THE UNIVERSE? DOES GOD EXIST? *Why is there suffering? Can there be an end to suffering?*

Kapila tried to answer these perennial questions as early as 600 or 700 BCE in a way that was radically different from the thinkers of his time. He was asking these questions a century before the Buddha (563–483 BCE), perhaps even before some of the Vedic seers, although in the epics Mahabharata and Ramayana, and the Puranas – such as Bhagavata, Brahmanda, Vishnu – he has been referred to as a Vedic sage who derived his theories from the Vedas.

We also find his name mentioned in the Upanishads. The Bhagavad Gita lauds him as the foremost among siddhas or sages, as adividvan, the primordial sage, and paramarishi, the supreme seer. It is quite likely that his name was co-opted and used in various texts for different spiritual entities. Buddhist texts, however, present Kapila as a leading philosopher who hailed from a place named after him, Kapilavastu, or present-day Tilaurakot in Nepal, where the Buddha lived until the age of twenty-nine.

Kapila rejected theistic monism, a view that all is of one essential substance – God – that is both immanent and transcendent, that had been popular in earlier schools of thought. He held that they were inadequate when it came to explaining the complex nature of life and the constantly changing world. Instead, declaring his preference for atheistic realism, he endeavoured to provide a lucid and logical interpretation of human existence and the world. His philosophy exhibited the complete independence and power of the mind to reflect upon and arrive at a comprehensible understanding of life without the need to involve a god or supernatural forces.

Centuries later, Kapila's sutras, or aphorisms, came to be called Sankhya philosophy. It was one of the saddarshanas, or the six systems of ancient philosophy, the other five being Yoga, Vaisheshika, Nyaya, Mimamsa and Vedanta. Sankhya philosophy has had the profoundest influence on subsequent schools of thought in India, including Buddhism. The concepts of Purusa and Prakriti, along with Yoga, for instance, occur in almost all Indian philosophical literature, although the twin concepts were sometimes expanded to mean different things with varied consequences.

The word 'Sankhya' is supposed to have originally meant 'number', but it eventually came to mean 'reflection' or 'the way', since Kapila's thought system laid emphasis on jnana, or knowledge, as the only means to liberation. The Sankhya philosophy marked a major departure from the God-centred religious conviction by bringing in the ideas of evolution and involution in place of creation and destruction.

Sankhyasutra, also called *Kapila Sutra*, was first composed as *Sankhyakarika* by Isvarakrsna in the fourth century CE. A broad summary of the sutras follows.

Purusa and Prakriti

Prakriti is the primordial principle or entity out of which evolves the universe in its infinite diversity. Prakriti is made up of three gunas or substances, namely, sattva, rajas and tamas; these gunas manifest themselves as illumination and buoyancy, action or mobility, and restraint or inertia respectively. Prakriti in the quiescent form is in a state of dynamic equilibrium, called a state of samya. But when this equilibrium is disturbed, it enters a state of vaisamya, or instability, and triggers creation and the evolution of the world.

Kapila had no use for a god or even for the notion of 'nothingness'. According to him, it is not god but Prakriti that is the material cause of existence. But the material cause and effect are not distinct, as in the Nyaya-Vaisheshika philosophy, for instance; rather, effect is always there in a potential form in its cause. In other words, even before their manifestation, the world or the universe and all its life forms were existent in its material cause, that is, the threefold Prakriti.

However, it is Purusa that triggers the (spiritual) principle or intelligence that, in turn, powers Prakriti to unfold and grow and evolve in its varied forms.

The physical and psychological features of the world are the manifestation of Prakriti, the primordial substance. But Prakriti, in and by itself, is jada – it has no consciousness. The three gunas of which Prakriti is made are in a perfectly balanced state or in a dynamic equilibrium. When there is samyoga or effective contact between Purusa and Prakriti, the trigunas lose their state of balance and set in motion the creative process of evolution.

Now, as a result of the inner turmoil of the gunas mixing with one another, the first product, the mahat or buddhi, the cosmic intellect, emerges from Prakriti. Further, from the mahat comes ahamkara, the cosmic ego, the principle of individuation; from the sattvic substance of ahamkara emerge manas, or the cosmic mind, along with jnanendriyas, the five organs of perception, and karmendriyas, the five organs of action; from the tamasic substance emerge the five tanmatras or the subtle elements: sound, touch, colour, taste and smell. All these in turn evolve into mahabhutas, or the gross elements, such as akasa, ether; vayu, wind; tejas, fire; apah, water; and prithvi, earth. This bewildering complex creation and its myriad forms of evolution are maintained by the inexhaustible source of Prakriti.

Bondage and Liberation

In Sankhya philosophy, cause and effect are not two different things; rather, there is pre-existence of effect in cause itself. There is no such thing as total destruction or annihilation; there is only a never-ending process of evolution and involution, anirbhava and tirobhava. It has no beginning, but it does have an end, santa. For humans, liberation from the cycles of birth and death is possible. No idea of a god as the liberator is posited here.

Life brings with it suffering and bondage, caused by aviveka, or ignorance. One can be liberated from suffering through right knowledge, jnana or vivekakhyati. This right knowledge – enabled by the sattvic guna of Prakriti – is attained by following the eight steps of Yoga, when the individual comes to realize the pristine purity of Purusa.

There are two kinds of liberation: the first is jivanmukti, where liberation is attained even while living. This occurs when the prarabdha-karma, the accumulated karma – the force created by a person's actions in the past – is exhausted; such a person continues to live in the world, unattached, free from the grip of karma. The second is videhamukti, the final liberation or 'final aloofness' which occurs after death; here there is no return to the world of samsara, the cycles of birth and death. In other words, the psychophysical complex is restored back to its source, Prakriti, and the Purusa remains in its eternal status of freedom.

Pramanas or Sources of Knowledge

Unlike other systems of thought, Sankhya admits only three pramanas or valid sources of knowledge, namely, pratyaksha or direct perception, anumana or inference, and sabda or verbal testimony.

Pratyaksha is the direct cognition of an object or the world through the sense organs. That is, knowledge produced through senses is perception. And there are two kinds of perceptions: nirvikalpaka or indeterminate, and savikalpaka or determinate; nirvikalpaka is more of a general nature, but when you make a closer observation you see more clearly, which is savikalpaka.

Anumana or inference is the second source of knowledge. You see smoke first and infer that there must be fire somewhere.

Sabda or verbal testimony is not a separate pramana but dependent on the testimony of the Vedas, that is, acceptance of the Vedas as a valid source of knowledge.

~

The Sankhya system was nourished and propagated by Kapila's disciple Asuri, and then by Asuri's disciple Panchasika. Over the centuries, this philosophy, and especially its twin concepts of Purusa and Prakriti and the dualism inherent in them, was found to be problematic by several philosophers, especially those who believed that the universe is non-dual in nature. At the same time, these concepts were borrowed and reinterpreted by several Indian schools of thought and sects.

Buddhism adopted the threefold idea of suffering and end of suffering into its noble truths, although its teachings on how to achieve liberation or nirvana were quite different from those of Sankhya philosophy.

While some Hindu texts depicted Purusa as the primordial being, the concept of Prakriti was reinterpreted by the Vedantins, such as Shankara, as maya and made part of Brahman, the ultimate reality underlying all phenomena. Patanjali's *Yogasutra* accepted almost every concept of Sankhya thought and added the idea of God to it. These ideas eventually entered the Mahabharata and the Puranas, where the concepts took on theistic colours. The philosopher Isvarakrsna (c. 350–450 CE), who described himself as a disciple of Kapila, wrote an influential commentary, *Sankhyakarika*, wherein he retained Kapila's atheistic position, with focus on causes of suffering and freedom from suffering.

Interestingly, in Chinese cosmology, the twin concepts of yin and yang, which developed some three hundred years after Kapila's Sankhya, were represented as the organizing principles of the universe. Yin, signifying the feminine, dark, soft, earth, water and so on, and yang, representing the masculine, light, hard, mountain, heaven, active and so on, constitute the world. It is this idea of duality that lies at the origin of Chinese classical science and philosophy and medicine, too. Taoism and Confucianism, too, are based on the concept of dualism, albeit interpreted in different ways.

We do not know for sure if Kapila's philosophy influenced these doctrines. However, twin concepts such as Purusa–Prakriti, yin–yang, jiva–ajiva and jiva–isvara, embodying the idea of active and passive, motion and stillness, like the concept of male and female, were used by ancient thinkers to construct a philosophy of balance, where two opposites coexist in harmony and are able to transmute into each other.

Kanada
(c. 2nd–4th centuries)

THERE IS AN INTERESTING STORY ABOUT HOW KANADA DEVELOPED THE theory of the atom that he is known for. Once, while nibbling at his food, Kanada kept throwing away small particles until it reached a stage when he found he could not divide the food into further parts. Thus was formed the idea of matter that cannot be divided further. Kanada called these indivisible, indestructible particles of matter paramanu, or atom. He used the idea of the atom to describe and explain the creation and dissolution of the world. Through the notion of the atom combined with the concept of Atman, the self or the soul, he developed, like Kapila, a non-theistic idea of the means to liberation from suffering. His philosophy, called Vaisheshika Darshana, remains one of the most significant schools of thought in Indian philosophy.

Kanada is believed to have lived between 2nd-4th centuries, or sometime around 300 BCE. Some scholars are of the opinion that his treatise could be older than the Sankhya and Mimamsa schools of thought by a couple of centuries, although this claim is difficult to ascertain. However, the name Kanada and his Vaisheshika sutras are cited in many ancient texts, notably in the Mahabharata, the *Vayu Purana*, the *Padma Purana* and the Buddhist text *Lankavatara Sutra*.

It is said that Kanada got his name because of his propagation of the theory of atoms. Alternately, as one story goes, it was a nickname because he lived on the unclaimed, scattered 'kana', or small grains collected from fields after a harvest. Kanada was also known as 'Uluka', a name by which he is referred to in several texts, including the second century philosopher Nagarjuna's *Ratnavali*.

Kanada was seen as a nastika, an atheist, because his treatise made no mention of a god. His sutras, however, have several references to the Vedas and Vedic rituals and customs, and in them Kanada accepts the authority of the Vedas in his own way. However, later commentators, who were theists, presented Kanada as a believer in God.

Kanada's *Vaisheshika Darshana* is divided into ten adhyayas, or chapters, and consists of 374 sutras, aphorisms.

These chapters give an account of the padarthas, or categories that inhere in substances; examine the bhutas or physical substances, such as space, time and so on; deal with sarira, the physical body and its accessories, tad-upayogin, and Atman, soul, and manas or mind; discuss Vedic dharma, dana dharma and ashramadharma; consider qualities or gunas, and inherence, samavaya; and the last two chapters discuss the nature of cognition, and anumana, inference.

What comes through is a system of physics and metaphysics of life and the world. According to Kanada, the empirical world is real. The world, made of padarthas, exists independent of the perceiver.

The saptapadarthas, or seven categories, are dravya, substance; guna, quality; karma, action; samanya, generality; visesa, particularity; samavaya, relation of inherence; and abhava, non-existence.

Dravya or substance, which inheres both quality and action, are nine in number: earth, water, light, air, ether, space, time, soul and mind. The first four exist in the form of paramanu, indivisible and eternal in nature. Dravya is the material cause of the world.

Vaisheshika posits two kinds of souls: the jivatma and Paramatma; jivatmas are infinite in number, whereas there is only one Paramatma, the Supreme Soul. A jivatma may be in bondage or free; but when liberated, it becomes free from its specific gunas or qualities, such as happiness, misery and so on.

Unlike Sankhya, which holds that the effect is already present in its cause, and the production of effect is nothing but the appearance of what is already potential or hidden in the cause, like, for instance, a tree or plant in a seed, Vaisheshika believes that effect is produced by cause and cannot pre-exist. Rather, Kanada theorised that the effect is caused by adrsta-karita, by unknown agents.

Vaisheshika was a blend of science, philosophy and religion, and possibly the earliest known systematic realism in human history based on an atomic theory of matter. Applying logic and realism, Kanada came to the position that everything can be subdivided, but this subdivision cannot go on forever, and there ought to be smallest particles, atoms, that cannot be further divided. That is the paramanu, indivisible and eternal. This was a brilliant imaginative explanation of the physical structure of the world, which, in large measure, is in line with the discoveries of modern physics.

Kanada's atomic theory had a great influence on thought systems of Buddhists, Ajivikas, Jainas, Naiyayikas, and quite possibly on Charaka, who wrote the medical text *Charaka Samhita*. Centuries later, philosopher and scholar of Mimamsa school of thought, Kumarila Bhatta (730 CE), accepted five categories, namely, substance, quality, action, universal and negation, and added sound and darkness to the list of nine substances. Kumarila's disciple Prabhakara, philosopher and grammarian in the Mimamsa tradition, accepted the nine substances, but added number, similarity and potency to the list. Vedantins generally refuted Kanada's categorical separation of cause and effect as distinct and independent. It is said Kanada's categorisation of light as a substance could have influenced modern physicist C.V. Raman in his work on the material character of light.

Patanjali
(born c. 200 BCE)

ACCORDING TO AN ANCIENT STORY, PATANJALI IS 'ONE WHO FELL INTO cupped hands'. The tale goes that when a sage was offering sacred water and praying to Surya, the sun god, a baby fell from the heavens into his cupped hands. He gave the baby to a woman called Gonika, who was childless. In another version, it was Gonika, the daughter of a sage, who was praying to Surya for a child when a baby dropped from the sky into her cupped palms. In effect, the story indicates that Patanjali was a boon given by the divine to fecundate the earth. Patanjali would go on to formulate the *Yogasutra*, a complete, holistic philosophy of life, seen by many as a gift to humanity.

It is important to note here that Indian philosophical systems are founded not only on pramana, or valid sources of knowledge, and on logic and reasoning, but are also grounded in experience. Hence, they are called darshana. Patanjali Yoga is a darshana. If theories of knowing offer methods of understanding, Yoga proffers methods for 'seeing' and 'experiencing' the truth. For, ultimately, truth is something to be lived. Yoga, then, is not just about maintaining bodily health but a complex discipline which is a means to the attainment of unitary consciousness.

Tradition ascribes three works to Patanjali: a treatise on the science of medicine, another on the science of grammar and lastly, the *Yogasutra*. Most scholars agree he could not have been the author of the first two works. As regards the *Yogasutra*, from the time of the Vedas to that of the Buddha, through the traditions of the saddarshanas (Sankhya, Vaisheshika, Nyaya, Mimamsa and Vedanta) and even thereafter, we come across references to yoga as a discipline and philosophy. It remained over centuries an integral part of the discipline of spiritual questers. Patanjali, who lived in the second century BCE, was thus not the originator of the science of yoga, but one who, through the *Yogasutra*, adopting ideas from Sankhya and Vaisheshika, systematized its philosophy and discipline into a coherent whole.

The text of the *Yogasutra* has four padas or chapters and 195 sutras. The philosophical foundation of the *Yogasutra* is largely based on Sankhya thought, with the notable addition of the concept of god or Isvara. According to Patanjali, existence rests and moves on three fundamental realities: Isvara, Purusa(s) and Prakriti. Isvara is the omniscient being, ever-free, untouched by Prakriti. Isvara is also considered to be the adiguru or primeval teacher. While Isvara is the primal Purusa, immaterial and free, individual souls, purusas, infinite in number, are bound to the prakriti, and subject to karmas, consequences of actions, and kleshas, afflictions or negative mental states.

It is by the will of Isvara and in accordance with karma, quiescent and emergent, that Prakriti, comprising three gunas or substances, namely, sattva, rajas and tamas, evolves into the living world. Jiva (Purusa), or the individual soul, is unalloyed and pure consciousness; however, once it gets involved with the substances of Prakriti, it forgets its own nature, is subjected to the joys and sorrows of the world and has to go through the cycles of birth and death. Following the eight steps of yoga, with the awakening of knowledge, the jiva is freed from the entanglement of samsara and returns to its primordial state of pure consciousness, or kaivalya.

Etymologically, yoga, derived from the verb 'yuj', means 'to yoke, join', or 'to bind together'. (We may note here that the term 'religion', derived from the Latin *re-ligio*, means to link back, to bind, to return to the source, to our natural state.)

Yoga offers eight graded disciplines, called the astanga, or eight limbs, to freedom. Of these, five are external aids, or bahirangas: yama, restraint; niyama, observance; asana, posture; pranayama, control and regulation of vital breaths or currents; and pratyahara, the state of withdrawal or inward gaze. The other three are internal aids, namely, dharana, concentration; dhyana, meditation; and samadhi, total absorption. Together, these disciplines build a necessary foundation for the attainment of self-awareness and liberation.

Yoga's eight disciplines are:

Yama

Yamas are further divided into five ethical vows:

- Ahimsa, abstinence from injury or violence to another.
- Satya, truth in thought, speech and act.
- Asteya, refraining from taking what belongs to another.
- Brahmacharya, celibacy and retention of sexforce without wasting it in any form, subtle or gross.
- Aparigraha, elimination of greed for things for one's own pleasure.

Niyama

Niyamas are five spiritual disciplines:

- Saucha, mental and physical purity.
- Santosha, contentment which keeps the body and mind free of stress and strain.
- Tapas, austerity of body, speech and thought.
- Svadhyaya, study of the scriptures.
- Isvarapranidhana, contemplation of and inner surrender to the divine.

Asana

Asana is the bodily posture in which one can sit steadily and at ease. Patanjali does not suggest any specific asana, except to say, 'posture one can hold with comfort and stillness'. Specific asanas, such as sirsasana, bhujangasana, savasana and so on, were added much later and came to be called Hatha Yoga. All these asanas help not only in keeping the body fit and healthy; more importantly, they are geared towards opening up or activating the kundalini chakras, the energy centres in the body, which enable transcendental states and, ultimately, liberation.

Pranayama

The body–mind and life force are closely linked with breath in the sustenance and growth of life. Through pranayama, or breathing exercises, once the incoming and outgoing breath is regulated, retained and steadied, it can calm a restless mind. Irregulated currents are set right, and nadis, subtle nerve channels, are purified and rejuvenated.

Pratyahara

This is the withdrawal of mental faculties and the sense organs from the sense objects and their habitual outward movement, turning the gaze inward.

Dharana

Dharana is concentration, or fixing the mental energies on a single object of one's choice. It could be a name, sound, a symbol or form, or an idea. The purpose here is to train oneself to withdraw from all other activities and remain focused on an object.

Dhyana

Dhyana is uninterrupted concentration upon an object – rather, on the nature of the object or the truth it embodies.

Samadhi

Once the practice of concentration is mastered, the distinction between the subject and the object, the knower and the known fades, the boundaries blur, and the deeper layers of consciousness and one's own being open up. At this stage, it's possible that one enters a larger, deeper awareness, a luminous consciousness. Eventually, the quester loses even awareness and remains absorbed in a bright light.

The three disciplines – dharana, dhyana and samadhi – are actually three continuous steps. Patanjali calls it samyama, and it should ideally be on the same object.

With the steady practice of yama, niyama, asana and samyama, the quester, or yogi, is likely to acquire occult powers, or yogasiddhis. Such powers may cause the yogi to develop the faculty to see into the past and future, read other's minds and so on. The temptation of attaining such powers distract one from the goal of yoga – liberation. Patanjali, therefore, warns questers from falling prey to such powers and advises against seeking for them, or ignoring them and moving on.

There is hardly any branch of Indian philosophy of which yoga is not an integral part. From the first millennium CE onwards, Tantra traditions in both Hinduism and Buddhism, by assimilating the essentials of astanga yoga, developed their own forms of Yoga, such as kundalini yoga, laya yoga, mantramarga, guhyamantra and so on. Adopting the essentials of Yogasutra, Sri Aurobindo developed a spiritual path called 'Integral Yoga', which he believed would enable supramental manifestation, the birth of a new human being.

The discipline of asanas or yogasanas, called Hatha yoga, which is just one limb of Yoga, has become hugely popular in the world today, offering posture-based exercises for physical fitness, stress relief and relaxation. However, it needs to be pointed out yet again that Yoga is much more than physical exercise; it is a complete philosophy of life and action, geared towards enlarging our consciousness, awakening the powers or faculties inherent in the body and enabling us to achieve a life of freedom and fullness, and that has been the greatest contribution of Patanjali Yoga to the world.

Mahavira
(born c. 599 BCE)

A STORY GOES THAT ONE DAY MAHAVIRA VISITED A VILLAGE ON THE
outskirts of which lived a cobra called Chandkaushik. The people of
the village lived in absolute terror of the cobra. Mahavira went into the
forest where Chandkaushik lived, sat down under a tree and meditated.
Feelings of peace and concern for the well-being of the people flowed
from his heart. Chandkaushik, coming out of his hole, hissed in anger,
but that did not disturb the meditating Mahavira. Getting angrier, the
cobra bit his toe. Mahavira opened his eyes and, compassion flowing
from his heart, said, 'Chandkaushik, shaant, let peace be with you.'
The cobra became calm and retreated to his hole.

There are many such Jain and Buddhist tales with messages of
love, peace and ahimsa, non-violence, where even wild animals, let
alone human criminals, turn calm and abjure violence. These are
metaphorical stories to bring home the ideal that through ahimsa
we can transform the world into an abode of joy and peace. There
are ample references to the ideal of non-violence in many ancient
texts of Hinduism, too, but it's only Mahavira, then the Buddha, who
expounded a comprehensive philosophy of non-violence.

Mahavira's emphasis on ahimsa as the supreme moral virtue was
perhaps one of the most significant contributions to Indian thought
and to the philosophy of the world at large. At the time – around 500
BCE – when battles between tribes and kingdoms and communities
and killings were seen as the natural order of life, when animals were
ritually sacrificed in Vedic and other traditions, when violence was
considered an inevitable part of existence even by religious people,
Mahavira taught non-violence as the way to freedom and joy.

The Buddha took this forward through his teaching of compassion,
anukampa, towards all forms of life. Centuries later, Jesus Christ
introduced the gospel of love into the warring Western world. In

modern times, Mahatma Gandhi renewed the gospel of non-violence and love as the path to not only individual freedom but the way to lokasangraha, welfare of the world.

Mahavira was born around 599 BCE to King Siddhartha (not to be confused with Siddhartha Gautama) and Queen Trishala of the Ikshvaku race. They named their son Vardhamana. Though historians have different opinions about the exact place of Mahavira's birth, they all agree that he was born in the kingdom of Vaishali, which is in modern-day Bihar.

Legend says his parents were followers of the twenty-third Jain Thirthankara, Parashvanatha. As in the story of the Buddha, we are told Prince Vardhamana too was brought up amidst luxury, but he led a very simple life. In accordance with the wishes of his parents, he married Princess Yashoda and the couple had a daughter, Priyadarshani. (The Digambara sect of Jainism, however, insists that Mahavira never married.)

His parents died when Vardhamana was 28, and his elder brother Nandivardhana succeeded their father. Two years later, at the age of 30, Vardhamana sought his brother's permission to renounce his royal life. It is said his brother tried to dissuade him from his resolve but a determined Vardhamana left home and embraced the ascetic life of a monk.

Over twelve years, Mahavira is believed to have practised complete silence and rigorous meditation. In the final stage of his sadhana, he put himself through immense hardship by discarding his clothes and going without food. This reminds us of the Buddha going through a similar rigorous ascetic sadhana only to soon give it up as not the way for him. But Vardhamana thought otherwise; it is said that he observed rigorous fasts, consuming food on a total of 341 days in his twelve and a half years of ascetic practice. Finally, he attained kevala jnana, omniscience or perfect knowledge, and was transformed into a Jina, the one who is victorious over attachment.

Vardhamana Mahavira is considered the last of the Jinas, or the last of the 24 Thirthankaras. He is not the founder of Jainism but a reformer, propagator and codifier of an already existing religious order. Mahavira is generally depicted in a sitting or standing meditative posture. His birth is celebrated as Mahavir Jayanti and his attainment of nirvana or kevala jnana as Deepavali, which coincides with the festival of lights celebrated by the Hindus.

For over thirty years, Mahavira travelled in and around the northern part of India and taught the way to liberation. He died in 527 BCE at the age of 72 in present-day Bihar.

According to some Jain texts, Mahavira's first disciples were eleven brahmins, with one Gautama (not the Buddha) as the leader of the group. These eleven disciples are believed to have remembered and orally transmitted Mahavira's teachings, which came to be called Jain Agamas. For several centuries after the death of Mahavira, the teachings were passed on orally from generation to generation and put down in writing on palm leaf sheets only in the first century CE. *Vardhamancharitra*, *Acharanga Sutra* and *Kalpa Sutra* are some of the major texts that give us accounts of his life, sadhana and teachings.

Mahavira considered men and women to be spiritual equals; in fact, he made no distinction between people, whether men or women, rich or poor, high or low caste. All were capable of attaining nirvana, liberation from cycle of birth and death, provided they worked towards it.

Historically, Jainism was probably the first religion to emerge with a clear set of beliefs and practices. The followers were organized into a fourfold order, known as Chaturvidh Jain Sangh: munis, male ascetic devotees; aryikas, nuns; sravakas, male lay followers; and sravikas, female lay followers. Jainism also had royal followers such as King Bimbisara of Magadha and King Chetaka of Videha. One of its striking features was the large number of women in the spiritual fold. At the time, it is said, hundreds of women renounced worldly life to become Jain nuns. Chandana, Mahavira's aunt, was believed to have been the head of the Jain order of nuns.

Centuries later, however, Jainism was split into two sects:

Digambara (skyclad) and Svetambara (whiteclad). While Svetambara monks dressed only in white, Digambara monks renounced all possessions, including clothing. The Digambaras decreed that women could not attain nirvana, and so they barred women from the order. But the Svetambaras made no such distinction between men and women aspirants and admitted both into their order, a tradition that continues to this day. It is estimated that there are about seven million people following Mahavira the world over, most of whom reside in India.

The Teachings

According to Jain cosmology, existence has neither beginning nor end and has six eternal substances, namely, soul, jiva; matter, pudgala; space, akasha; motion, dharma; rest, adharma; and time, kala. Aside from jiva, all the other five substances together form ajiva, the non-living. Everything in the world is produced by matter, except souls (jivas) and space. Even karma, which affects or taints jiva, is matter in a subtle form. Samsara is nothing but the entanglement of jiva in ajiva. What each person must strive for is nirvana, or the liberation of jiva from ajiva. This can be realized only by shedding karma by gradual means, and ultimately by absolute withdrawal from outward life which could result in fast unto death, or sallekhana. This absolute freedom from bondage of karma is the state of 'being without form', the state of perfection pervaded by a passionless, ineffable peace.

The attainment of liberation from the cycles of karma is possible through samyak darshana, right faith; samyak jnana, right knowledge; and samyak charitra, right character – and by practising five vratas, vows:

1. Ahimsa or non-violence, the mahavrata, the great vow, which involves eschewing all forms of violence in action, speech and thought.
2. Satya or truthfulness, in action, speech and thought.
3. Asteya or non-stealing: not taking anything that has not been properly given.

4. Brahmacharya or chastity, abstinence from sex and sensual pleasure for monks and faithfulness to one's partner for householders or lay people.

5. Aparigraha or non-possession/non-attachment, complete detachment from people, places and material things for monks, and for lay people, an attitude of non-attachment to worldly possessions.

Anekantavada and Syadvada

An important concept of Jain teaching is the concept of anekantavada, from which the concept of syadvada arose much later. However, the forms in which the two concepts are presented today developed over many centuries after the death of Mahavira.

Anekantavada may be translated as 'many-sidedness of reality', 'non-absolutism', 'relativity', or simply as multiple perspectives on the nature of reality and human existence. Truth and reality are always layered and complex which may be experienced in all its fullness, but it is impossible to express that completely in words. For instance, one can experience the 'truth' of a taste, say, a mango, but may not be able to fully express that taste through language. We do use language to express our experiences, our perception of reality, but these efforts cannot be absolutized since what an individual expresses about an experience, however valid, will always be just one perspective, incomplete and limiting.

Anekantavada may even be seen as an extension of the belief in ahimsa, since ahimsa is antithetical to absolutism which, if unrestrained, can turn tyrannical and violent. Therefore, some scholars, in the context of growing intolerance in the world today, see anekantavada as an appeal for religious tolerance, open-mindedness and pluralism.

'Syadvada' means 'perchance', 'perhaps', 'maybe', and is basically an extension of anekantavada. According to the philosopher Matilal, it is a 'conditional yes, or conditional approval' of any proposition, not a theory of uncertainty or doubt.

The Buddha, who lived and preached at a later time, had no use for these notions. Rather, he took the middle path that we simply cannot assert with certainty that something is so or not so. Later, in the second century CE, rejecting both the affirmative and the negative views, the Buddhist philosopher Nagarjuna maintained that there simply is no two – advaya. This view was derived from the philosophical position that all things have dependent origination (pratitya-samutpada) and therefore all things are empty (sunya).

Jain beliefs in anekantavada and syadvada were among the ideas that shaped Mahatma Gandhi's thought. Gandhi believed that on the level of faith, truth is pure consciousness; it is God, love, cosmic order. Truth reveals itself in the phenomenal world through love and ahimsa. However, humans are not given to know this absolute truth; for absolute truth would mean absolute ahimsa, incarnation of truth in totality. Relative truth is all that is given to us, hence we can but move from truth to greater truth and, in the light of this, manage and resolve human problems and conflict through non-violent means.

Sallekhana

The doctrine of non-violence is central to Jainism. With ahimsa as its great vow, and in its concern for avoiding harm or violence to any and all life forms, Jainism is unlike any other religion. In simple terms, when a person – a Jain monk or nun or even a believing Jain – feels that his or her mission in life has been completed or decides that he or she cannot or does not want to attain nirvana while alive, which is the ultimate goal of life, then the individual seeks it in death. There is religious sanction for this act of voluntarily embracing death.

Sallekhana is in fact seen as the ultimate form of ahimsa. Jains believe that eating and drinking involves some degree of violence for a selfish need, a seeker of nirvana, therefore, gives them up too. What it implies is that committing violence not only causes harm to others but injures one's own self and ultimately inhibits one's ability to attain nirvana. So a Jain ascetic is expected to uphold the vow of ahimsa even at the cost of his life.

Mahavira's thoughts continued to influence people long after his death. His concept of ahimsa was adopted and modified by various thinkers, including Buddha and Gandhi. While Buddhists thought of ahimsa as a supreme value that enjoins sentiments of benevolence, love and compassion towards all living things, Gandhi adopted it as a principle in the fight against exploitation, oppression and violence, and considered it the new-age dharma, the new yugadharma.

The Buddha
(born c. 567 BCE)

LEGEND HAS IT THAT ON THE LAST DAY OF THE BUDDHA'S LIFE, SEEING his master reduced to skin and bones, his disciple Ananda started crying. He broke down not only because his master was dying, but also because, as his closest disciple for more than forty years, he had come nowhere near attaining the perfection of wisdom. The Buddha stopped him and said: 'Ananda, do not grieve, do not lament. For have I not taught from the very beginning that with all that is dear and beloved there must be change, separation and severance? Now for a long time, Ananda, you have served the Tathagatha with loving kindness in deed, word and thought... Ananda! Now you should put forth energy and be a light unto thyself.'

Buddha's last words to Ananda was a timeless message to humankind as well. Much of our confusions and sufferings come from our search for solutions to the problems of living, for truth and for joy in external things, in scriptures and spiritual authorities, when in fact the answers lie within ourselves. This was the gist of his message: to put forth energy and be a light unto oneself, and every action of one's daily life then would spring from that light.

~

Scholars have called the period between 800 and 200 BCE the Axial Age because it was a period of great transformation in the history of humankind, especially in the spiritual realm. During this period, the world witnessed the coming of Zoroaster in Iran; the sages of the Upanishads, Mahavira and the Buddha in India; Confucius and Lao Tzu in China; Pythagoras, Heraclitus, Socrates and Plato in Greece. Their profound insights into the human condition and the nature of reality led to the development of new religions and philosophical systems that continue to challenge and inspire humanity to this day.

Among them stands out the Buddha, in whose life and teaching we witness the culmination of centuries of spiritual development. He declared the end of sorrow, took the open road and shared his insights with whosoever was ready to listen and enquire, irrespective of caste, creed and gender. He initiated, in true democratic spirit, what may be called 'jnana yajna' – offering jnana, knowledge, as an act of sacrifice. And he held back nothing.

As in the case of 'saviours' or messiahs in other cultures of the world, the birth of the Buddha too is suffused with myth and magical events. It is said he was born sometime in the fifth century BCE to Queen Maya and Suddhodana, king of the Shakyas, a scion of the solar race, in Lumbini, a part of modern Nepal. It is believed that on the seventh day after his birth, Maya died. The prince grew up under the care of her sister, Mahaprajapati. And the story goes that the brahmins, summoned by King Suddhodana, predicted that he would either become a Buddha or a chakravartin, a universal king. King Suddhodana wanted his son to become a chakravartin, not a spiritual master. So he made arrangements that Gautama would never see anything that could perturb his mind and compel him to take to the path of renunciation. In course of time, Gautama was married to the beautiful Yashodhara, who bore him a son, who was named Rahula.

Thus, Gautama lived a life of pleasure and comfort without a touch of worry or sorrow. But a life of such uninterrupted pleasure could not go on for long. And it so happened that one day he longed to see the world beyond the palace gates and asked Channa, his charioteer, to get his chariot. They set out and entered the common street, which, as per Suddhodana's orders, had been cleared of all disturbing sights. However, the story goes, the gods had other plans and they sent down sundry spirits in the guise of an old man, a sick man, a corpse and an ascetic, each a day for four days, to undo the king's plans and give the prince the much-needed nudge to begin his quest.

After being exposed to facets of life that he had never known existed, Gautama returned to his palace in a state of great agitation and withdrew into himself. Suddenly, it seemed to him that the life he had led so far was an escape from the realities of the world around him. Was there life beyond the triad of old age, illness, and death? His whole being burning with that question, legend recounts that the twenty-nine-year-old Gautama, turning his back on his young family and the right to be the king, left home quietly in the small hours and set off on the journey that would make him the Buddha.

Wearing a yellow robe and with his head shaven, which signified his renunciation of all affiliations to caste, family and native land, Gautama went in search of a guru. Under the guidance of Alara Kalama, his first guru, then Uddaka Ramaputta, his second and last, he experienced certain mystical states, only to realize that these experiences did not free him from desires and conflicts or enable him to attain freedom from the cause of sorrow. So he left both gurus and decided to strike out on his own.

He practised the extreme form of tapas, depriving himself of food and even water, hoping that would burn up the last vestiges of his negative karma and enable him to come upon the ultimate state beyond sorrow. That did not help him either; rather, it only pushed him to the brink of death. So, feeding himself with morsels of food, Gautama recovered his health and is said to have decided to undertake the final effort to attain nirvana. 'My flesh may wither away,' Gautama told himself with a firm resolution, 'and my blood may dry up until only skin, sinews and bones remain, but I will not give up... until I have found liberation, I will sit here unflinching and utterly still.'

All Buddhist traditions interpret his final effort as a heroic struggle, as a battle against temptation and the fear of death. Keeping silent and still against the ravings of Mara, the demon and tempter, Gautama crosses the last frontier of desire and fear. Warding off the temptation of Mara, it is said, Gautama looked deep into the heart of things, reflected upon the conditional nature of life, and then, freed of the process of becoming, entered the state of nirvana.

> When I knew and saw thus, my mind was liberated from the taint of sensual desire, from the taint of being, and from the taint of ignorance. When it was liberated there came the awareness: 'It is liberated.' I directly knew: 'Birth is destroyed, the holy life has been lived, what had to be done has been done, there is no more coming to any state of being.' (*Majjhima Nikaya*, 36)

The word nirvana suggests extinction of the self, rather, the annihilation of the fires of the self, the human passions that cause conflict and sorrow. It is considered the state of perfection, Buddhahood. That perfect state of being is also called Tathagata, the one who has passed from the world of samsara, the dualistic mode of living caught in the constant movement between pain and pleasure, good and evil and so on, and arrived as a Buddha, with no ego-consciousness because all frontiers have been dissolved. In positive terms, it is a state completely devoid of ego, full of peace, calm, bliss, purity and freshness.

After attaining the state of nirvana, it is said the Buddha passed through Varanasi and there he met with the five bhikkhus, his former companions during the time of his ascetic practice, and to them, according to the canonical texts, the Buddha gave his first sermon on the Middle Way:

There are two extremes, monks, which he who has given up the world ought to avoid. What are these two extremes? A life given to pleasures, devoted to pleasures and lusts – this is degrading, sensual, vulgar, ignoble, and profitless (unskilful). And a life given to mortifications – this is painful, ignoble, and profitless. By avoiding these two extremes, monks, the Tathagata has gained the knowledge of the middle way which leads to insight, which leads to wisdom, which conduces to calm, to knowledge, to Supreme Enlightenment, to Nirvana.

It is of crucial importance to note here that in his very first sermon the Buddha begins with a *feeling* rather than an *idea*. He does not talk of God, of good and evil, of the meaning and purpose of life, or promise salvation. There is suffering, dukkha, and there is an end to suffering. But we crave and cling to impermanent states and things only to reap dukkha. It is possible to get out of this circle of dukkha by treading the right and noble path and through skilful actions. There are no good and evil actions, only skilful actions that lead one to the path of liberation, and unskilful actions that bind one to a life of suffering.

Once the Buddha, while wandering through Kosala kingdom with a large community of bhikkhus, entered Kesaputta, a town where the Kalama people lived. The Kalamas had heard that Gautama was a fully enlightened person. They went to where the Buddha was, paid homage to him and one of the Kalamas said: 'Venerable sir, monks and brahmins visit Kesaputta and expound and explain only their own doctrines, while the other doctrines they criticize and loathe. We are not sure what to believe and what not to believe.'

'It is being unskilful, Kalamas, to live in greed, hate and delusion,' replied the Buddha. 'And it is being skilful not to take life, not to steal, not to tell lies, and such a man prompts another too, to do likewise.

'Listen, Kalamas. Do not believe something just because it has become a traditional practice, because it is what the scriptures say, or it sounds logical, or it accords with your thought. But, Kalamas, when you know for yourselves these things are unskilful, these things when performed and undertaken conduce to ruin and sorrow, then reject them. And when you know for yourselves these things are skilful, when performed and undertaken conduce to well-being and happiness, then live and act accordingly.'

Buddhism deals only with the 'self', the ego, the mind, and does not talk about a higher self. The Buddhist's position is that it is pointless to discuss whether the self or soul exists or not, because even if it exists, it cannot be known. It is avyakta, inexpressible. For, in the state of being where the dualistic mind is absent, who can tell what it is and what it is not? Therefore, in Buddhism, all assertions or affirmations about the soul or Atman are seen as projections of an insecure mind. In actuality, however, there is no centre, no self; it is only an illusion. The self is only a word, a label we attach for the aggregate of certain physical and psychical factors, but they have no independent existence.

The self or the mind is made of five elements or skandhas: rupa, vijnana, vedana, samjna and samskara; while rupa stands for the physical, the rest constitute the psychical elements of the self. What we call 'self-consciousness' or 'mental dispositions' is nothing but a combination of these factors or skandhas and is forever in a state of flux. There are only a series of sensations, a play of the biochemical, so to speak, which is put together by the mind into a form, a stream of ideas, and we imagine a common element or character underlying the stream and call it the self or Atman.

This leads to the question: Did the Buddha really deny an enduring self, and thereby the notion of rebirth as well? Ironically, the poignant Jataka tales narrate the previous births of the Buddha through several ages. Perhaps early Buddhism worked its way into the heart of the people by popularizing the conception of rebirth, though in actuality the Buddha himself never believed in the conventional notion of rebirth. What he has said of the soul, the nature of the mind and experience is so transparently sound and simple that there should be no confusion about his position with regard to the idea of transmigration.

O Brahmin, *there is only rebirth of character, but no transmigration of a self.* Your thought-forms reappear, but there is no ego-entity transferred. You are still cleaving to self. You are anxious about heaven but you seek the pleasures of self in heaven. You seek the life that is of the mind. Where self is, truth cannot be; yet when truth comes, self will disappear... self is death and truth is life. The cleaving to self is a perpetual dying, while moving in the truth is partaking of nirvana, which is life everlasting.

The Buddha had left home at twenty-nine in quest of truth, after nearly six years of rigorous sadhana, at thirty-five, his search came to an end when he 'was liberated from the taint of sensual desire, from the taint of being, and from the taint of ignorance'.

For over forty years thereafter, he took the open road and moved around the cities and towns and villages of Champa, Rajagriha, Savathi, Saketa, Kosambi and Benares, sharing his discovery of truth, teaching the way that led to the cessation of conflict and sorrow. During his last days, in his eighties, with Ananda as his companion, legend recounts he walked away from the 'civilized world' to a remote place called Kusinara (modern Kushinagar, Uttar Pradesh) and breathed his last sometime around 483 BCE.

Three months after his death, a group of his close associates, including Ananda, gathered in Rajagriha and held a council to recall and collate the *Buddhavachana*, the Buddha's teaching. The teaching remained in the oral form for about 400 years before it was written down in the Pali language from memory, sometime around the first century BCE. About a hundred years later serious differences arose within the Buddhist order over the true interpretation of the Buddha's teachings. Subsequently, this led to the formal division of Buddhism into the Hinayana, Mahayana and Vajrayana sects, representing three vital stages in the teachings of the Buddha.

Centuries later, under King Ashoka (c. 268–232 BCE), what had remained predominantly a spiritual sect grew into a full-fledged religion, but at a price. Compromises were made at the cost of losing its originality, and from the back door, as it were, were brought in the traditional beliefs in gods and heaven, good works, merit and the soul, to which the Buddha had not ascribed any spiritual significance. The way of the Buddha began to be predominantly interpreted in terms of 'performance' or 'engagement' with society rather than as one of contemplation and self-transformation.

It was this shift, one might say, from an apparently 'negative approach' to a 'liberal' and 'positive approach' – along with the portrayal of the Buddha as the Compassionate One, bodhisattva, preaching the way of Dhamma (the teachings of the Buddha) as the way of compassion for all and as the way to end suffering – that was instrumental in spreading Buddhism all over the world. There are over 520 million followers of Buddhism spread across the earth, largely in countries such as China, Sri Lanka, Myanmar, Malaysia, Thailand, Cambodia, Vietnam and Tibet.

Buddhism, not so much as a denominational religion but as a philosophy of life and a path of wisdom and compassion, has become a growing trend in the world today. In particular, the ideal of bodhisattva forms a vital part of the New Age movement, which aims to propagate spirituality without borders, without the need for divinity or a religious identity, for the development of human potential, spiritual growth and compassion.

Women Savants in Ancient Times

THE *MANU DHARMASHASTRA*, OR *Laws of Manu* DEALING WITH SOURCE of dharma, the dharma of the four social classes or castes, law of karma, rebirth and final liberation was composed sometime around 100 CE. The law denied women, along with shudras, access to brahmavidya, or spiritual knowledge, and condemned them to a life of submission and subservience to men in the name of stridharma, or wifely duties. For centuries this law marginalized women's place in family and society.

The Bhakti movement, which spread from the sixth to the seventeenth centuries CE across the Indian subcontinent, challenged the Manu Dharmashastra. Women made vital impacts during this period and played a crucial role in defying the Brahmanical ideology and structure that was based on Manu Dharmashastra. However, what is of interest for us here is that during the Vedic period there were no strictures against women treading the path of knowledge; in fact, we come across many women taking to the path of jnana, or knowledge, and asceticism. Such women were called brahmavadinis.

Brahmavadinis

During the early Vedic period (1500–500 BCE), the large number of women mentioned in the Vedas were ordinary women, not necessarily truth seekers; rather, only a few among them were known as brahmavadinis, expounders of Brahman or the Vedas. They were so called for three probable reasons: like men, they underwent the sacrament of upanayana, ritual of initiation restricted to the three upper castes, and studied the Vedas, though lived under their father or husband; they could recite the Vedas; and they participated in debates and discussions on Brahman, the ultimate reality underlying all phenomena.

Some of the notable women of this period were Gargi Vachaknavi, Vadava Pratitheyi, Sulabha Maitreyi, Romasa and Lopamudra, but, going by the texts, it appears that only Gargi and Maitreyi were brahmavadinis.

Sulabha Maitreyi
(c. 700 BCE)

It is said Maitreyi was the daughter of Sage Maitri, who was a minister in the court of King Janaka of the Videhas, Mithila. She was married to Yagnavalkya, a seer and teacher who makes a powerful presence not only in the *Brihadaranyaka Upanishad* but also in the Mahabharata and Puranas as a philosopher of Advaita, non-dualism. Interestingly, in the Mahabharata, Maitreyi is portrayed as unmarried, as an ascetic and a teacher who explains the non-dual philosophy to King Janaka.

However, it is in the *Brihadaranyaka Upanishad* that we see her as a person of substance and perceptiveness. Having completed the grihasth ashrama, the phase of life spent as a householder, Yajnavalkya decides to become a renunciant. He seeks Maitreyi's permission and tells her he wants to divide his property between her and his other wife, Katyayani.

'Maitreyi,' said Yajnavalkya, 'I am going to renounce this life. Let me make a final settlement between you and Katyayani.'

Maitreyi said: 'Sir, if indeed the whole earth, full of wealth, belonged to me, would I be immortal through that?'

'No,' replied Yajnavalkya, 'your life would be just like that of people who have plenty. Of Immortality, however, there is no hope through wealth.'

Then Maitreyi said: 'What should I do with that which would not make me immortal? Tell me, venerable Sir, of that alone which you know to be the only means of attaining Immortality.'

Yajnavalkya replied: 'My dear, come, sit down; I will explain it to you. Verily, not for the sake of the husband, my dear, is the husband loved, but he is loved for the sake of the self which, in its true nature, is one with the Supreme Self.

'As a lump of salt dropped into water becomes dissolved in water and cannot be taken out again, but wherever we taste the water it tastes salt[y], even so, my dear, this great, endless, infinite Reality is Pure Intelligence alone. This self comes out as a separate entity from these elements and with their destruction this separate existence also is destroyed. After attaining oneness it has no more consciousness.'

Then Maitreyi said: 'Just here you have bewildered me, Sir, by saying that after attaining oneness the self has no more consciousness.'

Yajnavalkya replied: 'Certainly I am not saying anything bewildering my dear. For when there is duality, then one smells another, one sees another, one hears another, one knows another. But when everything has become the Self, then what should one smell and through what, what should one see and through what, what should one know and through what? Through what should one know That owing to which all this is known? Through what, my dear, should one know the Knower?'

The dialogue continues, with Maitreyi at many points asking Yajnavalkya the right questions, seeking clarification on many a complex issue. The couple together explore the nature of Atman and Brahman, and their essential oneness. What is of significance here is that Maitreyi is not merely a part of the Upanishadic story but has character, refuses wealth, participates in the dialogue both as a student and as a truth seeker in her own right, exhibiting her intellectual growth and maturity. It is a remarkable 2700 years old story, especially considering the status or condition of women the world over at that time.

Gargi Vachaknavi
(c. 700 BCE)

Born sometime around 700 BCE, Gargi was the daughter of Sage Vachaknu in the lineage of Sage Garga. Gargi is supposed to have composed several hymns on the origin of existence. It is said Gargi acquired the knowledge of the Vedas at quite an early age. She was considered a learned women and an ardent seeker of truth, and was regarded as spiritually knowledgeable at a time when few women were in the spiritual fold.

Once, King Janaka of Videha organized a congregation of

philosophers. The participants sat around the fire sacrament and so the assembly was called Brahmayajna. Gargi was one of the prominent persons in the assembly. Yajnavalkya, considered a master of knowledge and wisdom, was also a part of the congregation. Not many there would doubt his ideas or dare to question him. However, learned men such as Asvala, Ushasta and Uddalaka asked him questions. And they all lost the debate one by one. At last it was Gargi's turn to take up the challenge with questions on the origin and nature of existence. Pointedly, she asked, 'Yajnavalkya, that of which they say is above the sky and below the earth, is between the earth and the sky as well, and which is the past, present, and future – tell me, in what is it woven, warp and woof?'

'In ether, Gargi.'

Thus the dialogue begins, Yajnavalkya answering her every question succinctly. And the catechism ends thus:

'By what is the World of Virij pervaded?'
'By the World of Hiranyagarbha, O Gargi.'
'By what, pray, is the World of Hiranyagarbha pervaded?'
'Do not, O Gargi,' said he, 'question too much, lest your head should fall off. You are questioning too much about a deity about whom we should not ask too much. Do not ask too much, O Gargi.'
Thereupon Gargi, the daughter of Vachaknu, held her peace.

It is interesting to note here that unsatisfied with Yajnavalkya's answers, Gargi keeps seeking clarification, which shows her intellectual tenacity, but Yajnavalkya unfairly silences her from further questioning him with a warning. Still Gargi praises him as insuperable expounder of Brahman. And Gargi too is praised as a Brahmavadin, and honoured as one of the navaratnas (nine gems) in the court of King Janaka. She is remembered today as a learned, courageous woman on an equal footing with learned men of her times, and as one who challenged the formidable Yajnavalkya.

Aryikas: Jain Nuns
(c. 500 BCE)

The tradition of women taking to the path of spirituality gained considerable momentum during Mahavira's time (599–527 BCE). Thousands of women, it is said, renounced worldly life to become nuns. Chandana, Mahavira's aunt, was believed to have been the head of the Jain order of nuns. When Jainism eventually split into the Digambara and Svetambara sects, the Digambaras barred women from the order on the grounds that they would not be able to go through the ascetic practices required of a monk to attain nirvana. The Svetambaras made no such distinction between men and women aspirants and admitted both into their order, a tradition that continues to this day. Female monastics are called sadhvis. We do not know of any sadhvi of substance from the past, except Mahavira's aunt, Chandana. In modern times, however, there are a few, Shakuntala, who took the name of Chandana after initiation, being the most famous one. It is an extraordinary story covered later in the book.

Shakyadhitas: Buddhist Nuns
(c. 500 BCE)

The Buddha (486 BCE), according to the Pali texts, was at first reluctant to admit women into the sangha. One day, Ananda, his cousin and constant companion, challenged the master thus: 'O Lord, tell me, are women capable of attaining nirvana?'

The Buddha said, 'Women are capable of attaining nirvana. With regard to nirvana, Ananda, there's no difference between men and women.' Thus cornered, he is believed to have asked Mahaprajapati Gautami, his stepmother and ardent devotee, who had been very keen to join the sangha, to go ahead with the initiation. Along with her, five hundred women are believed to have renounced worldly ties to undergo initiation and form the first Buddhist order of nuns – the

Shakyadhitas, or 'daughters of the Shakyan', the clan the Buddha belonged to.

The Shakyadhitas composed the *Therigatha: Verses of the Elder Nuns*. This collection was composed orally in Magadhi, the Magadh language, during the Buddha's lifetime, and after his death was put together in writing in 80 BCE. The *Therigatha* is arguably among the most ancient women's writing in the world and the earliest known anthology of women's literature in India. The *Therigatha*, which consists of 494 verses in 16 chapters, has been attributed to 101 bhikkhunis, fully ordained Buddhist nuns, out of which about 73 have been identified in the text.

These women speak with heartbreaking honesty about their trials and tribulations, and their ultimate escape from conflict and pain into a state of tranquillity. Here, we come across a mother whose child has died, a youthful woman who speaks poignantly about the unseemly changes wrought upon her by age, a former sex worker who becomes a bhikkhuni, male seducers and the sad fate of pregnant women, suffering typically associated with femininity and the woes of womanhood, dukkho ithibhavo.

However, the bhikkhunis know that they need to free themselves from not only attachment to things but also from their socially conditioned womanhood. And it's heartening to read in some of the poems the ecstatic cry of quite a few bhikkhunis when they find release from domestic servitude, from the burdens imposed on them by cultural and social structures on account of their gender.

Some of the outstanding women we encounter here are Mahaprajapati, Kisa Gautami, Sulabh, Ambapali and Supriya, to mention only a few, whose lives, utterances and spiritual attainments can in no way be ranked below those of the male monks.

These poems have a complex significance and encompass many strands of meaning. Significantly, as the Buddhist scholar Vijitha Rajapakse writes, 'they often bear witness in revealing terms to women's distinctive association with and appropriation of the Buddha's soteriological teachings'. Feminism as a struggle for the rights of women in the social world may not be seriously underscored in this text; however, the text 'does on occasion stress the equality of women and men in the mental sphere', and feminism in another sense is very much in evidence in the work, 'replete with articulations that record some characteristic viewpoints, experiences, attitudes, and thought patterns of women'.

Excerpts from *Therigatha*

A maiden, I, all clad in white, once heard
The Norm, and hearkened eager, earnestly,
So in me rose discernment of the Truths.

– Sulabh

~

Glossy and black as the down of the bee my curls once clustered.
They with the waste of the years are liker to hempen or bark cloth...
Fragrant as casket of perfume, as full of sweet blossoms the hair of mine.
All with the waste of the years now rank as the odour of the hare's fur...
Dense as a grove well planted, and comely with comb, pin and parting...
All with the waste of the years dishevelled the fair plaits and fallen...
Glittered the swarthy plaits in head-dresses jewelled and golden.
All with the waste of the years broken, and shorn are the tresses.

–Ambapali

~

So I forsook my world – my kinsfolk all,
My slaves, my hirelings, and my villages,
And the rich fields and meadows spread around,
Things fair and making for the joy of life –
All these I left, and sought the Sisterhood,
Turning my back upon no mean estate.

– Subha

~

For five-and-twenty years since I came forth
Not for one moment could my heart attain
The blessedness of calm serenity.
No peace of mind I found. My every thought
Was soaked in the fell drug of sense-desire.
With outstretched arms and shedding futile tears
I gat me, wretched woman, to my cell.

– Sama

~

One day, bathing my feet, I sit and watch
The water as it trickles down the slope.
Thereby I set my heart in steadfastness,
As one doth train a horse of noble breed.
Then going to my cell, I take my lamp,
And seated on my couch I watch the flame.
Grasping the pin, I pull the wick right down
Into the oil …
Lo! The Nibbana of the little lamp!
Emancipation dawns! My heart is free!

– Anonymous

Sarahapada
(c. 100–200 CE)

FOR OVER ELEVEN CENTURIES STARTING FROM THE SECOND CENTURY CE, there was a great churning of ideas, giving birth to some of the greatest minds in the Indian subcontinent. Among these were Sarahapada, Nagarjuna, Bhartrihari, Gaudapada, Adi Shankara, Abhinavagupta, Allama Prabhu, Akka Mahadevi and Ramanuja, to name just a few.

Sarahapada was a maverick mystic-philosopher, in a class of his own. He made fun of the monks for what he considered their pretence at renunciation, questioned Vedic authority and challenged the dominant narratives of his time. Yet, curiously, he was later revered as a mahasiddha, acharya of Tantrayana, guru of sahaja yoga, siddha of siddhas, yogishwara, Great Brahmana and so on.

Although he eventually came to be known as Sarahapada, originally his name was Rahula or Rahulabhadra. Sarahapada was an epithet he acquired once he came to be considered as an 'arrow shooter' or one who has shot the arrow into the heart of 'dualistic perceptions'. The weapon, in fact, became so significant a symbol of his life that in popular iconography he is depicted holding an arrow.

Sadly, not enough is known about his family and background. What we have is only a sketchy account of his life gathered from works available on him in the Tibetan language. Nagarjuna, the founder of the Madhyamaka philosophy, was one of his students, so we may confidently say that he lived around the first or second century CE in eastern India. It is said he was born to a brahmin family in Vidarbha, and was known as Brahmana Rahula. But as a young man he rebelled against his community, gave up his brahmin identity and disregarded its caste rules. He drank alcohol, associated with a low-caste woman and mocked everything Brahmanical. Enraged, the brahmin community is said to have complained to the king about his sacrilegious behaviour and sought his punishment, though nothing came of it. Later, he is believed to have taken to the path of a sramana and become a Buddhist.

Legend recounts that he joined the monastic university Nalanda as a student and became a teacher there. He is considered to be one of the founders of two Buddhist traditions, the Mahamudra tradition, and the Vajrayana tradition, on which he even wrote a treatise in Sanskrit. But he did not stay for long at Nalanda; he left the monastery and turned into a wandering yogi.

Two stories stand out during this phase of his life that indicate the radical shift in his life. What is most striking in these stories is that women were his instructors and companions in his spiritual journey.

Wandering about in search of a teacher, the story goes, he comes upon a woman making arrow shafts from reeds. Fascinated by her intense concentration and her dexterousness, he stands affixed to the place, watching her. A while later he asks her, 'So you are an arrow maker?' The woman raises her eyes to him and quips, 'You can understand the Buddha's tattva only through actions and symbols, not through words and texts.' It turns out that she is an arrow-making dakini, who in Vajrayana Buddhism is a sacred spirit, or a woman who has undergone extraordinary spiritual development. She could also be a human guru, a qualified Vajrayana master. In this instance she explains the inner or symbolic meaning of the arrow in the tantric language, or what is called *sandhyabhasa*, twilight language: a feature of esoteric traditions that use symbolic language incomprehensible to the uninitiated. It is said that Saraha, in that epiphanic moment, fully realized the state of Mahamudra. Mahamudra means 'great seal', or 'great imprint'. In Buddhism, especially in Tibetan Buddhism, Mahamudra refers to a body of teaching called Sahajayana, the vehicle of self-liberation. It is interesting to note here that there are communities following Sahajayana engaged in archery and arrow-making as a form of discipline.

To continue with the story, Sarahapada then abandoned his monastic vows and started his new life, taking the dakini as both his guru and wife.

It is upon learning and practising the art of arrow-making that

Rahula came to be called Sarahapada. The discipline of arrow-making, in effect, radicalized the understanding of what constitutes knowing, jnana or knowledge. According to Sarahapada, jnana involved not the use of words, talking, or transmitting information and so on; rather, it constituted doing, working, developing a particular skill.

As an aside, we see a similar understanding of spirituality developing among the Shiva saranas, devotees, in twelfth-century Karnataka. 'Kayaka' in Kannada means 'work', it could be whatever work or vocation one was involved in, be it ferrying, cobbling footwear, pottery or washing clothes, and it was held as sacred as the act of worshipping Shiva, or as a spiritual offering. This opened a radically new paradigm of spirituality and dignified the skills and hard work of the common people.

In another remarkable story of Sarahapada's life, the dakini, his teacher and consort, is referred to as 'radish curry dakini'. One day, Saraha asked the dakini to make him a radish curry. While she was preparing the curry, it so happened that he slipped into such a deep meditative state that he remained in samadhi for twelve years. Coming out of it after twelve years, he asked his wife and guru for the radish curry. The dakini told him, 'You sit in samadhi for twelve long years and the first thing you ask for is radish curry? Of what use is meditation if it did not diminish your desire for radish curry? Of what use is meditation if it did not enable you to transcend desires and fears, beliefs and concepts that create attachments and suffering?'

Both stories work as parables to highlight the nature of the mind and reality, and to bring home the message of Sahajayana, the natural way of living, free from all forms of attachment. Leave the mind in its most natural state, stated Sarahapada, pure and uncorrupted by conceptuality. In the freshness of the mind in its pure, unencumbered state, he assured, bodhi will naturally flourish.

In Indian and Tibetan Buddhist spirituality, 'sahaja' means spontaneous enlightenment, or spontaneous nirvana, the state of being where duality, separation, has ended and joy and peace is innate in every human being. Saraha made no distinction between a monk and a householder, for even a layperson, he said, could achieve nirvana in this lifetime through Sahajayana; therefore, there is actually no difference between nirvana and samsara, world, or worldly life.

Both in Buddhism and Hinduism at the time, renunciation was seen as superior to samsara, and it was believed that renunciation alone could lead one to the shore of anantasukkha, eternal happiness. Saraha questioned this assumption, and challenged all the formalities of sects and traditions. Truth cannot be attained merely through austere practices, studying scriptures, bathing in holy waters, or worshipping images of gods; to gain true knowledge one has to let go of all kinds of formalities and beliefs, and allow the mind to intuit its inner nature and just be, simply exist.

To be natural needs no effort. Children don't make an effort to be natural; they are born with an instinct for naturalness. Nobody tells a tree how to grow; it grows naturally in complete harmony with the laws of the universe. One needs to make an effort to become something or somebody else, not to be oneself. Nirvana, according to Sarahapada, is not the result of renunciation or sadhana. Awakening has nothing to do with what, who or where you are, but in looking deep into yourself and being able to see things for what they are and move beyond all forms of dualities.

Saraha's teaching was spontaneous and challenging, even irreverent and subversive. Take, for instance, his satirical dig at the spiritual significance associated with nudity and the practice of shaving heads by monks:

> If nudity can earn liberation, then dogs and foxes are most eligible,
> if having an absence of hair indicates spiritual perfection,
> then a girl's ass must have it.

He spared none. To his disciple, Nagarjuna, with whom he had a complex relationship, he once said, 'Come, but keep your philosophy of the middle path locked inside and then come.'

Sarahapada composed dohas, royal songs in poetic couplets, caryagiti or performance songs, and vajragiti or adamantine songs to teach the path of Sahajayana. 'Come,' he welcomed all in one of his songs, 'come, drop all that you are carrying, especially yourself, and all those concepts; come, prepared not to become anything.' It's not easy, though, for acquisitiveness is the nature of the mind, and so we gather things and keep building narratives, although it is like building a castle in the sky.

~

Sarahapada was a rebel, a spiritual maverick who fought against the stifling religious beliefs and conventions of his day. His insurrectionary approach and critique of tradition, leading to a decluttering and simplifying of philosophical beliefs and concepts, evoke the twelfth-century mystic Allama Prabhu, and U.G. Krishnamurti in the twentieth century. Both Allama Prabhu and Krishnamurti rejected all ideas and beliefs to give us a taste of that vast emptiness and great silence that is the natural mind.

Eventually Sarahapada's teaching came to be called Sahajayana, which flourished in Bengal and Odisha, and its followers were known as Sahajiyas. In due course, sahaja, the concept of spontaneous or natural spirituality, entered Hinduism with the Nath yogis and spread into other traditions and various forms of Sahajiyas emerged. The Vaishnava–Sahajiya sect became popular in Bengal. Sahaja sthithi, sahaja yoga, sahaja samadhi were some of the terms used in Hinduism, all of which mean natural state of being. Preferring the term sahaja over enlightenment, nirvana or moksha, U.G. Krishnamurti called the state of being he had come into as the 'natural state', a state of being where the mind is in a 'declutched state' of not knowing, and the body, in tremendous peace, is in tune with nature.

About 26 works are attributed to Saraha in three different languages: Old Bengali, Tibetan and Apabhramsa, a dialect spoken in the north

Indian plains. Interestingly, Apabhramsa also means 'corrupt', as the language deviated from the norms of Sanskrit grammar. It is significant to note here that although Saraha knew Sanskrit well, he composed his dohas in Apabhramsa. Among his most famous works in this language are the three cycles of doha-kosha. Variants of doha style of poetry appeared centuries later in the works of Kabir, Surdas and Tulsidas.

Excerpts from Sarahapada's dohas

Where is samsara? Where is nirvana?
Bodhi dwells neither in forest nor in home.
Recognize this point thoroughly,
Leave the mind in its stainless state,
Free from all conceptuality.

~

When the mind is purified as sahaj,
Then, dualities enter no more;
Just as how, when the lake becomes clear,
Bubbles dissolve into water, its very nature.

~

Like a brahmin taking rice and butter,
Offering sacrifice to the flame,
He who visualizes material things as celestial ambrosia,
Deludes himself that a dream is ultimate reality.

~

The relatively real is free of intellectual constructs,
And ultimately real mind, active or quiescent, is no-mind,
And this is the supreme, the highest of the high, immaculate.
    Friends, know this sacred high!

~

What, where and by whom are nothing,
Yet the entire event is imperative.
Whether love and attachment or desirelessness,
The form of the event is emptiness.

~

It cannot be denied nor yet affirmed,
And ungraspable it is inconceivable.
Through conceptualization fools are bound,
While concept-free there is immaculate sahaja.

~

No tantra, no mantra, no reflection or recollection –
Hey fool! All this is the cause of error.
Mind is unstained – don't taint it with meditation;
You're living in bliss: don't torment yourself.

❦

Nagarjuna
(c. 200)

ACCORDING TO A TIBETAN LAMA TRADITION, NAGARJUNA WAS BORN IN
the first century BCE, worked and lived for 600 years, thereafter went
into a spiritual retreat and eventually transmuted his body into a
glorious 'rainbow body'. In the Vajrayana, a Buddhist Tantra tradition,
usually translated as Diamond Vehicle or Thunderbolt Vehicle, it is
believed that one who attains ultimate realization shrinks until the
person disappears. Only their fingernails, toenails and hair are left
behind, as the person is transformed into light and a rainbow. The Lama
tradition thus holds that Nagarjuna is still alive. He can at will become
visible or invisible, and is still guiding people on the path to nirvana.
Somewhat in relation to this myth, there is the Indian story of

how Nagarjuna got his name and attained great wisdom. It is said he was a serious quester of truth. Dissatisfied with Brahmanical learning, he turned to Buddhism. After studying the three Pitakas, canonical Buddhist literature, he gave up all desires and lived humbly in retirement. It was at this time that he had an awakening of sorts, but still felt there was something lacking, that he had not achieved the state of nirvana he had sought.

Continuing his quest, he began wandering and reached the Himalayas. There, a mahanaga, a great serpent, who was a bodhisattva, took him to the netherworld and presented him with the text of the *Prajna-paramita Sutras* (the oldest and exegetical text of Mahayana Buddhism that majorly deals with the concept of voidness, shunyata). Nagas are considered a mythical race of serpents with magic powers, but scholars believe that the Nagas might have been a Prakrit-speaking people, who had a serpent as their totem and were deeply immersed in the way of the Buddha.

Both these myths tell us about the influential role Nagarjuna played in the revival of Buddhism in the second century CE. No wonder he was called the 'Second Buddha', who once again set in motion the wheel of dhamma. Historically, he was the founder of the Madhyamaka School, the Middle Way, of Mahayana Buddhism.

Using doubt as his method, Nagarjuna probed, questioned and negated ossified narratives to open up a radically new perspective to understanding that which cannot be perceived by the divided self. Through his works, he effectively counteracted the hegemony and dogmatism of Brahmanical schools of thought and the growing literalism and scholasticism of Buddhist sects, the Hinayana sect in particular. It is no exaggeration, therefore, to say that Nagarjuna's works have had tremendous impact on Indian thought, both Brahmanical and Buddhist, and he remains one of the greatest philosophers of all time.

Unfortunately, we know very little of his actual life, except for the hagiographical accounts that exist in the Chinese and Tibetan traditions. These narratives are at variance with each other on a number of counts, including the time and place of his birth. If the Tibetan account places his birth in 482 BCE, the Chinese tradition recognizes it as 212 BCE. Interestingly, Mahayana texts simply state that he was born 1,200 years after the Buddha's death. With regard to the place of his birth, Tamil Nadu, Vidarbha, Videha, Andhra Pradesh and even Karnataka are some of the locations identified by various scholars. However, since there are records of his associations with Nalanda and Nagarjunakonda, and his friendship with the Andhra Pradesh king Satavahana, we could fairly say he was active in both northern and southern India.

Going by available records, Nagarjuna was most likely born into a brahmin family in southern India, in what is today Andhra Pradesh. A story goes that at the time of his birth it was predicted that the boy would die at an early age, and so his parents, hoping to avert the terrible destiny, put him in a Buddhist order. He of course did not die; rather, as fate would have it, he grew up to be a healthy young man of prodigious talents and went on to live a long and great life.

By the time he came on the scene, exciting philosophical debates among and between Brahmanical and Buddhist schools of thought, alongside other competing philosophical systems such as Sankhya, Yoga, Vaisheshika and Nyaya, were at their peak. Nagarjuna deeply engaged with not only these different philosophies, but also with the many sects within the Buddhist stream, especially the Theravada sect.

Nagarjuna's notion of 'emptiness' and his contestation of Brahmanical theories and contemporary Buddhist thought were, in all probability, informed by his deep understanding of the binary nature of the mind and the fragmentary nature of all experiences. In light of this understanding, he employed and developed what is called the *Catuskoti*, 'four-corner' negation – a system of argumentation that involves systematic examination of each of the four possibilities of a proposition – to investigate and interrogate all the metaphysical schools of philosophy which were flourishing around him at the time.

His 'four-corner' negation technique worked like a double-edged knife to deconstruct all systems of thought and had a great influence in the development of Buddhist logic in general and the refinement of Tibetan Buddhism in particular.

In his most famous work, *Mulamadhyamakakarika* (Root Verses on the Middle Way), he deployed the technique of four-corner negation not to establish a new philosophy but to expose the limits of epistemology, theory of knowledge, and demonstrate the futility of all attempts to know what cannot be known. In other words, his negation of positions was no position but an awareness of the conditioned nature of all positions and views. It was not a philosophical treatise aimed at challenging and destroying other views, but an attempt to exhaust and reject all views as obstacles on the path to nirvana.

In order to make this difficult-to-comprehend idea of the fallacy of all views simpler, Nagarjuna offered two perspectives of reality as a sort of corollary to his sunyavada, the emptiness doctrine. These were samvritisatta, conventional truth employed for a practical purpose, and paramarthasatta, supreme truth or the truth of the void or emptiness. That is to say, samvritisatta, which is conventional truth, is the truth we use to transact in our social interactions. We need to accept the conventions of the logocentric world view to live in the world, but with the awareness that they are not permanent. Paramarthasatta, the truth that all our views – our very perception or experience of reality, shaped by knowledge acquired by the binary mind – have no basis in reality. Rather, the fact that they have only a functional value but no permanent basis or significance enables us to free ourselves from attachments and let go of all views.

It is interesting to note here that Western thinkers such as Friedrich Nietzsche, Schopenhauer, Edmund Husserl and Martin Heidegger, to name a few, were quite familiar with Buddhist thought and were probably influenced by it. Lately, a number of postmodernist thinkers have traced parallels between the French philosopher Jacques Derrida's theory of deconstruction and Nagarjuna's Middle Way and his notion of emptiness. Thinkers such as David R. Loy are of the opinion that while Derrida is considered quite radical, he is not radical enough when compared with Nagarjuna. He finds Derrida's type of deconstruction to be logocentric (language as fundamental expression of an external reality, or, a philosophy that all forms of thought are based on an external point of reference), which it tries to overcome, but cannot. 'What needs to be deconstructed,' he says, 'is not just language but the world we live in and the way we live in it.' In other words, one can deconstruct a text, but not dukkha, nor fear and anxiety, pain and pleasure. Nagarjuna's four-corner deconstruction is aimed not merely at exhausting all views but at doing away with the whole ideation process so that one gives oneself a chance to enter a state of being where the division between samsara and nirvana has ended, where there simply is no two, no separation – advaya.

Selected Verses from *Mulamadhyamakakarika*

I bow down to the most sublime of speakers, the completely awakened one who taught contingency (no cessation, no birth, no annihilation, no permanence, no coming, no going, no difference, no identity) to ease fixations.
No thing anywhere is ever born from itself, from something else, from both or without a cause.

Without letting go of seeing, a seer does not exist; in letting go of seeing, there is also no seer. If there is no seer, where can there be what-is-seen and seeing?

Because birth and remaining and perishing are not established, there is no conditioned. Because the conditioned is utterly unestablished, how can the unconditioned be established?

Like a dream, like a magician's illusion, like a city of gandharvas, likewise birth and likewise remaining, likewise perishing are taught.

When nirvana is not born and samsara not eliminated, then what is samsara? And what is considered as nirvana?

When one ceases thinking of inner and outer things as self and mine, clinging will come to a stop. Through that ceasing, birth will cease.

Through the ceasing of action and affliction, there is freedom. Action and affliction come from thoughts and they from fixations. Fixations are stopped by emptiness.

Everything is real, not real; both real and not real; neither not real nor real: this is the teaching of the Buddha.

Do not say 'empty,' or 'not empty,' or 'both,' or 'neither:' these are mentioned for the sake of conventional understanding.

The Dharma taught by Buddhas perfectly relies on two truths: the ambiguous truths of the world and the truths of the sublime meaning.

Those who do not understand the division into two truths, cannot understand the profound reality of the Buddha's teaching.

Without relying on conventions, the sublime meaning cannot be taught. Without understanding the sublime meaning, one will not attain nirvana.

Samsara does not have the slightest distinction from nirvana. Nirvana does not have the slightest distinction from samsara.

Whatever is the end of nirvana, that is the end of samsara. There is not even a subtle slight distinction between the two.

Bhartrihari
(c. 500)

IT IS SAID THAT AFTER SUFFERING HIS FIRST WIFE'S INFIDELITY, AND THE death of his devoted second wife, Pingala, Bhartrihari, the king of Ujjayini, disgusted by the endless cycle of pain and pleasure of samsara, abdicated his throne in favour of his younger brother Vikramaditya and sought to live a higher life. But as a man used to sensual pleasures and material comforts, it was not easy for him to transition into a simple, spiritual life. He made seven attempts to renounce worldly life and take to ascetic living but his weakness for women caused him to fail each time. A poem written by him eloquently indicates his state of mind.

> In this vain fleeting universe, a man
> of wisdom has two courses: first he can
> direct his time to pray, to save his soul,
> and wallow in religious nectar bowl.
> But, if he cannot, it is surely best
> to touch and hold a lovely woman's breast
> and caress her warm round hips, and thighs,
> and to possess that which between them lies.
>
> (Brough, trans., 1977)

When he finally turned his back on a life of debauchery, it is believed he left home and met with Yogi Gorakshnatha, the famous guru of the Natha tradition, and was initiated into a path of spirituality which eventually turned him into a yogi and helped him live a life of dispassion.

> When in the darkness of love,
> Ignorant, I wandered about, I saw nothing,
> Nothing in the wide world, but only women;

But just when I was cured of the blindness,
Through knowledge, the ointment for the eye,
Forthwith appeared all calmly over my eye,
And I saw in the world only one: Brahman!

(Sri Aurobindo, trans., 1969)

Bhartrihari, who is believed to have lived around the fifth century CE, is the author of the *Satakatraya*, a work of Sanskrit poetry, comprising three collections of about a hundred stanzas each, expressing different aesthetic moods or rasas: shringara (love / erotic), vairagya (dispassion) and niti (ethics and polity). These works are highly regarded in the literary world. His love poems in particular, teasing, sensuous and passionate, are as accomplished as the best in any language.

It should be noted here that Sanskrit literature is generally associated with the subject of religion and spirituality with texts such as the Upanishads, the Bhagavad Gita and Brahmasutras, but there is much that is not of or about religion, which may be called 'secular', that is of great literary value.

Another major work attributed to Bhartrihari, namely, *Vakyapadiya*, is on Sanskrit grammar and linguistic philosophy, but leading Sanskrit scholars are split in their opinions about its authorship. However, today, many are of the opinion that the same Bhartrihari is the author of both works. And why not, some have argued – the grammarian can also be a poet!

Vakyapadiya is an influential treatise on Sanskrit grammar, semantics and philosophy. Bhartrihari's position was that when single words are heard separately they may sound the same yet have different meanings, and it is only when a whole string of words or a sentence is heard that we can arrive at the correct meaning of individual words. In other words, padas, words, are understood unambiguously only in the context of the vakya, sentence, whose meaning as a whole is known.

Bhartrihari used the term 'sphota', which means 'to burst', at three levels: varna sphota, at the syllable level; pada sphota, at the word level; and vakya sphota, at the sentence level. Sphota, according to Bhartrihari, is the intuitive language capability of man. It is the intention behind an utterance and it arises both in the speaker and the listener. In the listener, it comes in a flash of recognition when a string of words, vakya sphota, is heard as a whole.

Bimal K. Matilal, an eminent Indian philosopher, believes that for Bhartrihari, thinking involves vibrations and that the mechanism of thought is the same as that of language. The sphota, therefore, is the carrier of thought, and no thought is possible without language. Interestingly, U.G. Krishnamurti, whose insights into the mechanism of thought and the nature of the mind are quite instructive, has said that thought, which is matter, is a vibration. Thinking is a vibration, too. The vocal chords are active when there is thinking, but we generally do not perceive it.

Naiyayikas, followers of the Nyaya system of philosophy (one of the ancient six schools of Indian philosophy), subscribed to Bhartrihari's position that everything knowable is expressible in language, and there is no knowledge beyond linguistic description. Modern scientists would gladly agree to this, for science works on that premise and as Sundar Sarukkai, a noted modern philosopher, says, 'For science, effability is given in the belief that there is no knowledge about the world which cannot, in principle, be accessed by science' (Sarukkai, 2005).

Buddhists and non-dual schools of thought, such as Advaita Vedanta within Hinduism, rejected Bhartrihari's stance that everything knowable is expressible in language. According to them, language could distort perception. Dignaga, a sixth-century Buddhist scholar, argued that there is a mode of perception or knowing which language cannot capture and express, and that it is inexpressible, ineffable. This is a view supported in varying degrees by most non-dual traditions.

Bhartrihari's sphota theory remains widely influential not only in Indian philosophy but also in Western thought. Ferdinand de Saussure (1857-1913), the linguist and semiotician who lectured on Sanskrit and Indo-European languages at the University of Geneva for three decades, may have been influenced by the sphota debate. His ideas of the sign (an object, quality, event, gesture or action), as composed of the signifier (underlying concept or meaning) and the signified (a concept or meaning as distinguished from the sign), might have been informed by the sphota theory.

Excerpts from the *Satakatraya*

Blinded by self-conceit and knowing nothing,
Like an elephant infatuate with passion,
I thought within myself, I all things knew;
But when by slow degrees I somewhat learnt
By aid of wise preceptors, my conceit,
Like some disease, passed off; and
Now I live in the lain sense of what a fool I am.

~

Idleness is a great enemy to mankind.
There is no friend like energy, for,
If you cultivate that,
It will never fail.

~

The clear bright flame of man's discernment dies
When a girl clouds it with her lamp-black eyes.

(Brough, trans., 1977)

~

The ugly vulture eats the dead,
Guiltless of murder's taint.
The heron swallows living fish
And looks like an ascetic saint.

(Brough, trans., 1977)

~

While describing to her best friend
Her adventures with her lover,
She realized she was talking to her husband,
And added, 'And then I woke up.'

(Brough, trans., 1977)

~

To the calm Light inviolable all hail
Whom Time divides not, nor Space measures, One,
Boundless and Absolute who is alone,
The eternal vast I am immutable!

(Sri Aurobindo, trans., 1969)

Gaudapada
(born c. 600)

GAUDAPADA WAS A SEVENTH CENTURY FOUNDER OF THE VEDIC
philosophy of Advaita Vedanta. He lived at a time when dialogue and
debate between Sramana traditions – non-Vedic movements such as
Buddhism and Jainism – and Brahmana traditions – Vedic Hinduism
– was common.

At the time of Gaudapada, it was possible to move from one stream
to the other and even return to the previous one, for there were many
examples of questers and monks doing this: for instance, Kumarila
Bhatta (seventh century CE) became a Buddhist seven times and as
often lapsed, the same is said about the famous poet-grammarian
Bhartrihari (fifth century CE). In his last avatar, Kumarila Bhatta turned
into a fierce Hindu, upheld the authority and infallibility of the Vedas
and grew critical of Buddhism. But Gaudapada, made of a different
mettle, absorbed the finer aspects of Buddhist philosophy, in particular
Madhyamaka, Middle Path, and incorporated some of its elements,
especially sunyavada, voidness, into his philosophy of Advaita.

Unfortunately, we know next to nothing about this great mystic's background and personal life, except that he was a paramaguru, supreme teacher, and a great exponent of Advaita Vedanta. He was the teacher of Govindapada, who in turn was the teacher of Shankara, the eighth century Acharya of Advaita Vedanta. In some of his texts, Shankara himself affirms this, quoting Gaudapada and referring to him as the master of Advaita Vedanta tradition.

Gaudapada's *Mandukya Karika*, also known as the *Agama Shastra*, is the earliest available systematic exposition of Advaita Vedanta. The *Mandukya Karika* is a treatise in verse form on the 13 verses of *Mandukya Upanishad*, in which Gaudapada establishes the non-dual nature of reality. Unsurprisingly, he mentions the Buddha with reverence, advances arguments similar to the Buddhist philosophers Vasubandhu and Nagarjuna in the course of his exposition to point out and explain the illusory nature of our phenomenal experience, but only to ultimately establish Atman-Brahman as the only reality.

Gaudapada refuted Sankhya's theory of causality. He argued that there is no cause per se, nor effect as such. Cause itself is born as effect; rather, cause-effect is a continuum. He proposed the theory of Ajativada, or non-origination, to explain that nothing is ever born, nothing is created, and there is no transactional reality. The argument was simple: if the eternal Self is the only reality, then whatever seems to exist apart from the Self must be unreal, maya, and hence non-existent. In other words, consciousness is the only reality but appears as material objects, like a burning firebrand that is waved in a circle – alatachakra – by the power of maya.

In actual fact, Buddhists used the metaphor of alatachakra to insist that the impression of a continuous circle is an illusion, and therefore, the circle has no svabhava or nature of its own. Gaudapada overturned this Buddhist metaphor to argue that the burning brand is itself the *substratum* of the burning circle. Actually, the burning circle is not an illusion even if it is considered so, and its svabhava is nothing other than that of the brand. In other words, while the Buddhists thought of the world and its objects as merely an illusion, Gaudapada insisted that this world-illusion was actually made up of consciousness.

Gaudapada thus deployed Buddhist metaphor and terminology to arrive at Vedantic conclusions regarding the ultimate presence of the Atman-Brahman as the substratum, adhishthana, of all experience. He asserted that Atman-Brahman is the only reality, and it is our attachment to unreality, caused by ignorance, which creates the duality which, in turn, causes bondage, fear and sorrow.

Selected Verses from the *Mandukya Karika*

Visva is all-pervading, the waking state where one experiences the external objects. Taijasa, the dream state, is where one experiences the subtle or internal objects. Prajna is deep sleep or a mass of awareness, where all experiences become unified.

Prajna knows nothing of self or non-self, neither true nor false. Turiya, the fourth state, pure consciousness, is forever and the all-seer.

Non-cognition of duality is common to the Prajna and Turiya. But Prajna is associated with the causal state of sleep, and that does not exist in Turiya.

Self-luminous Atman, by the power of its own Maya imagines itself in itself. He alone is aware of the objects. This is the conclusion of the Vedanta.

When the rope is realised to be a rope, all illusions about it cease, and only the rope remains. Realisation of the Self is just the same.

There is no cessation, no coming-to-be, none in bondage, no seeker after liberation and no-one liberated. This is the absolute truth.

From the standpoint of the Self the world does not exist; nor does it exist as independent – neither differentiated nor non-differentiated. This is what the wise know.

The Self is spoken of as existing in individual souls just as space exists encompassed by a pot. Its existence in composite things is like the space in pots.

When the pot is smashed, the pot-space merges totally with Space – in the same way souls merge in the Self.

On realisation that the Self is the Real, thinking ceases: it becomes Non-mind; in the absence of anything to perceive there is no perception.

It is totally ineffable and utterly inconceivable, completely peaceful, eternally radiant, ecstatic, immutable, fearless.

Supreme happiness is within, it is peaceful, it is accompanied by cessation, it is indescribable and birthless. Since it is identical with the Unborn Object of Knowledge, they declare It the Omniscient.

As a moving firebrand appears as a curve, consciousness when set in motion appears as the knower and the known.

As the firebrand when not in motion is free from appearances and from becoming, so too consciousness when not in motion is free of appearances and becoming.

When the firebrand is in motion, the appearances do not come from somewhere else; when it is motionless, the appearances do not go somewhere else, nor do they go into it.

They do not emerge from the firebrand since they are insubstantial. The same applies to consciousness, since in both cases the appearances are of the same kind.

When consciousness is oscillating, the appearances do not come to it from somewhere else, nor do they go somewhere else when it is at rest, nor do they enter into it.

They do not emerge from consciousness since they are insubstantial. They cannot be conceptualised since they are not subject to the relation of cause and effect.

For so long as there is attachment to cause-and-effect there is samsara; once the attachment ends, there is no attachment to samsara.

Having realised the truth of causelessness, and not accepting any individual cause, one attains freedom from fear, suffering and desire.

(Gambhirananda, 1987, and Nikhilananda, 2002)

Adi Shankara
(788–820)

LEGEND RECOUNTS THAT WHILE SHANKARA WAS AT SRINGERI, THROUGH his yogic power he came to know that his mother was seriously ill and dying. He rushed back to Kalady and was near his mother, Aryamba, at the time of her death.

But, if we are to go by the poem 'Mathrupanchakam', believed to have been composed by Shankara in memory of his mother, he was

not present at the time of her death. In the last of the five slokas, he
laments thus:

Neither did I give you water at the time of death,
Neither did I offer oblations to help the journey of death,
And neither did I chant the name of Rama in your ear,
Oh Mother supreme, pardon me for these lapses with compassion,
For I have arrived here late to attend to those.

To add to his distress, the Namboodiri Brahmins, the community to
which he belonged, are believed to have deserted him at a time when he
needed their help to perform his mother's last rites. Their contention
was that he had abandoned his mother and embraced sanyasa. As a
sanyasi who had severed all his ties with samsara, he had lost his right
to perform her last rites. So, they refused to assist him in carrying the
dead body to the place of cremation and even refused to give fire to
light the funeral pyre.

It is a terribly moving story that has been interpreted variously by
scholars and followers of Shankara, and his critics use it to dispute
Shankara's Advaita Vedanta. Among other things, Shankara believed
that individuals and the universal were one and the same, and the
world around us was only maya, an illusion, that binds us to itself. But
how could an absolute Advaita Vedantin, who has transcended the
divisive consciousness, to whom there is no such thing as 'I' and 'you',
perform his mother's funeral rites? In modern times, the philosopher
Aurobindo, who found Shankara's theory of maya problematic, joked
that Brahman laughed at the great non-dualist when he lit his mother's
funeral pyre.

Despite these criticisms, there is no doubt that Adi Shankara was
one of the most fascinating figures of all time. He was certainly one
of the great acharyas of Hinduism and remains the most significant
voice of Advaita Vedanta. In his engagements and debates with

different schools of thought such as the Charvakas, Kapalikas, Shaktas, Sankhyas, Jains and Buddhists, he absorbed and integrated the core ideas and insights from some of these philosophies, especially Buddhism, to formulate his philosophy of Advaita Vedanta as a *direct* interpretation of the Upanishads.

~

Shankara was born in the year 788 CE to a Namboodiri Brahmin couple, Sri Sivaguru and Aryamba, in the village then known as Sasalam. Sivaguru died when Shankara was hardly seven years old and he was brought up by his mother. It is said that he was a precocious child and, by the age of sixteen, he had mastered the four Vedas. On reaching his sixteenth year, Aryamaba wanted to get him married, but he refused and told his mother that he had resolved to renounce the world and become a sanyasi. 'But what would happen to me and who would perform the funeral rites after my death,' she lamented. Moved by his mother's plight, Shankara promised her that he would be there to serve her in her last days and perform the last rites. Before leaving home to find a guru and join the sacred order of sanyasa, he made arrangements that she would be taken care of by his relatives until he returned.

At Badrinath, he became Swami Govindapada's disciple and was initiated into sanyasa. After years of sadhana and training in Advaita philosophy under Govindapada, Shankara visited the holy city of Kashi. There he wrote his now famous commentaries on the Upanishads, the Bhagavad Gita and the *Brahma Sutras*. After this, Shankara is believed to have travelled from Gujarat in the west to Bengal in the east, challenging pandits and scholars from different schools of thought, including the Shaktas, Buddhists and Jains.

In almost all hagiographical works, these different schools of thought are projected as enemies of Vedic dharma and as seeds of evil, and Shankara is portrayed as a hero who overpowered them all and restored the Vedic Dharma and Advaita Vedanta to its pristine glory. Though this might be an overzealous narrative, there is no denying the fact that, like the Buddha, Shankara took an open road and initiated a jnana yajna – offering knowledge as an act of sacrifice – in public space, which led to the revitalization of Hinduism and its different spiritualties.

The most celebrated debate among many that Shankara had during his digvijaya, tour of conquest or victory in all directions, was the one with Mandana Misra, a ritualist, and his wife, Ubhaya Bharati. The great debate took place in Mandana Misra's house, with Ubhaya Bharati, known for her learning, as the referee. Mandana Misra was an authority on Vedic rituals, or Karmakanda, Karma Mimamsa school. The arguments and counter-arguments went on for several days, and in the end Shankara came through victorious, thus establishing the supremacy of Vedantic knowledge over rituals. While giving her verdict in favour of Shankara, Ubhaya Bharati added, 'But, Shankara, your victory remains incomplete. You know I am the other half of Mandana. So, you have defeated only one half of Mandana. For complete victory you need to defeat me as well.'

At first, Shankara was reluctant to engage in a debate with a woman, but when Bharati quoted instances from the past where men and women had debated with each other freely, he agreed. The debate went on for seventeen days and it seemed there was no way the master of the Vedas could be defeated unless there was a change of subject. Finally, Ubhaya Bharati silenced Shankara by introducing the subject of sex: 'Discuss the science and the art of love between the sexes. Enumerate its forms and expressions. What is its nature and what are its centres?'

Shankara took up the challenge and asked for a month's time to answer her questions. With his yogic powers, it is said, he left his 'gross body' behind in a cave (to be taken care of by his disciples) and in his 'subtle body' entered the corpse of Raja Amaruka, just before it was to be cremated. In the form of Raja Amaruka, Shankara lived a life of pleasure with his wives and was so full of joy that he forgot all about the debate with Ubhaya Bharati. Eventually, his disciples, disguised as dancers, came into the royal court to remind him of his unfinished debate. Shankara then left the court in his subtle form, re-entered his body and returned to resume and win the debate, armed with his newly acquired knowledge of sexuality.

Shankara's followers believe that Shankara knew all about kamashastra, the science of sexual love, yet he went through the debate only to effectively bring home the truth of Advaita Siddhanta or Advaita Doctrine. However, Shankara was not the first one to propound the Advaita Siddhanta. Gaudapada's *Mandukya Karika*, also known as the *Agama Shastra*, a treatise on the *Mandukya Upanishad*, was the first attempt to develop a systematic exposition of Advaita Vedanta. Shankara harmonized Gaudapada's non-dual philosophy with that of the Upanishadic texts and built a systemized foundation for Advaita Vedanta.

Shankara maintained that there exists the Satyasya Satyam, the Truth of all truths – namely, Brahman – that is unborn and eternal, that is the source and ground of all existence, that which creates, maintains and withdraws within it the universe. And this ultimate reality or truth has two sides to it, namely, Atman and Brahman. Atman is the perceptible personal particular, while Brahman is the unlimited universal, but in actuality, both Atman and Brahman are identical.

Further, he maintained that through sadhana, which includes study, reflection and meditation, a sincere quester can gain self-knowledge and self-realization, which in effect is the realization of one's real nature as Brahman. This supreme realization of the identity or unity of Atman and Brahman is moksha, liberation, or Jivanmukti, and the one who has achieved this supreme state of being is a Jivanmukta.

Realization of Brahman or the attainment of Jivanmukti, release from the cycles of birth and death, is the highest goal of human existence. One is prevented from achieving this goal due to ignorance, avidya, which in turn is caused by maya. Maya, according to Shankara, is the empirical reality that entangles human consciousness. It is the power of maya that creates a bondage to the empirical world, preventing the unveiling of the true, unitary Self – Brahman.

To explain maya, Shankara introduced the notion of two kinds of truth: vyvaharika satya, phenomenal reality, and paramarthika satya, ultimate reality. According to Shankara, Brahman is the absolute, ultimate reality. It is the Infinite Being, Infinite Consciousness and Infinite Bliss, without form, qualities or attributes. It is the Ultimate Truth – beyond the senses, beyond the mind, beyond imagination. From the point of view of the experience of this Ultimate Truth, Brahman, Shankara asserted, the material world, its distinctness, the individuality of the living creatures, and even Isvara (the Supreme Lord) itself, are all untrue, maya, a mere dream.

Shankara died young, at the age of thirty-two, at Kedarnath, and what he achieved within the short span of his life was most remarkable. He founded four mutts, one each at Sringeri, Badrinath, Puri and Dwaraka. It is believed that his teachings – through numerous works and commentaries about Advaita Vedanta and the four mutts he established – helped in the historical revival, development and propagation of Advaita Vedanta. His teachings continue to influence almost all contemporary monastic lineages and Advaita Vedanta discourses today. His assertion that empirical existence is mere Maya, an illusion, and his idealism that the Self is the only reality, that the Self and the Absolute are identical, have been compared and contrasted with modern idealism – which states that reality is inseparable from human perception and is a mental construct connected to ideas – of Western philosophers, such as George Berkeley, Immanuel Kant, Henri Bergson and so on. His non-dual philosophy that boldly declares the oneness of life is in fact a notable theme of modern New Age Spirituality.

Aphorisms

Knowledge, Jnana, is the only direct means to liberation.

~

The phenomenal world seems to be real, but ... only until Brahman is realised.

~

One should understand the self to be the witness of the organism's activities.

~

The self is absolute consciousness as distinguished from buddhi, individual consciousness.

~

By mistaking the Self to be the individual self, one only imagines that the individual self knows, does and sees everything well. The Self illumines the consciousness.

~

I am other than the senses. I am not the mind. The Self is neither the senses nor mind, but is unconditioned.

~

I am that reality or knowledge that is ever unconditioned and ever free.

~

Sitting in a lonely place one should contemplate the one self, one-pointedly.

~

Meditate on that whose nature is reality, bliss, and knowledge and which is the witness of consciousness, as yourself.

～

All creatures are born of Brahman, the Supreme Self.

(Collated from *Upadeshasahasri* and *Sankara the Missionary*)

⋚⋙

Abhinavagupta
(950–1016)

ABHINAVAGUPTA SAW HIS BIRTH AS COSMIC, A MOMENTOUS EVENT IN the world, a manifestation of Shiva tattva or principle. His passing, too, was cosmic, an awakening into an ethereal state of being: the story goes that, sometime in 1020 CE, when he was over 70 years of age, he entered the Cave of Bhairava (a fierce manifestation of Shiva who destroys fear) in Srinagar with 1,200 disciples. Sitting with the disciples and chanting the hymn of Bhairava, 'Bhairavastrotam', he turned into a blaze of light, like an 'unsetting arisen sun', luminous, ever awakened.

Abhinavagupta was considered an earthly incarnation of Bhairava. Through his life, works and in the manner of his leaving his physical body, Abhinavagupta taught that the entire cosmos is itself the Body of the Divine. There is no death but only awakening into the recognition that one is Bhairava, ever awakened and luminous.

Abhinavagupta (c. 950–1016 CE), a Shaivite sage, was undoubtedly one of the greatest philosophers, mystics, writers and visionaries of India. An aesthetician, poet, musician, dramatist and exegete, he was a terrific polymath. He is the author of over 40 works, the most famous and influential of which are *Tantraloka*, Light on Tantra, *Tantrasara*,

Distillation of the Tantra, and *Abhinavabharati*, a commentary on the *Natyashastra*.

Abhinavagupta was born in Kashmir to a learned and illustrious family. His mother, Vimalakala, and father, Narashima Gupta, were devotees of Shiva. His mother died when he was just two years old and he was raised by his large family, which consisted of learned members, including aunts, uncles, his elder brother Manoraatha and sister Amba. It is said he was born of Tantric sexual union of his parents. So he was called yogini-bhu, born of an awakened yogini, endowed with exceptional spiritual and intellectual prowess. Acknowledging this, Abhinavagupta began his *Tantraloka* with a verse honouring his parents:

> My mother Vimala is she for whom the birth of Abhinava was a festival of joy; my father is renowned as Simhagupta, full of the state of Shiva. May my heart, formed from the emissions of the ecstatic state of their union, embodying the nectar of the Absolute, shine forth.

> (Wallis, 2007)

Abhinavagupta was not his real name, which Abhinava himself reveals in his *Tantraloka* (1.50), though without revealing his real name. In recognition of his brilliance, one of his masters is said to have called him 'Abhinava', which means 'ever new', or 'ever vigilant'. Ever yearning for new knowledge, ever renewing himself, he took as many as 15 teachers, all mystic philosophers and scholars – including Vaishnavas, Siddhanta Shaivas, Buddhists, Jains and Trika kula, Tantra of the Embodied Triad. He was like a bee, flying from flower to flower, collecting the nectar from each.

His father was his first teacher, from whom he learned grammar, logic and Sanskrit literature. From Lakshmanagupta he learned several systems of non-dual philosophy, from Bhaskara the spanda (vibration) system, from Bhutiraja the karma (sequence) system, from Bhatta

Tauta aesthetics and philosophy of language, from Vamanatha dualistic Shaivism and so on. Sambhunatha, Lord Shiva himself, is believed to have been his most beloved teacher, from whom he learned all about what is called 'Kaula' or 'Embodied tradition', where the body is seen as the seat of enlightenment or Shiva principle. At Shiva's behest, Abinavagupta composed the massive compendium on Tantric practice, *Tantraloka*.

He remained unmarried and is believed to have used the vital force of his energy to be in communion with Shiva-Shakti. He travelled widely and met with several yogis and gurus until the age of 35. By then, he was finished with his studies, ranging from grammar to logic, Buddhist philosophy to Tantra Yoga, art and music to aesthetics, and fully grown in his sadhana; he had attained the highest state of being as per the Kaula tradition.

He turned his home into a unique ashram, a centre of spiritual learning and practice. A painting depicting his spiritual home shows him seated in virasana, Hero Pose, a kneeling asana, with two yoginis standing behind him, and surrounded by family members and disciples, while he plays on his veena, simultaneously dictating verses of *Tantraloka* to a devoted scribe.

His ashram was a radical space that ran counter to the orthodox Brahmanical schools that laid restrictions of caste and gender on spiritual study and practice and made the spiritual quest for enlightenment the right of only a chosen few. Abhinavagupta questioned the privileging, in the spiritual realm, of sanyasis and monks over householders. According to him, it did not matter if one was a monk or householder, a brahmin or an outcast, so long as one was pure of heart and serious in one's spiritual pursuit. In a concluding verse of his *Patanjali's Paramarthasara*, he took to pieces the prevailing orthodoxy thus:

O my devotees! On this path of supreme Bhairava, whoever has taken a step with pure desire, no matter if that desire is slow or intense; it does not matter if he is a brahmin, if he is a sweeper, if he is an outcast, or if he is anybody; he becomes one with Para-bhairava.

(Wallis, 2007)

He wrote prolifically until the age of 66 and produced over 40 works, of which only about 21 are available. Some of his major works are mentioned below:

Tantraloka is his most important work, a twelve-volume encyclopaedic tome, translated into many Indian languages. It is an extraordinary synthesis of the Trika system. Trika Kaula or Embodied Triad philosophy, known today as Kashmir Shaivism, considered the body a means to attaining the non-dual state, termed Bhairava or Paramesvara.

Tantrasara, as the name suggests, is a summarized version of *Tantraloka* in prose.

Isvarapratyabhijna-Vimarsini, Reflections on Recognition, commentary to the verses on the recognition of the Lord, is a treatise on the Pratyabhijna School, a branch of Kashmir Shaivism.

Abhinavabharati is a long and complex commentary on Bharata Muni's *Natyashastra*. Abhinavagupta's fame rests on this work, wherein he discussed the theory of rasa and aesthetic savour, as much as on *Tantraloka*.

Kashmir Shaivism, also known as Trika Kaula or Embodied Triad philosophy, or Trika Shaivism, is a non-dualist tradition of Shaiva-Shakta Tantra which originated sometime in 850 CE. The much older Shaivism was called Kula and it was a dualistic tradition, while Trika, whose great exegete was Abhinavagupta, was a non-dualistic tradition. The defining feature of the Trika, which distinguishes it from other non-dual traditions – for instance, Advaita Vedanta – is its idealistic and monistic Pratyabhijna (recognition) philosophical system propounded by Utpaladeva and Abhinavagupta. Another distinguishing factor was the centrality of the three goddesses of Trika: Para, Parapara and Apara. Para is depicted in brilliant white in a benevolent form, considered as Supreme Shakti. Parapara in red and yellow, and Apara in black are both shown as wild and terrifying, wearing garlands of skulls and sporting tridents, representing energies or powers of life. All three goddesses are supposed to be forms of Kali.

Shiva, often referred to as Bhairava, Paramashiva or Paramesvara, is the sole reality and both the material and efficient cause of the universe, and expresses himself in the world in five forms: as chit, consciousness; ananda, bliss; icha, urge; jnana, knowledge; and kriya, action. Liberation happens with the recognition of the presence of the atma or the supreme reality. While Vedanta rejects the dualistic world and experience as unreal, as maya, in Kashmir Shaivism realization comes with the recognition that the whole universe is a manifestation of Paramashiva and that the Self itself is an embodiment of every aspect of the universe.

In other words, it was not necessary to negate and renounce the world as unreal. Abhinavagupta declared that freedom from suffering comes not by renunciation or denying the world but by embracing it as Shiva, by seeing and experiencing Paramashiva in everything. It is the complete awareness of the totality of being here and now.

His writings on Tantra, philosophy, art, poetry and aesthetics interpenetrated each other as different forms and expressions of the same divinity. Tantra, mantra and poetry blend in his discourses. Art or artistic expression is life itself and is an aid to spiritual realization, which is the recognition of the supreme fact that the individual is non-distinct from the ultimate Artist, Paramashiva, who is the source and very ground of creation itself.

One who realizes that [the powers of] knowledge (jnana) and activity (kriya) are but manifestations of the svatantrya [independent power of God] and that these manifestations are nondistinct from oneself and from the very essence of the ultimate, whose form is the Lord (isvararupa)—a person [in this way] "resonating" entirely with the

awareness that knowledge and activity are really one—whatever
this person desires he or she is certainly able to accomplish.
Such a person abides in a state of complete mystical absorption
(samavesa), even though still in a body. Such a person, while still in
the body, is not just liberated while living (jivanmukta) but has in
fact attained the ultimate realization of identity with the supreme
lord (paramvesvara).

(*Isvarapratyabhijna-Vimarsini* 4.1.15; Sanderson, 2005)

Abhinavagupta was influenced by Buddhist philosophy, especially
Buddhist logic, yet his position was different when it came to what
constituted enlightenment or nirvana. In that, he was an adherent
and an apostle of Kaula Shaivism. The Buddhist's position was that it
is pointless to discuss whether the Higher Self exists or not, because,
even if it exists, it cannot be known, it cannot be spoken about; it is
avyakrta, inexpressible, ineffable. For, in the state of being where the
(dualistic) mind is absent, who can tell what it is and is not?

Shankara's position was that Brahman is knowable, realizable, for *It*
or the Real is svamprakasha – self-evident, svasamvedya – self-revealed.
However, Abhinavagupta asserted – which is the central tenet of Trika
Kaula – that one's own I-awareness is itself that supreme awareness
of one's identity with God. In other words, enlightenment or self-
realization is a cognitive act, an act of recognition in which divinity
itself recognizes its own presence.

He classified liberation under three categories: aparamukta, those
united to or still attached to the Supreme in its manifested phase,
namely, the body; jivanmukta, those liberated while living in the
body; paramukta, final liberation. Abhinavagupta was supposed to
be a paramukta, one in whom the remaining karma was destroyed to
gain the final liberation.

Abhinavagupta's influence on Indian, especially Shaiva and Shakta
schools, has been deep and lasting. In fact, many Shaiva schools accept
him as their spiritual head, indeed an incarnation of Bhairava himself.

His influence went beyond Kashmir and even reached down south to Karnataka and Tamil Nadu. It is well known that the Shiva saranas, the twelfth century mystic poets of Karnataka, such as Allama Prabhu, Basavanna and some of their contemporaries, were familiar with Kashmir Shaivism.

❦

Basavanna
(1134–1196)

BASAVANNA WAS A REBEL, MYSTIC POET AND ONE OF THE GREATEST reformers of India. He was irreverent towards authority, even as he worked as a minister under King Bijjala I of the Kalachuri dynasty. His attitude is aptly demonstrated by the following anecdote from his life:

Once, after a long meeting with the king over administrative matters, Basavanna stood up from his chair to leave, when Devarasa, the king's trusted minister and confidante, said sharply, 'Basavanna, one last question. I have observed that you do not actually bow to the Maharaja, but bow to the image of the Shivalinga on your ring. What does that mean? Disregard for the Maharaja? Or, are you questioning the authority of the Maharaja?' (Rao, 2010)

Basavanna replied: 'I bow only to Lord Shiva. I don't mean to disrespect our Maharaja. I work under him; he is my master and my King, but not my God. Kings come and go and they serve a need. We have created a world where kings and governments are considered necessary. Otherwise, there could be anarchy and danger. But a time will come, and when it comes, we shall be in no need of kings and states. We should work towards building such an enlightened society. I'm sure our Maharaja would agree that the king's role lies in creating such a world where Dharma and peace will reign supreme.' (Rao, 2010)

Basavanna was born sometime around 1134 CE in Bagevadi, a town in Bagalkot district, Karnataka, to Madalambike and Madiraja.

It is said that even as a boy he was quite a rebel. He revolted against orthodox beliefs and practices, especially against the caste system and Brahmanic ritualism. Around the age of ten or so, legend has it that he tore off the sacred thread, left Bagevadi and went to Kudalasangama in Bagalkot, and became a disciple of Guru Eshanya, the head of Sangamesh Monastery, a Shaivite school of learning.

It is at this monastery, over the next twelve odd years, that he studied the Vedas, the Agamas – non-Vedic texts – and was introduced to Kashmir Shaivism and the Shaivism of the Nayanaras, a group of Shiva devotees during 3rd to 8th centuries CE in Tamil Nadu. It was here at Kudalasangama, exposed to different spiritual cosmologies and through rigorous sadhana, that Basavanna came upon his calling and became a spiritual radical. Kudalasangamadeva, a Shivalinga and the deity of the temple at Kudalasangama, became his chosen God and the closing signature line of his vachanas, prose-poems.

Subsequently, he went to Kalyana, Bidar district, and married Gangambike, the daughter of a minister in the court of Bijjala. He started working as an accountant in the court of the king, and later as prime minister. He later also married the king's foster sister, Neelambike, who was close to Gangambike. And it was at Kalyana, as the king's minister, that he started out as a religious reformist. Distressed at and critical of the religious structures and practices built on and around the Brahmanical traditions, he initiated a religious movement – a new, vibrant form of Shaivism with egalitarian ideals, challenging and rejecting Brahman orthodoxy, the caste system and gender discrimination.

This new kind of Shaivism came to be called 'Virashaivism' in the fifteenth century and later, Lingayatism. It was derived from the word 'Virashaivas', the 'brave or heroic devotees of Shiva'. This new Shaiva Siddhanta was a creative mix of Buddhist and Hindu philosophies as well as Kashmir Shaivism, combined with a critique of Brahmanism from within Hinduism.

This new religious doctrine rejected the Vedic ritual of fire worship, the practice of Brahmanical impurities (the pancha-sutakas or the five kinds of pollution), the authority of the Vedas and the priestly caste, as well as the varnashrama dharma, based on birth, heredity and privilege. It encouraged widow remarriages and departed from the Vedic ritual of cremation, instead they buried the dead. To these new dispensations, some of which were not entirely new but pressed into service with greater vigour and direction, Basavanna added a firm rejection of temple worship and devised a new ritual for worshipping the Shivalinga.

Like Narayana Guru, the modern Dalit spiritual teacher and reformer, and Mahatma Gandhi, Basavanna was a 'critical insider'. While on the one hand he rejected the spiritual authority of the Vedas and oppressive features of the Brahmanical tradition, on the other, he developed what may be called a spirituality of liberation from within the Hindu spiritual traditions.

The rich will make temples for Shiva.
What shall I, a poor man, do?
My legs are pillars, the body the shrine,
the head a cupola of gold.
Listen, O Kudalasangamadeva,
things standing shall fall,
but the moving ever shall stay.

(Ramanujan, 1973)

This vachana of Basavanna succinctly summarized the central concern of this new cult of Shiva. According to scholar A.K. Ramanujan, the temple is a 'static standing thing that has forgotten its moving originals', and the poem 'calls for a return to the original of all temples, preferring the (human) body to the embodiment'.

Basavanna introduced the practice of linga-dharana, literally wearing the linga on the body, thereby challenging temple culture, the ritual, social and spiritual authority of the brahmin priests and pandits, and yet upholding the spirit of bhakti. This linga, worn on the body, was called 'ishtalinga', 'dear linga', as opposed to 'sthavara linga', the fixed linga, installed and established in temples. Saranas wrapped the ishtalinga in a piece of cloth or set it in a small silver casket and wore it round their neck in such a way that it rested on their chest. Twice a day the devotee would take it out, hold it in his palm and worship.

At the forefront of this resurgent Shaivism were people traditionally belonging to the 'lower castes', including boatmen, washermen, tanners, cooks, shepherds, labourers, fishermen, toddy sellers, prostitutes and peasants. For instance, among Basava's close associates, Jedara Dasimayya was a weaver, Shankar Dasimayya a tailor, Madivala Machayya a washerman, Myadar Ketayya a basket-maker, Kinnari Bommayya a goldsmith, Vakkalmuddayya a farmer, Hadap Appanna a barber, Jedar Madanna a soldier, Ganada Kannappa an oilman, Dohar Kakkayya a tanner, Mydar Channayya a cobbler, and Ambigara Chowdayya a ferryman.

Vachana means 'thing said', not smriti or what is remembered, not sruti or what is heard or received, but thought–feelings and insights, uttered here and now. No metrical or prosodic patterns were used in the vachanas, but they combined the lucidity of prose with the rhythm of poetry. And among these saranas sprang poets, both men and women, of great spiritual depth and understanding. And each one brought his or her unique insights and idiom into the rich repertoire of vachanas. If some were direct and even candid to a fault, some were profound, complex and mystical.

Through the technique of irony, paradox, abuse, assertion and drawing images from their vocation and everyday experiences, they spoke of their perception of things, about pretensions and false devotion, the absurdity of orthodoxy, and false consciousness. Their work, their vocation – called kayaka – whether it was cow-herding, cobbling sandals, or washing clothes, was considered as sacred as the worship of Shiva.

To the saranas, bhakti was supreme, the mantra, the way and the goal. Sometimes the vigour and passion with which they took to their beliefs and practices bordered on fanaticism: they considered it sacrilegious to worship any form or symbol of God other than the linga. Their faith demanded that there be no caste discrimination amongst the Shiva-bhaktas, and to show their solidarity, it was essential to dine together, a practice which came to be called dasoha. Dasoha actually means charity given with a sense of service. Similar to the Sikh langar, at the Lingayat Mutts, free meals are served to all, irrespective of religion, caste and gender.

What undid this revolutionary movement was the open challenge the saranas threw at the then political power and Brahmanic order, in the form of a marriage between a brahmin girl and an ati-shudra, untouchable, boy. This marriage, between the tanner Haralayya and the brahmin Madhuvarasa, let loose the destructive forces from within the ancient Hindu order. It was a historical marriage and a marriage that would change history. It was a fearless and thunderous expression of their faith as much as a denunciation of the varnashrama dharma, which viewed marriage between a brahmin woman and an untouchable man the most heretical of all possible inter-caste marriages. To the saranas, however, the day Haralayya and Madhuvarasa received their diksha and wore lingas on their bodies, they had severed their links with the caste they had been born into. They were Shiva saranas now, plain and simple, with no caste identity and therefore no caste duties to be followed.

But the Brahmanical authority viewed the marriage as a threat to its ancient order and prompted the king take action against the revolutionaries. The parents of the newly-wed couple were arrested, tortured and killed. In retaliation, Jayadeva, a militant young sarana, assassinated King Bijjala. The king's son, Somadeva, then let loose his army on the hapless Virashaivas. Thousands of saranas, including

Basavanna, had to flee the city of Kalyana, thus bringing to an end one of the most inspiring, socio-philosophical revolutions in Indian history. Subsequently, after losing their revolutionary zeal and vision, the large and still growing community of Virashaivas devolved into yet another caste within the Hindu caste structure, claiming a status higher than the brahmins.

There are today hundreds of Lingayat mutts, big and small, spread across the state. Some of them have entered the social field to open hospitals, establish educational institutions and provide hostel facilities to poor children. However, not surprisingly, all the divisive beliefs and practices that Basavanna criticised as not being conducive to build a casteless, just society and come upon anubhaava, the direct experience of God, have now been reintroduced into the lives of Lingayats and their many mutts.

Nevertheless, the lives and vachanas of some of the saranas, especially Basavanna, Allama Prabhu and Akka Mahadevi, have inspired a considerable corpus of extraordinary writing that deals with issues of social justice, gender equality, religious transcendence and spiritual liberation. Their vachanas continue to evoke a vision of society and life beyond borders, bringing home the possibility of self-realization, here and now.

Basavanna's Vachanas

You exist
like light hidden in the horizon,
like a frame in a picture,
like meaning in a word,
O Kudalasangamadeva!

~

Lord, your sacred feet
cover the earth and sky,
extend to the underworld and beyond.

The crown of your head
touches the boundaries of the boundless space.
O, Kudalasangamadeva,
both visible and invisible,
mysterious is your form,
now come alive as Linga in my palm.

Without *anubhaava* bhakti is empty;
Without *anubhaava* linga is unattainable;
Without *anubhaava* one understands nothing.
When such is the truth, why call
anubhaava an invention of thought,
O, Prabhudeva?

(Translated by author)

∽

Allama Prabhu
(c. 1100)

ALLAMA PRABHU WAS AN AVADHUTA, ONE WHO HAS SHAKEN OFF ALL
worldly attachments, a jangama, wandering monk, a mystic poet
and a maverick sage all rolled into one. To use a line from one of his
vachanas, he was like a butterfly with 'no memory of the caterpillar'
and his life was like the flight of an eagle in untrammelled air.

A fascinating story of Allama Prabhu's encounter with Gorakanath
offers a vivid description of Allama's intriguing mystic personality.
Gorakanath, who lived sometime around the eleventh century CE,
is considered a Mahayogi and founder of the Natha tradition. This
encounter, described in fifteenth century Kannada spiritual texts, is
imaginary yet philosophically real. When a spiritual master appears
on the scene, he needs to check out the different schools of thought

or traditions, and if they are found wanting and failing, he confronts them in a philosophical debate in order to awaken them. Many philosophical debates and quarrels have been of this nature in India, though, sometimes, spiritual traditions have used this technique to claim superiority over other traditions or sects.

So one day, while passing through the land of the Siddhas, Allama Prabhu came upon Gorakanath, grinning and blocking his path. It is said Gorakanath challenged him to a duel, but Allama showed no interest and only wanted Gorakanath to get off his path. But when Gorakanath mocked him and persisted, Allama accepted his challenge. Thus, the terrific contest between the two masters began. Taking out a deadly sword that shone liquid-white like silver, Gorakanath gave it to Allama and said: 'Strike me and cut me in two, that is, if you can. Come on, don't hesitate.'

Allama swung the sword at Gorakanath, but the blade clanged on the body that was hard like diamond. And Gorakanath roared in triumph.

Returning the sword to Gorakanath, Allama said, 'Try it on me now. Let's see.'

Gorakanath swung the sword at Allama with all his strength. The sword swished through Allama's body, as if through space.

'You are empty,' cried Gorakanath in utter amazement, and down from his hand fell his sword and lay near Allama's feet. (Rao, 2010)

Allama Prabhu was born in Shivamogga in Karnataka, to Sujnani and Nirashankara. We do not know the exact year he was born, but since he was a contemporary of Basavanna, we could assume it was sometime in the early part of the twelfth century.

Allama was born into a low-caste family. His father, Nirashankara, was a dance teacher and Allama, as a young man, worked as a temple drummer. The story goes that he madly fell in love with one Kamalathe, a temple dancer, and got married to her; but, as fate would have it, within a short period after their marriage, she caught a fever and died, leaving Allama heartbroken. Suffering her memory, it is said, Allama drifted from place to place. One day, he happened to discover a shrine, entering which he came upon a yogi, Animisayya (the one without eyelids, or the open-eyed one), sitting in a trance in the heart of the temple. Legend recounts that Animisayya handed over a sacred linga to a stunned Allama and vanished into thin air. It was an explosive moment that burned away his suffering: Allama found himself totally transformed.

From then on, Allama turned into a jangama, singing his song of life. About 1,300 vachanas are attributed to Allama. But he was not a bhakti poet in the conventional sense of the term. His vachanas end with his signature: Guheshvara or Lord of Caves, signifying light and darkness, that which *is* and *is not*, and that which cannot be comprehended by the divided mind.

His vachanas are marked by explosive images and bewildering metaphors that break and leap over the limitations of language. The mind is stunned reading about 'the toad that swallowed the sky', a 'black koel eat up the sun', a 'blind man catch a snake', and the many gods reduced to a heap of ash. He was, like Nagarjuna of the second century and U.G. Krishnamurti of modern times, the ultimate negator of everything that can be expressed, for all expressions are an interpretation of life and the world, mere constructs. Borders and boundaries fall away and one realizes that there is nothing to seek, no yonder shore to reach, rather there is only the vivid, living, ineffable present.

Allama is believed to have visited Kalyana, where Basavanna lived and taught, presided over the famous Sunya-Shimasana, the Throne of Void, at Anubhava Mantapa, the Hall of Experience, and engaged himself in conversations with the Shiva saranas. He rejected Vedic tradition and questioned and ridiculed image worship, the caste system, religious customs and rituals. Most vachanakaras, composers of vachanas, including Basavanna, Akka Mahadevi, Siddarama and others, spoke of him in their vachanas in glowing terms and with worshipful attitudes, referring to him as Prabhu, master – indeed, as the guru of gurus, yet one who had no wish to offer a teaching, establish a sect or have disciples.

His teaching, if his vachanas are to be considered as embodying teaching at all, is in the mode of anti-teaching: geared towards stunning or silencing the mind and emptying it of all ideas. In Allama's vachanas, gods die, their spouses become widows, and the Vedas get dismissed as mere gossip, pandits and monks are fools and bhakti is so much noise. All this leads to questioning and puncturing all frames of thought to give us a taste of the void.

We do not know how Allama Prabhu died, all we are told by the texts is that after his last visit to Kalyana, he left for Srisaila, located in Nallamala hills in Kurnool District of Andhra Pradesh, and was heard no more. Today, Allama Prabhu is seen as a Lingayat, belonging to the Virashaiva faith. And there are mutts, though few, where he is worshipped as an incarnation of Shiva. Unlike most Lingayats, Allama did not wear a linga on him; in fact, he was critical of image worship. 'When there is no outside or inside, when there is no I or other,' he challenged, 'where is the sign, where is the need for any sign or symbol?' (Rao, 2010)

Selected Vachanas of Allama Prabhu

I saw the toad swallow the sky,
the blind man catch the snake.
I saw the heart conceive,
the hand grow big with a child,
the ear drink up the smell of camphor,
the nose eat up the dazzle of pearls, and
hungry eyes devour diamonds.

~

In a blue sapphire,
I saw the three worlds hiding.
Yet, looking for your light,

I went hither and thither,
in and out, and it was like
a sudden dawn of
a million million suns,
a ganglion of lighting,
O Lord of the Caves.
But tell me,
if you are light, what am I?
O, there can be no metaphor...

~

I saw the corpse of samsara
alive with swarming worms.
I saw dogs come to devour
the reeking body, start a fight.
But I didn't see you anywhere there,
O Lord Guheshvara.

~

Whence this great tree,
whence the koel bird?
Whence and what kind of relationship?
Gooseberry from the mountain,
salt from the sea,
whence and what kind of relationship?
O, Lord of the caves,
between you and I,
whence and what kind of relationship?

~

Your Vedas are mere words,
Your shastras and puranas a gossip,
Your bhakti so much noise...

~

The one who knows joy is not the happy one,
the one who knows sorrow is not the unhappy one,
the one who knows both joy and sorrow
is not the jnani, only the one who grasps
the sign of the dead and
of the one who was never born,
knows Lord Guhesvara.

If there is no desire,
there is no imagination;
if there is no imagination,
there is no thinking;
if there is no thinking,
there is no Guheshvara;
if there is no Guheshvara,
there is no truth,
no void, either.

(Translated by author)

Akka Mahadevi
(1130–60)

TREKKING HUNDREDS OF KILOMETRES, AKKA MAHADEVI REACHES
Kalyana to meet with Allama Prabhu and Basavanna. But she must pass
one more hurdle before she can do so. She is stopped from entering
Anubhava Mantapa, the Hall of Experience at Kalyana, by Kinnari
Bommayya, a noted poet and highly respected Shiva sarana. Why has
she discarded her clothes and come naked as the day she was born?

He suspects her spiritual maturity and wants to test her. He decides
that if she has really experienced union with the linga, he would
surrender and accept her as his mother, but if he saw any sign of shame,

anxiety and fear, then he would know that she is a fake. Brazenly, he walks towards her and demands she submit to the physical test.

Akka Mahadevi pushes him away and cries: 'You look an unabashed hypocrite, come abandoning your spiritual path. What are you shamelessly leering at? These sagging breasts, untied hair, sunken cheeks, withered arms, and this thing, a mere passage for urine. You fool, get off my path.' But Kinnari Bommayya won't let her go. Realizing the pointlessness of fighting him, Mahadevi surrenders herself to the situation, saying, 'In truth I'm not a woman. What do you think? Uniting with lord Chennamallikarjuna I have ceased to be woman.' Kinnari Bommayya touches her face, arms and other parts of her body. He realizes that her body, without any trace of strain or anxiety, had become the receptacle of Divinity. And he notices traces of vibhuti, ash, on her body, on her yoni.

Akka tells him, 'Brother, what you see, the vibhuti, is nothing but the desires burnt to ash.'

Kinnari Bommayya offers his remorseful apology and surrenders to her like a devotee to a god, and then himself proudly escorts her to the Anubhava Mantapa to meet Allama Prabhu and Basavanna. (Rao, 2018)

If on the one hand, Akka Mahadevi was like a unique fragrant mountain flower, a gift of nature, on the other, she was the ultimate archetypal quester, who, literally walking naked, moved beyond all binaries – I and other, male and female, even devotee and god – into a life of freedom and fullness. In other words, her life brings home the wonder and mystery of life, indicating the possibility of transcending the divided, gendered self, and living as one with the cosmos.

Mahadevi was born around 1130–1160 CE, at Uduthadi, in Shivamogga in Karnataka. Her parents, Nirmala Shetty and Sumati, were ardent devotees of Lord Shiva. Legend recounts that at quite an early age Mahadevi took to worshipping the Shivalinga. Perhaps she was initiated into the worship of the Shivalinga by her guru and, like Andal, the seventh century saint of Tamil Nadu, she considered herself betrothed to her god.

She spent her adolescence in his worship and composed vachanas, prose-poems, that spilled over with fervent longing for her Beloved, whom she called 'Chennamallikarjuna', the name of Shiva in her hometown's temple. At the early stage of her devotion, her Lord Shiva has a name and form. He is saguna, one with attributes. The vachanas are intensely iconic, relational; there is rasa or aesthetic emotions: love and lovelornness, hope and despair, agony and ecstasy.

Shiva, the Lord of the Peaks, was her real husband, but, like Meera Bai, she was forced to marry an earthly man. One morning, at the time when the family had set out to a nearby Shiva temple, King Kaushika happened to be on his way to the next town. Kaushika saw Mahadevi among the crowd and, smitten with love for her, decided to have her as his wife. The next day, he sent a marriage proposal through his emissary. Nirmala Shetty, Mahadevi's father, refused to agree to the proposal because Kaushika was a Jain, a bhavi, a non-Shaivite, but eventually, fearing the possibly dangerous consequences, he gave his consent. Mahadevi knew Kaushika was capable of putting her parents to sword if she rejected the offer, so she finally agreed to marry Kaushika.

She put three conditions before him: one, Kaushika should not come in the way of her devotion to Lord Shiva and her sadhana; two, she should not be prevented from meeting her guru and visiting maheshwaras, devotees of Maheshwara, Shiva; three, she should have the freedom to live as she wished. If he were to violate the conditions laid for her to stay at the palace, she would walk free.

Kaushika had no objection, for he was elated that Mahadevi herself would willingly wed him and come to the palace. The conditions she had laid for her stay did not bother him, and he believed that it would be just a matter of time before she would turn into a devoted wife.

Mahadevi did not. Instead, she spent most of her waking hours immersed in prayers, or spent whole days with the wandering monks who came and went like flock of birds. She lived in the palace like an ascetic. But come evening, Kaushika would send for her, and the darkness would descend upon her world and she would go numb. There was no escape, she was his formally wedded wife and she had voluntarily agreed to the sacrifice.

How did Mahadevi bear this contrary union? Going by her vachanas, Mahadevi did not convert this tension into a religious conflict between the flesh and the spirit; rather, given her ineluctable circumstances, in all probability, she took a practical view of things, prayed and waited for a sign.

> Why do I need this dummy
> of a dying world?
> Illusion's chamberpot,
> hasty passions' whorehouse,
> this crackpot
> and leaky basement?
> Finger may squeeze the fig to feel it,
> yet not choose to eat it.
> Take me, flaws and all,
> O Lord Chennamallikarjuna.

(Ramanujan, trans., 1973)

As her fate would have it, the marriage did not last long. One day, a few maheshwaras arrived at the palace and sent word for her. It so happened that Mahadevi was resting at the time, so Kaushika shouted at the maid not to wake her up and sent the saranas away. The clamour awakened Mahadevi and she went wild with anger at Kaushika for coming in the way of her meeting with the Shiva devotees. The first condition she had laid upon him was thus broken, but upon his imploring her, legend says, she forgave him.

Another day, while Mahadevi was in Kaushika's chamber, her guru happened to come to the palace to see her. Kaushika would not let her go, insisting that as his wife it was her duty to be with him. She stood firm and demanded that he let her go so that she could see her guru right away. In a fit of rage, Kaushika shouted at her to leave that very moment if she could not be his wife. The second condition was broken but Mahadevi forgave him yet again.

Yet another day, the third condition too was breached. When, after her morning bath, Mahadevi sat in meditation, the sacred linga cupped in her raised left palm, Kaushika broke in on her sacred hour and tried to take her by force. Thus, he broke even the last condition that had been laid upon him.

Mahadevi walked free. Like a bird at last freed from her cage, Mahadevi walked away and out of Kaushika's life, from her hitherto incarcerated existence as the queen in the palace, from her past that now seemed a heap of mere ash. Like a snake that sheds off its old skin, Mahadevi shed her needless modesty and cumbersome sari. Like Shiva who walked naked through the pine forest looking for Sati, his skin burning and shining like burnished gold, Mahadevi, giving a strange twist to the tale, walked sky-clad past the civilized world in search of Shiva, the Lord of the Peaks.

Legend recounts that from Uduthadi, Mahadevi trekked nearly 800 kilometres to meet with Basavanna, Allama Prabhu and other saranas. After braving her trial by fire at the hand of Kinnari Bommayya, no sooner had she entered the Anubhava Mantapa, when she was quizzed about her personal integrity and spiritual merit by none other than Allama Prabhu himself.

It is said that Allama had to interrogate her not to clear his own misgivings about her spiritual maturity but to dispel the possible doubts of the saranas. However, that did not ease Mahadevi's experience; the questions were stinging and testing:

'Why have you come here? The whole world knows that you were married to King Kaushika, that you betrayed his trust in you and ran away. Why?'

Mahadevi answered: 'Of what use have I of husbands who die and decay? Throw them into the kitchen fires. The One with no bond nor fear, no clan nor land, no birth nor death, no place nor form, my Lord Chennamallikarjuna, He is my husband.'

And to the question about her nudity and why, if there was nothing to hide, she had to hide her body behind her tresses, Mahadevi said: 'Prabhu, are you really troubled by my young age and body? Men and women blush when a cloth covering their shame comes loose. But when the entire world is the eye of the Lord overlooking everything, what can you cover and conceal? Still I cover myself with my hair for the sake of the world, lest people see in my body what is not there. And it is to protect others and not myself, nor to hide anything.

(Rao, 2018)

Convinced of her answers, Allama Prabhu praised her spiritual achievement and maturity and called her 'elder sister' – akka. From then on, she was always referred to as Akka Mahadevi.

~

Akka Mahadevi lived her last days in the deep and mountainous part of the forest at Srishaila in Nallamala hills in Kurnool, Andhra Pradesh. She lived in one of the caves there, away from prying eyes and chattering tongues, with the forest and hills and River Krishna flowing by as her companions. Just as she settled down in the forest to an uninterrupted life of prayer and contemplation, legend recounts that first her parents, then her husband, Kaushika, visited her and pleaded with her to return home. But Mahadevi told them that she was safe and at peace with herself and at home in the company of her Lord, and bluntly asked them to go back and never bother her again.

Akka Mahadevi continued to live in the cave and is believed to have attained the state of tranquillity, or wholeness. Going by her later vachanas, she even ceased speaking of Chennamallikarjuna, or of her agony of separation and yearning for union. The search, the struggle,

the yearning, had ceased. It was a journey from bhava to anubhaava –
the unmediated experience or vision of the Absolute Infinite Principle.

> I am a bhakte,
> but I cannot tell
> there is a devotee and lord.
> I do not know vows and rituals
> or what even anubhaava means.
> I am a sarane
> but there's no surrender nor holding on to anything,
> the thought sarana-sati linga-pati means nothing,
> there is no separation,
> all that exists is one.
>
> (Translated by author)

All she knew was to go where her heart took her, and with single-
minded, burning devotion to her Lord, she moved swiftly, shedding
the 'unessential' as she moved from Uduthadi to Kalyana to Srishaila.
From bhakti to awareness – arivu – to emptiness – bayalu; from what
may be called Saguna Brahman to Nirguna Brahman. We do not know
for how long she lived thus at Srishaila. The story ends abruptly, and
the manner of her passing remains a mystery.

Akka Mahadevi continues to occupy a significant place in the
spiritual history and popular culture of India today. Her life lived in
defiance of religious tradition and conventional notions of sex and
gender has made her a complete rebel and a foremost feminist. In
Karnataka, she remains a force active in the writings of women poets in
particular, and in Kannada literature in general. In fact, Akka Mahadevi
is a household name in the state, remembered and commemorated in
literature, films, music videos, and with roads and universities named
after her.

A Selection of Akka Mahadevi's Vachanas

Not seeing you,
in the hill, in the forest,
from tree to tree,
I roamed,
searching, crying: Lord, my Lord,
where is your kindness?
Give me a clue to your hiding place,
come, show me your face,
O Lord Chennamallikarjuna.

~

People,
male and female,
blush when a cloth covering their shame
comes loose.
When the lord of life
lives immersed without a face
in the world,
when all the world is His eye,
looking on everywhere, what can you
cover and conceal?

~

Sagging breasts, untied hair
sunken cheeks and withered arms,
brothers,
why do you leer at me?
I'm a woman who has lost
caste and pride,
is dead to the world
and become a devotee.
Fathers,

why do you stare at me
I'm a woman who
uniting with Chennamallikarjuna
has lost status and pride.

~

Look,
the Veda and Shastra
Agama and Purana
are mere powdered grain-chaff
on the pounding stone.
If one can sever
the head of the mind
that hops around
then,
O lord Chennamallikarjuna
there is nothing
but utter void.

~

I do not say it is the Linga,
I do not say it is oneness with the Linga,
I do not say it is union,
I do not say it is harmony,
I do not say it has occurred,
I do not say it has not occurred,
I do not say it is You,
I do not say it is I,
After becoming one with
Chennamallikarjuna,
I say nothing what[so]ever.

(Translated by author)

Thiruvalluvar
(c. 500)

ONCE, A SPIRITUAL ASPIRANT ASKED THIRUVALLUVAR WHICH OF THE two ashramas, stages of life, was better: grihastha, householder, or sanyasa, renunciate. It was, in a way, an irrelevant and silly question to ask one who was leading the life of a householder. Thiruvalluvar, however, did not answer the question. They were having lunch at the time, and Thiruvalluvar told his wife, Vasuki, that the rice was very hot and asked her to bring a fan to cool it. The rice had been cooked in the morning and couldn't have been hot; still, the wife obeyed her husband's command without demur. The aspirant was amazed and intrigued by the strange behaviour of the master and his wife. Then it dawned upon him that it was meant to be the answer to his question. The perfect harmony between the husband and wife and their cordiality showed that it was possible to live a householder's life in perfect harmony and peace, yet be spiritual, engaged in the pursuit of knowledge. Indeed, in the very first chapter of his great composition, *Tirukkural*, Thiruvalluvar says: 'There is more penance in the life of a householder who does what should be done and avoids any lapse from dharma, than in the privation of hermits.' (Rajagopalachari, 1996)

Thiruvalluvar was commonly known as Valluvar. His birth year uncertain, although a considerable number of scholars agree that he most likely lived sometime around fifth century CE in Madurai, and later in the town of Mylapore, Tamil Nadu. His mother, Adi, and father, Bhagwan, had three sons, including Valluvar, and four daughters. However, there is considerable debate about this, and indeed all aspects of Valluvar's life. Since he extols agriculture in his work, some scholars believe he belonged to the agricultural caste Vellalars, while others think he was a Paraiyar, possibly a weaver or royal drummer caste.

And what profession did he pursue? Again, opinions are divided. An agriculturalist, drummer, priest, poet, soothsayer or healer. But one thing we can be certain about was that he was an extraordinarily intelligent and wise man, a keen observer of life and a great visionary. He was very much a married man, and he and Vasuki made an ideal couple. Legend has it that he was devastated when Vasuki died. He turned hermit, devoted to religious contemplation. Here is a moving poem, he wrote after her death:

Dost thou depart, who did'st prepare
My savoury food with skilful care;
On whom alone of womankind,
In ceaseless love, I fixed my mind;
Who from my door hast never stirred,
And never hast transgressed my word;
Whose palms so softly chafed my feet,
Till charmed I lay in slumbers sweet;
Who tended me with wakeful eyes–
The last to sleep, the first to rise?
Now weary night denies repose:
Can these eyes know sleep again?

(Robinson, 2001)

Tirukkural, literally Sacred Verses, or tersely the *Kural*, was written in Tamil and contains 1,330 couplets or kurals, divided into 133 sections of 10 couplets each. It is truly a compendium of aphorisms on almost every aspect of ethical, social, political, economic, religious, philosophical and spiritual life. It covers not only the problems of everyday life and their possible solutions, but also deals with the follies and vices of kings, education of princes and the destruction and chaos wreaked by war, famines and epidemics, with emphasis on the vital principles of non-violence and the path of righteousness and truth.

Universal in its appeal, *Kural* is considered to be the modern Veda or Tamil Veda, and has been translated into about 82 languages, including several Indian ones. Owing to its universality and non-denominational character, many religious groups see their own moral codes, values and philosophy of life reflected in the work. Though Valluvar was born a Hindu and was immersed in Hindu philosophy, it is quite likely that he was inspired by Jain teachings, especially their principles of non-violence and vegetarianism, and drawn to the life of Jesus Christ and his 'Sermon on the Mount', which only proves the catholicity of the work and its author. Jainism as an old religion had a presence in Tamil Nadu, and it is possible that Valluvar was well exposed to Christianity, which had begun to spread across the state at the time.

Legend has it that Valluvar took his work to the Pandiyan king's court at Madurai, and presented it to an assembly of 49 scholars who had assembled there to assess the works of several poets. Valluvar's work was praised and accepted unanimously as a work of the highest quality and of universal relevance. At the assembly, Avvaiyar, the celebrated Tamil poet, is believed to have described the power of the *Kural* thus: 'Valluvar pierced an atom and injected seven seas into it and compressed it into what we have today as *Kural*.'

Selections from the *Kural*

> Where there is no tenderness of heart,
> Life is barren of purpose.
> Can a tree that is dried up in the desert sun
> Put forth leaves?

$\sim$

> Truly it is strange that people speak harsh words,
> When they have themselves felt the joy
> That kindly speech begets.
> You may neglect everything else,
> But be ever vigilant in restraining your tongue.

$\sim$

If one wrongs you, put up with it,
Better still to forget it, if you can.

~

The gruel that children's little hands have stirred
Is sweeter than nectar.

~

To use bitter words, when kind words are at hand,
Is like picking unripe fruit when the ripe fruit is there.

~

The wound that's made by fire will heal,
But the wound that's made by tongue will never heal.

~

Real kindness seeks no return;
What return can the world make to rain clouds?

~

How can kindliness rule that man
Who eateth other flesh to increase his own?

~

Anger kills both laughter and joy;
What greater foe is there than anger?

~

Whatever things a man gives up,
By those he cannot suffer pain.

~

Even the ignorant may appear very worthy,
If they keep silent before the learned.

~

Reasoning with a drunkard is like
Going under water with a torch to seek for a drowning man.

(Rajagopalachari, trans., 1996)

❧

Nandanar
(c. 700–800)

'DALIT' MEANS 'BROKEN', ONE WHO IS EXCLUDED FROM THE four-fold caste system. In many parts of India where the caste system was followed stringently, and any violation of its rules were severely punished, a Dalit had to announce his arrival in public streets and public spaces, so as to not 'pollute' the members of the upper castes. In the musical play based on the work *Nandanar Charitam* (1861) written by the poet Gopalakrishna Bharati (1810–96), in the opening scene a Dalit character cries out, 'May I come in?' apparently seeking the permission of the audience to step onto the stage.

It took centuries before the Dalits would protest against such inhuman discrimination and start the fight for equality and justice, before they could replace the hapless cry 'may I come in' with a self-confident, thunderous warning:

Clear the way, the Dalits are coming,
their hearts and minds ablaze,
with a million dreams
voiced in the language of earthquakes,
burning torches in their hands,

sparks of revolution in their eyes,
exploding like balls of fire,
the Dalits are coming,
rewriting history with their feet.

(Dalit poet Dr Siddalingaiah, 1975)

~

Nandanar lived sometime around seventh or eighth century CE. His life was truly a moving tale of untold suffering and redemption. After his death, he was deified as a spiritual luminary, a worshipful Nayanar (Shaivite saint), and he became an inspirational figure for the Dalits. But in actual life he bore the cross of suffering stoically till his death. In 1927, on a visit to Chidambaram, Tamil Nadu, to lay the foundation stone of the doorstep of a temple, recalling the life story of Nandanar, Gandhiji called him a true practitioner of satyagraha: 'Nandanar broke every barrier and won his way to freedom, not by brag, not by bluster, but by the purest form of self-suffering...he shamed his persecutors into doing justice by his lofty prayer, by the purity of his character he compelled God Himself to descend and made Him open the eyes of his persecutors.'

Gandhiji's words do capture the spirit of Nandanar's life, but it is an excruciatingly painful fact that over the centuries suffering has been the lot of the lower castes, Dalits in particular, and any protest against the brutal caste discrimination and the bigotry of the upper castes was fated to be passive and non-violent.

Nandanar's story is told in *Periya Puranam*, a twelfth-century hagiographical Tamil work on 63 Nayanars, who were Shaivite saints. The more popular *Nandanar Charitam* is a more objective and realistic account of Nandanar's life and the tyranny of the upper castes, and this work has been the basis of many later retellings.

Nandanar was from Mellanallur, a village in Thanjavur district of Tamil Nadu. He was born into the Pulaiya caste, who were considered untouchables. Pulaiyas were agricultural labourers, leather makers, artisans and drummers. They made drums and other musical instruments from wood and cattle skin. Nandanar was skilled in making drums; he also worked as a labourer on the fields of a Vedhiya, an upper-caste landlord. Whenever a kettledrum had to be made for the temple, Nandanar himself would take the required leather to the temple people.

Since he belonged to an untouchable caste and was not allowed inside the temple, he would stand at the gate for a glimpse of the Shivalinga. The story goes that the Nandi idol that sat in the direction of the sanctum sanctorum blocked his view. Moved by his devotion, Shiva himself commanded the giant stone bull to move aside so that the bhakta, devotee, could view the linga. Promptly, Nandi moved a little to the right and Nandanar could catch a glimpse of the god.

Nandanar was a Shiva bhakta. Even standing at the gates of the temples filled him with joy. It was the varnashrama dharma that prevented him from going inside for a closer view of the linga, let alone offer puja to the god. But he yearned to enter the temple, to come face to face with the Lord of the universe. Returning home in great joy after having a glimpse of the linga, it is said, he decided to go to Chidambaram and try his luck there at the Thillai Nataraj Temple, dedicated to Nataraj, the Lord of Dance, a vibrant aspect of Lord Shiva. But he was not able to muster enough courage to leave for Chidambaram. When asked when he planned to go there, he would say, 'I'll go tomorrow.' When a few such tomorrows had passed, he came to be called 'tiru nalai povar' – 'one who will go tomorrow' and the name stuck.

Finally, one day, a determined Nandanar approached the landlord for permission to go to Chidambaram. The landlord laughed at the idea and advised him to stick to his caste and community deities. Even his own people warned him against the trip and asked him to leave the brahmin gods alone. But Nandanar persisted with his plan. The story takes a metaphysical turn here and we are told that the landlord at last agreed to grant permission, provided Nandanar ploughed his large tract of land for cultivation before leaving for the temple. Lord Shiva smiled, for he knew what had to be done in favour of his devotee. The next day morning, the landlord was shocked to see the entire land ploughed and the soil prepared for sowing. He realized Nandanar was no ordinary person and gladly let him go to Chidambaram.

At Chidambaram, Nandanar could not, of course, enter the temple. A determined Nandanar waited at the gate, praying to Shiva, and pleading with the priests to let him go in and have just one glimpse of the lord. The brahmin priests snorted and scoffed at his request; didn't he know people of his caste were not allowed into the temple? That night, the lord appeared in the dream of the temple dikshitar, priest, and commanded him to let Nandanar enter the temple after a ritual purification through a holy fire.

The next day, the brahmin priests prepared a pyre outside the temple and Nandanar entered the sacred fire and came out purified, looking bright like a brahmin sage, a sacred thread across his lustrous chest and his limbs smeared with holy ash. As the gods above showered flowers on him and the now enchanted brahmins cheered, Nandanar walked into the temple, entered the garbhagriha, sanctum sanctorum, merged and became one with the image of Lord Nataraja.

This story of Nandanar was later appropriated into *Periya Puranam*, a religious narrative depicting the lives of 63 Nayanars, canonical poets of Tamil Shaivism. Nandanar was canonized as the 18th Nayanar saint.

However, there are different ways of reading myths, folktales and legends, and it is crucial to know the likely sources and authors of these tales. Sometimes, these tales hide cruel truths in order to fit them into the mainstream. Non-canonical narratives put forward a different, rather, a more probable version. Nandanar was most likely burnt at the stake to put fear of God in the hearts of the lower castes. And by transforming Nandanar into a brahmin through the fire trial, the superiority of the brahmin was reinforced and the legitimacy of the varnashrama dharma, that denies Dalits access to temples and religious texts, was upheld. The fire trial metaphor here works in two ways: one, it is an attempt to clean up the evil deed or sublimate the negative, purify and spiritualize what is otherwise a repulsive story, and project it as a great tale of pure bhakti, to instruct and inspire. Two, it is a technique to confuse, confound and redirect the anger of the victim community and domesticate their energy in the service of the orthodoxy.

Today, Nandanar is worshipped as a great saint in many Shiva temples. There is even a sacred water tank, called Nandanar thirtha in Chidambaram at the place where Nandanar supposedly went through the fire purification. Nandanar's tale of suffering and redemption continues to be retold through folk tales, plays, stories, art forms and feature films. Today, he is an icon of protest in the Dalit rights movement, as much as an inspirational and worshipful figure in the saga of bhakti and freedom.

෴

Andal
(c. 700–800)

OVER A SPAN OF TWELVE CENTURIES OF THE BHAKTI MOVEMENT, starting from the sixth to seventeenth century, we come across many women devotees who chose to remain unmarried; rather, they refused to be betrothed to any mortal man for they considered themselves already wedded to their beloved deities. If married, as in the case of Meera Bai and Akka Mahadevi, the 'earthly' husbands were 'secondary' husbands and didn't count in their spiritual journey. These women saw themselves as nitya sumangalis, eternal wives, and they could never be widowed. In the realm of bhakti, the stories of Sitas and Savitris didn't serve as ideal models; in fact, pativratadharma, moral and religious duty of a married woman, was subverted and rendered irrelevant.

Andal's marriage with Lord Ranganatha (the reclining form of Lord Vishnu) is one such story. She lived 1,300 years ago but is still alive today in the hearts of millions of people through her story, songs, music and art forms. To this day in Tamil Nadu, it has been a tradition to recite and sing verses from her composition, *Thiruppavai*, in temples and musical concerts in the winter festival season of Markhazi. She has, in fact, become a deity worthy of worship in many temples. She holds a prominent position among the 12 Alvars, the Vaishanvite saint-poets who inaugurated the bhakti culture that spread across the Indian subcontinent and democratized the sacred communion with Divinity, which the priestly caste had arrogated to itself.

The extraordinary story of the 12 Alvars, Tamil poet-saints, who were supreme devotees of Lord Vishnu and popularized Vaishnavism, began in the second century CE. The poetic works of these saints in Tamil, compiled as *Nalayira Divya Prabandham*, containing 4,000 verses, and is considered a Tamil Veda, along with the more popular *Tirukkural*. Most of these have been rendered into songs and are sung in Vaishnava temples and on religious occasions.

Not all Alvars were from the brahmin or upper castes; in fact, some of the well-known ones came from the lower castes. For instance, Thiruppaan Alvar was from the paanar community of musicians and song makers, who were traditionally treated as untouchables and not allowed into temples. Thirumangai Alvar was from the kallar caste, supposed to be robber community. Kulasekara Alvar was a kshatriya, Thirumazhisai Alvar an ati-shudra, untouchable, and Nammalvar, considered the greatest among the Alvaras, was a shudra. The Alvars were instrumental in promoting the Bhagavatha cult, the worshipping of Krishna as Bhagavan, and spreading Vaishnavisim in the South.

Andal was the lone woman among the 12 Alvars. We know nothing about her parents and caste. Legend has it that she was found under a tulsi plant by a brahmin named Vishnuchittar, who was a devotee of Lord Krishna, an avatar of Lord Vishnu. He adopted and named her Kodhai. Vishnuchittar lived in Srivilliputtur, a village close to the historic city of Madurai in Tamil Nadu, and would later be known as Periyalvar, eldest Alvar.

Vishnuchittar made garlands of choicest flowers plucked from his own flower garden and offered them every morning and evening to the local deity. The young Kodhai, who had by then considered herself betrothed to Lord Krishna, would deck herself with the garlands intended for the temple deity, Sri Ranganatha of Srirangam in Tiruchirapalli. Studying herself in a mirror, she would place it back in the basket only after feeling satisfied that it would look grand on the Lord too. This she did every day and felt filled with inexplicable joy. One day, the priest at the temple saw a strand of hair in the garland and was shocked. He reprimanded Vishnuchittar and asked, 'How did this happen, and now how can I offer a desecrated garland to the Lord?' Distraught, Vishnuchittar returned home, made a fresh garland and took it to the temple.

The next day, Vishnuchittar caught Kodhai in the act of wearing the flowers and scolded her. That night, Lord Ranganatha appeared in his dream and commanded him to let Andal wear the flowers before offering them to Him, since the scent of Andal's hair emanating from the garland was dearer to him than anything else. Kodhai felt accepted and blessed by Lord Ranganatha, and now she had no doubt He was her husband. As years rolled by and she came of age, her father brought up a proposal of marriage. To Andal, the very thought of being married to a mortal felt like a sacrificial offering to God being violated by jackals in the forest. She flatly refused and declared, 'I intend to marry the Lord alone.'

Here are two of the outpourings of her divine frenzy for spiritual communion with Lord Krishna.

O glorious God of love!
I pray thee understand the penance
I perform with the body foul, hair dishevelled,
eyes pale and a single meal a day.

To thee I wish to wed,
grant me the boon to touch your feet,
O Lord Krishna!

~

My lustre and hue,
mind and sleep have deserted me
in my lonely affliction.
The sense of shame is of no avail now,
for all and sundry know the truth.
Come, my lord, don't tarry.
Come, save my life,
take me to Gokula…

How does one give a mortal in marriage to the immortal God, the Lord of the universe? Clueless, Periyalvar was caught in a dilemma. It was out of the question; a marriage to God would be nothing short of a miracle enacted on human stage, blessed by the grace of Sri Ranganatha Himself. And so it happened that Lord Ranganatha appeared in Periyalvar's dream and assured him that Andal would be accepted by Him as the divine bride if brought to His presence in the temple.

Finally, as per her wish and in accordance with Sri Ranganatha's bidding, Andal was taken in a ceremonial procession to the temple and was given away in marriage to the Lord of Srirangam. Legend says that Andal walked straight into the sanctum sanctorum and stood beside the idol of Lord Ranganatha, and then, to the utter amazement of Periyalvar and other devotees, she vanished in a sudden burst of blinding light.

Andal's legacy consists of two literary works she composed in Tamil verse form: *Thiruppavai* and *Nachiar Tirumozhi*. It is said Kodhai listened to her father singing every morning and evening, and was familiar with his compositions, and that was how she got imbued with poetry from a young age. She would imagine herself among the gopis in the Brindavan and Gokul, feeling lovelorn like Radha, waiting for the arrival of Krishna, her breasts swelling with love, and poetry flowed out of her.

Thiruppavai, The Song Divine, is a collection of 30 verses in which she sees herself as a cowherd girl, a gopika, in love with Lord Krishna. The poems articulate devotional fervour, metaphysical symbolism and artistic excellence. *Nachiar Tirumozhi*, Sacred Utterance, a longish poem of 143 verses, deeply autobiographical, expresses her bold sensuality and intense longing for Lord Krishna. It is an audacious work, frank and free, expressing bridal love and the burning desire to seek union with her Lord – an erotic genre of love poetry akin to Jayadeva's *Gita Govinda*. While *Thiruppavai* is widely endorsed and sung in many Vaishnava temples, verses from *Nachiar Tirumozhi* are not as favoured, especially by orthodox Vaishanava sects, because of their erotic content.

My life will be spared
Only if he will come
To stay for me for one night
If he will enter me,
So as to leave
the imprint of his saffron paste
upon my breasts.
Mixing, churning, maddening me inside,
Gathering my swollen ripeness
Spilling nectar,
As my body and blood
Burst into flower.

(Dalrymple, 2015)

Andal remains a living legend and one of the most popular poet-saints in the religious history of South India. Almost every Vaishnava temple in Tamil Nadu has a shrine dedicated to her and her songs from *Thiruppavai* are sung in most Hindu Tamil households. *Thiruppavai*, considered the nectar of the Vedas, embodying ethical values, love and devotion, has been translated into many languages of India, and the work has been commented upon by innumerable scholars in different languages.

Extracts from *Thiruppavai*

Did you not hear, Oh slow witted girl,
The twittering sound of black birds of the morn,
Which sounds like a talk between them,
Did you not hear the tingling sound,
When the big and small coin like pendants,
Rub against each other,
Did you not hear the sound of vigorous pull,
Of the curd churner being pulled,
By the flower bedecked cow herdesses,
Did you not hear the sound of twirling curd,
When churned using the mixer,
Oh, leader among girls, how can you sleep,
When they sing the names sweetly.
Of Narayana and Kesava.

~

In the pond in the backyard of your house.
The lily in the ponds have opened,
The night flowers have closed,
The white toothed sages,
Who wear clothes as red as
The powder of brick,
Are going to their temples
To sound the conch.
You who promised to wake us up, please wake up,

Are you not ashamed,
You chatter box,
Let us all sing about the lotus eyed one,
Who has a holy conch and disc in his hands,
Oh Lord Vishnu.

(Ramachander, trans.)

Extracts from *Nachiar Tirumozhi*

Andal whilst admiring herself wearing the garland
which was meant for the deity,
the guilt glazed love lay on her breasts
thick and heavy as him.
Frightened with force
and locked away, she conjured him every night,
her lord Krishna.

My surging breasts long to leap to the touch of his hand
which holds aloft the flaming discus and the conch.
Coax the world-measurer to caress my waist,
to encircle the twin globes of my breasts.

(Sarukkai and Shankar, trans, 2016)

Ramanuja
(1027–1137)

ONE DAY, KEEN TO LEARN THE HITHERTO SECRET ASTAKSARI, EIGHT-syllable mantra – om namo narayanaya – Ramanuja went to the guru Gosti Purna. It was supposed to be a powerful mantra which had been revealed to only a few, and the guru did not think Ramanuja was ready for it. Ramanuja, however, persisted with the request and, at last, Gosti Pura initiated him into the sacred mantra. The story goes that right after the initiation, Ramanuja climbed the temple tower and announced the secret mantra at the top of his voice to all those interested. Gosti Pura was furious and cursed him to hell. Ramanuja accepted the curse and said that if the sacred mantra could uplift people and lead them to liberation, he would gladly go to hell. Touched by Ramanuja's concern for the well-being of people, the guru took back his curse and blessed Ramanuja.

Among the acharyas, religious teachers, namely Shankara, Vallabha, Madhva and Nimbarka, Ramanuja stands out not only as one of the greatest spiritual masters but also as one who endeavoured to translate the spirit or the core teaching of Vedanta, which is the oneness of life and equality of Atmans, into social practice. And his Sri Vaishnavism, the doctrine of bhakti and prapatti, devotion and surrender to God, laid the foundation for the flowering of different colours of Vaishnavism across the country and made bhakti the major force within Hinduism.

The growth of Vaishnavism – the belief that Lord Vishnu is the supreme god – is traced to the Vedas; to the Puranas, such as *Bhagavata Purana*, their myths and stories, views of God, cosmogony and social order; to the Ramayana, wherein Sri Rama is seen as an avatar of Lord Vishnu; to the Mahabharata, the Bhagavad Gita in particular, which laid emphasis on the path of bhakti for liberation; and Bhagavatism, which identified Lord Vishnu with Bhagavan, the lord of the universe and source of goodness.

Over centuries, drawing inspiration from these texts, different forms of Vaishnavism developed in tune with the aspirations of people and their religious and cultural background. Some of these were styled after their respective founders, Madhva, Nimbarka, Chaitanya Mahaprabhu, Jnaneshvar and so on. We call Ramanuja's kind 'Sri Vaishnavism' to distinguish it from others. His was one of the earliest Vaishnava traditions after the 12 Alvars, and their lives and compositions, compiled in *Divya Prabandham*, had a considerable influence in the development of Ramanuja's vibrant form of bhakti and Vishishtadvaita, qualified non-dualism.

Ramanuja was born to Kanthimani and Asuri Kesava Somayaji in Sriperumbudur, Tamil Nadu, sometime in 1027 CE. It is said he lost his father while he was still young. He married young and moved to Kanchipuram, where he studied Vedanta under the guru Yadava Prakasa. But he found the guru's interpretation of the Vedic texts, particularly the Upanishads, problematic and disagreed with him on several issues. So he left him and met Periya Nambi, also called Mahapuran, considered the best of the Vaishnava teachers. He renounced his married life and was initiated into Vaishnavism by Periya Nambi. He was 32 years of age when he took sanyasa, settled down at Srirangam and began his long life as a philosopher and preacher of Sri Vaishnavism. There he composed *Vedantasara*, commentaries on *Brahma Sutras* and the Bhagavad Gita. He came to be known as Yatiraja, the prince of ascetics, and his fame grew far and wide.

Ramanuja believed that Adi Shankara, in his Advaita Vedanta, non-dual philosophy, did not deal justly with the relation of the devotee to God. Ramanuja built a strong philosophical case against what he considered the unwarranted abstractions of Advaita Vedanta, especially the notion of maya, illusion. Ramanuja did not believe that the world should be dismissed as merely an illusion. The jivas, individual souls, and the world are both real and independent, but their reality is dependent on that of God, Brahman. Neither of them is the same as Brahman. Yet the world, jivas and Brahman form a unity – the world and the souls have their existence as the body or expression of Brahman. The world of matter and the jivas are the glory of God. But they are nothing apart from Brahman. In other words, Brahman, the souls and the physical world are all real and distinct, all different and equally eternal, and at the same time inseparable. Brahman is both Nirguna and Saguna, transcendent and immanent. Ramanuja accepted Advaita, non-dualism, but with a qualification, visesa, hence his philosophy is called Vishishtadvaita, qualified non-dualism.

To Ramanuja, the claim of oneness and sameness with Brahman and denial of the existence of the world was an error, even blasphemous. In effect, as the philosopher, S. Radhakrishna says, it was a sorry substitute for intelligent devotion. True being of Atman or an individual soul consisted not in an absorption in the Supreme, but in fellowship with Him. In centuries, Ramanuja was the first to systematically counter Adi Shankara's Advaita Vedanta and offer an alternate, cogent interpretation of the Upanishads and other ancient spiritual texts.

He argued that the Upanishads, including the *Brahma Sutras* and the Bhagavad Gita, have to be seen as an integrated corpus of jnana, knowledge, as expressing a consistent philosophy, rather than taking isolated portions to interpret and bolster one's own doctrine, as Shankara had done. The Upanishads uphold both plurality and oneness; therefore, he asserted, the truth must combine both pluralism and non-dualism, that is to say, qualified non-dualism as opposed to Shankara's unqualified non-dualism.

More importantly, by bringing in the urge for bhakti, or devotional worship, Ramanuja gave bhakti an intellectual basis. The goal of the human being is to love and serve God, anything that detracts from this truth detracts from His glory. This form of bhakti or Vaishnavism is called Sri Vaishnavism. The prefix 'Sri' is related to the presence of Sridevi, otherwise known as Goddess Lakshmi, who, along with Lord Vishnu, form the basis of ultimate reality. This was the belief of the Alvars as well.

It is said Ramanuja's enemies made two attempts on his life, both unsuccessful. The third time, on learning the king Chola I, who was a Shaivite and hated the growing popularity of Sri Vaishnavism, could put his life in danger, Ramanuja prudently left Srirangam and went to the then Hoysala kingdom in Karnataka. There, he is believed to have converted the Jain king Bitti Deva to Hinduism, and with the help of Bitti Deva, who changed his name to Vishnuvardhana, he had a temple of Lord Thirunarayanaswamy built on the hills of Melkote, in present day Mandya district, Karnataka. Today, Melkote is a popular temple town with a Sanskrit academy. Ramanuja lived in and around Mysore for 22 years, and by the time he left the place, Sri Vaishnavism had spread all around Mysore.

Meanwhile, King Chola I died and his successor, Kulothunga Chola, who was favourable to Ramanuja, wanted him to return to Srirangam. Ramanuja went back, and completed his most influential work, *Vedanta Sutra*, also referred to as *Sri Bhasya*. It is Ramanuja's most famous work, wherein he refuted Shankara's notion of non-dualism or Advaita Vedanta and his theory of maya, and presented the fundamental philosophical principles of Vishishtadvaita with particular focus on bhakti as a means to liberation.

Ramanuja is believed to have lived for another 22 years, teaching his way of bhakti. On approaching 120 years of age, legend recounts, Ramanuja prayed to his beloved Lord Narayana to let him depart from his mortal body. He had done his best to preserve the essence of the Vedas and it was time to go. But it was unbearable for his disciples to let him go and they begged him to stay for some more years at least for their sake. But the decision could not be changed and to appease their grief, Ramanuja is believed to have given the following final instruction:

Always remain in the company of and serve those souls devoted to Godhead just as you would serve your own spiritual preceptor. Have faith in the teachings of the Vedas and in the words of the great saints. Never become the slave of your senses; always strive to conquer the three great enemies of self-realization: lust, anger, and greed. Worship Narayana and take pleasure in uttering the holy names of God as your only refuge. Sincerely serve the devotees of Godhead; by service to the great devotees, the highest service is done and one quickly gains the supreme mercy. Remembering these things you should live happily in this world for the attainment of the next.

(Gaudiya History: Ramanujacharya)

During his time, Ramanuja himself had initiated many from non-brahmin communities into Sri Vaishanvism; there had been no bar on the lower castes to join the new faith. However, after Ramanuja's passing, a section of the Sri Vaishnavites devolved into a closed community. In the sixteenth century, Sri Vaishnavism mutts split into two: Thenkalai (southern) tradition and Vadakalai (northern) tradition, both of which are still active today, following their own hagiographical versions of Ramanuja's life and teaching.

Thenkalai is a liberal, Tamil-based tradition, headquartered at Srirangam, with nine mutts in different parts of Tamil Nadu, Karnataka and Andhra Pradesh. It was at Srirangam that Ramanuja spent many years, where he welcomed the outcastes and involved them in the temple activities. Thenkalai continues to follow Ramanuja's liberal tradition. They worship Vishnu, follow Tamil texts, such as the *Prabandhas* of Alvars with primacy to rituals in Tamil language. Anybody, regardless of caste, can become a Sri Vaishnava and a spiritual teacher.

Vadakalai is more a conservative, Sanskrit-based tradition, headquartered at Kanchipuram, with three mutts, one each in Tamil Nadu, Karnataka and Andhra Pradesh. They follow the Sanskrit Vedas and caste rules prescribed by the Manusmriti.

❦

Madhvacharya
(1238–1317)

THERE IS AN INTERESTING STORY ABOUT HOW MADHVA HAPPENED TO establish the temple of Krishna at Udupi, Karnataka, 800 years ago. It goes like this. A ship from Dwaraka, Gujarat, was caught in a storm while sailing in the western coast of Malpe. That morning, Madhva was on the seashore performing his daily rituals. It is said, by his aparoksha or divine knowledge, Madhva knew what had to be done, and guided the ship safely to the harbour. The captain of the ship, immensely grateful to Madhva for saving their lives, told him to take anything he wanted from the ship. The ship was carrying many valuable things, but Madhva's eyes fell on a heavy lump of gopichandana, holy sandalwood, and he asked for it. Amused and surprised, the captain offered the lump of gopichandana to Madhva. The story goes that Madhva found an idol of Bala Gopala, the infant Krishna, in the sandalwood lump and took it to the sea to purify it. Then he had a temple built and installed the idol in the sanctum sanctorum. To ensure regular worship of the Lord without any hindrance whatsoever, he gave the responsibility to his eight disciples to carry on the sacred task, each for a two-month term. In the sixteenth century, this rotational system, known as Paryaya, was modified to two years each, a practice that continues to this day.

Interestingly, the name of the town, Udupi, is derived from 'Udupa', one of the names of Lord Shiva, who carries the moon on his head. Udupi lies on the Arabian Sea and is a famous pilgrim centre as well as a tourist spot today. Even before Madhva's time, Udupi was a holy site of two Shiva temples, Sri Chandramauleshvara and Ananteshvara, where Lord Vishnu is believed to reside in the Shivalingas established in both the temples. Today, however, the place is most famous for the Sri Krishna Temple established by Madhva.

Madhva was born in 1238 to Madhyageha Bhatta and Vedavati, a Tulu speaking Vaishnava Brahmin family, in Pajaka near Udupi in the coastal district of Mangaluru. He was named Vasudeva, after Lord Krishna, and came to be called Purnaprajna when he became a sanyasi, Anandatirtha on becoming head of the Vaishnava monastery, and finally Madhva, which stuck, and today he is widely known as Madhvacharya.

Even as a boy, he was extraordinarily intelligent, with a phenomenal memory. He became a sanyasi as a teenager and went to study under Achyutrapreksha, pontiff of a monastery near Udupi and a noted guru of Advaita. But serious differences rose between the master and the disciple in their understanding of the philosophy of the

Upanishads. Madhva could not accept the philosophy of non-dualism (the perspective that all things are interconnected and ultimately one) which, according to Madhva, cancelled out man's relation with God and shut out bhakti. Achyutrapreksha was astounded by the brilliance of his disciple, and it is said, years later, the guru became a disciple.

In the next few years, Madhva is believed to have engaged himself, like Shankara and Ramanuja during their time, in debates with several scholars and converted them to his view of Vedanta. Among the different schools of thought, such as the Buddhist, Jain, Virashaivites and others, his criticism was mostly focused on Advaita. Steadfast in his mission to discuss, debate and spread his view of Vedanta, he went on a long pilgrimage in South India, visiting the holy places. During this tour, a story goes, he was challenged by pandits to explain the scriptures. By the dint of his scholarship and eloquence, 'Madhva showed that each Vedic sukta, hymn, had three meanings, the Mahabharata ten, and that each name of Vishnu in the *Saharsanama*, wherein the deity is remembered by 1000 names, had a hundred.' (Swami Harshananda)

Shankara declared that Atman is the perceptible personal particular, Brahman is the unlimited universal, but essentially, both Atman and Brahman are identical. Brahman alone is real, the ultimate Truth, while the material world, its distinctness, the individuality of the living creatures, and even Isvara, the Supreme Lord itself, are all untrue, maya, a mere fantasy.

Ramanuja countered Shankara thus: God is real and independent, the jivas, individual souls, and the world are real, but their reality is dependent on that of God. Neither of them is the same as Brahman. Yet all three – the world/matter, jivas and Brahman – form a unity. The goal of the human being is to love and serve God rather than become one with God, to taste the sugar, not become the sugar.

If Ramanuja took one step away from Shankara, Madhva took one step away from Ramanuja and two from Shankara. Madhva's Dvaita system resembles Ramanuja's Vishishtadvaita in its emphasis on bhakti as the way to liberation and in identifying the supreme God with Lord Vishnu, or Narayana. But its metaphysical position differed, in that the Dvaita was more explicitly pluralistic. Like the other two schools, Madhva too claimed his philosophy to be as old as the Vedas. But, unlike the other two acharyas, he asserted that the ritual part, karma-kanda, and the Upanishads, jnana-kanda, were equally valid and interconnected.

Further, according to Dvaita metaphysics, reality is plural; however, there are only two tattvas or categories of reality: svatantra tattva, independent reality, and asvatantra tattva, dependent reality. God, or Narayana, is the cause of the world and the only independent reality. The created world of jivas, individual souls, and jada, material things, are plural, different, distinct and dependent realities. In other words, God, souls and matter are all different and distinct from each other. Everything is unique, there is no soul like another, no thing or object like another; for that matter, even liberation, the highest state of bliss, which can be achieved only with the grace of Narayana, is different for each one.

According to Dvaita, liberation or moksha is not absolute freedom or coming upon the awareness that one is Brahman, tat tvam asi or thou art that; rather, you realize atat tvam asi, thou are not that, develop an attraction, attachment, loving devotion to God, and by complete surrender to Him and by His grace attain the state of bliss. Not through jnana or karma yogas but only through bhakti yoga and by Divine grace can the human experience the highest state of being, which involves the actualization of a deep personal engagement with the Divine.

Madhva wrote commentaries on the *Brahma Sutras*, the Bhagavad Gita and the Upanishads, Rig Veda, Mahabharata and Bhagavata Purana. His *Anu-Vyakhyana*, commentaries on *Brahma Sutras*, is considered to be his masterpiece. He established eight mutts, monasteries, in Udupi, and a total of 24 mutts all over India. His illustrious successors, Jayathirtha (1356-1388), Vyasaraya (1478–1589) and Raghavendratirtha (1595–1671) wrote copiously and kept the Dvaita Vedanta tradition alive.

In modern times, the International Society for Krishna Consciousness (ISKCON) founded by A.C. Bhaktivedanata Swami Prabhupada, which owes its allegiance to the Gaudiya Vaishnavism of Chaitanya Mahaprabhu, is essentially derived from Madhva's Dvaita Vedanta.

¢¢¢

Lalleshwari
(1320–1392)

A STORY GOES THAT ONE MORNING, LALLA STAYED AT THE RIVER GHAT for an unusually long time. Her mother-in-law, who waited for the slightest opportunity to find fault with her and punish her, told Lalla's husband to go find her and bring her home. On reaching the river ghat, the husband was intrigued to see Lalla fill the pot with water from the stream and then pour it back. Fill and empty, fill and empty, it seemed like the making of a song, a poetic act! This went on for a while and then finally Lalla filled her pot with water and, carrying it on her head, proceeded home.

The husband, mean and with cruel intentions, reached home first and as she entered the house, he smashed the pot with a stick. The earthen pot broke into pieces, but the water did not spill: it remained frozen in its place. Now Lalla moved, and as the frozen water melted and flowed down her arm and through her fingers, she started filling the empty pots and vessels in the house. Once all the vessels were filled with water, Lalla turned to her mother-in-law and asked if there were any more vessels to be filled. Witnessing the miracle, both mother and son were speechless. Lalla then went out and threw the excess water on to the field, which transformed into a little pond.

Lalleshwari was born in 1320 CE in Pandrethan, near Srinagar, in a Kashmiri Pandit family. She is known as Lalla Arifa to Muslims, and

Lalla Yogishwari to Hindus, but more popularly referred to as Lal Ded, which means 'Grandmother Lal', or simply as Lalla. She was married off at the young age of 12. It was an ill-matched marriage. Even though she was obedient and performed her wifely duties scrupulously, both her husband and mother-in-law were disapproving of her meditative absorptions and visits to shrines. It is said they even treated her cruelly and often starved her by way of punishment.

According to a popular story, when she was given food, her mother-in-law would keep a stone on her plate and cover it with rice; this was to show others how well she took care of her daughter-in-law. Lalla would quickly finish the scanty rice, wash her plate and the stone and put them back. She never complained nor told others. Whether there was a feast at home, or a big sheep was killed, she wrote in one of her vakhs: '...Lalla will have her lump of stone always.' (Razdan, 1998) She put up with this unhappy situation for twelve long years, then, at the age of 24, she left the family, renounced all her ties with the world and took to a life of sanyasa. There was no looking back. When her husband came to see her and take her back home, she plainly told him: 'There is no light like the Light of God, no pilgrimage like the journey with Him, no relative and source of happiness like the Lord. Go to Him, love Him. As far as our bond is concerned, it ends here.' (Razdan, 1998)

She joined the ashram of Siddha Srikantha, a Shaivite guru, and sought his spiritual guidance. She probably stayed at the ashram for some years before she came into her own and became a wandering yogini. Indifferent to social strictures, like Akka Mahadevi, we are told that she walked nude, oblivious to the world around, singing and dancing in a state of ecstasy.

Her compositions are called 'vakh', corresponding to Vedic-Sanskritic 'vak', 'speech', and to 'vachana', utterance, of the twelfth century saranas. They are marked by vehemence, fervour, even fury and apparent pride, and bring to mind the vachanas of Allama Prabhu. Her vakhs express the agony of separation and longing to unite with her lord, and her eventual leap from bhakti bhava to the non-dual state of being, run parallel to Akka Mahadevi's spiritual journey from bhava to anubhaava, unmediated experience or vision of truth.

In her early vakhs, like most bhaktas agonizing over their separation from God and longing for union, Lalla too describes her life as sailing in a boat through the murky waters of samsara and struggling to cross over to the shore of joy and freedom. Her life, she laments, is like an unbaked earthen pot with water slowly seeping through it, threatening to fall to bits, but she will not give up the fight. In her later poems, we see the agony of separation and feverish longing giving way to reflection, meditation and the celebration of 'the Supreme Self within'.

Lalla was not just a bhakti poet. Her vakhs, about 250 of them, were not mere outpourings of her devotion to God; rather, there was bhakti as well as jnana, knowledge, and these two streams merged perfectly in Lalla. More importantly, unlike other women bhaktas, Lalla did not consider the body a liability, nor a weakness or obstacle to be overcome on the path to self-realization; rather, the body was the field of light and energy, the source and ground of intelligence and enlightenment. To bring home the truth of the oneness of reality and the irrelevance of beliefs and rituals, tantras and mantras in the quest for self-realization, she creatively deployed expressions from Sankhya philosophy, Shaiva Sidhhanta, Tantra Yoga and the Mahayana philosophy of sunyata.

Lalla died in 1392 CE and her vakhs were committed to writing 400 years after her death. Nund Rishi, also known as Sheikh Nuruddin, who belonged to the Rishi Order of Kashmir, was deeply influenced by Lalleshwari. In one of his poems, Nund Rishi calls her an 'avatar' and prays to God to grant him the same boon as He had to Lalla, of immense love for God. While Lalla, along with Nund Rishi, remains a shining example of what is called Kashmiriyat, she stands out among the women saints and mystics of India, such as Akka Mahadevi, Meera Bai and Anandamayi Ma, as one who blazed a path all her own. Her vakhs continue to speak to people today and illumine the path to the fullness of life.

A Selection of Lalla's Vakhs

That thou art my destiny.
Learning by rote, my tongue and palate dried,
I found not the right way
to act and reach thee.
Telling the beads,
my thumb and finger
wore out; and, my friend,
I couldn't get rid of
the duality of mind.

~

I, Lalla, searched and sought Him,
and even beyond my strength I strove.
Finding His doors bolted and barred
I longed to see;
firmly resolved, I stood just there
with tears and love,
fixing my gaze upon His door.

~

The idol is but stone,
the temple is but stone,
from top to bottom all is stone.
Whom will you worship, O foolish pandit,
let go and let prana and the mind unite.

(Kaul, 1972)

~

Not by ascetic practices is the Self realised,
nor by any other means.
In contemplation you may stay absorbed
as salt in water,

yet it is hard for you to gain
the true knowledge of the Self.

~

Shiva is present everywhere.
Where lies the creek to distinguish
between a Hindu and a Mussalman?
Quick witted if you are,
recognise yourself and realise God!

~

Tantra dissolved and
the mantra remained.
The mantra disappeared,
consciousness remained.
Consciousness vanished,
nothingness merged with
nothingness of the Void.

~

Should you, in this body, seek
the Supreme Self that dwells within,
remove greed and illusion,
lo, a halo of glory will surround
this very body of yours.

~

Here there is neither word nor thought,
Transcendent nor non-Transcendent.
Vows of silence and mystic mudras
cannot gain you admittance here.
Even Shiva and Shakti remain not here.
What remains is the Truth

to know and realise.
Here there is neither thou nor I,
nothing to contemplate,
not even God.

(Razdan 1998)

Kabir
(born 1398)

ONCE, A YOUNG MAN NAMED RAM DAS, WHO CONSIDERED HIMSELF
an earnest seeker of God, went to Kabir the mystic-poet and said,
'Master, you are a jnani, you have performed many miracles and
helped people to see God. Kindly help me, too, to see God.' Kabir
could not refuse the sincere request of the young aspirant and asked
him to come after two days. He also told him to arrange a festive lunch
for people, since it was going to be an occasion for celebration. And,
'Come prepared to meet God,' he warned cryptically.

Overjoyed, Ram Das sold his property and with the money he got
he made elaborate arrangements for the lunch party. On the fixed day,
varieties of delicious food were prepared. People gathered in large
numbers. If some came to partake of the festive food, others came
feeling blessed to have the opportunity to see God. All the invitees were
told that food would be served to them only after God had appeared
before Ram Das, so they waited for the blessed moment.

Hours passed but God did not appear. Some of the invitees started
feeling very hungry and very irritated, those who were hoping for
the darshan of God felt disappointed, while some others started to
wonder if Kabir was playing a practical joke on them. It was almost
evening and tempers were rising high. Suddenly, they heard a loud
noise coming from the kitchen. A buffalo had entered the kitchen

and knocked down the pots of cooked food. Rice, various dishes and sweets lay scattered on the floor.

Enraged, Ram Das picked up a stout staff and started beating the animal mercilessly. Wailing in pain, the buffalo escaped from the kitchen. Now the crowd, including Ram Das, much annoyed and angry and cursing Kabir, went looking for him. He was there, at one end of the garden, hugging the animal and weeping bitterly. 'O my lord,' Kabir cried, 'you were not so injured even while fighting Ravana! How could anyone do this to you?'

God always responds, eager to meet his bhaktas, but sometimes the bhaktas, full of themselves, fail to recognize him. But when duality ceases, one knows that the buffalo was Rama and the one who beat the buffalo was also Rama! It is the same all-pervading Universal Self. This is the real darshan, holy sight, in Kabir's book.

According to scholars, Kabir was born in 1398 and breathed his last around 1448 or 1455. He was born into or adopted by a Muslim family of weavers, julahas (Farsi), so he was well acquainted with Islam, but going by his poems, called bijaks, it appears that he had an intimate knowledge and understanding of Hindu thought and mythology as well. However, he was critical of religious orthodoxy and authoritarianism and chided Hindus and Muslims alike. To Muslims who accused him of becoming a kafir, he said: 'He who uses wicked violence or robs the world by deceit, who eats or drinks intoxicants, or seizes the goods of others, he is the kafir...' And to the brahmins who protested his applying tilak on his forehead and posing as a Vaishnavite, when in reality he was a Muslim and so a mlechcha, an untouchable, he answered: 'On my tongue Vishnu, in my eyes Narayan, and in my heart Gobind dwells.' (Tagore, 1915)

On the one hand, if Kabir's bijaks or poems sound like critiques of religious orthodoxy and chicanery, on the other, they are like a finely woven tapestry of queries, wonderment and assertion of the oneness of reality. His Rama was not the mythological Ram, but One without attributes, Nirguna Brahman; his Hazrat not a god with a religious identity but the formless Eternal Presence. His spirituality brooked no barriers and no borders. All is one, for there is no two.

> Brother, whence came two divine masters of the world?
> Who has led you astray?
> Allah, Rama, Karim, Keshava, Hari, Hazrat, are but names given.
> Jewels and jewels are made of one gold bar; but in it is one nature only...
> One reads the Vedas, another Khutbas; one is Maulvi, another is Pande.
> Kabir says, both alike have gone astray; none has found Rama.

(Shabda 30. Tagore, trans., 1915)

To Kabir, true bhakti needs no mediation, for all the mediating agents – priests and temples, mullahs and mosques – and all the beliefs, practices and identities enforced on people by religious authorities have unfortunately created walls of separation between believers, between individuals and God. They are mere substitutes for the real thing, that great vibrant presence which is all pervasive and beyond name and form. His was a call to return to the unmediated vision of *That* which has no attributes and to the experience of the oneness of life. In other words, his was a call for a return of all temples and mosques and churches to the original, namely, the spirit within. In his words, 'Search your hearts...that's his abode... He's the very Breath of our breaths.' (Shah, 1977)

Kabir did not live long; he probably died when he was in his fifties. Legend has it that after his death a dispute arose between Hindus and Muslims with regard to the funeral and they both laid claim to his body. It is said that when the dispute between the two threatened to turn violent, an old man appeared on the scene, appealed for calm and told the disputants to go and look for Kabir's body under the sheet of cloth that covered it. They removed the shroud only to find a heap of flowers in place of the corpse. The Hindus and Muslims divided the flowers between them. Half of the flowers were buried in Maghar and the other half was cremated in Kashi.

Kabir's Bijak Granth is considered a sacred book by Kabir Panthis, followers of Kabir, who have been instrumental in popularizing Kabir's songs, especially in the North. Kabir Panthis practise forgiveness and compassion, and the universal brotherhood of all beings, but, ironical as it may sound today, they worship the idol of Kabir, and even wear sacred thread and sandal paste, practices against which Kabir taught all his life. His bijaks have a vital presence in the *Guru Granth Sahib*, the holy book of Sikhs, and with many of his bijaks translated and circulated in several languages, he is probably the most widely read and quoted mystic-poet in India today.

A Selection of Kabir's Songs

The Kazi is searching the words of the Koran, and instructing others. But if his heart not be steeped in that love,
what does it avail, though he be a teacher of men?
The Yogi dyes his garments with red, but if he knows naught of that colour of love, what does it avail though his garments be tinted?
Kabir says: 'Whether I be in the temple or the balcony, in the camp or in the flower garden, I tell you truly that every moment my Lord is taking His delight in me.'

~

O servant, where dost thou seek Me?
Lo! I am beside thee.
I am neither in temple nor in mosque:
I am neither in Kaaba nor in Kailash:
Neither am I in rites and ceremonies,
nor in Yoga and renunciation.
If thou art a true seeker, thou shalt at once see Me:

thou shalt meet Me in a moment of time.
Kabir says, 'O Sadhu! God is the breath of all breath.'

(Shah, trans., 1977)

~

I have found the key of the mystery,
I have reached the root of union.
Travelling by no track, I have come to the sorrowless land:
Very easily has the mercy of the great Lord come upon me.
They have sung of Him as infinite and unattainable, but I in my
meditations have seen Him without sight.
That is indeed the sorrowless land, and
none know the path that leads there.
Only he who is on that path has surely transcended all sorrow.
Wonderful is that land of rest, to which no merit can win.
It is the wise who has seen it, who has sung of it.

~

The images are all lifeless, they cannot speak:
I know, for I have cried aloud to them.
The Purana and the Koran are mere words:
lifting up the curtain, I have seen.

(Tagore, trans., 1915)

Varkaris

ONE DAY, THE GOD VITTALA WENT TO SEE HIS DEVOTEE PUNDALIKA.
Pundalika was attending to his old parents when Vittala arrived at
his door. He could not possibly leave his parents unattended and
go to Vittala. Because of heavy rains, the river was in spate and the
water level was rising, so, throwing a brick for Vittala to stand on

safely, Pundalika promised to see him after finishing his chores. The god stood on the brick, waiting. Pundalika never emerged, since he remained completely engaged in serving his parents. The god, hands on his hips and still waiting for his bhakta, turned into stone. It is this Vittala, now called Vithoba, who stands, arms akimbo, waiting for his bhaktas in the temple at Pandharpur in Maharashtra.

It is not uncommon in bhakti narratives for gods to seek out bhaktas, just as bhaktas yearn for the company of their lords. It's an intense 'love affair', so to say, where the god and devotee rely on each other for the bhakti to flourish and ultimately merge in union. It is also said that Vithoba, standing with his arms akimbo, symbolizes the Kundalini Shakti, Serpent Power, worshipping which could raise the divine energy of the devotees.

Pundalika is considered the founder of the Vithoba-centric Varkari sect. 'Varkari' means the 'one who makes the journey' to Pandharpur to worship Vithoba – a Vaishnava deity identified with Vishnu and Krishna. Devotees, cutting across castes, make this pilgrimage to Pandharpur, usually in groups, singing abhangs, hymns, composed and sung by the saints who were devotees of Vithoba. The popular abhangs sung by people today are by the saints Namdev, Tukaram and Jnaneshwar, and from compositions such as *Bhaktalilamrita* and *Bhaktavijaya* by Mahipati, and *Pundalika-Mahatmya* by Bahinabai. To Varkaris, Vithoba is the ultimate truth and He lives in the hearts of every devotee, so they bow to each other in recognition of the belief that everybody is Vithoba.

Generally, pilgrimages to Pandharpur are undertaken in the Hindu months of ashadh, June–July, and karthik, November–December. There is collective singing, dancing and chanting by devotees drawn from different castes, high and low, and they carry padukas, sandals of the saints, notably Jnaneshwar and Tukaram, in palkhis, palanquins. The palkhi festival was started by Tukaram's son, Narayan Maharaj, in 1685. It is a unique festival, for one ceremoniously carry not the image or idol of the god but the (symbolic) sandals of his devotees. If, on the one hand, this unique practice bestows an honour on the saints, on the other hand it enacts the long journey undertaken by the likes of Jnaneshwar and Tukaram to worship Vithoba at Pandharpur; it's as if the devotee, singing and dancing, is accompanying their beloved saints to meet the lord.

Jnaneshwar
(1275–1296)

There is an interesting story of Jnaneshwar making a buffalo chant the Vedas. Long before he became a yogi, when he was a young boy of twelve, he saw a man thrashing an old buffalo. Moved by the animal's silent suffering he pleaded with the man to stop. The priests, who happened to be at the spot, ridiculed him for being more concerned about a beast than about the teachings of the Vedas. 'But I know,' the boy replied sharply, 'the Vedas hold all life to be sacred and a manifestation of the Brahman.' The priests laughed and asked if the buffalo too was sacred and a manifestation of the same Brahman. Jnaneshwar then placed his hand on the animal's head and it started reciting a Vedic verse in a deep voice. This fantastical tale, like most stories of miracles by saints and sages, embodies a pointed spiritual message, and is told to teach the ignorant, haughty priests a lesson.

Jnaneshwar was born sometime in 1275 in a brahmin family in Apegaon, a village in Maharashtra. His father, Vitthalapant, was a Kulkarni, an accountant, who maintained land and tax records of Apegaon and surrounding villages. At an early stage of his married life, Vitthalapant is believed to have turned spiritual, left his family, visited Kashi and became a monk. Upon knowing that he was a married person before taking the initiation into sanyasa, his guru reprimanded him and commanded him to relinquish his sanyasa and go back to his family. Vitthalapant came back to his wife, Rakhumabai, and in the course of time the couple had four children, Nivruttinath, Jnaneshwar, Sopan and Muktabai.

The brahmin community viewed his return to family life a heresy, a betrayal of the sanyasa tradition, and the couple were excommunicated. Weighed down with guilt and worried about the future of their children, both Vitthalapant and Rakhumabai committed suicide by throwing themselves into Indrayani River in the hope their children would be free of persecution. The story goes that the brahmin community accepted Vitthalapant's children after putting them through ritual purification, and on the condition that they would all observe celibacy for life.

The siblings took to the spiritual path and became noted bhakti poets. Among them, Jnaneshwar was a gifted yogi. At the young age of 16, he composed *Dhyaneshwari*, 'Divine Knowledge', a commentary on the Bhagavad Gita, which became one of the major texts of the Varkari sect. A couple of years later, in his other work, *Amrutanubhava*, he discussed Advaita siddhanta, non-dualism, and talked about his own understanding and experience of the divinity. Both works are considered milestones in Marathi literature. Incidentally, *Dhyaneshwari* was one of the favourite texts of Nisargadatta Maharaj (1897-1981), the great non-dualist of modern times. Jnaneshwar writing these works in Marathi was a major departure from the prevailing hegemony of Sanskrit as the language of the divinity, the language in which major religious works were written and had remained inaccessible to common people.

Jnaneshwar was possibly influenced by the two prominent spiritual movements of his time, namely, Mahanubhava and the Nath Yogi tradition. Followers of Mahanubhava worshipped Krishna, rejected the varnashrama dharma, the caste system, and the authority of the Vedas. The Nath Yogi tradition, founded by Yogi Gorakshanath, laid emphasis on yoga and the oneness of Vishnu and Shiva. It is said that Jnaneshwar's brother, Nivruttinath, initiated him into the Nath tradition and Jnaneshwar in turn initiated his sisters Sopan and Muktabai, who went on to become noted yoginis. Jnaneshwar was a non-dualist but did not discount the importance of bhakti; rather, he advocated what he called jnana-yukta bhakti, devotion guided by knowledge.

Not only yogis, even common people, he affirmed, would come into self-realization by surrendering one's will to God and renunciation of the fruits of one's actions. More importantly, he asserted that Shiva and Vishnu were essentially the same, representing the creative principles of the universe. Further, his criticism of the misguided priestly authority, his spiritual egalitarianism and celebration of ordinary family life shaped the character of the Varkari sect.

Legend has it that Jnaneshwar and Namdev met at Pandharpur and became great friends. They are believed to have travelled together to many holy places, spreading the message of jnana and bhakti. After completing the pilgrimage, Jnaneshwar decided to enter sanjeevan samadhi, a practice to voluntarily leave one's mortal body after entering into a deep meditative state or samadhi, an account of which is available in a set of abhangs composed by Namdev. There are several instances of saints entering into jeeva samadhi, also called bhoo samadhi (underground burial). But what is extraordinary is that Jnaneshwar was only 22 years old when he felt the mission of his life was complete and it was time to go. His samadhi in the Siddheshwara Temple complex in Alandi is considered a holy place to this day.

According to tradition, after completion of the mission in life, a saint stops the functions of the body voluntarily by uniting the individual mind with the Lord's. The body is then buried. It is believed that the place around such a samadhi has very high spiritual magnetic force. Incidentally, almost all the Siddhars of Tamil Nadu are believed to have entered into jeeva samadhi.

Then there was the practice of jala samadhi, sacred drowning or water burial, and again, there are several instances of saints walking into rivers or streams and ending their lives. For instance, the twelfth century mystic-poet and social reformer, Basavanna, sought jala samadhi at the confluence of the rivers Ghataprabha and Krishna in Karnataka. Chandrashekara Bharati, the 34th Acharya of Sringeri

Sharada Peetham, walked into River Tunga at the age of 64, and Chidananda Bharati, who took jala samadhi in Mandakini River near Kedarnath, was only 24 years old.

Namdev
(1270–1350)

In bhakti narratives, gods, like human beings, seek food from their devotees to satiate their hunger; at times, they even eat from their devotees' hands. Namdev's mother didn't believe Vithoba ate the plate of eatables Namdev had offered to the god. One day she hid herself behind the temple door and couldn't believe her eyes when she saw the god himself sitting by the side of his stubborn bhakta, eating from the plate the bhakta offered to him.

Namdev, born Namdeo Relekar, came from a family of tailors and is believed to have lived between 1270 and 1350. The tailors belonged to the shudra caste and lived near Pandharpur, in a village on the banks of the Bhima River. They were devotees of Vithoba and went on pilgrimage to Pandharpur twice a year.

At a young age, Namdev was married to Radha Bai and had four sons and one daughter. Unlike the devoted wives of many a saint, Radha Bai, it is said, was not moved by Namdev's devotion to Vithoba. She often quarrelled with her husband because he neglected the family and spent most of his time immersed in worshipping his Lord. Legend recounts that, in order to protect his bhakta from his wife's ire, the god himself took up a human form to attend the naming ceremony of Namdev's child, posed as Namdev's friend, and offered generous gifts to Radha Bai.

Namdev is believed to have met and become friends with Jnaneshwar at Pandharpur. It is very rare to find two saints in deep friendship. Over five years, it is said, the two friends went on a long journey, visiting sacred places and meeting with holy people. During this pilgrimage, they supposedly met the great saints Narsi Mehta,

Tulsidas, Kabir and Gorakhnath. They were all not contemporaries, and the two couldn't have met them all; even so, the story reveals that it was a period of great spiritual regeneration across the Indian subcontinent.

After their return to Pandharpur, Jnaneshwar entered sanjeevan samadhi in Alandi. Before that, he advised Namdev to take a guru in order to deepen his spiritual pursuit and come upon self-realization. Namdev hesitated because he didn't want his mind to ever be distracted from the name of his lord Vithoba. But when he met Visoba Khechara, a disciple of Jananeshwar and a follower of the Nath tradition, he was so inspired that he surrendered to the man and became his disciple.

After the initiation and instructions from Visoba, there was a deepening in Namdev's understanding of spirituality. Vithoba was not merely the idol standing with arms akimbo in Pandharpur temple, but an all-pervading divinity that was everywhere and in everything. And the guru had taught wisely: we are here for a short while, like the potter's wheel which goes on rotating even after the potter has left. Namdev sang:

> He is the One in many,
> countless are His shapes and forms.
> He pervades all that exists;
> wherever I look, He is there.
> But very few perceive this reality,
> for Maya ever enchants us
> with her multiple reflections
> of colour and alluring beauty.
> Everything is Gobind,
> Gobind is everything...

(Nirmal Dass, 2000)

Namdev did not compose any philosophical work, nor did he found a sect, but his abhangs, short devotional poems/songs, composed in lucid Marathi, are extremely popular, and 61 of these hymns find a place in the Guru Granth Sahib, the holy book of Sikhism. Along with the abhangs of Jnaneshwar and Tukarama, Namdev's hymns hold a pride of place among the songs sung by the Varkaris to this day.

In his last days, he is believed to have settled down at Pandharpur with a large number of devotees. Legend recounts that he had for company Kanhopatra, a dancing girl, Gora, a potter, Savata, a gardener, Sena, a barber, Chokhamela, who was an ati-shudra, untouchable, and Janabai. He died at the age of 80.

Janabai's story forms an integral part of Namdev's biography. A staunch devotee of Vithoba and a devoted follower of Namdev, she might have been his neighbour, a friend, a sister, but in her abhangs she called herself his maid, and for births to come, she wrote, she wanted to be at Pandharpur and serve Namdev.

Here is a beautiful story where Jnaneshwar, Namdev and Janabai come together to bring home the mystery and truth of the non-dual nature of life and reality.

One day, as Namdev sat outside, as usual immersed in thoughts of Vithoba, his wife, Radha Bai, came out and lambasted him for not doing any work to make a living. Would Vithoba feed the family? Janabai, who witnessed the ugly scene, suggested that Namdev take a loan from a merchant and sell clothes to earn some money. Namdev complied and went from village to village, selling clothes. At one village, he saw people wailing and crying bitterly. They told him that they were looted of all their belongings by bandits. Moved by their plight, Namdev gave away all the money he had earned so far as well as the unsold clothes, and returned home empty-handed. Radha Bai flew into a rage, and along with her children, left for her parents' home.

Janabai burst into tears thinking of her master's endless troubles. But why should such things happen to a great devotee like Namdev? She demanded of Vithoba bitterly. Just then Jnaneshwar arrived there and asked Janabai why she was weeping.

Janabai explained, and cried, 'Oh brother, does it make the Lord happy to see his children suffer? Don't you see how mercilessly the Lord has treated Namdev?'

'It is only a dream, Jana,' responded Jnaneshwar, smiling. 'All is maya of Vithoba. He who looted is Vithoba, he who is looted is Vithoba, Namdev who helped them is Vithoba, you who is weeping now is Vithoba, the whole world is Vithoba. When you realize this, Jana, who will you blame, who will you weep for?' ('Sant Jnaneshwar Visits Namdev').

Chokhamela
(c. 1400)

Chokhamela was a devotee of Vithoba but was barred from entering the Vithoba Temple at Pandharpur because he was considered 'untouchable'. Like Nandanar, the Shiva devotee of seventh century Tamil Nadu, and Kanaka Dasa, devotee of Krishna of the sixteenth century Karnataka, Chokhamela too stationed himself at the gate of the Lord's temple, hoping against hope that one day he would be allowed inside to come face to face with the Lord.

One night, as usual, the priest locked the door of the temple and left, while Chokhamela, praying, not wanting to return home, slept at the gate. Moved by his unalloyed devotion, Vithoba came out, hugged him and then led him into the sanctum sanctorum, and the god and his devotee stayed in union the whole night. At the break of dawn, Vithoba removed the tulsi mala, a garland made of basil seeds, put it around his bhakta's neck, brought him out and left him at the gate.

In the morning, the priest noticed that the mala was missing from the neck of the idol. The search party found the garland around Chokhamela's neck, who was still immersed in bliss. This was nothing less than blasphemy, a grave sin that could not go unpunished. Chokhamela was whipped and tied to bullocks to be dragged to a painful death. The bullocks, however, refused to move because Lord Vithoba held them by their horns.

Chokhamela belonged to the Mahar caste, considered untouchable because they were given the 'impure' tasks of cleaning the village, which included removal of carcases. Their touch, even their proximity, was considered polluting. They were condemned to live on the outskirts of villages, denied access to facilities and education, especially knowledge of the scriptures.

Since he was a contemporary of Namdev, we could say Chokhamela lived in the fourteenth century. He was born in Mehuna Raja, a village in Buldhana district, then later lived at Mangalvada in Maharashtra. He married early to Soyarbai and they had a son, Karmamela. He worked as a farm labourer for an upper caste landlord.

As a devotee of Vithoba, he visited Pandharpur regularly. Once, he listened to Namdev's kirtan and was so moved by it that he became Namdev's disciple. Chokhamela himself acknowledged Namdev as his guru in some of his poems. It is said that when Namdev started living in Pandharpur, he gathered around him a large number of Vithoba devotees who came from all castes.

This may bring to mind the twelfth century poet-saint and social reformer Basavanna of Karnataka, around whom gathered a large number of people from the lower castes. There were potters, barbers, tailors, weavers, cobblers, and many others. He was their anna, elder brother, and around him grew the vibrant community of saranas, challenging the orthodoxy of Vedic brahmins and rejecting traditional gender discrimination and varnashrama dharma.

Namdev was neither a revolutionary nor a social reformer, but he was certainly something of an elder brother to the devotees of Vithoba. To him people of all castes were equal before the eyes of God. Chokhamela could join Namdev's kirtans, sing and compose abhangs, but he would not be allowed inside the Vithoba Temple. We might ask: why didn't Namdev take Chokhamela along with him inside the temple? Perhaps Namdev lacked total conviction, or he was not the type to start a social fight seeking entry of low-caste people into the temple, or the stranglehold of the priestly class over the temple was such that they could not break it. Chokhamela's poems refer to his standing at the gate, but with no self-pity or rancour, except a deep prayer for Vithoba's darshan.

Legend has it that while he was working on the construction of a wall in Mangalvada, a wall collapsed, crushing to death several workers, Chokhamela among them. When his guru, Namdev, went there to get his remains, it is said, his bones were heard chanting Vittala, Vittala. Today, however, the tomb of Chokhamela lies in front of the temple. The only solace one might derive from this, if any, is that devotees have to visit Chokhamela's shrine before going in to have the darshan of the Lord.

Chokhamela's abhangs are sung to this day, not only by the lower castes but also by others. He did not of course receive as much prominence as Namdev or Tukaram, but remains popular, his body buried under the tomb, at the entrance of the Vithoba Temple.

Here is one of his abhangs, in a rather ironic tone, questioning the notion of caste pollution.

Vedas and the shastras
polluted; puranas inauspicious
impure; the body, the soul
contaminated; the manifest
Being is the same.
Brahma polluted, Vishnu too;
Shankar is impure, inauspicious.
Birth impure, dying is impure:
says Chokha,
pollution stretches
without beginning
and end.

(Mokashi-Punekar, trans., 2002)

Tukaram
(1608–1650)

Legend has it that Tukaram repeatedly tried his hand at business to make a living and failed every time. He was innocent of the shrewd ways of the world. He was no help in household tasks, either. His wife, Jijabai, having tried every trick and failed to get him to work and support the family, at last gave up and decided to follow him in his path of bhakti. Upon his advice, she gave away all her belongings to the poor, including her sarees, and kept just one for her use.

One day, while she was taking a bath, a poor woman happened to come and beg Tukaram for a piece of cloth to cover herself. Tukaram gladly gave her his wife's last saree. Enraged, Jijabai flung the choicest abuses on him, but the words only bounced off deaf ears. She decided that there was no use punishing her husband, for it was not his fault but Vithoba's, who had turned him mad.

The story goes that she picked up a stone and rushed inside Vithoba's temple to take the Lord to task. Rukmini, Vithoba's spouse, studying Jijabai's anger, advised Vithoba that they run from there. That would be disgraceful, said the Lord, and it would amount to letting Tukaram down. Instead, as Jijabai entered the sanctorum, her hand raised, she saw Rukmini smiling at her affectionately, holding before her a basket full of gifts, that included gold coins and silk sarees.

Tukaram Bolhoba Ambile was born in 1608 in Dehu, a small village near Pune in Maharshtra. He belonged to the Kunbi caste, traditionally farm labourers, but the family was into trade and money-lending business. His parents were devotees of Vithoba and he inherited the love for the god from them. He was about 17 when his parents died, and the responsibility of the family fell upon him.

He married Rukmabai early in life, and they had a son named Santu. Legend has it that later she fell very sick and was bedridden, and so Tukaram took a second wife, Jijabai, to take care of the family. Around those years, 1630–32, a terrible famine, due to failure of monsoon and as a result of consecutive staple crop failure, swept across Gujarat and Maharashtra, causing untold misery and deaths due to starvation and disease. Millions died, among them Tukaram's first wife and son.

The widespread dire poverty, deaths of millions and loss of his first wife and son had a profound effect on Tukaram. Hitherto he had led a conventional life, performed the rituals and worshipped the family deity Vithoba, but the horrid turn of events made him withdraw into himself and turn spiritual. One day he left home and did not return for 15 days. Only later did people realize that he went up the Sahyadri Hills (Western Ghats) and stayed there, contemplating, meditating on the intricacies of life and the enigma of existence – most likely torn between pravriti, passion for life, and nivriti, the urge to renounce everything and seek moksha – and praying to Vithoba to show him the right path. It is believed Tukaram came into self-realization during this intense period of meditation on the hills.

He came down only when his wife, Jijabai, went up in search of him and brought him home. It was a different Tukaram who returned, one who had lost that old zest for business and taste for money; now his gaze turned inward, his thoughts fixed on the Almighty Lord. One day, he gathered all his old account books, along with the promissory notes people had given on taking loans from his father, and threw them into the Indrayani River. He thus emptied himself of the non-essentials of life and turned his attention on God.

During this period, he found a guru in Babaji Chaitanya, a disciple of Jnaneshwar, as R.D. Ranade suggests; or, going by Tukaram's reports, he had a vision of Guru Babaji who taught him the Japa of Ramakrishna Hari. Tukaram now spent most his time in bhajans or kirtans and the study of the scriptures and works of Jnaneshwar, Namdev and Ekanath. He came to be seen as a saint and people flocked to listen to his abhangs and participate in kirtans.

A small but powerful group of brahmins resented his growing popularity and audacity to give spiritual instruction to laypeople. More importantly, as one belonging to the shudra caste he had no right to interpret the scriptures. One Rameshwar Shastri, scholar and leader of the brahmin community, refused to accept Tukaram's innocence in the matter or that it was Vithoba working through him. He ordered him to stop composing abhangs, collected all his poems, tied them into bundle and drowned it in the river. But, to the surprise of everyone present, the bundle came up to the surface of the water and start floating towards the bank. The poems were recovered. The brahmins realized their folly and begged for Tukaram's forgiveness.

There are two views about Tukaram's philosophy. One, that during his later days he turned into a worshipper of Nirguna Brahman, God without form or attributes; the other is that initially he was a worshipper of Saguna Brahman, God with form and attributes; that he extolled bhakti as the joy-filled, right path to liberation; that he was critical of both elaborate rituals and asceticism. One of his abhangs reads: '...even dogs come in saffron and bears have matted hair. If living in caves is being spiritual, then rats who inhabit caves and crevices are great sadhakas.' ('Tukaram') Elsewhere, he even calls an advaitin a 'bufoon'. On the other hand, here is an abhang which celebrates Advaita, the union of the Self and the Brahman: 'When salt is dissolved in water, what is it that remains distinct? I have thus become one in joy with thee. When fire and camphor are brought together, is there any black remnant left? Tuka says, thou and I are one light.' (Bhandarkar, 2014)

There is a third way to understand: he did not oscillate between dvaitic and advaitic positions; rather, he did not care to offer a systematic philosophy. He moved and sang as per the dictates of his heart. We may call this kind of bhakti Dvaitadvaita, dualistic monism. Vithoba or Vittala is both here and beyond, both tangible as a person and intangible as a principle. *That* is not either/or, but both.

Poetry would be impossible without the presence of both attitudes. The poets need images, languages, the world of gunas or qualities, the very elements they may reject in their mystical heights. In short, by its very nature, bhakti or bhakti poetry is intensely iconic and a powerful bhava, yet the impulse, the deep urge within it, is defiantly aniconic, often rising towards the state of union, of oneness with God.

> Saintliness is not to be purchased in shops,
> nor is it to be had for wandering, nor in cupboards, nor in
> deserts, nor in forests.
> It is not obtainable for a heap of riches. It is not in the heavens
> above, nor in the entrails of the earth below.
> Tuka says: It is a life's bargain, and if you will not give your life
> to possess it, better be silent.
> The essence of the endless Vedas is this:
> Seek the shelter of God, repeat His name with all thy heart.
> The result of the cogitations of all the Shastras is also the same.
> Tuka says: The burden of the eighteen Puranas is also identical.
> Merit consists in doing good to others, sin in doing harm to
> others. There is no other pair comparable to this.
> Truth is the only freedom; untruth is bondage,
> there is no secret like this.
> God's name on one's lips is itself liberation,
> disregarding the name is perdition.
> Companionship of the good is the only heaven,
> indifference is hell.
> Tuka says: It is thus clear what is good and what is injurious,
> let people choose what they will.
>
> (Gandhi, trans.)

Legend has it that Tukaram knew when he would shed his mortal body. Hours before his departure he is believed to have thanked his wife for being kind and loving, advised his people to continue with the Japa of Ramakrishna Hari and then went up the hills of Sahyadri. There, he climbed into the chariot sent by his Lord, and as people who had followed him watched in a daze, the chariot rose into the skies in a blaze of light.

Tukarama's abhangs, in simple, direct, folksy style, composed in the vernacular Marathi, fuse stories from the Puranas with deep spiritual messages. About 4,600 abhangs are ascribed to him. Compared to the abhangs of other Varkari saints – Jnaneshwar, Namdev, Bhanibai and Mahapati – Tukaram's compositions are quite large in number. His abhangs are hugely popular not only in Marathi speaking regions, but also in the South and they have been translated into several Indian languages, including English. There are feature films on him in Marathi, Kannada and Tamil. He remains one of the most popular saints across India.

Even during his time, his fame as a poet-saint spread far and wide. Politically, it was a stormy period. Muslim rule had spread across the continent and frequent battles between kingdoms threw people's lives in danger. And spiritual values were on the decline. Tukaram himself said: 'The Brahmins had given up their pious deportment, the kshatriyas were bleeding the vaishyas and forcible conversions were the rule of the day' ('Prevailing Political, Social and Religious Situation'). In spite of his critique of the ruling powers, he had a great admirer in Shivaji Maharaj. The Varkari tradition and abhangs, it is believed, helped forge the Marathi identity and contributed to Shivaji's rise to power. In effect, Tukaram's teaching and abhangs marked the culmination of the Varkari tradition which began with Jnaneshwar, Namdev and Ekanath, and inspired millions to take to the path of bhakti for the attainment of blissful being, among them, the great Bahinabai.

Bahinabai
(1628–1700)

Bahinabai's husband, Ratnakar, did not like her being immersed in her devotion to Vithoba, meeting with saints and participating in kirtans. His reprimands and even physical punishments did not stop her from her devotional activities, so he decided to leave her. Bahina begged him to desist from it, or she would give up her life. Ratnakar was determined to leave her, but before he could leave the house he suddenly fell ill and was in great pain. Bahina nursed him day and night and, we are told, Ratnakar eventually realized his mistake. Here is Bahina's abhang, describing her dilemma and resolve:

> I'll serve my husband, he's my god.
> He is my guru, his way is my way
> this is my heart's true resolve.
> With my husband renouncing the world,
> Panduranga, what good will it do me?
> My husband's the soul, I'm the body.
> He is the water, I'm a fish in it.
> Why should the stone god Vitthal
> and the dream sant Tuka
> deprive me of the happiness I know?

(Feldhaus, trans., 1982)

Bahina is quarrelling with Vithoba and Tukaram here. It is because of Vithoba and Tukaram, because of her devotion to them, that she had neglected her husband and become indifferent to his needs. She'll have to mend and heal her relationship, and she even threatens to leave the god and the guru and devote herself entirely to her husband. Gods take such threats from bhaktas seriously and do generally work out a splendid solution. They need their bhaktas as much as bhaktas need them. Bhakti is like a seesaw, especially in the case of married women devotees, who get torn between their duty towards their family and devotion to their god, though eventually, with a little help from their god, they achieve a fine balance between the two.

Generally, in bhakti narratives, a woman bhakta would be happier if the husband leaves, which they seldom do, so it's often the woman breaking the norm and leaving the husband in quest of her god. In female spirituality, all patriarchal values are subverted or rejected:

women walk out of marriage or tell their husbands to go find another willing woman and leave them alone and refuse to wear the garb of the widow when their husbands die.

For, in the realm of bhakti, a married woman's earthly or worldly husband is a 'second' husband and doesn't count. Bahina is one of the rare exceptions who surprises us by breaking the norm in bhakti narratives. To her, family life is not a prison, and the husband is not a burden. The way of bhakti is varied and complex and deeply subjective, often breaking through the framework we try to impose on it.

Bahina was born to Audeo Kulkarni and Janikibai in 1628, in Deogaon, a town in Maharashtra. Kulkarni was a brahmin and worked as a village accountant. It is said Bahina was born to the couple after many years of prayer to Lord Vithoba. After Bahina, they were blessed with two sons. Bahina was only five years old when she was given in marriage to one Ratnakar Pathak, a widower aged thirty. Ratnakar had to wait for her to join him after her attainment of puberty.

In the meantime, her father, who was in heavy debt, was imprisoned. Ratnakar intervened to get him released from prison. The family left the village and moved from place to place for over two years before they settled down in Kolhapur. It was when Bahina visited Pandharpur that she heard the abhangs sing at the temple and fell in love with Lord Vithoba. Thus started her spiritual journey, as well as her troubles with her husband.

The couple owned a cow and a calf, gifted to them by a learned brahmin. The calf took a great liking to Bahina and followed her everywhere. Once, a well-known guru came to Kolhapur and performed kirtans at the temple. Bahina attended the kirtans and so did the calf, who wouldn't leave her alone. It is said the guru was moved by the bond between the calf and Bahina, called them to where he was sitting, patted both the calf and Bahina with affection and blessed them. Some people, who resented Bahina and the presence of the calf, went and complained to Ratnakar. He came there in a rage and dragged Bahina home by her hair, beat her and locked her up in a room. The story goes that on witnessing this horrendous scene, the calf gave up eating and eventually died. Grief-stricken, Bahina swooned and slipped into an unconscious state for three days.

The death of the calf, whom she had identified herself and become one with, catapulted her into the near death experience. She came upon a vision of Lord Vittala and Tukaram, who instructed her on the way of supreme bhakti and gave her the sacred mantra. After three days, when Bahina awakened from the unconscious state, say, a state of samadhi, she found herself transformed. The guru summoned Ratnakar and told him that Bahina was no ordinary woman but a yogini and that he should let her be.

Ratnakar refused to abide by the guru's advice. As Bahina started composing abhangs and her popularity spread far and wide, the jealous Ratnakar decided to leave her. In anguish, she blamed not her husband but Vithoba and Tukaram for not letting her serve her husband. As it happened, Ratnakar fell sick and could not leave. With care and affection, Bahina nursed him back to health. Ratnakar realized his mistake and became a devotee of Tukaram. In course of time, Bahina gave birth to a daughter and son.

In her abhangs, Bahina talked about her troubled relationship with her husband and its resolution. If she extolled the merits of pativrata, moral duties of a married woman, in some, in others she went into raptures over pure devotion to God. She did not believe in the need to renounce samsara in order to experience God. A fine balance between pravriti-marg, path of samsara, and nivriti-marg, path of renunciation, was possible, and her life was an embodiment of that balance. Her abhangs also dealt with other subjects, such as atman, the importance of the guru, true brahmanhood, pure devotion and so on.

She remained happily married, and her son, named Vithoba, became a noted poet. Apart from an autobiographical work and large number of abhangs, she composed *Pundalika-Mahatmya*, a hagiographical work on Pundalika, the founder of the Varkari tradition. She also became something of a guru and initiated several aspirants into the spiritual path. Legend has it that she had a premonition of her death and sent word to her son, Vithoba, who had gone out of town, to return home in time to perform the last rites. Her prediction came to pass, and she died at the age of 72 when her son was back home. Bahina Bai remains one of the noted Varkari saints, whose abhangs swung between nivriti and pravriti marg and came to rest at a midpoint between the two.

❦

Sankardev
(1449–1568)

SANKARDEV'S LIFE AND TEACHINGS MAKE ONE OF THE MOST SIGNIFICANT chapters in the religious and cultural history of India. He was something like the remarkable polymath Abhinavagupta, the great philosopher-poet Rabindranath Tagore, and the saint-poet and social reformer, Basavanna – all rolled into one. He was a scholar, poet, playwright, artist, saint and social reformer. He wrote in Assamese, Sanskrit and Brajavali, a dialect based on Maithili, blended with the local/Assamese vocables and idiomatic expressions. He created new forms of music, Borgeet and Bhatima; theatre, Ankia Naat Bhaona; dance, Sankari and Sattriya; and Vaishnava sect, Ekasarana Dharma, which inaugurated a social, cultural and religious renaissance in Assam.

Sankardev, named Sankaravara, was born in the year 1449 to Shiromani Kusumvar Bhuyan and Satyasandhya Devi at Alipukhuri, presently in Nagaon district of Assam. The family belonged to the Kayastha caste. Sankardev lost his parents at the tender age of seven and was brought up by his grandmother, Khersuti.

He was a precocious child, but was sent to Mahendra Kandali school (a boarding school named after the famous Sanskrit scholar) only at the age of 12. For over eight years he studied the Vedas, epics, Puranas, grammar, lexicon and kavyas, and even composed a long poem *Harichandra Upakhyana*. After schooling, at the age of 20, he married Suryavati, and around the same time became the chief of Shiromani Bhuyan – a loosely independent confederacy of warrior chiefs and landlords. Three years later, Suryavati gave birth to a girl and died soon after. Her premature death affected Sankardev deeply and he lost interest in Shiromani Bhuyan. When the daughter, Manu, came of age, he got her married to a young Kayastha man named Hari. He handed over the power of administration of the Shiromani to his uncles Jayanta and Madhav Doloi and went on a long pilgrimage.

For over 12 years, accompanied by 17 close associates, including his friend Ramaram, Sankardev travelled in northern India, visiting holy places and meeting with many saints and scholars. Some of the places he visited were Varanasi, Prayag, Vrindavan, Mathura, Dwarka, Gaya, Puri and other major centres of Vaishnava cults. At Badrikashram, he is believed to have composed his first Borgeet in Brajavali – 'Man Meri Ram Charanahi Lagu'. His long stay at Puri and Varanasi, and interactions with spiritual masters such as Jagadish Misra, profoundly influenced the neo-Vaishnava movement he founded.

Sankardev was 44 years old when he returned home, with plans to start a new life. His grandmother, however, wanted him to remarry and resume the leadership of Shiromani Bhuya. He objected at first, then, three years later, he deferred to her wish and married Kalinidi, but refused to have anything to do with Shiromani Bhuya. He moved back to his native place, Bordowa. There, he built a Devagriha – was not a temple, but a Home of the Divine, a sacred space, where he could meet with people to hold prayers and discuss spiritual matters. This was similar to Basvanna's Anubhava Mantapa, Hall of Experience, where he met his followers and other Shiva devotees for discussions and recitation of vachanas.

The *Bhagavata Purana,* also known as *Srimad Bhagavata* or simply *Bhagavata*, which deals with bhakti or devotion to Krishna and a wide range of topics including cosmology, music, dance, yoga and culture, has been the foundational text for many a variety of Vaishnavite cult. At Varanasi, the religious teacher Jagadish Mishra's recitation and explanation of *Bhagavata* had a profound impact on Sankardev. It was an epiphanic moment, giving birth to a new cult of bhakti which came to be called Ekasarana Dharma, literally, 'Shelter-in-One-religion'. It believed in surrendering to and taking shelter under one God, Krishna, and worshipping Him with pure devotion. Like most bhakti traditions, it followed the dasya attitude: the bhakta considers herself to be a servant of God. It differed from other Vaishnava cults in that Radha is not worshipped along with Krishna. In fact, there was no idol worship. Realization of God was an internal matter, idol worship and other religious paraphernalia were seen as quite unnecessary. In the places where devotees sat together to chant and sing, they did not keep any idol of Krishna; instead, a book was kept, usually the sacred *Bhagavata*, symbolizing God.

Sankardev taught universal love for all beings as God resided within all beings. He rejected the varnashrama dharma and made a major departure from the prevalent system in society by initiating people from all castes – shudras, tribals, even Muslims – into Ekasarana Dharma. The conversion of Madhavdev – a sakta, a worshipper of Devi/Shakti, and a talented poet and thinker with a wide following– into the new faith helped Sankardev spread Ekasarana far and wide.

Sankardev composed the *Kirtan Ghosha*, celebrating the glory of Krishna, and wrote and produced *Chihna-yatra*, a musical play on Krishna, in order to popularize Ekasarana Dharma. He introduced different musical elements like anka, a single act or multiple acts in a play, and slokas, poetic form, along with songs, accompanied by mridangas and different types of cymbals which he himself had designed. He also played an active part in the performance, often taking on the role of the sutradhara, narrator of the play. In Sanskrit plays, the sutradhara usually introduced the topic of the play and then departed from the stage, but here, in *Chihna-yatra*, after introducing the theme of the play, Sankardev stayed on stage and even participated in singing, acting and playing the musical instrument. A great innovator, he brought something new into everything he did.

During this time the Bhuyans had become politically weak, caught in the conflict between the Ahom king, Suhungmung, and the Koch king, Biswa Singha. To complicate matters, the Brahmins, alarmed by the growing popularity of the Ekasarana, conspired to crush Sankardev's new religious movement. Persuaded by the enemies of Sankardev, Suhungmung's successor Sulenmung, had Sankardev's son-in-law Hari and follower Madhavdev arrested. While Hari was executed, Madhavdev was imprisoned for a year. In 1541, on Madhavdev's release, feeling unsafe in the kingdom of Ahom, Sankardev and his family moved to the Koch kingdom, to a place called Patbausi.

The trouble did not end here for Sankardev. On a complaint by the priestly class of the Koch, King Naranarayana, son and successor of Biswa Singha, ordered Sankardev's arrest. But on the intervention of Chilari, the general of the Koch army and brother of the king, Sankardev was given an audience with the court. The priestly class failed to prove their complaint and Sankardev was declared innocent. Further, the king was so impressed by Sankardev's arguments and his pious views on religion and God that he extended his support for the new religion. Eventually, large sections of people of both the Koch and the Ahom kingdoms came to accept the new faith and Sankardev as their guru.

Sankardev passed away in 1568; he was 120 years old. Hindus believe that 120 years is the maximum life span of a human being, but that only perfect beings with a perfect body can live for that many years. Incidentally, Gandhiji desired to live for 120 years in order to fulfil his mission of Sarvodaya, rising or emancipation of all, and Lokasangraha, universal welfare, and come upon moksha, liberation.

Sankardev was a colossus and his contribution to the world of art, culture and religion was immense, to say the least. The cultural and spiritual renaissance Sankardev inaugurated continues to echo throughout the length and breadth of Assam today.

He integrated the divided ethnic groups and different castes into one cultural and religious unit, originated two classical dance forms, created new ragas, wrote plays in modern Assamese language and introduced elevated stage and drop-scene, which was the first of its kind. He designed the Vrindavan vastra, the cloth of Vrindavan, a rectangular tapestry richly woven with embroidered design on silk, depicting the the lila, play, of Krishna at Vrindavan; this is now preserved in the Victoria and Albert Museum of London.

Above all, he was a great spiritual master, on par with some of the greatest of this land. Sattras, monasteries and assembly of devotees, form an important socio-religious institution in Assam to this day, carrying forward the Ekasarana Dharma started by Sankardev.

Works of Sankardev

Poetry: *Kirtana-ghosha, Harischandra-upakhyana, Rukmini-harana, Ajamilopakhyana, Bali-chalana, Kurukshetra-yatra, Gopi-uddhava-samvada, Amrta-manthana, Krishna-prayana-pandava-niryana, Kamajaya*

Treatises: *Bhakati-pradipa, Anadi-patana, Nimi-navasiddha-samvada, Bhakti Ratnakara* (in Sanskrit)

Translation: *Bhagavata* and *Ramayana*

Drama: *Patni-prasada, Parijata-harana, Kali-damana, Rukmini-harana, Keli-gopala, Srirama-vijaya*

Cihna Yatra, his first play, along with two other plays, *Janma-jatra; Kangsa-badha,* have been lost.

Songs: *Borgeet* and *Bhatima*

Dance: *Sattriya* and *Sankari*

Krishna Chaitanya
(1486–1534)

AS AN INFANT IN HIS MOTHER'S ARMS, A STORY GOES, KRISHNA CHAITANYA wept continually and wouldn't stop. The mother tried to breastfeed him, then tried all the tricks she knew to stop his crying, but in vain. One day, a neighbouring woman happened to be there when he broke into a long wail. Both women tried many upayas, tricks, to quieten him but to no avail. Irritated, the neighbouring woman cried, 'Hari Bol'. Instantly the child stopped crying. Thus, the house, from his childhood days, was filled with the sacred utterance 'Hari Bol'. It was an indication of things to come.

Years later, after Krishna Chaitanya moved away from the path of knowledge to one of pure devotion, the very utterance of the Lord's name would transport him to a state of ecstasy. He would shout and chant: 'Krishna, Krishna! Hari Bol, Hari Bol!' With tears streaming down his cheeks, he would laugh, weep, jump and dance in a state of mahabhava, ecstasy.

It is believed that going to temples, performing pujas and so on are at best rituals of bhakti, mechanical and superficial. These rituals work like floodgates that restrain, hold back bhakti-bhava from bursting forth. But once the floodgates open, the bhakta is swept off in its current and she is no more herself but a channel for the divine. Krishna Chaitanya was one such divine channel through which bhakti-bhava, devotion to Krishna, inspired the modern-day 'Hare Krishna' movement that spread across the world.

Chaitanya was born in the year 1486 to Jagannath Mishra and Sachi Devi. If according to some scholars he was born in the village of Dhakadakshin in Bengal, according to *Chaitanya Charitamruta*, written by Krishnadasa Kaviraja, he was born in Mayapur village, located on the banks of the Ganga, near Nabadwip in the Nadia district of West Bengal.

Before Krishna Chaitanya's birth, Sachi Devi had lost a number of children, so he was called 'Nimai' after the neem tree, which is supposed to protect against evil forces. He had a fair complexion, so he was also sometimes called 'Gauranga'. It is said he was a child prodigy and could recite mantras and other religious hymns at a very young age.

As a young man, he is believed to have pursued the path of jnana, knowledge. His father was a pandit and had many philosophical works at home. Chaitanya studied most of these texts on his own, especially, the Nyaya system of philosophy. Then he underwent training under the famous Pandit Raghunatha Siromani. Soon, Chaitanya came to be considered the best pandit in Nadia.

Around this time, he married Lakshmi, the daughter of Vallabhacharya, and became a family man. Soon after his marriage, when Krishna Chaitanya was 23 years old, his father died. He went on a pilgrimage to Gaya, in northern India, to perform a religious ceremony to pay homage to his deceased father. There, he met Isvar Puri, an ascetic who belonged to Madhvacharya's school of thought, and accepted him as his guru. It marked a turning point in Krishna Chaitanya's life. The young pandit was completely taken in by the discourses on bhakti. It was something like a revelation and it wholly changed his outlook on life. Isvar Puri gave him the mantra of Lord Krishna. Bhakti became his way of life and Lord Krishna the supreme God, ultimate guru and companion.

On returning home, he heard that his wife, Lakshmi, had died of snakebite. At his mother's insistence he took another wife, to woman named Vishnupriya, but his married life did not last long. At the age of 24, he decided to embrace sanyasa. His mother and wife were heartbroken. He loved them, but the calling was stronger. He took his initiation into sanyasa as Krishna Chaitanya from Swami Keshava Bharati. As a sanyasi now, head tonsured, clothed in his bare kaupina, loincloth, and a bahirvasa, outer covering, carrying a danda, stick, in one hand, and a kamandala, hermit's water-pot, in the other, he left home and Nadia for Odisha.

He was accompanied by a few close associates. It was a long journey, they had to cover about 500 kilometres. They walked through forests and valleys, towns and villages, and in many places he held sankirtans, songs or chants praising God, that attracted hundreds of people to the way of bhakti. He is believed to have resided with one Sarvabhauma, a Sanskrit pandit, near the Jagannatha Temple at Puri, Odisha, for 18 long years.

During his stay at Sarvabhauma's house, upon the pandit's request, Chaitanya gave his interpretation of the *Brahmasutra*, arguing for the supremacy of bhakti marg and won over the pandit and his followers. Then, through his sankirtans and discourses, hundreds of people are believed to have accepted him as their guru and Lord Krishna as the supreme deity. To this day, Puri Srikhetra in Odisha remains an important pilgrim centre for Chaitanya Vaishnavism, also known as Gaudiya Vaishnava tradition, with its focus on the devotional worship of Radha and Krishna.

During his long stay in Odisha, he is believed to have gone on a long tour to the South of India. He visited Tirupathi Hills, Kanchipuram, the famous Srirangam on the banks of Cauvery, Madurai, Kanyakumari, Udupi and Pandharpur. It is said that at these religious centres, he not only had dialogues with Vaishnavites and Advaitins, but also with Buddhists and Jains, winning over the hearts of many and instilling in them the spiritual love of Krishna.

Chaitanya's death remains shrouded in mystery. According to some scholars he died of natural causes on 14 June 1534, at Tota Gopinath Temple in Puri; some reason he suffered from epilepsy and that it might have been the cause of his death; others suggest he was probably murdered and his body disposed by his rivals; while legend has it he just mysteriously disappeared. Before his death, however, he is believed to have given the following instruction to his followers:

The chanting of Krishna's Name is the chief means of attaining Krishna's feet in the Kali Yuga. Chant the name while sitting, standing, walking, eating, in bed and everywhere, at any time. (Hindupedia)

Chaitanya did not leave behind any writings, except for a series of verses known as the *Siksastaka*, or 'eight verses of instruction', which he had spoken and were recorded by one of his close associates. These eight verses are considered to contain the complete philosophy of Gaudiya Vaishnavism in condensed form:

1. Krishna is the Supreme Absolute Truth.
2. Krishna is the source of everything.
3. The jivas or individual souls are all separated parts of the Lord.
4. In bound state the jivas are under the influence of matter, due to their tatastha nature (nature of the soul).
5. In the liberated state the jivas are free from the influence of matter, due to their tatastha nature.
6. The jivas/atman and the material world are both different from and identical to the Paramatman.
7. Pure love of Krishna is the ultimate goal.
8. Krishna is the only lovable blessing to be received.

Legend has it that Chaitanya requested his close associates, who later came to be known as the Six Goswamis of Vrindavan, to systematically present the philosophy of bhakti he had taught them in their own writings. These Goswamis were responsible for systematizing the Gaudiya Vaishnava doctrine.

Chaitanya's Gaudiya Vaishnavism is a living tradition in Bengal, Odisha and Uttar Pradesh. Sri Ramakrishna, who, like Chaitanya, used to often slip into a state of samadhi, encouraged the bhakti marga of Chaitanya, whom he referred to as 'Gauranga'.

In the twentieth century, the teachings of Chaitanya were taken to the West by A.C. Bhaktivedanta Swami Prabhupada, who belonged to the Bhaktisiddhanta Sarasvati branch of Chaitanya's tradition. He founded the movement known today as The International Society for Krishna Consciousness (ISKCON) to spread Chaitanya's teachings throughout the world.

❧⸙❧

Ravidas
(born 1371)

ONCE, THE BRAHMINS OF VARANASI APPROACHED THE CHIEF OF KASHI, Naresh Hardev Singh, and complained about Ravidas breaking caste rules. Ravidas was summoned by the chief and asked to explain. Ravidas said that everybody had the right to worship God and that he was a true worshipper of God. The brahmins questioned his claim and proclaimed themselves as the true worshippers of God as per tradition. The chief decided to put them to a test. He asked Ravidas and the brahmin pandits to get their Thakurs, idols of God, to the river Ganga the next day. The party whose idol floats on water would be declared the true worshipper of God. The next day morning, a large crowd gathered at the ghat, bank, of the river to witness the likely miracle. Indeed it was a miracle when they saw the Thakur of Ravidas, which was quite heavy, floating gently on the water, while the Thakurs of the brahmin priests sank no sooner than they had placed them on the surface of the water.

Ravidas belonged to the Chamar caste, who were tanners and cobblers and considered untouchables because they dealt with the skin of dead animals. Ravidas was born in 1371 to Raghuram and Ghurbinia, in the village Goverdhanpur near Varanasi in Uttar Pradesh. Living close to the holy place, Kashi, otherwise called Varanasi, spirituality might have come naturally to Ravidas. The stigma of untouchability never bothered him; rather, he was proud of his vocation and carried on with his profession of making and repairing sandals and shoes even after he came to be revered as a guru and had a wide following cutting across castes.

Ravidas was married at an early age to Lona Devi and they had
a son named Vijaydas. He lived in a small hut and set up a shop for
mending footwear. He had a shrine built by the side of his house,
where he is believed to have installed an idol made out of animal hide.
Initially, there was much resentment from the upper castes, even stiff
opposition from the brahmin priestly class to his religious observances.
Undeterred, he carried on with his meditations, compositions of
hymns and mending of shoes. His spiritual maturity and pious nature
drew many to his place. Gradually, as more and more people flocked
around him and his spiritual stature grew, even brahmin pandits, it is
said, would bow to him with reverence.

> What shall I sing?
> I am unable to sing in praise of God,
> for I have attained the state of spiritual calm.
> In the state of ecstasy,
> there is neither sky nor earth.
> The splendour of Ram and Krishan exist no more,
> I am telling you the truth.
> I do not rejoice in the Vedas or Puranas,
> lost in the state of ecstasy.
> Between me and you and you and me,
> all differences have gone.
> To whom should I reveal this secret?
> Fully absorbed in Him,
> All my songs have finished, says Ravidas.
>
>   (Arsh, trans.)

In Ravidas's philosophy there was a creative blend of the devotional
and the transcendental, the saguna and nirguna, God with attributes
and God as formless or without attributes, which, in some ways, link
him to the Nath Yoga philosophy. He often used the term sahaj, natural,
to highlight the truth that tranquillity and love are the natural attributes

of a being. His teaching of equanimity and love, sahaj bhao, drew people from all castes to him, and, centuries later, his large following developed into a new religion.

Unlike Kabir, who lambasted the brahmin priests and the mullahs for their false religiosity, Ravidas was a gentle, compassionate sage. And in his own gentle, loving way he rejected the authority of the Vedas and the spiritual power of the brahmins, though he was quite persistent in his critique of the caste hierarchy. By continuing to work as a cobbler and expressing his pride in his caste identity, he brought dignity to the work a chamar performed, which, in many ways, is analogous to Basavanna's philosophy of kayaka, one's work or vocation being equivalent to worshipping God. It is this spirit of self-assertion that drew millions of lower-caste people, especially chamars, to look upon him as their liberator.

Several hagiographical works on Ravidas emerged centuries after his death, notable among them are *Premambodha* in the Sikh tradition, *Bhaktamal* of the saint Nabhadas and *Parchais* of the guru Anantadas. The Guru Granth of the Sikhs, and *Panchvani* of the Hindu Dadupanthis, followers of the sixteenth century Saint Dadu Dayal, remain the two important sources of Ravidas's literary works. In the Adi Granth, about 40 of his verses are included. The Ravidassia sect in Punjab proclaim themselves 'putt chamar di', 'sons of chamars'. There is even a new religion called Ravidassia Panth. The Ravidassia Panth was launched out of Sikhism, when Guru Ramanand Dass, a leader of the Dera Sach Khand and a follower of Ravidas, was murdered in Vienna in 2009 by a radical group. They have their own holy book, *Amritbani Guru Ravidass Ji*, containing the writings and teaching of Ravidas. Every year, devotees of Ravidas from all over India, Europe, UK and US gather at Shri Guru Ravidas Janam Asthan Mandir in Goverdhanpur, Varnasi, to celebrate Ravidas Jayanti in the month of February. During the festive period, Ravidas meets Ambedkar in shops on the ghats of Varanasi, where calendars, pictures and T-shirts carrying the images of these two great icons are sold.

Ravidas dreamt of a world where there would be no sorrow, no discrimination and no inequality, and people would live in harmony and peace. It was a revolutionary idea conceived hundreds of years before Karl Marx would come up with his ideal of a stateless state. Ravidas called it Begumpura Shehr – a land without sorrow, full of peace and humanity, where there would be no discrimination on the basis of caste, where nobody would pay taxes, and people would live in harmony and loving kindness.

> The regal realm with the sorrowless name
> they call it Begumpura, a place with no pain,
> no taxes or cares, none owns property there,
> no wrongdoing, worry, terror, or torture.
> Oh my brother, I've come to take it as my own,
> my distant home, where everything is right...
> They do this or that, they walk where they wish,
> they stroll through fabled palaces unchallenged.
> Oh, says Ravidas, a tanner now set free,
> those who walk beside me are my friends.

(ravidassiadharam.in)

Guru Nanak
(1469–1539)

A STORY GOES THAT ON HIS TRAVELS TO DIFFERENT SPIRITUAL CENTRES, Guru Nanak once went to a scared place high in the Himalayan mountains, where spirits of different powers lived. Seeing him enter their realm, they assumed he was there to join them and so put him through a series of tests which he had to pass before gaining admittance. Soon, fearful, ghoulish figures appeared from everywhere and tried to scare him. Nanak paid them no heed, thus passing the first test. Then a benign looking spirit approached him and said, 'Before you proceed further, take this urn and fill it with water from the nearby lake and come back.' Nanak took the urn, went to the lake and found it filled with gems, rubies and diamonds instead of water. He returned with the empty urn and said, 'Forgive me, there was no water in the lake.' He was not tempted by the riches of the world; he had passed the second test as well. The yogis now stepped in and one of them spoke thus to Nanak: 'This is the way of spirituality. You really are great. But there's just one thing left. Renounce the world, give up everything, then you can join us.'

Nanak smiled. 'Who told you I came here to join you? I came here to ask you why, when you see the world on fire, when you know how to cool it, you choose to be indifferent and remain here. One should renounce the world while being in it, not away from it. Tell me, has your yoga really brought you closer to God? I don't think so.' And, not wanting to waste any more time there, Nanak left the forest and went back into the world to continue with his mission of spreading the message of love and service (Khalsa).

'The world is on fire' is a striking metaphor, and reminiscent of the Buddha's 'Fire Sermon' to his disciples. The Buddha used the image of fire to speak about the fires of greed, hate, sorrow and delusion, how it was burning humanity and how liberation from these passions constituted nirvana. Nanak, too, spoke about the possibility of freeing oneself from the fires of pride, anger, greed, attachment and lust, while living in the world, not outside of it; while being compassionately engaged with the world, not by renouncing it.

Nanak was born in a Hindu family, to Mehta Kalu and Mata Tripta, in the year 1469, in the village Talwandi, now known as Nankana Sahib, situated near Lahore, Pakistan. His father was a village accountant. It is said that as a child Nanak had a sharp, questioning mind. When he came of age and had to be invested with the sacred thread, janeu, as per tradition, he refused to go through the ceremony. His parents and the priest were shocked but could not force him to go through the ritual. Years later, in one of his poems he explained:

Let mercy be the cotton, contentment the thread,
Continence the knot and truth the twist.
Oh priest! If you have such a thread,
Do give it to me.
It will not wear out, nor get soiled, nor be burnt, nor lost.
Blessed are those who go about wearing such a thread.

('Guru Nanak', Sikhwiki)

Nanak was attached to his sister Bebe Nanaki. When she married Jai Ram and moved to Sultanpur, he, too, went with her to Sultanpur. There, at the age of 16, he took up a job under the employer of his brother-in-law. This was a formative period for Nanak, and he was turning more and more inwards. It was during this time that he went through a life-changing experience. In the morning he used to go to the river to bathe and meditate. One morning, he left home as usual and didn't return. It is believed he went deep inside the forest to meditate and stayed there for three days. This may bring to mind the story of the 'transformations' the sages or prophets such as the Buddha, Jesus, Mohammad and so on underwent when they were in solitude. Without generalizing this phenomenon, we may suggest that the would-be sage comes upon the vision of truth and then later gives expression to the vision in her or his own way, and in the context of the needs and aspirations of the people of his or her times.

On his return, Nanak did not speak for some time, and when he did, his first few words were: 'There is no Hindu and no Mussalman.' The teaching that would emerge in the following years was, in a sense, an exegesis of these words, which was in effect a call to transcend all forms of division through love and selfless service.

In 1487, he married Mata Sulakkhani and the couple had two sons,

Sri Chand and Lakhmi Chand. Sri Chand received instructions from his father and lived an intense spiritual life, and then went on to become the founder of the Udasi, a religious sect centred in northern India. Their religious faith and practices border on a syncretism of Sikhism and Hinduism. The Udasis worship Shiva, Vishnu, Durga, Ganesha and Surya.

Nanak worked during the day, but in the morning and evening hours, he would meditate and sing hymns, accompanied by Bhai Mardana, on the rabab, a stringed instrument. Mardana was his childhood friend, and a Muslim. Later, Mardana even accompanied him on his long travels for 30 years, and remained his close associate till the end.

Nanak's teachings are contained in the form of 974 poetic hymns recorded in Gurmukhi in the Guru Granth Sahib, the holy text of Sikhism. The book is considered an eternal, living guru. The whole text, containing the teachings of the Sikh gurus, the teachings of non-Sikh gurus such as Ravidas, Ramanand, Kabir and Namdev, and one hymn from Mardana, was compiled by the tenth guru of Sikhism. It consists of 1,430 angs, pages and 6,000 sabads, line compositions, poetically rendered and set to a rhythmic music. The scripture is not considered a revelation or voice of God and Nanak is not regarded a prophet or an incarnation of God, but an illumined soul.

According to Nanak the everyday world is part of the infinite reality, there is no division between a spiritual life and a householder's life. In fact, they are intertwined; all that we need to develop is an increased spiritual awareness in the day-to-day living, cultivate truthfulness, fidelity, self-control and purity in one's being.

He advocated the existence of one God and taught that every human being can reach out to God through meditation and other pious practices. In his words:

There is but One God, His name is Truth, He is the Creator, He fears none, He is without hate, He never dies, He is beyond the

cycle of birth and death, He is self-illuminated, He is realized by
the kindness of the True Guru. He was True in the beginning,
He was True when the ages commenced and has ever been True,
He is also True now.

('The First Master')

He condemned the prevalent caste system, the treatment of some
as high and others as low, slavery and racial discrimination, idolatry and
worship of demigods. Instead he emphasized the importance of seva,
selfless service as against tyaga, renunciation, equality between man
and man, and man and woman. With regard to women in particular,
he appealed to his followers to respect them. He said:

From woman, man is born; within woman, man is conceived; to
woman he is engaged and married. Woman becomes his friend;
through woman, the future generations come. When his woman
dies, he seeks another woman; to woman he is bound. So why call
her bad? From her, kings are born. From woman, woman is born;
without woman, there would be no one at all.

('Guru Nanak's Message')

It was a new religion in the making, and within a few years of his
passing, his teaching matured into a full-fledged religion based on
egalitarian values and selfless service to humanity. Selflessness, honest
living and meditation on God and repetition of the sacred mantra were
the three pillars of this new faith:

1. Vand Chakna, spirit of sharing and giving, and giving to those
   who are less fortunate. But, also a selflessness of attitude –
   avoiding the pitfalls of egoism, pride and jealousy.
2. Kirat Karni, earning and living an honest life. Not only earning
   one's living without deceit, exploitation or fraud, but also
   accepting both pains and pleasures as God's gifts and blessings.

3. Naam Japna, meditation on God – Waheguru – through reciting, chanting, singing and constant remembrance followed by adherence to Dharam, righteousness.

Starting in 1496, at the age of 27, Guru Nanak, with Mardana as his companion, travelled extensively with his message of one God, love and selfless service. It is estimated that for over 30 years he covered a staggering distance of 28,000 kilometres by foot on five major tours. He travelled in different parts of India, then in Kashmir, Nepal, Sri Lanka, Arabia and Persia, and held discussions with leaders of various religious sects, such as Hindus, Jains, Buddhists, Parsis and Muslims. He spoke in the temples and mosques, at various pilgrimage sites, and everywhere he spoke out against empty religious rituals, dependence on priests and books, caste and racial discrimination, the sacrifice of widows and oppression of women. It is important to note here that he did not seek conversion of people into his path; rather, he asked the Muslims to be true Muslims, the Hindus to be true Hindus, the Parsis to be true Parsis.

After completing his mission, he settled in Kartarpur, the City of God, on the banks of River Ravi in Punjab. People came from far to listen to his discourses and take part in the kirtans. Langar, free communal kitchen, was started. Regardless of caste or social and economic status, people could mingle and partake of the food. Before his passing away in 1539, at the age of 70, he installed Bhai Lehna, Guru Angad Dev, as his successor, the Second Nanak.

Selected Sayings from Guru Granth Sahib

No one knows the state of the Lord. The Yogis, the celibates, the austere penitents, and all sorts of clever people have failed. In an instant, He changes the beggar into a king, and the king into a beggar. He fills what is empty, and empties what is full. Such are His ways. He Himself spread out the expanse of His Maya, and He Himself beholds it. He assumes so many forms, and plays so many games, and yet He remains distinct and detached from it all. Incalculable, infinite, incomprehensible and immaculate... So give up all your doubts; prays Nanak, O mortal, focus your consciousness on His Feet.

~

Says Nanak, the Guru has revealed God to me, and now I see that there is no such thing as birth or death. No one dies; no one comes or goes.

~

Burn worldly love,
rub the ashes and make ink of it,
make the heart the pen,
the intellect the writer,
write that which has no end or limit.

~

He who has no faith in himself can never have faith in God.

~

Even Kings and emperors with heaps of wealth and vast dominion cannot compare with an ant filled with the love of God.

~

The world is a drama, staged in a dream.

~

For each and every person, our Lord and Master provides sustenance. Why are you so afraid, O mind? The flamingos fly hundreds of miles, leaving their young ones behind. Who feeds them, and who teaches them to feed themselves? Have you ever thought of this in your mind?

~

What should the yogi have to fear? Trees, plants, and all that is
inside and outside, is He Himself.

~

Nanak, the whole world is in distress. He, who believes in the
Name, becomes victorious.

~

The Lord of man and beast is working in all; His presence is
scattered everywhere; There is none else to be seen.

('The Guru Granth Sahib')

❧

Meera Bai
(born 1498)

MEERA WAS FOUR YEARS OF AGE, WHEN HER MOTHER, VEER KUMARI,
took her to a royal wedding. Fascinated and drawn by the joyful mood
that throbbed around her, the invitees in colourful dresses, the bride
decked in silk and jewels and the play of music, the little girl asked
her mother, 'Dear mother, am I too going to be married this way?'

'Of course, dear,' said her mother, 'and on a grander scale.'

'But who will be my bridegroom, mother?'

'Who else?' the mother replied playfully, 'the most beautiful Krishna
will be your bridegroom.' (Goetz, 1966)

The little girl took her mother's words seriously and from then
on looked upon Krishna as her bridegroom and lord. Two years later,
her mother passed away. She was brought up by her grandfather, Rao
Dudaji. One day, a sadhu came to the palace to see Rao Dudaji and
stayed overnight. Next day morning, Meera saw the sadhu sing songs
and perform puja to a beautiful little idol of Krishna. Charmed by

the idol, she wanted it for herself, but the sadhu wouldn't part with it. Meera insisted, like children often do, even kicked up a racket, to obtain the icon. The sadhu, though quite reluctantly, gave her the idol, and taught her how to worship the lord. According to another version, the sadhu was none other than the famous saint Ravidas, who gave her the idol by way of initiation.

Thus began Meera's 'love affair' with Krishna. We cannot explain with any certainty why saints such as Andal, Akka Mahadevi, Lalleshwari, or Meera, took a passionate liking to their respective gods, looked upon themselves as 'brides' of and sought union with their lords, just as we cannot explain why at an early age some boys and girls exhibit extraordinary talent for music or painting or such arts.

Meera was born in the year 1498 at Kudki, a village near Merwa city, which is presently in the Nagpur district of Rajasthan. Her father, Ratan Singh, was the youngest son of Rao Dudaji, ruler of Merwa, and her mother, Veer Kumari, was the princess of Zola Rajput Sultan Singh. As a princess, apart from her training in sewing and embroidery, good manners and court etiquette, dancing and singing and playing musical instruments, she was taught horse riding and possibly even sword fighting. She knew how to read and write and was quite conversant with religious texts such as the *Bhagavata Purana* and the great epics, Ramayana and Mahabharata. Such education certainly would have contributed to the development of her exceptional independence and self-reliance. It stood her in good stead when she took decisions that went against social norms and the fiercely patriarchal Rajputana tradition.

She was married at the age of 13 to Prince Bhojraj, the son of Rana Sanga of Chittor, a political arrangement between the Merwa and Chittor kingdoms. Such political alliances through marriages were a common practice. But it was an unhappy marriage. Legend has it that the marriage was never consummated, perhaps because her devotion to Krishna was so total that she couldn't have borne any physical connection with her husband. Krishna was her 'first' husband, the husband of her soul, Bhojraj, a mortal, 'second' husband was of no consequence.

How did this rebellion pan out in a patriarchal household where it was a woman's duty to bear children? According to one account, Bhojraj appealed to her to give up her foolish love of Krishna and live according to the conventions of the royal household, but when she paid no heed to the advice and continued to spend her time in prayers and meeting with sadhus, he was moved by her unalloyed devotion to Krishna. He left her alone to do as she pleases, and took a new bride.

Generally, women of Meera's rank, queen dowagers and older women of the royal family, lived in a different wing of the palace, sometimes even in a separate house, and had their own household establishment. They spent much of their time in religious activities, such as bhajans, meeting with religious gurus or feeding religious mendicants, or attending social events and so on.

So it's quite likely that Meera was living independently in a separate house. And by then she had started composing her padas or poems on Krishna, whom she variously referred to as Satguru, Prabhu Ji, Giridhar Nagar or Giridhar Gopal. It was a time when the Mughal rule was fast spreading across North India and the Rajput kingdoms were under grave threat of attack from the Mughal kings.

Family conflicts and power struggles within and among the royal families of Mewar, Chittor and Jodhpur had made them vulnerable to such attacks. Meera was willy-nilly thrown into the thick of these political conspiracies and conflicts and wars between them and against the Delhi Sultanate. How she negotiated these troubles and kept herself unaffected and pursued her spiritual quest is in itself a great story.

In 1518, in a surprise attack by the army of Ibrahim Lodhi on Mewar, Meera's husband Bhojraj was gravely wounded in the fight. He never recovered and died two years later. In keeping with the Rajput Kshatriya tradition, Meera, merely 22 years old, was asked to perform sati, that is, to immolate herself on the funeral pyre of her husband. As per the custom, a widow was expected to willingly give up her life and join her husband in heaven as his devoted wife. Meera refused, even though she had examples of women in the family, who had performed sati after the deaths of their husbands. Bhojraj may have been her husband but, in her heart, she was Lord Krishna's bride: nitya sumangali, the eternal wife, she could never be widowed. However, by refusing to perform sati, she incurred life-long resentment from the family members, especially her mother-in-law.

Within a few years of her husband's tragic death, she lost both her father and father-in-law in a war with the army of Babur, the founder of the Mughal Empire in the Indian subcontinent. Her brother-in-law, Vikram Singh, became the ruler of Chittor and did not take kindly to her rebellious behaviour and zealous devotion to Krishna. But, studying the available information, Hermann Goetz, a German art historian and writer, thinks that Meera was persecuted not for religious reasons but for possible political ones. Meera used to meet with religious gurus and mendicants quite regularly. The king suspected that these religious people could be spies, secret messengers and conspirators in religious garb.

Two attempts were made to eliminate her. Once, her drink of milk was laced with poison, and on another occasion a basket of flowers with a deadly snake hidden under it was sent to her as a gift. We do not know how she escaped the two attempts on her life except that she survived miraculously on both occasions and decided to leave Chittor.

O Lord Krishna
there's no home for me in the three worlds.
You are my refuge.
Says Meera, I am Your slave,
forget me not,
I beseech You.

~

Meera danced with ankle-bells on her feet.
People said Meera was mad.
You ruined the family reputation,
screamed my mother-in-law.
Rana sent me a cup of poison and Meera
drank it laughing.
My body and soul lie at His feet,
I seek refuge in Him,
my lord Giridhar Nagar.

(Shekhawat, trans., 2019)

In defiance of tradition, Meera had refused to commit sati. Now, abandoning worldly comfort and security, she left the palace and went on a pilgrimage, singing and dancing with anklets on her feet, and in the company of seekers and holy men. Her lyrical padas in the Rajasthani language combined defiance, forlornness and yearning for union with Krishna. Some 1,300 padas are attributed to her, though all of them may not have been composed by her. These padas were written down only after some 150 years after her passing away.

Fastening the bells of his love to my feet
I'll dance in front of Giridhar.
Dancing I will please his eyes.
My love is an ancient one,
that is the only truth.
I care not about social norms
nor of family's honour.
I belong to Hari,
am dyed in His colour.

(Shekhawat, trans., 2019)

In the poetry of nirguna bhaktas, such as Allama Prabhu and Lalleshwari, we sense an intense urge to transcend into 'nothingness', which is also 'fullness'. Generally, bhakti poetry is intensely iconic and a powerful bhava, yet the impulse, the deep urge within it, can be defiantly aniconic, often rising towards anubhaava, unmediated experience of reality. However, among the saguna bhaktas, Andal and Meera for instance, there is a relentless play of different bhavas, of lovelornness, yearning for union and surrender; it remains relational, the bridge is never crossed. It is a case of *seeking and being with god*, not becoming god.

Coming back to the story, after fleeing Chittor, Meera is believed to have visited several holy places. At Brindavan, legend recounts, she sent a message to Rupa Goswami, who was a renunciate and a celibate, a disciple of Chaitanya Mahaprabhu and considered a great saint of Vrindavan at the time, expressing her wish to meet him. Goswami is believed to have refused to meet her because as a sanyasi he would not meet a woman. Expressing her surprise, the story goes that Meera sent another message, asking him, 'Are you competing with god? I thought the lord is the only true man, purush, in the universe, everyone else is only a female devotee of Krishna.' There was no response from Rupa Goswami. Undeterred, Meera danced her way through Vrindavan and then moved from village to village.

From Vrindavan, Meera went to Dwarka. All through her travels, and at Dwarka in particular, Meera mixed freely with people from the lower castes. She taught them songs and danced with them with abandon. In the words of Hermann Goetz, 'Meera had developed into a revolutionary, not by attacking the social order and official religion, but by ignoring them, and appealing, in the name of her religion of the heart, directly to the lower social classes and the women. In a time of political disruption such teachings and [coming from the royal Rajput family] her free intercourse with all classes and with sadhus from everywhere could easily stamp her as a dangerous anti-social force.'

Abandoning her identity as the princess of Merwa, Meera settled down in Dwarka, leading the simple life of an ascetic. In these years, she is believed to have composed *Raag Soaratha*, *Raag Govind* and *Govind Tika*, and also had a hand in getting the Krishna temple at Dwarka rebuilt. In 1546, Rana Udai Singh, who had succeeded Vikram Singh, sent a deputation of brahmins to bring Meera back to Chittor. According to one version, Udai Singh wanted her back not because she had become an embarrassment, or because she had turned a renegade, but because he believed her spiritual powers could help his kingdom.

After many battles with the Muslim rulers and the death of Ratan Singh and Vikram Singh, Mewar had fallen to pieces and Chittor was in ruins. It seemed like a curse had fallen upon them. It could be because they had ill-treated a saintly Meera and even tried to murder her. To remedy the scourge, they needed to accept and honour her; also, Udai Singh believed, Meera's presence amidst them could help him rebuild Chittor.

Meera refused to return, and the brahmins went on a fast to force her. One night, she quietly disappeared from the temple of Ranchhodji. Only her clothes were found in the sanctum sanctorum. It was believed Lord Krishna had granted her the supreme union by absorbing her into his image. Hagiographical accounts of her life usually end here in supernatural mystery. But in reality, it is said, Meera fled Dwarka that night because she didn't want to be forced to return to Chittor. She is believed to have travelled to Amber, Mathura, Puri and such holy place as an ordinary woman and meet with Tulsidas, Tansen and Man Singh, Akbar's trusted general, during this period. Then we hear of her no more. She probably died around the age of 65.

Selected Songs of Meera

Gopal is mine and I'm His.
The Dark One
the mountain-holder,
who wears the peacock-crown:
He alone is my husband...

Now with love
He carries me across to the further shore.

~

When I'm dead
Crow, eat me up
Eat up every part,
But spare my two eyes
They long to see Him!

~

So madly in love,
None can fathom my ache, my pang
Only a wounded would know
The pain of wounded
Not any onlookers.
How to meet my Swami?
His abode is on the gallows!

~

Meera, afire in love
and longing
Came to streets
to sing His songs
Reared in palaces,
Walked out an ascetic
Queen Meera is now
Called Crazy Meera!

Don't stop her
Don't interrupt her
Meera sings Govind, Gopal
In company of saints

Dyed in hues of Mohan

Meera, in love, celebrates her Beloved

(Shekhawat, trans., 2019)

❦

Kanaka Dasa
(1509–1609)

MOST BIOGRAPHIES ON KANAKA DASA AGREE THAT HIS TEACHER Vyasaraya Swami treated all his disciples equally irrespective of the caste they belonged to. However, his brahmin disciples threatened to leave if Kanaka, who was from the shepherd caste, was allowed to sit with them. To save his guru from trouble, Kanaka volunteered to sit some distance away in a corner. Vyasaraya was not happy with this arrangement but he was helpless.

One day, he decided to put his disciples to a test. After his sermon on the nature of Brahman in *Isavasya Upanishad*, he gave a banana to each disciple and asked them to eat the fruit in a place where no one could see them eating. The disciples quickly dispersed to complete the task and then returned after a while, each one beaming in triumph, except Kanaka, who still carried the uneaten banana. After the other disciples described in vivid details the secret spots where they had consumed the fruit, Kanaka placed the banana in front of his guru and said, 'Sir, I could not find a place where Brahman did not exist, where his divine eye could not see me.'

On the last day of the class, Vyasaraya Swami wanted to know how much progress each disciple had made during the course. He said, 'My dear students, you have learnt all that had to be learnt and have grown wiser. Tell me, who among you is now capable of going to Vaikunta, the abode of Lord Vishnu?'

The disciples looked at each other not knowing how to answer the tricky question. For, to assert that one was capable would be a mark of arrogance, and to admit that one was incapable would mean defeat. They held their silence, but then Kanaka stood up to answer, while some sneered at him and others broke into laughter. Kanaka joined his palms in reverence and said, 'Swami, I may go if "I" can go.'

'Explain,' said the teacher.

'Swami, I did not mean I can go, rather what I meant was one can go to the abode of god if one could let go one's "I-ness" or "ego".' (Naikar, 2016)

The above incidents show that even as a young sadhaka, student, Kanaka Dasa had a philosophical bent of mind and the flair of a mystic.

Generally, saint-poets such as Meera Bai, Purandaradasa or the Alvars, find a sense of completeness in seeking and being with God, in being immersed in saguna bhakti, devotion to and worship of God in form, while mystic-poets such as Jnaneshvar, Kabir and Lalleshwari yearn to go beyond seeking and being with God to seeking and becoming one with God. Their bhakti may be characterized as nirguna bhakti, devotion to and worship of God as formless or without attributes. Kanaka Dasa swung between saguna and nirguna bhakti. There was a strong philosophical streak in him that animated his kirtanas and mundiges, verses or lyrics, peppered with questions, wonderment and bemusement at the way of life and the mystery of God.

Kanaka Dasa was born as Thimmappa Nayaka in 1509 to the couple Beerappa and Bachamma at Bada village, near Bankapura in Karnataka. He was named Thimmappa because he was born by the grace of Lord Venkateshwara of Tirupati, sometimes called Tirupati Thimmappa in Kannada. His father Beerappa was the head of 78 villages that were part of the Vijayanagara Empire.

Thimmappa was a smart and intelligent child and his father made arrangements for his education at quite an early age under the reputed teacher Srinivasacharya of Bankapura. By the age of 10, Thimmappa was introduced to poetry, drama and epics such as Ramayana and

Mahabharata, and started composing poetry at that tender age. He was naturally drawn to music, like duck to water, and took to singing devotional songs. Lord Adikeshava, a form of Lord Vishnu, was the village deity and Thimmappa, who now saw himself as a devotee of the Lord, spent long hours at the temple.

The untimely death of his father, just when he had stepped into his thirteenth year and was growing to be a singer, affected him deeply. The family was forced to leave Bada for Kaginele, a wealthy town with many temples. Thimmappa started visiting these temples with great devotion. During the day he tended their sheep and goat and come evening, he would immerse himself in devotional songs, even participate in folk plays which were based on mythical stories. During this time, he composed *Hari Bhakta Sara*, Essence of Devotion to Hari.

There was a major turn in his life at this stage when his reputation as a disciplined, spiritual person and an accomplished poet reached the ears of the King of Vijayanagara. The King, Krishnadevaraya, appointed him as Dandanayaka, administrator of Bada and Bankapura. His post as Dandanayaka was higher than what his father had held during his time. He was now called Kanakanayaka and he took to this new life with enthusiasm and responsibility and plunged into the developmental activities of Bada and Bankapura, constructing canals, reservoirs and roads and renovating old temples.

His mother now wanted him to get married. He married Lakshmidevi and in a year's time the couple had a son, who was named Biranayaka. Kanakanayaka must have been a highly disciplined person, otherwise it would have been impossible for him to carry out his responsibilities as a householder and administrator and yet in equal measure continue with his spiritual and aesthetic pursuits. For, it was during this period he composed his now famous *Mohana Tarangini*, Ocean of Beauty. It was a lyrical work containing 42 chapters with 2800 verses in the *sangatya*, metric metre, inspired by stories from the *Bhagavata*, *Mahabharatha* and other various puranas.

At a stage when he was at the height of his powers both as an administrator and in his poetic achievement, tragedy struck him, like a bolt from the blue. Both his wife and child died one after another, leaving him devastated. His mother, Bachamma, wanted him to get married again but he refused. His anguish didn't end there. The Vijayanagar Empire began to fall apart and he lost his job as the administrator of Bada and Bankapura.

In time, the deep sorrow changed into devotional passion. In a dream he saw the Lord of the seven hills, Lord Tirumalesha, and himself running towards the god, but before he could reach he was awakened. This dream with some variations occurred again and again, and in one of them the god himself asked him to trust in himself and follow the divine path. These visions freed him from the grip of sorrow and he found himself dancing in ecstasy, singing his troubles away!

> Enough of the worldly service, O Lord,
> and of serving men of grass,
> I am done with the world,
> ready to meditate upon thy lotus feet.

> (Translated by author)

He discarded his fine clothes, clad himself in a white dhoti and crowned his head with a turban. With a woollen blanket over his left shoulder, he carried the ekanada or ektara, single-stringed musical instrument, on his right, and wearing a pair of rough slippers, set out from Kaginele to Bada. Thus, Kanakaraya changed into Kanaka Dasa. Dancing and singing the end of sorrow, he is believed to have carried the idol of Adikeshava from Bada back to Kaginele and got a temple built for the Lord there, which came to be called as 'Adikeshava of Kaginele'. As the dasa, servant, of Adikeshava, the temple as his abode, he began to compose padas, poems, and in the evenings, sing kirtans and discourse on the path to joy and freedom.

Thus, he immersed himself day and night in devotional activities;

then, one fine morning, he left Kaginele on a long tour. Still thirsty for spiritual knowledge, he sought a wise guru. He went to the Sosale Ashram at Tiruma-Kudalu, situated on the banks of the confluence of Kapila and Kaveri rivers, where the famous Vyasaraya Swami, taught. He was stopped at the gate of the ashram. With his matted hair, beard and coarse turban and dhoti, the ektara hanging by his shoulder, he looked a picture of a mendicant. The men at the gate wanted to know about his background and caste. The whole cosmos as his home and Lord Narayana as his master, he belonged to no caste nor clan, he said. The brahmin disciples of Vyasaraya were not impressed. 'Reveal your caste,' they insisted. Thrumming the string of his ektara, Kanaka Dasa sang:

Shepherds, we are, brothers, and
Birayya is our Lord,
who guards the herds
of human sheep.

(Translated by author)

Vyasaraya Swami, who heard the commotion, came out and instantly knew who the stranger was. To the chagrin of his disciples, Vyasaraya took him by hand into the ashram and they got into a long conversation. Kanaka Dasa said he wanted to learn from him, Vyasaraya replied that it would his honour to teach him. But the brahmin disciples raised an objection. 'He belongs to the kuruba caste,' they said, 'he can't be our classmate.' Before Vyasaraya could react, Kanaka Dasa said he would sit away from the disciples and not pollute them, all that he desired was to listen to the guru's discourses.

The story of Kanaka Dasa's stay at the ashram, his interactions with the teacher and his disciples and the many incidents that took place there read like illuminating parables, two of which have been narrated at the beginning of this chapter.

Later, from the ashram, Kanaka Dasa is believed to have travelled to many religious centres and holy places both in the south and north, singing his kirtans and teaching people the path of liberation through bhakti. Tirupati, Gokarna, Chandragutti, Banavasi, Gadag, Hampi, Belur, Gaya, Mathura, Kashi and Dwarka are some of the places mentioned in the hagiographical accounts. His visit to the town of Udupi, in the coastal district of Mangaluru, famous for the Krishna temple and as a holy place, stands out as the crowning glory of his career as a saint-poet.

At the entrance of the Krishna temple he was stopped from going inside. He looked a mendicant in rags, or probably the brahmin camp there knew that Kanaka Dasa was a kuruba, a shepherd, who had turned into a wandering dasa. The ringing of the bells and chanting inside was enchanting to his ears and he desired to go in and witness the puja and have darshan of the Lord. When his pleading didn't work, he quietly walked to the back side of the temple, and standing there, behind the wall of the sanctum sanctorum, thrumming the string of his ektara, began singing a kirtan in praise of Krishna.

The wall cracked, bricks fell off creating a large hole in the wall, and Lord Krishna turned around on his pedestal to see and listen to the melody of his great devotee. To this day there exists a hole in the back of the temple wall, famously called Kanakana Kindi, Kanaka's Peep Hole. Visiting devotees first take a look at Krishna through this little window before going in for the darshan. Whether Krishna turned around to give darshan to or have darshan of his parama bhakta continues to be a debating point in discussions on the miraculous incident.

From Udupi, Kanaka Dasa is believed to have travelled in the North before returning to Kaginele. His last days were spent in Kaginele, singing hymns to his lord Adikeshava. He died at the age of 98.

Besides Kanaka Dasa's 240 musical compositions – such as kirtanas, devotional and philosophical songs, and mundiges, poetic riddles – his other works include mythological stories with philosophical undertones, such as *Nalacharitre*, Story of Nala; *Haribhakti Sara*, Essence of Devotion to Hari; *Narasimhastava*, In Praise of Lord Narasimha; *Mohanatarangini*, Ocean of Beauty; *Ramadhanya Charite*, Story of Rama-Grain or of Ragi/Millet.

Ramadhanya Charite is a philosophical piece on the quarrel between two food grains, Rice and Ragi, each claiming superiority over the other, and the story works like an allegory on the conflict between the socially and politically powerful castes, whose staple food was the expensive rice, and the working, economically weak lower castes who subsisted on eating the cheap and simple ragi mudde, ragi balls. Both Rice and Ragi come before Rama and argue out their cases. Rama, who is on his way back to Ayodhya after the victory over Ravana, could not give his verdict that instant. He needed time and so he asked the two grains to wait for some days.

After his coronation ceremony in Ayodhya, Rama remembered the duel and summoned Rice and Ragi to his court. In this interim period of six months, the Rice looked wasted and spoiled, while Ragi beamed, strong and healthy as always. Rama declared Ragi as superior to Rice. Clearly, the story was an indictment of the higher castes and their oppression and exploitation of the people of the lower castes in the name of varnashrama dharma. And this parable marked, probably for the first time in the Kannada literary history, the beginnings of protest literature by the downtrodden.

Selected Kirtanas

> Do not fret, O mind, have patience,
> He shall take care of all, keep faith!
> Behold the tree atop the hill,
> Now who watered it? Just consider.
> He who gives us life takes ownership
> And will protect us, have no fear.
> Who feeds every bird and beast
> In the woods each day? Give it a thought.

Like a mother would guard her child He guards
Every life form, be assured.
Who painted the peacock in colours grand?
And chose the lovely hue for the ruby red
And for the parrot that exact shade of green?
Leave your worries to him instead.
When the frogs that live in the stone pond
Croak in hunger, whose magic wand
Brings to them a morsel? Fret not
When Keshava of Kaginele is in command.

(Ravikumar, trans.)

~

Lord, tell me, are you in maya/illusion, or the maya is in you?
Are you in the body, or the body is in you?
The space dwells in the house, or is it the other way round?
Or, is it that both exist in the seeing eye?
Lord, tell me, is the eye in the mind, or the mind in the eye?
Or, both the mind and the eye reside in you?
Is sweetness in the sugar, or sugar in the sweetness?
Does fragrance lie in the flower, or flower in fragrance?
Or do both exist in the nostril?
O Lord Adikeshava, do not all things abide in you?

(Translated by author)

A Mundige—Riddle

A bird swallows a tree,
Has come into the house.
Tell me the meaning of this.

The bird has a single horn, but no entrails inside.
Three throats it has, but no nose.

It sits in the house like a lame one
And gobbles the food of eight or ten men.

It eats while rumbling
With its mouth on its top
And produces loud music.

Born in a wild forest,
It has split into two.
It protects you in poverty.

It plays at the hands
Of lotus-faced belles.
It feeds the humanity
With its victuals.
Lord Adikeshava sitting
On the gem-studded throne
Knows the secret.

(Naiker, trans., 2016)

Tulsidas
(c. 1600)

THERE IS AN INTERESTING TALE ABOUT HOW TULSIDAS, AN ORDINARY
married man pursuing the simple pleasures of life, was transformed
into a poet of the highest order. One evening, the story goes, Tulsidas
grew desperate to see his wife, who had gone to her parents' house.
He could not wait until her return and decided to take the ferry to his
in-laws' place. It was a stormy night and the river was in spate. The
boatman refused to ferry him across the turbulent river and advised
Tulsidas to go home and try his luck the next morning. There was no

going back, come what may, he simply had to go see her. Despite the boatman's warning, he got into the choppy waters and started to swim as the rain pelted down once again.

He had no idea how he reached the other shore, he scrambled up the bank and hurried towards his in-laws' place. His wife, Ratnavali, was shocked to see him all drenched and panting. He simply said, 'I had to see you.' Realizing he had swum across the stormy river, she was too stunned to speak for a while. Then she said, 'You risked your life just to see me?' She laughed, and teased, 'If only you had developed for Lord Rama even half the love that you have for my body, you would have certainly crossed the ocean of samsara and attained immortality and eternal bliss.' She chuckled and added, 'Come in now and dry yourself.'

Tulsidas refused to go in. There he stood at the entrance of the house, suddenly emptied of the passion that had driven him to her door. He turned and walked away, never to return to his wife.

It is the story of Tulsidas's awakening into the spiritual dimension retold by many biographies on him. Some, however, maintain that he remained unmarried, completely dedicated to worshipping Rama. Strangely, we never get to hear about Ratnavali again. It's as if she was given a short but powerful role to play and then taken off the stage.

The biographies on Tulsidas's life are based on five old hagiographies composed between the seventeenth and eighteenth centuries, namely, *Bhaktamal*, *Bhaktirasbodhini*, *Mula Gosain Charit*, *Gosain Charita* and *Gautam Chandrika*. In all these works, Tulsidas was looked upon as the reincarnation of Valmiki. The story goes that after Rama's passing, Hanuman retired to the Himalaya and there he scripted a play on the life of Rama called *Mahanataka* or *Hanuman Nataka*. He engraved the script on the rocks there using his nails. But when Valmiki said that Hanuman's play would eclipse his own Ramayana, Hanuman cast all the engraved rocks into the sea and instructed Valmiki to take birth as Tulsidas in the Kaliyuga and compose the Ramayana in the vernacular.

Tulsidas was a legend during his lifetime, and his fame rested on the prodigious work he produced, especially the *Ramacharitamanas* and the *Hanuman Chalisa*. There are too many differences of opinions regarding the year of his birth, but he was born sometime in the sixteenth century, in a brahmin family in Sukarkhet, a village on the banks of the Ganga in Uttar Pradesh. His parents, Hulsi and Atmaram Dubey, called him Rambola.

Strange and ironical as it may sound, legend has it that this boy, who was to become one of the greatest writers of all time, was born under a bad star and would cause the death of his father. So the parents decided to abandon him, but fortunately their maidservant Chuniya adopted the boy and took him to her village. She nurtured him for five years and then died of illness, leaving Rambola an orphan.

He was adopted yet again, by Narharidas, a follower of Ramananda's monastic order. Rambola was given a new name, Tulsidas, and initiated into the monastic order. As a matter of fact, Tulsidas himself narrates these events in his work *Ramacharitamanas*, and how he came to be exposed to the Ramayana. At the time, he says that he was too young to be able to appreciate the great epic. Years later, he went to Varanasi and over 16 years, studied Sanskrit grammar, the Vedas, astrology and the six darshanas, or philosophical schools of thought, such as Sankhya, Vaisheshika, Yoga and so on, under the guru Shesha Sanatana.

According to some sources, sometime during this period he is believed to have married Ratnavali, while according to other accounts, he remained a sadhu after his initiation into sanyasa. However, if we believe the former version and the story narrated at the beginning of this chapter, the teasing words of his wife Ratnavali seemed to have awakened him to his mission in life. He renounced samsara and went on a pilgrimage to the holy places such as Badrinath, Dwarka, Puri and Rameshwaram. After his return from the long tour, he settled down in Varanasi.

During his travels and then back at Varanasi, he produced voluminous work. Many stories of miracles are attributed to him during this time. He is believed to have brought a dead Brahmin back to life. At the time, Akbar ruled over most of northern India, and, it is said, much impressed by Tuslidas's strong personality and the miracles he performed, became his great admirer and turned into an appreciator of other faiths.

There is a story about why Tulsidas, although well versed in Sanskrit, wrote in Awadhi. One night, it goes, Lord Shiva appeared in Tulsidas's dream and instructed him to go to Ayodhya and there compose poetry in Awadhi. Awadhi is a variety of Hindi spoken in northern India, Ayodhya in particular, regarded as the homeland of Sri Rama, situated on the banks of the river Saryu in the present-day Indian state of Uttar Pradesh.

So to Ayodhya he went and, working for almost three years, Tulsidas completed the *Ramacharitamanas* in 1633. Returning to Varanasi, at the Kashi Vishwanath Temple, Tulsidas recited in Awadhi the story of Rama to Lord Vishwanath. Not all the brahmins of Varanasi liked the rendering of the Sanskrit Ramayana in Awadhi. Attempts were made to steal the manuscript of *Ramacharitamanas* from Tulsidas's house. Legend has it that Rama and Lakshman themselves stood as guards in protection of the manuscript.

Ramacharitamanas is neither a straight retelling nor an abridged version of the Sanskrit epic Ramayana by Valmiki. There are in fact interesting differences between the two Ramayanas, with two major differences mentioned here. In Valmiki's book, the story ends with the passing of Sita, Lakshmana, and ultimately, Rama, too, while in Tulsidas's rendering it ends with the happy event of the birth of Lava and Kusha. In the Yudha Kanda of Ramayana, Valmiki brings in Lord Brahma who reminds Rama of his divine nature, that he is the Lord Narayana himself, otherwise, for the most part, Rama is portrayed as a human being with excellent virtues, as maryada purushothama, ideal man. In *Ramacharitamanas*, Rama is seen more as the Supreme Being, as an incarnation of God, and his portrayal is shot through with unfaltering bhakti, devotion to Rama.

Tulsidas actually drew his inspiration from various sources, including the Puranas, Upanishads, Ramayana, *Adhyatma Ramayana*,

Prasannaraghava and *Hanuman Nataka*, though the text is only around one-third the size of Valmiki's Sanskrit Ramayana. Divided into seven kandas, books, likened to the seven steps leading into the holy waters of Lake Manasarovar, the work is structured around three conversations: between Shiva and Parvati, sages Bharadwaja and Yajnavalkya, and finally between Kakbhusundi and Garuda, the king of birds. *Ramacharitamanas* is acclaimed as the greatest book of all devotional literature.

Major Works

Dohavali, Collection of Dohas, consisting of 573 aphorisms on topics related to tact, political wisdom, righteousness and the purpose of life.

Sahitya Ratna or *Ratna Ramayan*, Collection of Kavittas, Ramayana rendered in Braja language.

Gitavali, Collection of Songs, Ramayana rendered into songs in Braja.

Krishna Gitavali, Collection of Songs to Krishna.

Vinaya Patrika, Petition of Humility, consisting of 279 hymns in Braja, in the form of a petition to Rama praying for his blessings.

Besides these, Tulsidas has written six more works in Awadhi and Braja, along with three works celebrating Lord Hanuman: *Sankatmochan Hanumanashtak*, *Hanuman Chalisa* and *Hanuman Bahuka*. Among these, *Hanuman Chalisa*, 40 hymns in Awadhi in obeisance to Hanuman, is one of the most widely read and recited short religious texts in northern India.

In bhakti, Tulsidas argued that Nirguna Brahman, formless, invisible and indescribable, becomes the visible Saguna Brahman with qualities, like formless water solidifies to become snow. Rama to him was the ultimate, greater than nirguna and saguna aspects of God, higher than even Vishnu. In short, all the aspects of God, the four states of being, the power of maya and the entire universe is the lila, play, of Rama, and all these abide in him.

Tulsidas venerated the Hindu pantheon, to him there was no incompatibility between devotion to Rama and Shiva; however, the name and sound 'Rama', conjunction of the consonants *ra* and *ma*, was to him the most magical, powerful mantra, repetition of which in pure bhakti could take one to liberation and bliss. Indeed, to many saint-poets over the centuries Ramanaam – the chanting of Ram – was the supreme mantra that could release one from bondage and suffering. To Kabir, however, Rama was not the mythological, Dasaratha Rama, but a symbol of Nirguna Brahman. More recently, for Gandhi, too, who did not believe in idol worship, Rama symbolized the ultimate truth.

Just as there is a difference of opinion among the biographers regarding the year of his birth, there is uncertainty about the exact date of Tulsidas's death. However, most agree that he died in ripe old age after a prolonged illness. Tulsidas is a legend to this day. He did not found any sect, nor are there followers of Tulsidas – like there are in the case of Ramanuja, Vallabhacharya, Kabir and many such saint-poets – but the abundant bhakti literature he produced and the philosophy he expounded have permeated all shades of Vaishnava sects in particular, and the bhakti culture in general. Ramlila, the popular dramatic folk re-enactment of the life of Rama, is based on *Ramacharitamanas*, and the *Hanuman Chalisa* is an immensely popular hymn chanted by millions of Hindus even today.

Vemana
(born 1652)

ONCE, VEMANA'S MOTHER DESIRED TO GO ON A PILGRIMAGE TO KASHI. Vemana was critical of such religious practices, it did not help people;

rather, he held, it only helped the brahmin caste to strengthen their stranglehold on religious matters. However, he did not stop his mother from going to Kashi. He hung a copper penny around her neck and said that if there was any merit in bathing in the River Ganga there, the copper would turn to gold. A week later, his mother returned, with the copper penny unchanged. 'So what's the merit you gained by going to the so-called holy city? None!' cried Vemana. Then he said that what she could not achieve by going to Kashi, he would accomplish without going there. He took the copper from her, urinated on it and turned it into gold.

Some people may feel repelled by the story but that is to be expected, is even necessary to free oneself from the futility of orthodox beliefs and practices. In one of his dohas, poems, the second century mystic and philosopher Sarahapada stated that for the one in whom the duality has ended, the sacred rivers Yamuna, Ganga, and holy places such as Banaras exist everywhere. Echoing a similar view the eleventh century saint-poet of Karnataka, Devara Dasimayya, declared that 'to the utterly at-one with Siva... his front yard is the true Banaras.' No such soft approach for Vemana, rather, he deployed shock tactics to drive home the truth that for the one pure in heart and one with God, everything is sacred and every place is holy.

Vemana's poems challenged, ridiculed and even subverted orthodox religious beliefs and practices. It is not surprising, therefore, that the priestly class and orthodox people in his native Andhra Pradesh did not take well to him at all, something that continued into the twentieth century. In 1918, when one Charles Phillip Brown, a British official and a polyglot, came to Andhra from England to conduct research on Vemana and bring out a translation of Vemana's poems, there was a palpable resistance to his work not only from the brahmin pandits but also from many scholars and professors of the universities.

They not only refused to cooperate but even created obstacles in his research activities. Charles Phillip Brown writes that a so-called learned brahmin, enlisted by Charles to translate the poems, 'attempted to expunge every rustic phrase and malignant rhyme, even striking out whole lines and substituted others of his own composing. I put a stop to his edition and dismissed him.' (Narla, 1969)

Vemana was born in 1652, in the Kapu or Reddy caste. He was the third son to Kumaragiri Vema Reddy and Mallamamba. His elder brother Komati Venkareddy was the ruler of the Reddy kingdom. Vemana was neither interested in the political affairs of the kingdom, nor in family life; he was the black sheep of sorts of the royal family. He mixed with rogues, had a relationship with a courtesan and spent most of his time and monies on her. Years later, reflecting upon his carefree days, in one of his verses he wrote:

> I joined rogues and wandered about,
> and, not acquiring wisdom for a long time,
> I lived in the company of a prostitute,
> thinking it to be Release.

(Moorty and Roberts, trans., 1995)

The turning point in his life came when he agreed to manage the goldsmith workshop run by the royal family. He was happy with the job and his workers, except for one Kondaviti Abhiramayya, who used to come late to the shop every day. One day, he confronted Abhiramayya and asked for an explanation. Abhiramayya's answer did not sound true and it seemed he was covering up something. Curious to know the truth, one early morning, Vemana hid himself near Abhiramayya's house. He saw him going out and followed him. He watched him quickly bathe in the river, then pick some flowers and enter a nearby cave. Inside the cave lived a Shiva yogi, who, after accepting the flowers, told Abhiramayya that the next day would be his last day on earth and so Abhiramayya should come without fail if he wanted to receive a secret mantra.

It seemed like a sign from the heavens and Vemana wanted to

receive the mantra himself. That evening, he made such arrangements that Abhiramayya would be held up with work at the shop. Early morning the next day, while Abhiramayya was still at the shop, Vemana went to his place, picked some flowers and went into the cave to meet the yogi. He told the yogi that Abhiramayya was entrusted with some important work by the king himself and so he had to take Abhiramayya's place.

It was the yogi's last day and he wanted to pass on the secret mantra before he left. The yogi looked at Vemana and saw the spiritual greed in his eyes, and the light that lay concealed behind it. He smiled, more at the mysterious way of life than at Vemana's longing, which seemed genuine. He called Vemana to sit by him and taught him the sacred mantra by writing the secret syllables on his tongue.

Supremely happy but with a guilty conscience, Vemana returned to the shop. He had deceived Abhiramayya and the bad karma would stick to him all his life if Abhiramayya didn't forgive him. Vemana held his feet and begged for forgiveness. 'It's because of you I was blessed by the guru,' he pleaded, 'you'll always be my first teacher.' Abhiramayya forgave him. And Vemana never forgot Abhiramayya's kindness. In one of his poems he remembered, '...the honourable guru, Abhiramayya, drew me to my teacher.' (Moorty and Roberts, trans., 1995)

It seems his initiation into the secret mantra triggered a spiritual transformation in him. It is of course true that unless one is ready for change, nothing, no mantra, no guru, can bring about any change. Vemana was ready for the change in him and he did mature into a radical sage. A knowledgeable sage, too, whose knowledge ranged from the esoteric to the commonplace, epics such as the Ramayana and the Mahabharata to yoga and tantra, Vaishnavism and Shaivism to Islam. He was well aware of the practices and occupations of the people around him and knew the machinations of the caste system. He spared none and attacked, especially, the external preoccupations of religious people with rituals, image worship and pilgrimages; condemned caste distinctions; ridiculed respectability, pretentiousness and miserliness; and questioned the worth of scriptural learning and intellectual gymnastics (Moorty and Roberts, 1995).

About 3,000 poems in Telugu language are attributed to him, though scholars think that all of them may not have been authored by him. His poems, written in simple, unpretentious language and in native idiom, may not be popular today, but the sharp and pithy lines from his poems have become colloquial phrases of the everyday Telugu language. Large collections of his poems have been translated into Kannada, Tamil, Sanskrit and English. In many old paintings and sculptures, he is depicted sitting naked with one arm placed on his right knee. It's quite possible that like the Jain Digambaras, Akka Mahadevi and Lalleshwari, he wandered naked and taught.

Vemana's death is shrouded in mystery, although there is a headstone marking his grave in Kadiri town of Anantapur district in Andhra Pradesh. There are two versions of his death; in one, the place of his burial was struck by a thunderbolt and he arose from the tomb, holding the thunderbolt in his hand. In the other, he was struck by a thunderbolt and died while working in a field. Then on the eighth day, he came alive and resumed his work. It's a terrific metaphor and it suits well the fiery sage that he was.

Unlike mystic-poets such as Sankara, Ramanuja or Basavanna, he did not found a school or establish a sect after him, nor was he a pious bhakti poet like a Tukaram or a Meera; rather, he was more akin to the likes of the nirguna bhaktas and spiritual rebels such as Allama Prabhu and Kabir. In other words, it is difficult to define his philosophy in terms of a particular school of thought. Since he rebelled against the spiritual authority of the brahmins, elaborate rituals, idol worship and the caste system, one may be tempted to fit him into one of the non-Brahmanical traditions such as Buddhism or Tantrism or Virashaivism, but we shall not do that. Let Vemana walk free and continue to teach us.

Selected Poems

O, you fools,
do not make an image
out of stone,
set it up in a dark house,
and bow to it.
Know that Brahman resides
in your hearts.

~

Spiritual debates
without Siva's grace
will not remove doubt
in seekers.
Can a lamp in a painting
dispel darkness?

~

You need a lamp
only till you find your jewels;
after you find them
what need for the lamp?
After you have become god,
what need for your body?

~

Why revile a pariah
again and again?
Aren't his flesh and blood
the same as yours?
What is the caste of Him
who moves in him?

~

What won't come
won't,
even if you wish.
What will come
will,
even if you wish not.
However much you worry,
what will happen
will not
not happen.

(Moorty and Roberts, trans., 1995)

❧❦❧

Shishunala Sharifa
(1819–89)

GOVINDA BHATTA, NOTORIOUS AS AN UNCONVENTIONAL GURU AND AN eccentric master who knew the scriptures inside out, came from a brahmin family but followed none of the traditional Brahmanical caste rules or rituals. One day, Sharifa's father, who looked upon Govinda Bhatta as a genuine guru, took his son to him. 'Master, please accept my son as your student,' said the father. Govinda Bhatta studied the boy with keen interest and asked, 'Hey, Sharifa, who is your father?' The villagers broke into laughter, for it seemed a ridiculous question to ask when the father stood right beside the son. Sharifa, however, stunned everyone with his reply, 'Sir, why do you ask such a question? You know that your father and mine are the same.'

Govinda Bhatta laughed, patted the boy on his back, then turning to the father, said, 'Imam Saheb, the land is fertile, the seed will sprout well. I'll take care of him, from today he is my son.'

The seed did sprout well and grew into a gigantic tree of great splendour. As a poet and saint, at home both with Islam and Hindu philosophy, Sharifa was a shining example of the great hermeneutical tradition of India, a tradition that transcends religious identity and dwells in the realm of mystic spirituality.

Sharifa was born on 7 March 1819 in Shishuvinahala, a village in Dharwad district of Karnataka. His parents Hazrat Saheb and Hujuma called him Mohammad Sharifa. Hazrat Saheb was an imam and a disciple of the famous saint Hajaresha Qadri. The Qadri was a devotee of Shiva, and as per the Virashaiva or Lingayat tradition, he gave 'linga deeksha', or initiation by tying a linga around the neck of his disciples. That was how Hazrat Saheb was initiated into the study of Hindu scriptures, especially the poetry and philosophy of the Shiva saranas such as Allama Prabhu and Basavanna. And it was through his father that Sharifa was exposed to Hindu philosophy at an early age.

There were no madrasas at Shishuvinahala at the time. The Lingayat gurus ran schools called 'Ayyanavara Shaale', where children were taught to read and write, and given a grounding in logic, grammar and aesthetics. The imam sent Sharifa to one such school, where he also learnt about Lingayat tradition, the Ramayana, the Mahabharata and the Puranas. Sharifa was a brilliant student, a quick mind.

It was around this time, when he was about 14 or 15 years of age, that the famous maverick guru, Govinda Bhatta, happened to visit Shishuvinahala. The orthodox brahmin community held him in contempt because he drank liquor, smoked ganja and mixed with low-caste people. They dubbed him a heretic and barred him from their community. Govinda Bhatta did not care; a true avadhuta, one who has shaken off all worldly ties, he wandered from place to place, slept in village squares or temples and broke all caste rules by mixing with and teaching the way of spirituality to those who were intent on acquiring knowledge, irrespective of caste or creed.

Imam Saheb wanted Sharifa to be taught by Govinda Bhatta. Govinda Bhatta saw that the boy was quite sharp and intelligent and ready for higher knowledge. It was a case of a student in search of the right teacher and vice versa. Sharifa took to Govinda Bhatta like duck to water. The many incidents during their time together as master and disciple read like lessons in spirituality. We narrate two of them here.

One day, the guru with his disciples went to a Mahakali temple which was situated outside the village. At one place, their path was blocked by a huge thorn bush. Govinda Bhatta stepped on the bush with his sandals and went over to the other side. The others were barefoot and there was no way they could cross over without injuring themselves badly. Govinda Bhatta removed his sandals and threw them over to the other side and said, 'Use them to cross over.' The disciples hesitated. 'Master, we are sorry we can't do that,' one of them said, 'a guru's paduka (sandals) is a sacred thing and a symbol of the guru, it must be kept on the head, not worn on the feet.' Bhatta looked at Sharifa and asked, 'What's your stand? Are you joining me or not?' Now, without hesitation, Sharifa wore the sandals and climbed over the bush. The guru and disciple then walked towards the temple. Ever ready to learn and with a mind of his own, Sharifa was the kind of disciple gurus yearned for.

Another story goes that once, Govinda Bhatta and his disciples were resting under a banyan tree at the village square. A group of brahmins, who happened to come that way, saw Govinda Bhatta sitting beside Sharifa, his arm over Sharifa's shoulder. They stopped and one of them said, 'Hey Bhatta, why are you sitting so close to that Musalman? What is he to you? Don't you have any sense of propriety?'

Govinda Bhatta laughed and said, 'What gives you the right to speak such nonsense? Just because you are a brahmin by birth doesn't make you a brahmin.'

Another man from the group gibed, 'O, to you we are not brahmins but that thuruka (Musalman) is, no? Are you also going to conduct upanayana for him?'

Govinda Bhatta took off his sacred thread and, chanting the Gayathri Mantra, put it on Sharifa and declared: 'Listen, one who is in quest of Brahman is a true brahmin, in that sense, Sharifa is a true brahmin and he is a greater brahmin than all those who are brahmins merely by birth.' Sharifa, overwhelmed with gratitude and reverence, prostrated at the master's feet. The master lifted him up and hugged him with affection (Bhatt, 2011).

We do not know for how many years Sharifa trained under Govinda Bhatta; however, it was while living and travelling with the guru that he matured into a poet, studied Shaiva philosophy in depth and took a great liking to Allama Prabhu. His veneration of Allama was such that, wherever he went, he carried a copy of *Prabhulingalile*, a text on the life and times of Allama Prabhu.

After he left Govinda Bhatta, Sharifa worked as a teacher in several schools in and around Shishuvinahala. It seems he had a passion for educating children. He started a number of schools in surrounding villages and came to be recognized as an excellent teacher. He was in his twenties then, and the parents thought it was high time he got married. Sharifa resisted the proposal, for he believed marriage could disrupt his spiritual quest. When his parents persisted, he went to Govinda Bhatta for advice. The guru laughed and said, 'Sharifa, why do you have such apprehensions? However much it rains, would wind become wet, or light become soaked? Stop worrying and go and get married.'

Thus, Sharifa married Fatima. In course of time a daughter was born to them, but his happy family life was cut short when cholera swept through the village and took the life of both, the child and mother. Sharifa was devastated, but he had to accept the tragic inevitable and move on with his life. Alone now, he began to travel and meet with spiritual masters and hold discussions with them on various philosophical concepts he needed to explore and understand. Then he went and spent many days with Govinda Bhatta. He composed some of the finest poems during this period, many of which were on Advaita philosophy.

Sharifa came to be known as Shivayogi Sharifa. Around 300 poems, generally referred to as tattvapadas, philosophical utterances, are attributed to him. The subjects ranged from the notions of atman,

Brahman, guru and renunciation to sex, anger, pride, perils of wealth, spiritual vision of life and so on. His padas are peppered with everyday, common experiences in native idioms, but they are very different from the dohas, vachanas and padas of other saint-poets in their rhythm and sweep; and, notably, almost all of his padas are richly metaphorical. Monkey, pests, garments, mad dog, snake, scorpion, horse and leaking roof are some of the powerful metaphors he deploys to speak about the nature of the mind, sexual desire, suffering, ignorance, awakening from ignorance and so on.

On completion of his sixtieth year, Sharifa sang, 'I'll leave this body, leave this body and give it back to earth...' and decided to end his mortal existence as per the sarana tradition. The ritual involved worshipping the feet of a Jangama, a wandering Shiva sarana, and then the Jangama was supposed to place his foot on his head as a sign of approval and blessing before he breathed his last to the chanting of Shiva mantra. No Jangama was prepared to go through such a ritual and place his foot on a Shivayogi of the stature of Sharifa. Finally, Karibassayya of Hiremutt, a well-known monastery, moved by Sharifa's request, agreed to perform the ritual. On 3 July 1889, to the chanting of Shiva mantras, Shishunala Shivayogi Sharifa offered his body to the earth and turned empty.

The last rites that followed his passing were something unique in the history of our spiritual narratives. After much debate and discussion between the Hindus and Muslims, it was decided the body would be buried according to the rites of both religions. The crowd sang, 'Iva nammava'– he is ours, he is ours – while on one side of the tomb Muslims recited lines from the Quran and on the other side the Hindus chanted verses from the Vedas.

Sharifa's gaddige, tomb, at Shishuvinahala is a pilgrim centre today, visited by both Hindus and Muslims. And at the heart of Shishuvinahala, under a huge peepul tree, there is a concrete square on which sit the stone figures of the guru and his disciple, Govinda Bhatta and Sharifa, their hands raised in abhaya mudra, the gesture of fearlessness, protection, friendship and peace. During annual fairs, people gather at the tomb and the square in hundreds and spend the whole night singing Sharifa's tattvapadas. His tattvapadas are very popular across the state of Karnataka, a considerable number of which have been rendered into songs by some of the major singers of the state.

A Selection of Sharifa's Padas

The Temple of the Body

Look at the temple, brother,
look at temple of the body
look at the body where
the lord of the earth
sits hiding in great light.
Look at the temple, brothers,
look at the temple of the body.

He alone is solid who rises
reining in sixes and threes
in the primal rhythm of trumpets,
bugles and conches, he shines,
the bliss of the beyond.
Look at the temple, brothers,
look at the temple of the body.

The days are passing. Hurry up
and live where king of yogis
the lord of Shishunala lives
in the form of Brahma
the supreme beyond.
Look at the temple, brothers,
look at the temple of the body.

On The Field

How they trouble me,
these kabbakki birds!
I am all alone
on the field.
Three birds from this side
six from the other side
they lie in wait and ambush me again
till I get exhausted.
The birds that come are all rogues
they come in gangs
of three, six and nine
always to muddle up the mind,
the most roguish is the one there
I am tired of shooting stones
from the sling.
Lord Shishunala's old bird is snoring
after eating up all the grains
they come and beg
Guru Govinda for salvation.

Bamboo

I am bamboo, I am bamboo
is there anyone I am not for?
I was born as grass
and grew up into a tree
I became a cradle for beautiful mothers,
a winnowing board in the hands of girls,
a support for the canopy,
a basinga for the bridegroom,
a walking stick to help the old,
a mace for the young
while hunting.

I became a beam for the palanquin,
a basket for flowers
and for sweets in huge monasteries,
I became a flute in Krishna's hands
a stick for boys to play with,
I became a staff in the hands of monks.
Born in the dung heap I grew big
and turned, in the hands of saints
in Lord Shishunala's sacred shrine,
a lute with a single string

Pot

What kind of pot is this?
What a lovely pot!
The pot that went past
three sisters
the pot with which sported
six sisters
the pot that went to the mela
on Shiva's night
and had the vision of Siddharama!
Alas! It disappeared
in the bazaar on the way back
when six sisters went together
to draw water from the well.
Alas! It slipped out of their hands
and was blown to bits
the pot that Lord of Shishunala
moulded with care.
What is it? Find out,
You wise people.

(Shivaprakash, trans., 2019)

Sri Ramakrishna
(1836–86)

SOMETIME AROUND HIS THIRTIETH YEAR, RAMAKRISHNA WAS INITIATED into Advaita Vedanta by Totapuri, an itinerant monk and Naga sanyasi well-versed in non-dual philosophy. Totapuri did not approve of Ramakrishna worshipping the idol of Kali, the Divine Mother. Brahman is formless, he insisted, and bhakti bhava, emotion, was an aspect of maya, illusion, and Ramakrishna should free himself of it if he wishes to enter the non-dual state.

And he instructed Ramakrishna to chant and meditate as per the mahavakyas, great utterances, that is: *Brahman alone is real, and the world is illusory. I have no separate existence, I am that Brahman alone.* Nirvikalpa samadhi is considered to be the highest state of spiritual realization, where the whole gamut of thought-feeling, which constitute a living being and the world, are dissolved, where even awareness is absent.

Ramakrishna did as instructed, but, when he was on the threshold of nirvikalpa samadhi, there was a break because, as Ramakrishna reported later: '...the Mother's form stood in my way... Then, with a stern determination I used my discrimination as a sword and with it severed it in two. There remained no more obstruction to my mind, which at once soared beyond the relative plane, and I lost myself in samadhi.' Ramakrishna remained on and off in the state of nirvikalpa samadhi for six months, and then as his fate would have it, the Divine Mother appeared and commanded him to 'remain on the threshold of relative consciousness for the sake of humanity'. (Nikhilananda, trans., 2002)

Ramakrishna was one of the most remarkable and lively sages of modern times. When Ramakrishna said that all spiritual paths ultimately lead to the same goal, namely, the experience of Godhood, he was speaking from his experience and not merely espousing a philosophy, since he himself had gone through all the different varieties of religious practices and experiences. In him, the great debates among the different religions and sects were ingeniously reconciled and united. And, paradoxical as it may sound, the teachings of Advaita, Dvaita, Vishishtadvaita and Dvaitadvaita permeated and found vibrant expression in the unrelenting play of his 50 years of existence in Kolkata.

Ramakrishna – named Gadadhar after Lord Vishnu – was born on 18 February 1836, in the village of Kamarpukur, in the Hooghly district of West Bengal, into a poor and pious brahmin family. His parents were Kshudiram Chattopadhyay and Chandramani Devi. His father died when Ramakrishna was hardly seven years old and he was brought up by his mother and eldest brother, Ramkumar. It is said that as a boy he was given to spells of spiritual trance. After about 12 years of schooling, he dropped out and went to Kolkata to assist his brother, who worked as the head priest of Dakshineswar Kali Temple. A year later, Ramkumar died, and Ramakrishna was asked to be the priest of the temple. At first, Ramakrishna did not agree, for he thought the heavy responsibility of the temple as a priest would come in the way of his sadhana, but when Hriday, his nephew, agreed to assist him in the work, he accepted the job.

Once he assumed the duties of the temple priest, his life changed forever. Goddess Kali was no more just a figure in stone but his virtual mother, and day and night he began to yearn for Her darshan. He was so consumed by his desire to *see* the Divine Mother that one day, unable to bear the agony of separation from the goddess, he decided to kill himself with the sword that was kept in the temple. He jumped up like a madman and seized it, when suddenly the blessed Mother revealed Herself to him. He fell unconscious on the floor. It was the beginning of a series of such experiences he would undergo over the next few years.

Prior to going into the state of nirvikalpa samadhi, Ramakrishna had moved through different forms of bhakti, such as shanta (serenity, calm), sakhya (friendship), dasya (the relation of servant to master) and vatsalya (fondness, affection or the love a mother feels for a child).

One time, behaving like the monkey god, Hanuman, he lived on fruits and passed most of his time sitting naked on trees, calling out for Lord Rama. And he did have a vision of Lord Rama. The temple authorities thought he was going mad because of his spiritual practises and arranged for his treatment by an expert physician. But it did not help.

Back home, his mother and his elder brother, Rameshwar, were worried and decided to get Ramakrishna married. They believed that marriage would be a good steadying influence upon him. Ramakrishna, now 23 years old, was married to a five-year-old bride, Saradamani, later to be known as Sarada Devi, the Holy Mother. After the marriage, for 13 years or so, Saradamani stayed at her parent's place and then joined Ramakrishna in Dakshineswar, at the age of 18. The marriage was never consummated because Ramakrishna, who was in his mid-thirties at the time, had embraced the monastic life of a sanyasi. Saradamani became Ramakrishna's devoted follower and his first disciple, and he in turn regarded Saradamani as the Divine Mother in person, addressing her as Sree Maa, Holy Mother.

There were other experiences Ramakrishna had. On one occasion, dressed like an Arab, he lived like a Muslim devotee outside the temple complex, chanting the name of Allah, reciting the namaz five times daily. Thus immersed in Islamic practices, he had a vision of the Prophet merging with his body. After this experience, he took to Christianity like a zealous follower. And he is believed to have had a vision of the Madonna and Child, and then of Jesus Christ, who, too, is supposed to have merged with his body.

It is important to reiterate here that during this period he explored all the well-known modes of spiritual practices and sought to experience the Divinity in all its forms and manifestations. If, on the one hand, his experiments with different forms of bhakti, and his visions of Rama, Jesus Christ and Prophet Mohammad bear testimony to his catholicity, on the other, he became an embodiment of the truth that all spiritual paths ultimately lead to the same goal, namely, the experience of Godhood.

As news of his mystical experiences spread, people, cutting across class and caste, even prominent cultural leaders and scholars, intellectuals and writers, visited the garden house of Kali Temple in Dakshineswar to see and meet with Ramakrishna. And with them came spiritual seekers and sceptics, among them Narendra (who became Swami Vivekananda), Rakhal, Yogin, Tarak and Kali, to name a few, who were to be transformed by the magical touch of Ramakrishna and then go on to become torchbearers of Ramakrishna Mission, which was set up in 1897 by them with Vivekananda in the lead.

Ramakrishna lived an open life and taught whoever cared to listen to him. His method of teaching was simple, straightforward, and informal. He used rustic Bengali, reminisced about his spiritual journey and experiences, narrated tales, cracked jokes, broke into songs and even used 'abusive' words to drive home a point. He explained what are considered tough Vedantic concepts in simple, lucid terms and by drawing examples from everyday life. And he never failed to point out that the different paths to God-realization need not have to be contradictory, rather they are only complementary, being suited to people with different outlooks and mental dispositions.

Perhaps Ramakrishna knew he would not live for long. Two days before his death, he is believed to have passed on his spiritual energy and knowledge to Vivekananda, who would fulfil his unfinished mission of spreading the Vedantic truth of the oneness of life in the world. Weeks before that happened, when Ramakrishna fell seriously ill, at first it seemed a recurrence of sore throat he had suffered in the past, but on clinical examination it was found to be throat cancer. All sorts of medications, including Ayurveda and homoeopathy, were tried but with no success. It seemed the recurrences of his samadhi aggravated the disease.

In the early hours of Monday, 16 August 1886, Ramakrishna fell unconscious and his body turned stiff. The stiffness was something unusual but some of the disciples thought that the master had merely entered into a state of deep samadhi. It was not to be, and hours later, the doctor declared him dead. He was 49 years old.

Ramakrishna remains one of the most powerful influences in the spiritual world today. He belonged to the tradition of the great rishis with a fine blend of the brilliant intellect of a Shankara and the wonderfully expansive heart of a Krishna Chaitanya. 'The story of Ramakrishna Paramahamsa's life,' as Gandhi put it succinctly, 'is [truly] a story of religion in practice.' (Nikhilananda, 2008). And, expanding on Gandhi's remark, as it were, Arnold Joseph Toynbee (1889-1975), English historian and philosopher of history, says, 'Sri Ramakrishna's message was unique in being expressed in action. Religion is not just a matter for study, it is something that has to be experienced and to be lived, and this is the field in which Sri Ramakrishna manifested his uniqueness. His religious activity and experience were, in fact, comprehensive to a degree that had perhaps never before been attained by any other religious genius, in India or elsewhere.' (Ghanananda, 1970)

A Selection from his Teachings

I have practised all religions—Hinduism, Islam, Christianity—and I have also followed the paths of the different Hindu sects. I have found that it is the same God toward whom all are directing their steps, though along different paths. You must try all beliefs and traverse all the different ways once. Wherever I look, I see men quarrelling in the name of religion—Hindus, Mohammedans, Brahmos, Vaishnavas, and the rest. But they never reflect that He who is called Krishna is also called Siva, and bears the name of the Primal Energy, Jesus, and Allah as well—the same Rama with a thousand names.

~

Truth is one; only It is called by different names. All people are seeking the same Truth; the variance is due to climate, temperament, and name. A lake has many ghats. From one ghat the Hindus take water in jars and call it "jal". From another ghat the Mussalmā·ns take water in leather bags and call it "pani". From a third the Christians take the same thing and call it "water". Suppose someone says that the thing is not "jal" but "pani", or that it is not "pani" but "water", or that it is not "water" but "jal", it would indeed be ridiculous. But this very thing is at the root of the friction among sects, their misunderstandings and quarrels. This is why people injure and kill one another, and shed blood, in the name of religion. But this is not good. Everyone is going toward God. They will all realise Him if they have sincerity and longing of heart.

～

It's enough to have faith in one aspect of God. You have faith in God without form. That is very good. But never get into your head that your faith alone is true and every other is false. Know for certain that God without form is real and that God with form is also real. Then hold fast to whichever faith appeals to you.

Aphorisms

Great men have the nature of a child. They are always a child before Him; so they are free from pride. All their strength is of God and not their own. It belongs to Him and comes from Him.

～

I am everybody's disciple. All are the children of God. All are His servants.

～

You must regard other views as so many paths leading to God. You should not feel that your path is the only right path and that other paths are wrong. You mustn't bear malice toward others.

～

One cannot think of the Absolute without the Relative, or of the Relative without the Absolute.

~

Brahman and Sakti are identical. If you accept the one, you must accept the other.

~

The vain man of intellect busies himself with finding out the "why" and "wherefore" of creation, while the humble man of wisdom makes friends with the Creator and enjoys His gift of supreme bliss.

~

As a piece of rope, when burnt, retains its form, but cannot serve to bind, so is the ego which is burnt by the fire of supreme Knowledge.

~

As a boy holding to a post or a pillar whirls about it with headlong speed without any fear or falling, so perform your worldly duties, fixing your hold firmly upon God, and you will be free from danger.

~

The more you dwell on worldly things, the greater will be your attachment. Smear your finger with oil if you want to open the jackfruit, or the milky exudation will stick to them. Devotion to God is like this oil.

~

So long as the bee does not sit on the flower, it buzzes. When it has begun to sip the honey, it is quiet. Sometimes, however, after drinking its fill, it hums out of sheer joy.

(Collated from Gupta, 2002 and Nikhilananda, 2008.)

Vivekananda
(1863–1902)

SOMETIME IN 1881, VIVEKANANDA, THEN CALLED NARENDRA OR NAREN, met Ramakrishna for the first time and was not particularly impressed. He was still a student at a college then and, influenced by Western philosophy and the Brahmo Samaj, he saw himself as a rationalist with a scientific bent of mind.

The day he met Ramakrishna for the first time, Ramakrishna caught hold of his hand as soon as Vivekananda entered his room, and began to shed tears of joy. And he cried out, 'Ah, you came so late! How could you be so unkind as to keep me waiting for so long? Oh, I am panting to unburden my mind to one who can appreciate my innermost experiences.' Narendra was taken aback. What kind of a man is this? He must be raving mad, he thought.

Later, he keenly watched Ramakrishna and heard his words carefully. There seemed nothing wrong in his words. Could this man be a great teacher? Vivekananda thought he was a 'monomaniac' and took leave of him and returned home. But he couldn't help meeting him again, and when he did, it changed his life completely. The sceptic turned into a believer. In his words, '…slowly he drew near me and in the twinkling of an eye he placed his right foot on my body. The touch at once gave rise to a novel experience within me. With my eyes open I saw that the walls, and everything in the room, whirled rapidly and vanished into nought, and the whole universe together with my individuality was about to merge in an all-encompassing mysterious void! I was terribly frightened and thought that I was facing death.' Yet again, in the third meeting, the touch of the master transported him into a realm he had no clue about, his mind underwent a 'complete revolution', he felt 'there really was nothing whatever in the universe but God' (Chetanananda, 1999).

It was not the words of the master, but his magical touch, the blast of energy from him, that transformed Narendra. Transformed into what? What did he become? It is difficult to describe or explain. For he was not a regular saint or mystic, though he was always referred to as Swami Vivekananda. He was an orator, writer, musician, mystic – all rolled into one. He was a phenomenon, who lived for less than 40 years, but what he accomplished and the legacy he left behind in that short span reads like a fairy tale.

Once, after his talk on Yoga, which was deeply philosophical without any reference to pranayama and dietary restrictions, a lady asked Vivekananda, 'Swamiji, what do you think of breathing and eating?' He answered, 'I assure you madam, I am in favour of both.' (Chetanananda, 2018). Indeed, he was fond of spicy dishes and meat and ate heavily, smoked, or went without these for several months. Though deeply spiritual, he was against blind faith, religious taboos and social restrictions. He was an intellectual giant, yet one with a melting heart. A renunciant who wept like a child at the sight of poverty and suffering, and loved his mother dearly.

Endowed with phenomenal memory, he could quote verbatim chapters and verses from books he would have finished reading at an incredible speed. Whatever he did, he did it with great intensity and honesty and without fear or reservation. He was a live wire whose words electrified and transformed people. There is no doubt he was a major force in the revival of Hinduism, and there was not a single freedom fighter who was not inspired by the life and teachings of Vivekananda.

Vivekananda was born Narendranath Datta on 12 January 1863, in a Bengali Kayastha family. He was one of eight children to Vishwanath Dutta and Bhubaneswari. His father was a successful attorney at the Calcutta High Court and the family lived in comfort. As a child he was so naughty and energetic that his mother is believed to have once quipped, 'I prayed to Shiva for a son and he sent me one of his ghouls.' (Nikhilananda, 1953)

As a young man, Narendra was an all-rounder of sorts, with a strong spiritual streak in him. He was fond of music and loved to sing. He excelled in his studies and actively participated in sports and tried his hand in gymnastics, wrestling and body building. By the time he graduated from the Presidency College in Calcutta, he had acquired a vast knowledge of both Western and Indian philosophy and was known for his sharp intellect. In Western philosophy he was particularly attracted to the English philosopher and historian David Hume (1711-1776), the German philosophers Immanuel Kant (1724-1804), Friedrich Hegel (1770-1831) and Schopenhauer (1788-1860), and French philosopher Auguste Comte (1798-1857), and was so fascinated by the famous biologist and sociologist Herbert Spencer's (1820-1903) theory of evolution that he even corresponded with him. In Indian philosophy, he was drawn to the Vedas, the Upanishads, the Bhagavad Gita and was well acquainted with the Puranas and the epics, namely, the Ramayana and the Mahabharata. And he was not yet 20!

In his twenties, he joined the Sadharan Brahmo Samaj, a breakaway faction of Rammohan Roy's Brahmo Samaj, started by Keshab Chandra Sen and Debendranath Tagore. Inspired by Western notions of universalism and Unitarianism that stressed individual freedom of belief and emphasized personal spiritual experience over theology, and as a member of the Sadharan Brahmo Samaj, he came to believe in a monotheistic, formless God, and was against polytheism, idol worship, ideas of reincarnation, karma and so on. He was a modern young Indian in search of a rational, intelligible view of human existence and a radically new vision of society based on a fine combination of Western ideas and Indian thought.

It was in such a frame of mind in 1881 that he met Ramakrishna in his room at the temple garden at Dakshineswar. He had heard people praise Ramakrishna highly but on meeting him in person, he was not impressed. Nevertheless, he asked him, 'Sir, have you seen God?' Lately he had posed the same question to quite a few religious people, including Debendranath Tagore. He was very earnest to know if there was anyone who had really come face to face with God. None of the answers he had received so far had satisfied him. In fact, many had skirted the question instead of giving him a direct answer. Ramakrishna answered directly, 'Yes, I see him just as I see you here, only in a much more intense sense.' (Chetanananda, 1999). Narendra was stunned, for the first time he found somebody who dared to say that he had seen God. But somehow, he could not reconcile Ramakrishna's words with his strange behaviour.

However, on his second visit, the magical touch of the master dissolved all his doubts and he experienced the presence of God. It changed the course of his life. Wherever he went and whatever he did seemed suffused with God. Everything was God, nothing else but God. He lost the sense of division. The food he ate, the streets he crossed, even the carriage rushing towards him, was himself. There was no separation. Thus began Narendra's spiritual life. In his words, 'It is impossible to give others any idea of the ineffable joy we derived from the presence of the master. It is really beyond our understanding how he could train us, without our knowing it, through fun and play.' (Chetanananda, 1999)

From that point onwards, Narendra immersed himself in Ramakrishna's always enlightening chats, sometimes by asking questions, narrating stories from his side, even singing songs at the bidding of the master.

Early in 1884 Narendra's father died of a heart attack, leaving behind heavy debts. Overnight, the family was plunged into penury. Narendra was the eldest son and the responsibility of the family naturally fell on him. Creditors knocked on the door, demanding repayment of loans. Some relatives tried to usurp their ancestral home. Narendra was in desperate need of a job to support the family, but, in spite of being a qualified graduate, he was unsuccessful in finding a job.

This was the most painful phase in his life, constantly torn between his spiritual calling and the responsibility of supporting his mother and younger siblings. There were days when he went without food, wandering about town, looking for a job. All that he could find were temporary jobs. For some days he worked in an attorney's office as a clerk, translated books, even sang in parties and earned a little money to tide over the dire situation at home. He started to lose faith in God. 'Does God actually exist?' he asked himself, 'If so, does he hear the plaintive prayer of man?' (Chetanananda, 1999).

One day he ran to Dakshineswar, hoping the master would surely help him. He explained his dismal situation and requested Ramakrishna to pray on his behalf to Goddess Mother Kali to alleviate the family's suffering. He was sure the Goddess would grant the master's prayers. Ramakrishna said, 'My child, I cannot say such words, you know. Why don't you yourself pray?' So Narendra himself went to the temple to pray. Suddenly a firm conviction gripped him that he would see the Mother and he was beside himself with joy. He went in, made salutations and prayed, 'Mother, grant me discrimination, grant me detachment, divine knowledge and devotion.' And he felt flooded with peace (Chetanananda, 1999).

On his return to the room, Ramakrishna asked, 'Did you pray to Mother for the removal of your problems?' Only now he remembered he had made no such request. 'Go quickly again and make that request,' said Ramakrishna. Narendra went back and once again prayed for divine knowledge and returned. Ramakrishna drove him back again. Yet again, Narendra couldn't bring himself to pray for the removal of his financial problems. Ramakrishna smiled and said, 'You are not meant for worldly happiness. What can I do?' A still worried Narendra begged, 'You must utter the prayer for my sake.' At last, Ramakrishna gave in with a smile and said, 'All right, they will never lack plain food and clothing.' (Nikhilananda, 1953)

Thereafter, Vivekananda's family never lacked food and clothing, the basic necessities of life, but never attained economic stability and security either. After he left home to become a sanyasi, he could not be of any help to his family at all. The thought that he did not do enough for his family, that he did not live up to the expectation of his mother and keep her happy, troubled him till his last days.

In 1884, Ramakrishna fell seriously ill and was diagnosed with throat cancer. There were now a large number of disciples, including Narendra, around him. Ramakrishna was not a rich man's guru and he got a paltry pension as a 'retired' priest of the Dakshineswar Temple. He had to be moved to a new place on health grounds and the disciples had to raise funds, sometimes even pledge their belongings, to pay the rent and meet household expenses. Ramakrishna knew his days were numbered and he had a couple of tasks to be completed.

One day, he presented saffron robes to the inner circle of his disciples and initiated them into sanyasa with mantra diksha (bestowing them a sacred mantra each). Thus Narendra became Vivekananda. Two days before his passing, Ramakrishna made Narendra sit in front of him, and gazing at him, fell into samadhi. Vivekananda felt a force like an electric current penetrate his body and lost consciousness. In his words, 'When consciousness returned I found Sri Ramakrishna in tears. On questioning him, he said, "Today, giving you my all, I have become a beggar. With this power you are to do much work for the good of the world before you return."' (Nikhilananda, 2008)

After Ramakrishna's passing, the disciples lived together in a building at Baranagar in North Calcutta, which later became Ramakrishna Math. In 1888, Vivekananda left Calcutta on a long tour across the country in order to meet with people and study the Indian social and economic condition, similar to what Gandhiji would do in 1916. It was a learning experience to meet with people from different strata of society. Vivekananda was deeply moved by the problems faced by the poor people and vowed to dedicate his life for the alleviation of their suffering and build the country with ennobling spirituality.

In 1893, with the support of his admirers and Ajit Singh Raja, king of Khetri in Rajasthan, he attended the World Parliament of Religions in Chicago, America. His eloquent speech, starting with the famous opening line, 'Sisters and brothers of America', and his elucidation of the principles of Vedanta and the profound catholicity of Hinduism marked the beginning of the spread of Hindu thought, especially

Vedanta, in the West. In fact, Vivekananda founded the Vedantic Society of New York in 1894, which introduced Hindu philosophy in general, and Ramakrishna's teachings in particular, to Americans. And it was only a beginning of a series of such centres that were to open in different parts of America and other European countries in the next few years.

Back in India, he founded Ramakrishna Mission at Belur Math, Calcutta, in 1897. And yet again he travelled across India, giving a series of lectures on Vedanta. If in the West he spoke eloquently about India's great spiritual heritage, in India he repeatedly addressed the issues of widespread poverty, the curse of the caste system, the need for promoting education among the masses, science and industrialization, and ending colonial rule. Many branches of Ramakrishna Mission sprang up in different parts of India, headed by monks from Belur Math. The mission was dedicated to various forms of social service which was the need of the hour, and in propagation of practical tenets of Vedanta.

In 1899, for over four years he toured Western countries again, meeting with prominent people, and giving lectures at Paris, Vienna, Istanbul and Egypt. Returning to India, with declining health, he settled down in the monastery at Belur Math. It wouldn't be an exaggeration to say that there was hardly an ailment he did not suffer from, including migraines, asthma, insomnia, diabetes and heart problems, and yet, with steely resolve, he travelled everywhere with the message of love and freedom. He was a great presence wherever he went and his words, profound and insightful and urgent, had a tremendous impact on people who were fortunate enough to be in his presence: 'Each soul is potentially divine. The goal is to manifest this Divinity within. Do this either by work, or worship, or mental discipline, or philosophy—by one, or more, or all of these—and be free. This is the whole of religion. Doctrines, or dogmas, or rituals, or books, or temples, or forms, are but secondary details... Arise, awake and stop not till the goal is reached.' (Dhar, 1975)

The rich tribute paid by the French dramatist and historian Romain Rolland (1866-1944) must succinctly describe the electrifying personality that Vivekananda was: 'If you want to know India, study Vivekananda. In him everything is positive and nothing negative. His words are great music... I cannot touch these sayings of his, scattered as they are through the pages of books, at thirty years' distance, without receiving a thrill through my body like an electric shock. And what shocks, what transports, must have been produced when in burning words they issued from the lips of the hero!' (Rolland, 1931)

On 4 July 1902, Vivekananda awoke early, lectured to his pupils about Yoga, and later, discussed with his colleagues the plans of starting a Vedic college in the math. In the evening, at about 7 p.m., he went into his room and never came out. Sometime during the night, either his heart stopped beating, or he slipped into mahasamadhi. He was 39 years old.

Swami Vivekananda was undoubtedly one of the most influential spiritual teachers of modern India and his great legacy is the stuff of a thousand stories, both in India and abroad. Almost the whole generation of social reformers, political and spiritual leaders and activists who fought against the British Raj, and worked for social reforms and spiritual transformation, including Gandhi, Subhas Chandra Bose, Rabindranath Tagore, Bal Gangadhar Tilak and Aurobindo, drew inspiration from his teaching. After India's freedom from colonial rule, innumerable writers, poets, artists, intellectuals and thinkers, who all envisioned, wrote and worked towards developing a new society founded on spiritual and egalitarian values, took their ideas and drew stimulus from Vivekananda. Today, however, his legacy is a subject of hot debate between the Hindu nationalists and the votaries of a plural, inclusive society based on democratic values and practices. While the right-wing ideologists lay claim to Vivekananda and project him as the pioneer saint of Hindu supremacy, social and political activists, artists and intellectuals, continue to contest this appropriation of Vivekananda by highlighting his criticism of religious superstitions and restrictions, economic poverty and caste division, his condemnation of all forms of narrowness, fanaticism and bigotry inherent in Orthodox Hinduism, and by showing him as the champion of religious equality, social inclusion and service to the needy.

Aphorisms

The greatest error is to call a man a weak and miserable sinner. Every time a person thinks in this mistaken manner, he rivets one more link in the chain of avidya that binds him, adds one more layer to the 'self-hypnotism' that lies heavy over his mind.

~

This is the gist of all worship: to be pure and to do good to others. He who sees Shiva in the poor, in the weak, and in the diseased, really worships Shiva; and if he sees Shiva only in the image, his worship is but preliminary. He who has served and helped one poor man seeing Shiva in him, without thinking of his caste, or creed, or race, or anything, with him Shiva is more pleased than with the man who sees Him only in temples.

~

This I have seen in life—those who are overcautious about themselves fall into dangers at every step; those who are afraid of losing honour and respect, get only disgrace; and those who are always afraid of loss, always lose.

~

Why are people so afraid? The answer is that they have made themselves helpless and dependent on others. We are so lazy, we do not want to do anything ourselves. We want a Personal God, a Saviour or a Prophet to do everything for us.

~

Take up an idea, devote yourself to it, struggle on in patience, and the sun will rise for you.

~

Education is the manifestation of perfection present already in man. Religion is the manifestation of the divinity already in man.

~

We must approach religion with reverence and with love, and our heart will stand up and say, this is truth, and this is untruth.

~

Give me few men and women who are pure and selfless and I shall shake the world.

~

Condemn none: if you can stretch out a helping hand, do so. If you cannot, fold your hands, bless your brothers, and let them go their own way.

~

This life is short, the vanities of the world are transient, but they alone live who live for others, the rest are more dead than alive.

~

You cannot believe in God until you believe in yourself.

~

When we really begin to live in the world, then we understand what is meant by brotherhood or mankind, and not before.

~

Feel like Christ and you will be a Christ; feel like Buddha and you will be a Buddha. It is feeling that is the life, the strength, the vitality, without which no amount of intellectual activity can reach God.

~

The moment I have realized God sitting in the temple of every human body, the moment I stand in reverence before every human being and see God in him — that moment I am free from bondage, everything that binds vanishes, and I am free.

~

The Vedanta recognizes no sin, it only recognizes error. And the greatest error, says the Vedanta, is to say that you are weak, that you are a sinner, a miserable creature, and that you have no power and you cannot do this and that.

~

All is the Self or Brahman. The saint, the sinner, the lamb, the tiger, even the murderer, as far as they have any reality, can be nothing else, because there is nothing else.

(Collated *Complete Works of Swami Vivekananda*, 1907, 2001)

~

Narayana Guru
(1856–1928)

ONE EVENING, WHEN IT GOT TOO LATE TO GET BACK TO THE ASHRAM before nightfall, Narayana Guru and his close disciple Nani Asan decided to spend the night in the forest. The night was cold and they started a small fire to keep themselves warm. Except for the wind among the trees and the continuous chirping of the cricket, the forest lay immersed in silence. His legs crossed, Narayana Guru sat in stillness by the fire, while Nani Asan curled up in a blanket and went to sleep. After some time, Narayana Guru gently prodded Asan with a stick and asked him to get up. Asan woke up after a few more jabs from the guru.

Up he sat and was struck with terror when he saw a tiger and a cub on the other side of the fire, watching them with unblinking eyes. Narayana Guru said, 'Don't panic, they wouldn't harm us. If you feel no fear or animosity against anyone or anything, you can calm down all animosity to you from any quarter.' (Kunhappa, 1982). It was not possible for Asan to control his fear; he curled back on the ground and pulled the blanket over his head. After a while, his fear gave way to curiosity, and he put his head out only to see that the tiger and the cub had disappeared.

Later, Asan reported this story to his fellow disciples. There are many such fascinating stories about Narayana Guru, but this one effectively reveals his way. This incident stands out as a powerful metaphor to bring home the message that not through anger and hatred but through love and non-violent means it is possible to transform people and society. His two great contemporaries, Gandhiji, the apostle of non-violence, and Tagore, the visionary poet, thought of him as a revolutionary sage and held him in high esteem.

Narayana Guru was born around 20 August 1856, in the village of Chembazanthi near Thiruvananthapuram, the capital of the then State of Travancore. His mother was Kuttiyamma, and father, Madan Asan, was a teacher and physician. They belonged to the Ezhava caste. Numerically, Nairs and Ezhavas formed the largest castes in Kerala; while Nairs were shudras within the caste hierarchy, Ezhavas were considered ati-shudras, beyond the pale of the caste system. They were traditionally toddy tappers and agriculturalists and were considered 'unapproachable'; nevertheless, they were quite distinct from the 'untouchable' castes elsewhere.

Though generally Ezhavas were the downtrodden and economically backward caste, there were quite a significant number of Ezhava vaidyas, physicians and Sanskrit scholars. They practised Ayurveda and all their medical texts were in Sanskrit, and so were naturally well versed in Sanskrit language. The brahmins claimed themselves to be the repositories of the Shastras, including Ayurveda, but they were inaccessible to the common people.

As a boy Narayana Guru was affectionately called 'Nanu'. Nanu, it is said, was quite mischievous and loved playing pranks on elders. He was also quite intelligent, with a philosophical bent of mind. There were no schools nearby and so he was sent to Chembazanthi Mootha Pillai, famous astrologer and educationist, for learning Sanskrit. Pillai found him to be a fast learner and enjoyed teaching him.

In the evenings, Nanu continued his studies under his uncle Krishnan Vaidiar, a noted poet in Malayalam, who was equally impressed by his grasp of things. Occasionally, he took the cows out for grazing and also worked as a help on their agricultural land. As the years rolled by, he turned more and more inwards and became a wanderer of sorts. He would disappear from home for several days and go visit houses of relatives and friends. But he would stay in their houses only briefly and then move on. He was growing; his inner state was undergoing change, turning him into a serious seeker of truth.

One time when he went away for many days, his parents assumed that he was off on one of his usual mysterious wanderings. He returned after 18 days, looking emaciated and a much-changed man. He had not gone far; more exactly, he had spent all 18 days in an old temple of the Goddess situated inside the forest. On returning home from his previous wanderings, he had realized he had contracted smallpox. He knew it was an infectious disease, so informing none at home, he went into the forest and decided the old temple would be the right place to rest and recover from the disease.

Pujas were offered to the goddess only once a year during the festival and so no one noticed his presence. He suffered through day and night the rise in body temperature and the terrible discomfort. In the dark of the night and throwing a cloth over his head, he sometimes went to nearby houses to get alms. Thus, he survived the disease and returned home. It appears that these 18 days of suffering, and being alone in deep contemplation, brought about a profound change in his outlook on life.

After this incident, one day, noticing that the boy had a good grasp of Sanskrit with an ability to explain complex ideas in simple ways, Krishnan Vaidiar insisted Nanu be sent for higher studies and offered financial help. In 1876, at the age of 20, Nanu left home for Kayamkulam, a town in the district of Alappuzha, Kerala, to study under Kummanpally Asan, who was a great Sanskrit scholar. He could not find a place in the gurukula's hostel run by the upper caste, but fortunately he got a place to stay at a house-cum-hostel run by a rich Ezhava family for poor Ezhava students. At the Sanskrit school, he was taught the Vedas, Upanishads and Sanskrit texts such as Kalidasa's *Raghuvamsa Mahakavya*. He did extraordinarily well in his studies; in fact, he was so far ahead of his classmates in his grasp of the lessons that the impressed teacher let him sit with senior students. But unfortunately, his studies were cut short when he fell seriously ill by a severe attack of dysentery in 1879 and had to return home.

Back home, after recovering from his illness, he himself started schools at Meerakandavu and Anchuthengu for young boys. At Anchuthengu, where he lived now, he spent his free time at the Jnaneswaran Temple, and also conducted Gita classes in the temple precincts for those interested. It was the time when the impulse to renounce the world and take to a life of contemplation was gathering momentum in him, but he couldn't bring himself to take the plunge. Expressing this dilemma in one of the poems he wrote at the time, he asked of Shiva:

There is none equal to thee,
Knowing this truth well

am I still straying
among puzzling thoughts that
lead me, to what?

(Kunhappa, 1982)

His parents thought it was time he got married, and relatives persuaded him to agree to the proposal, which he came to regret later. He went through the wedding ceremonies, but he did not go to the bride's house for the nuptial ceremony and so the marriage was not consummated. Yielding to family pressure, when he did finally visit his wife's house, he did not enter it. Instead, he sat in the veranda of the house, ate the sweet and banana brought to him by her, and then said, 'People are born in this world with diverse objectives. You and I have different paths to tread. You would do well to follow yours and let me follow mine.' And he walked away (Kunhappa, 1982).

He started on his wanderings again, mostly spending long hours on hills, inside caves, in forests and by riverbanks, living off fruits, leaves and roots. He spent a long period of time in a cave known as Pillathadam on Maruthwa Hill, doing his sadhana. Maruthwa Hill is situated on the southernmost tip of the Western Ghats in Kanyakumari district. It is known as the abode of medicinal herbs, and a holy land where spiritual aspirants and yogis performed tapas. After coming down from the hills, he was loved and revered as Nanu Swami by the people. He let them take him on a celebratory procession and then went off again, this time to Kanyakumari, Kovalam and Thiruvananthapuram, spent time with fishermen at the beaches, met with Muslims and Christians and shared food with them.

Moving from one seashore to another, in 1886, he went to Aruvipuram, an enchanting place by the river Neyyar in Kerala. There, on the lap of lush green nature, he found a shelter and got engaged in his tapas. Word spread that he was a siddha, who performed miracles. People came from nearby villages and towns to have his darshan and brought with them offerings of fruit and rice and curry.

It was decided to build a Shiva temple there in the heart of the forest. One night, Nanu Swami dived into the river and came up with a stone resembling a Shivalinga. The linga was consecrated and a temple was built around it. It was a momentous period in Kerala history that would change the destiny of the Ezhavas and other lower castes of Kerala. On a slab of granite, the swami got the following message engraved:

Here is a model abode
Where men live like brothers:
Bereft of the prejudice of caste
Or the rancour of religious differences.

It was here that Narayana Guru gave the clarion call: 'One caste, One religion, One god for man.' And he assured his followers: 'Our ideals serve us, as the Pole Star guides the navigator at sea. His ship may never reach the Pole Star, but it reaches a safe harbour all the same.' (Kunhappa, 1982)

Narayana Guru's spontaneous spiritual act that defied the caste rules and went against the Brahmanical Shastras sent shock waves through the state of Kerala. How could an Ezhava, who was denied entry into a temple, build a temple for Shiva? Narayana Guru silenced the protest by simply stating: 'I consecrated the Ezhava Siva.' That was his approach, always creative and persuasive, never confrontational.

In the following years, Narayana Guru got about 30 temples built one after another, most of them in Kerala, a couple each in Karnataka, Tamil Nadu and Sri Lanka. Ezhavas and other lower caste people did not worship gods from the Hindu pantheon, instead worshipped ancestors, tribal heroes, hills and brooks, snakes and spirits, and female deities who demanded animal sacrifices. Narayana Guru did not condemn them, but was against mass consumption of liquor during festivals, drunken brawls and sacrifice of animals, which he wanted to end.

Most people understood the Guru's direction and moved over to worshipping Shiva, Subramania, Ganesh and other such gods. So, in a few of the temples built by Narayana Guru, idols of Shiva, Subramania and Ganesh were installed, but not all of them were consecrated with idols. Karamukka Temple has only a lighted lamp as an icon; at the Murukumuzha Temple the words satyam (truth), dharmam (faith and duty), daya (compassion) and sneham (love), were engraved on a slab and placed in the sanctum sanctorum; in Kalavamcodam temple, a mirror with 'Om' etched on it was displayed.

In effect, Narayana Guru did not seek permission from brahmin priests or fight for the right of the people of low castes to enter temples and worship the deities; instead, he took the temples to them. This was nothing less than a revolution, but it had to be completed and strengthened by education of the masses and training them in skills that would enable them to earn their living through decent means and lead a life of dignity and autonomy. The Sree Narayana Dharma Paripalana Yogam, or SNDP, was founded in 1903, and under its aegis, many schools, colleges and technical institutes were started to cater to the needs of the downtrodden. Narayana Guru was now recognized as a revolutionary sage. Distinguished personalities, religious leaders and writers travelled to Kerala to meet the great man.

Adi Shankara had propagated Advaita Vedanta, the oneness of life, and Brahman – the ultimate principle of life, source and cause of all existence – as the only truth, but he had failed to overcome the divisive caste system and put this truth of Oneness to action.

Narayana Guru, who looked up to Shankara and followed his Advaita Vedanta, fulfilled the sacred task. Many a saint-poet of the bhakti movement, which spread across India from the sixth to seventeenth centuries, had wrestled with the caste oppression in their own personal lives and propagated equality of all men and women before God. Narayana Guru's message of 'One caste, One religion, One God', his act of throwing open the temple doors to people of all castes and taking education to the hitherto unlettered and marginalized lower castes marked the social culmination of the teachings of these saint-poets and Advaita Vedanta.

In February 1928, Narayana Guru fell seriously ill and died seven months later. He was 72 at the time.

Teachings

Whichever the religion,
It suffices
If it makes a better man.

~

Acts that one performs
For one's own sake
Should also aim for the good
Of other men.

~

Love of others is my happiness,
Love that is mine is happiness for others.
And so, truly, deeds that benefit a man
Must be a cause for other's happiness too.

~

Devoid of dividing walls
Of caste or race
Or hatred of rival faith
We all live here
In Brotherhood.

~

Whatever may be the difference in men's creed, dress, language etc., they all belong to the same kind of creation, there is no harm at all in their dining together or having marital relation with one another.

~

Hindu religion contains the principles of all religions. For spiritual attainment Hindu religion is more than enough.

~

My religion is also Buddhism. I am a Buddhist because I am an Advaitin (believer in non-dualism).

~

During Christ's time love was a necessity. Christ, therefore, gave more prominence to love. One should have patience like Christ.

~

Advice of Mohammed Nabi is also good. During Nabi's life feeling of brotherhood might have been a necessity. Islam is therefore giving more prominence to brotherhood.

~

Wrong knowledge gives rise to divisive tendency. This generates discriminatory and hierarchal feelings and leads to quarrels and confrontations. Such people can be reformed only by those who have immense spiritual strength and purity of the soul. Buddha, Jesus Christ and Prophet Nabi succeeded in achieving this.

~

God is pure consciousness or the embodiment of Absolute knowledge (chit purushan) Who sees sans eyes, hears sans ears, feels sans skin, smells sans nose and tastes sans tongue.

(Teachings of Narayana Guru, 2017)

Anandamayi Ma
(1896–1982)

YEARS BEFORE TUSHAR CHAUDHURI BECAME A CLOSE ASSOCIATE OF MA, as a rational-minded college student she had doubts about the miracle stories surrounding her. However, one day she decided to find out for herself if Ma had any extraordinary spiritual powers. It was said that just by looking at people Ma could know their thoughts and feelings. Tushar devised a plan to test if Ma really possessed that kind of power.

Generally, during darshan hour, Ma asked a devotee or two to sing. Tushar was gifted with a good voice and practised a particular song thoroughly at home. Thus prepared, she decided to go for Ma's darshan with a strong desire in her mind to sing before her, but only if Ma asked her to sing. She did not divulge this decision to her parents, who were Ma's devotees, nor to anybody else.

Next day, she went for Ma's darshan with her mother, and on purpose took a seat in the back row. It seemed all too simple, the test. If Ma invited her to sing, it proved she had the power to read people's thoughts; if she didn't, then it proved she didn't have any such powers. An hour ticked by, and Ma did not even cast a single glance in her direction. Ma asked a woman to sing a song. After her singing, Ma asked another song to be sung to mark the end of the darshan time. Just as the song ended, people started leaving one by one, after making pranams to Ma.

Tushar had wished for Ma to win the test, but sadly, it was not to be. Feeling disappointed, Tushar got up to leave, went near Ma and made her pranams. Ma looked up in her eyes and asked, 'Are you leaving now? Won't you let me hear your song?' Tushar was too stunned to react. 'Just sing at least one song for me,' Ma added earnestly. Tushar sat down and just as she was getting ready to sing, Ma smiled and said, 'Sing that song which you have practised all these days.' (Chaudhuri, 2006)

Anandamayi Ma was born as Nirmala, on April 30, 1896, in

the village Kheora of East Bengal, now a part of Bangladesh. Her parents, Bipin Bihari Bhattacharya and Moksada Sundari, were devout Vaishnavas, worshippers of Vishnu. She was the second child and they called her Nirmala, 'immaculate beauty', which she was till her last days.

Nirmala was different from girls of her age, both in her behaviour and reaction to things around her. She did hardly two year of schooling and showed no interest in learning to read and write, nor in things children of her age were generally interested in. She was different but always looked cheerful and was of such a happy demeanour that she was called Hasi Ma, mother of smiles, or Khusir Ma, happy mother. This cheerful temperament that was her nature in all circumstances earned her the sobriquet Anandamayi Ma, joy or bliss-permeated mother.

She was cheerful, and obedient too. She performed household chores without complaint. But, at times, she used to fall into trance and her parents took it as 'absentmindedness' and not as something 'abnormal' or 'supernormal'. In 1909, at the age of 13, she was married to Raman Mohan Chakravarti, who was older to her by several years. At the time he worked as a clerk in the police department at Atpara, East Bengal. Five years later, 18-year-old Nirmala moved in with him to set up the family in Astagrama, also in East Bengal, where he had taken a new job with the Land Settlement Department. She called him Bholanath, and the name stuck.

The marriage was never consummated. Every time Bholanath approached her, she would fall into a trance or death-like state. He took her to be a typical village girl, illiterate, but a little moody and melancholic. As a dutiful wife, she scrubbed and cleaned the house, washed his clothes and cooked his meals with an endearing smile on her face. But when it came to sex, she was dead to his touch. She was obedient but not submissive.

Kundalini Yoga asserts that with the rising of Kundalini energy the body-mind get transformed. The sexual glands undergo a radical change and the individual is freed from the grip of sexual desire. Did Nirmala know about the changes taking place in her and attribute any spiritual quality to it? She had no guru, nor any learned person around her to consult with. Perhaps she subliminally understood that her body was being transformed into a field of divine energy. But Bholanath and his relatives took exception to her slipping into samadhi now and then. His relatives and friends urged Bholanath to separate from Nirmala and find a suitable wife.

To his credit, Bholanath never thought of breaking the marriage, but he eventually agreed with his relatives that it could be the work of evil spirits. An exorcist was brought home, who, upon realizing Nirmala was no ordinary woman, prostrated in front of her and sought her forgiveness. Next, a distinguished physician was called to examine Nirmala. The doctor, after studying her behaviour and examining her, is believed to have assured Bholanath and his relatives that Nirmala did not suffer from any mental illness, rather her 'eccentric' behaviour was a sign of 'God intoxication' (Lipski, 2000).

Things began to change as more and more people came to know about her exalted spiritual state and started to come for her darshan. Bholanath let her meet them and gradually he too was drawn to her 'divine' presence, although he did not, like others, prostrate himself in front of her and address her as 'Ma' or as 'Goddess Durga'. Nirmala continued to perform household tasks, though she was found in a withdrawn state of ecstasy much of the time. She was now regularly invited to grace public pujas and kirtans, where people directly witnessed her going into the state of samadhi. As her fame as a new avatar of Divinity, Anandamayi Ma, spread all around, people from all walks of life, including prominent government officials, medical doctors, Sanskrit scholars, professors from universities, writers and serious spiritual seekers as well as gurus came to have her darshan and meet with her for spiritual advice.

Anandamayi had no guru, had no formal religious education, did not go through scriptural study or any training in spiritual sadhana.

Grace descended on her, or what may be called the inner nature or immanent potential opened up spontaneously and transformed her. She offered no teaching as such; rather, she taught what had to be taught through telling stories with spiritual messages, through kirtans and her cheerful, smiling presence.

She believed in the spiritual equality of women and encouraged them to wear the sacred thread, but she did not encourage renunciation. Although she did not advocate any specific method or sadhana, she quite often asserted that Self-realization was possible, not in the distant future, but here and now, provided one worked towards it with sincerity until the veil of ignorance fell away and *That* which is eternal, self-luminous, shone forth.

Anandamayi Ma was recognized as an embodiment of joy and compassion, as a sage of the highest order during her lifetime. Prominent political and cultural leaders, including Pandit Nehru, sought her company. Spiritual seekers, even gurus from Shaivite, Tantric and Vaishnava sects sought her counsel. People from Islam, Christian, Zoroastrian and Buddhist faiths too found her company endearing, and her teaching as embodying the essential philosophy of their own religion or faith.

Her informal talks and conversations with people in Bengali were recorded by her devotees, some of which were later translated into English and other languages. In 1928, an ashram was built at Siddhesvari in Dacca, in present-day Bangladesh. It was only the first of a network of ashrams that were later established all over northern India to carry forward Anandamayi Ma's message. Ma died at the age of 86, on 27 August 1982, in Dehradun.

Selected Sayings

As you love your own body, so regard everyone as equal to your own body. When the Supreme Experience supervenes, everyone's service is revealed as one's own service. Call it a bird, an insect, an animal or a man, call it by any name you please, one serves one's own Self in every one of them.

~

With earnestness, love and goodwill carry out life's everyday duties and try to elevate yourself step by step. In all human activities let there be a live contact with the Divine and you will not have to leave off anything. Your work will then be done well and you will be on the right track to find the Master.

~

Whatever work you have to do, do it with a singleness of purpose, with all the simplicity, contentment and joy you are capable of. Thus only will you be able to reap the best fruit of work. In fullness of time, the dry leaves of life will naturally drop off and new ones shoot forth.

~

The lute of man's short life is strung with so many strings; they have to be cut asunder. There is no real substance to these many strings. It is futile to let one's thoughts be occupied with the ties by which one is bound. Why behave like a fool and return again and again to this world of illusion?

~

Man appears to be the embodiment of want. Want is what he thinks about and want indeed is what he obtains. Contemplate your true being—or else there will be want, wrong action, helplessness, distress and death.

~

Why speak of Self-realisation in the future? It *is* here and now—only the veil that hides it has to be destroyed. That which in any case is doomed to destruction is to be destroyed. When the veil falls to pieces *That* which eternally *Is* shines forth—*One*, Self-luminous.

(Collated from Narayan, 2006 and Mangalananda, 2016)

❦

Sufism and the Illustrious Indian Sufis

ONCE, WHILE MOHAMMAD AND HIS COMPANIONS WERE PRAYING IN A masjid, a Bedouin came in, went near a wall and started urinating there. Aghast at what the Bedouin was doing, the companions of Mohammad cried, 'Stop! Stop it!' A couple of them jumped to their feet and were about to attack the Bedouin. Mohammad stopped them and said, 'Do not interrupt him, leave him alone.' So they kept quiet until the stranger finished urinating. Then Mohammad got up, went over to the Bedouin and said, 'In a Masjid it is not right to do anything like urinating and defecating. This is a sacred place for remembering Allah, praying and reading Quran and for such pious activities.' Then he went and brought a bucket of water and washed the place clean, after which he said to his companions, 'Come, let us go and complete the prayer.' (Malik, Hadith I)

This account from the Hadith carries a powerful message of love and service. Perhaps such pious acts and wise words of Mohammad gave rise to Sufism, but we cannot fix its origin in definite terms. However, as is rightly said, Sufism is an aspect, or a mystical dimension of Islam and not a sect of Islam. It was referred to as *Tasawwuf* in Arabic, meaning 'to dress in coarse woollen garb' as a sign of penitence and renunciation of worldly life. Only centuries later did it come to be called 'Sufism' and its practitioner a 'Sufi', sometimes called *faqir* or fakir in Arabic, and *darvish* in Persian.

There are many 'Tariqas', Sufi orders, and all of them trace their teachers back through generations to Mohammad himself. Although

Sufism is quite different from mainstream Islam – in that it transcends religious sectarianism and seeks to find the truth of divine love through direct personal experience of God – it has played an important role in the historical spread of Islam and in shaping regional Islamic cultures in Africa and Asia. And the literatures produced by Sufi-mystics such as Jalal ad-Din Muhammad Rumi, Omar Khayyam and Al-Ghazali have contributed immensely to the appreciation of Islamic mysticism in the non-Muslim world.

Historically, Sufism – propagated by notable figures such as Ali Ibn Abi Talib, Hasan and Rabiah in Bhaghdad, Iraq – began to spread in South Asia when the practitioners travelled to Iran and Afghanistan and then to India. It came through the scholars, poets and mystics when Turkic military rule spread in Indian Punjab in 1027 CE, then in Delhi and Ajmer and later in Bengal, Benaras, Rajasthan and Bihar. By 1186, it is said, the vibrant Islamic culture and its mysticism had become a significant presence in northern India. The translations of the Quran, Hadith and Sufi philosophy and poetry into vernacular languages further helped the already gathering momentum of Islamization in India.

However, we need to note that Islam had already arrived in southern India in the seventh century, when Arab traders came on business to coastal Malabar in Kerala. Immigrant Arabs from the Persian Gulf began settling in Kerala. Historically, therefore, Islam as a religion first spread in the Malabar region. The first mosque, Cheramaan Juma Mosque, was built in 629 CE in Methala, in Thrissur district of Kerala, by Malik Deenar. And Mappilas were the first Indian community to convert to Islam.

The Sufi teaching of love and harmony and divine communion resonated with the people of India and, by the twelfth and thirteenth centuries, Sufi brotherhoods had a vital presence in northern India. The Sufis ran the Khanqah, a hospice and dormitory which offered free food, spiritual guidance and counselling. It drew people from depressed castes and classes in thousands into their fold. The spiritually hungry, psychologically deprived and socially exploited and oppressed lower-caste people found in the Islamic faith a way out of suffering and a path to their liberation.

So, it is a historical fact that the depressed castes took to Islam voluntarily and not because they were forced to convert, although it cannot be denied that certain kings and fanatical religious leaders indulged in forced conversions. Politically, some Sufi orders played an important role in strengthening the powers of Mughal rule in India, while culturally, a good number of Sufis engaged themselves creatively with Hindu and Buddhist thought and practices, and contributed to the growth of syncretic mysticism and the unique forms and styles of art and music that form a vital part of Indian culture today.

Characteristics of Sufism

According to the doctrine of Sufism, Haq (God) and Khalaq (Soul) are the same, and union with God can be achieved through love of God, prayers, fasts and rituals. Sufi mysticism is associated with the liberal interpretation of Quran called Tarikat, in contrast to Shariat which is the conservative interpretation of Quran. In practice, however, it surpassed religious and cultural beliefs and identities and stressed on discovering deeper identity or connection with God. Although Sufis opposed materialistic life, they were not in favour of complete renunciation. And music formed an integral part of their devotion to God.

Sufism has many similarities to Vaishnavism, especially in its emphasis on love/bhakti as the way to God; and in its doctrine it is much closer to Vishishtadvaita, qualified non-dualism, than Advaita, non-dualism, although some Sufis, such as Baba Farid, Sarmad Kashani and Bulleh Shah, may offer a taste of Advaita in some of their songs. However, most Sufis, who related to God or the Absolute with qualities, though without form, were, to use the Hindu terms, saguna bhaktas, like Tukaram and Meera, and not nirguna bhaktas, such as Kabir or Lalleshwari.

Some of the major Sufi orders that spread across India were Madariyya, Shadhiliyya, Chistiyyah, Suhrwardiyyah, Naqshbandiyyah and Qadiriyyah. Among them, the Chisti order is most visible and spread its roots all across India.

Chisti Order

Khwaja Moinuddin Chisti introduced the Chistiyyah order of Sunni mysticism in India. He was born in 1141 CE in Persia and came to India around 1192 and settled down at Ajmer. Before that, he is believed to have travelled for almost 20 years across northern India, meeting some of the Sunni mystics of the time, including Abdul Qadir Gilani and Najmuddin Kubra. He was initiated by the famous saint Khwaja Uthman.

Back in Ajmer, he married late and had three sons and one daughter. He had a large number of followers who were drawn by his simple ascetic life and message of love, equality and universal brotherhood. He was notably the first Islamic mystic who allowed the use of music in their hymns to God, which had a particular appeal to Indians.

He died in his nineties, leaving behind not any significant composition but a liberating, ecumenical tradition and a band of dedicated disciples, through whom the Chistiyyah order spread to many parts of the subcontinent. Farid-ud-din Ganj-i-Shakar, Nizamuddin Auliya and Amir Khusrau were some of the famous Chistiyyahs. The tomb or dargah of Moinuddin in Ajmer, which was visited by Emperor Akbar about fourteen times, continues to be one of the holy sites not only for Sunni Muslims but also Hindus who look upon Moinuddin as a great saint. It has also become a tourist destination and people from all over India and the world go and visit the tomb.

Baba Farid
(1179–1266)

Farid-ud-din Ganj-i-Shakar, more popularly known as Baba Farid, was born in a Sunni Muslim family in 1179 in a village of Punjab region in present-day Pakistan. He received his education at Multan, a noted education centre at the time, and at 16 went on the Hajj pilgrimage with his parents. Later, he moved to Delhi and was introduced to mystical Islamic doctrine by the Sufi saint Qutbuddin Bakhtiar Kaki. After his master's death, he became his spiritual successor, moved from Delhi and settled in Ajodhan (in present-day Pakistan). He had five sons and three daughters from his three wives.

In the later period of his life, however, he led an extremely ascetic life. A folk legend has it that once he went into a nearby jungle to meditate and lived without food; he chewed on a piece of wood he had taken with him whenever he felt very hungry and took nothing else. His greatest contribution was that he wrote in Punjabi when there was hardly any literature in that language, and it was considered a coarse folk dialect, while Sanskrit, Arabic, Turkish and Persian languages were deemed the languages of the learned. His writings laid the foundation for the later development of Punjabi.

He was highly respected for his syncretic outlook and catholicity. He had a wide following and inspired many a devotee to tread the path of perfect renunciation and total absorption in God. Today, his chillas, shrines, are found in many parts of northern India, the most important being the shrine in Pakistan, considered one of the holiest Sufi shrines. His poetry, brimming over with devotion to God and transcending boundaries of religions, appealed to spiritual questers everywhere. It is not surprising, therefore, that over a hundred of his hymns to God were included in the holy Guru Granth Sahib by the fifth guru of Sikhism, Arjan Dev.

Here are a few of the hymns translated by Shri Mata Krishnaji (of Brindaban), quoted by author Bankey Behari in his *Sufis, Mystics and Yogis of India*:

The day a man is born, the date of his death is inscribed
on his forehead. This writing cannot be effaced; the
marriage with the God of Death must come on the

appointed day, entreaties are of no avail. The path by which the
soul has to pass is subtler than the thickness of a hair.

~

Despise not the earth, for none is greater than it.
So long as you are alive, you tread it under your feet,
but on your death it lies over your head.

~

To what avail is your seeking Him amidst thorns and
brambles that prick your feet?
He dwells in your heart.
Seek Him there.
So says Farid.

~

When I heard the gong being struck in the temple,
The sight pained me, for the thought occurred to me,
'When this faultless thing is being struck mercilessly for no fault,
what punishment would I not have to endure in the end,
when I have so many faults to my account?' So says Farid.

~

The world is held by Him, and He dwelleth in creation.
Knowing this, do not look with disdain on any trivial
object for He pervadeth all of them. So says Farid.

~

The body is shrivelled up and turned into a skeleton.
The crows peck and are eating off the sole of the foot and
the skin of the hands. Alack! Very unlucky am I, not to
have met the Lord yet. So says Farid.

~

Why entangle thyself in 'I' and 'My-ness' and waste
time over thy relations of the body. Believe me, he alone
renounces the world on whom He confers His grace.
So says Farid.

~

His grace may fall on us at any time.
There is no definite rule regulating it.
Some do not get it even after performing
great austerities and nightlong vigils,
whilst it is forced on those who lie asleep.

Nizamuddin Auliya
(1238–1325)

Nizam-ud-din Auliya was one of the most famous Sufis on the Indian
subcontinent and unarguably the most famous of the Chisti saints.
He was born in 1238 at Badayun, a village in Uttar Pradesh. He had
a brother and a sister. Their father, Syed Abdullah, died when he was
five years old, and the family moved to Delhi.

Even as a young boy, he was of spiritual bent of mind. At 16 years
of age, when he was still a student engaged in the study of scriptures,
he happened to hear about Baba Farid and felt flooded with feelings
of love and respect for the saint. The love kept burning like a fire
until, after completing his studies four years later, he went to Ajodha
(presently Pakpattan Sharif in Pakistan) to meet with Baba Farid and
became his disciple. Years later, he was to tell his disciples that he had
never felt the same after meeting with any other Sufi. Baba Farid, too,
took a great liking to Nizamuddin. Every year, Nizamuddin visited
Ajodha and spent the month of Ramzan with his teacher. On his third
visit, Baba Farid made him his successor.

After Baba Farid's death, Nizamuddin made his home on the
outskirts of Delhi in Ghiyaspur. Unlike other Sufis, Nizamuddin

remained unmarried, totally dedicated to the teachings of the Chisti order. He started a khanqah, a spiritual retreat which also served as a hospice, in Ghiyaspur, where people were offered free food, shelter and spiritual education. His emphasis on love, brotherhood and mystic personality drew hundreds of people, rich and poor alike, to him. He initiated people from other faiths into the Chisti order without converting them into Islam. His unreserved love towards all, his remarkable catholicity and religious pluralism made him the most endearing of all Sufi saints.

While continuing with and expanding on the teachings of Moinuddin and Baba Farid, he laid emphasis on the belief that it was possible to know and experience God within this life, provided, of course, one was capable of perfect renunciation and complete trust in God. He denounced distinctions based on social, economic and religious status, and avoided mixing with the Sultans and the nobles. In his lifetime, seven Sultans ruled over Delhi, but he never cared to meet them nor allowed them to visit him. Once, the story goes, when the Sultan Alauddin Khilji sent word that he wished to meet him at his place, Nizamuddin said: 'I have two doors in my home. If the Sultan would enter through one door, I would go out through the other.' (Bhattacharjya, 2011)

Besides having a wide following, Nizamuddin had around 600 khalifas, disciples, who were given the authority to take their own disciples and propagate the spiritual lineage. Among them, Nasiruddin Chiragh Dehlavi was made his successor. Amir Khusrau was his most loved disciple, just as Nizamuddin was of Baba Farid. It was his wish that Khusrau should be buried with him in the same grave after his death. His tomb, Nizamuddin Dargah in Delhi, is one of the most famous dargahs in the country, visited by people of all faiths.

Aphorisms

Women are equally endowed with spiritual power and talent. They are equal to men in spiritual discipline.

∼

The purpose of prayer is to get rid of self-conceit. One who is ego-centric and selfish cannot achieve anything spiritually.

∼

There should be no expression of anger when points of difference are discussed.

∼

Self-criticism and quarrel with one's own self is better than seventy years of prayer.

∼

A man is in his worst state when he considers himself good and pious.

∼

One should pray for the salvation of all. There should be no discrimination in it.

∼

Fasting is half the prayer, the other half is patience.

∼

Whatever one does not like for himself, he should not under any circumstances, suggest for others.

∼

Resignation to the Will of God is the real key to peace and satisfaction in life.

(Nizami, 2004)

Amir Khusrau

(1253–1325)

A story goes that when Amir Khusrau was born, his father took him to a mystic for his blessings. The mystic looked at the baby and exclaimed, 'Amir Lachin, you have brought to me one who will go two steps beyond Khaqani.' It wouldn't be incorrect to say that Amir Khusrau, who was undoubtedly one of the most incredibly gifted poets of all time, went several steps ahead of Khaqani, the famous twelfth century Persian poet who is placed in the front ranks of Persian literature.

Khusrau was not only a poet but also a wonderful musician and composer, and is said to be the inventor of many musical instruments, including the tabla. His mastery over different forms of poetry was unparalleled. He is said to have created six forms of music, namely, qaul, qalbana, tarana, naqsh and gul, and then of course qawwali, a hugely popular musical form sung widely in India and Pakistan today. Perhaps he is unequalled in the volume of poetry he produced – nearly a hundred works of different forms of poetry in Persian and Hindavi – and was instrumental in developing the Urdu language. He was also the most loved disciple of Nizamuddin.

Khusrau was born in 1253 at Patiyali in Uttar Pradesh. His father, Amir Saifuddin Mahmud, belonged to the Lachin tribe from what is today Uzbekistan. When the country was invaded and ravaged by the army of Genghis Khan, Amir Saifuddin, along with other members of the tribe, fled their home and came to Delhi via Afghanistan, seeking refuge. The then Sultan of Delhi, who too was a Turk, granted them land at Patiyali. Amir Saifuddin married Bibi Daulatnaz and the couple had a daughter and three sons, one of whom was Khusrau. Amir Saifuddin died when Khusrau was eight years old. Bibi Daulatnaz left Patiyali and moved to her father's house in Delhi with her children. Her grandfather was a Rajput and thus the children grew up in a household where both Islamic and Hindu culture and traditions prevailed.

Khusrau learnt to read and write at quite an early age. He started writing poetry at the age of eight. At 17, he produced his first collection of poems, *Tuhfat us-Sighr*, The Gift of Childhood. Three years later, in his twenties, he joined the army of the reigning Sultan, Ghiyas ud-Din Balban. The news about his poetic accomplishment spread in the army and reached the ears of the Sultan. The Sultan's second son, Bughra Khan, who was the ruler of Bengal, invited him to Bengal and became his patron. Later, the eldest son of the Sultan, Khan Mohammad, invited him to his court in Multan.

This way, Khusrau enjoyed the company of the members of the royal family and served under seven Sultans. During this long period, he was also a witness to several battles, conspiracies and assassinations. How he negotiated these political upheavals and possible psychological pressures and yet produced prodigious poetical works one after another is an intriguing story. Between 1279 and 1296, he produced several masanvis – extensive poems on the lives, deaths and heroic deeds of kings and Sultans – and also wrote diwans – collection of poems on a variety of subjects, set to music. The famous masanvi *Laila-Majnu* was composed during this period.

In 1300, when he was 47 years old, he was grief-stricken by the death of both his mother and one of his brothers. He wrote:

A double radiance left my star this year
Gone are my brother and my mother,
My two full moons have set and ceased to shine
In short week through this ill-luck of mine.

(allpoetry.com / Amir-Khusro)

He had seen many tragic deaths over these years and had even composed poetry on sorrows that death causes, but the demise of his mother and brother seemed to have turned him inwards and to a contemplative life. In 1310, he met Nizamuddin Auliya and became his disciple.

What a Glow Everywhere I See
What a glow everywhere I see, Oh mother, what a glow;
I've found the beloved, yes I found him,
In my courtyard;
I have found my pir Nizamuddin Aulia.
I roamed around the entire world,
looking for an ideal beloved;
And finally this face has enchanted my heart.
The whole world has been opened for me,
Never seen a glow like this before.

('Amir Khusro')

Chisti Order gurus, especially Nizamuddin, as a rule, avoided any contact with the Sultans and the wealthy class. As said earlier, Nizamuddin witnessed the reign of seven rulers of the Delhi Sultanate, but never entertained any of them, although they all revered him. In contrast, Khusrau served seven Sultans and three princes from the times of Sultan Balban to Mohammad Bin Tughlaq, and even composed masanvis on them.

Given this apparent contrast between the guru and his disciple, how this extraordinarily deep relationship between them panned out should really be an interesting story in itself. Perhaps it had something to do with Khusrau's terrific talent and charming personality. In 1315, he swung back to his poetry and wrote a romantic masanvi about the marriage between Alauddin Khilji's son Khizr Khan and princess Duval Rani. However, four years later, he came back to Nizamuddin and produced a work of prose *Afzal ul-Fawaid*, Greatest blessings, on the teachings of the guru.

Nizamuddin died in 1325, at the age of 90. On hearing about his guru's death, Kushrau, who was out of town on work, is believed to have rushed back to Delhi.

Oh Khusrau, go back now,
The dark dusk settles in four corners...

                                        ('Amir Khusro')

Utterly inconsolable, in deep sorrow over his teacher's passing,
Khusrau died six months later and was buried close to the tomb of
Nizamuddin. He was 72 years old. Before his passing, Nizamuddin
had said that people should first offer their respects to Khusrau at his
tomb, before visiting his; such was the love and high regard for his
dearest disciple.

Khusrau's playful riddles, qawwali and ghazals, his long and short
poems rendered to music, are a part of the popular culture in South
Asia. Amir Khusrau remains an iconic figure in the cultural history of
the Indian subcontinent. He called himself a 'Hindustani Turk', and
people called him 'Tuti-e-Hind', Parrot of India.

Selected Poems and Couplets

Every sect has a faith, a direction (Qibla) to which they turn,
I have turned my face towards the crooked cap (of Nizamudin
    Aulia)
The whole world worships something or the other,
Some look for God in Mecca, while some go to Kashi (Banaras),
So why can't I, Oh wise people, fall at my beloved's feet?

I am a pagan and a worshipper of love: the creed (of Muslims)
    I do not need;
Every vein of mine has become taut like a wire,
the (Brahman's) girdle I do not need.
Leave from my bedside, you ignorant physician!
The only cure for the patient of love is the sight of his beloved –
other than this no medicine does he need.
If there be no pilot in our boat, let there be none:

We have god in our midst: the sea we do not need.
The people of the world say that Khusrau worships idols.
So he does, so he does; the people he does not need,
the world he does not need.

(allpoetry.com/Amir-Khusro)

Oh Khusrau, the river of love runs in strange directions.
One who jumps into it drowns, and one who drowns, gets across.
The creaking of the chain of Majnun is the orchestra of the lovers,
To appreciate its music is quite beyond the ears of the wise.
If I cannot see her, at least I can think of her, and so be happy;
To light the beggar's hut no candle is better than moonlight.

~

My heart is a wanderer in love, may it ever remain so.
My life's been rendered miserable in love, may it grow more and
more miserable.

~

People think they are alive because they have soul in them,
But I am alive because I have love in myself.

~

My beloved speaks Turkish, and Turkish I do not know;
How I wish if her tongue would have been in my mouth.

~

Old age and lovemaking do not go together;
But O Khusrau, you still remain a proof against this reasoning.

~

If there is a paradise on earth,
It is this, it is this, it is this...

('Amir Khusro')

Bulleh Shah
(1680–1758)

Legend has it that even as a young boy, Bulleh Shah was of spiritual bent of mind, and no sooner had he completed his education than he went in search of a teacher in Lahore. Both Islamic and Hindu mystical traditions believe that one needs a guru to guide one on the path of spirituality. In the intellectual circles of Lahore, Bulleh Shah heard of Shah Inayat as an able teacher, but none could guide him to the teacher's place. It was summer and roaming around in the hot sun, he looked for a cool place to rest. To his luck, he saw a mango grove nearby and went in.

Innumerable succulent mangoes hung from every branch. He was hungry and thought perhaps he could have a couple of mangoes. He looked around for the keeper of the garden to seek his permission, but finding none, he decided to help himself. He looked at the ripe fruits and prayed, 'Allah ghani', and down fell a mango into his hands. He repeated the magic words and collected a few more mangoes. Just when he was about to feast on them, there came the keeper of the garden and accused him of stealing the mangoes.

Bulleh Shah said, 'No, I have not stolen the mangoes, but they have fallen into my hands.' And to demonstrate the truth, he uttered, 'Allah ghani,' and yet again a mango fell into his hands. Instead of getting angry, the gardener laughed and said, 'You do not know how to pronounce the holy words properly and so you have reduced their power.' So saying, he uttered, 'Allah ghani,' and down fell all the fruits on the ground, and when he uttered the magic words again, up they flew back on to the trees.

Unable to believe his eyes, Bulleh Shah cried, 'Sir, may I know whom I'm speaking to?'

'Shah Inayat, head gardener of the Shalimar gardens of Lahore.'

Bulleh Shah fell at his feet and begged to be accepted as his disciple and shown the way to God (Karishna, 2008).

Bulleh Shah was born in the 1680 in the village Pandoki of Kasur in Lahore. He belonged to a highly conservative Saiyid community. After completing his education, he became a disciple of Shah Inayat. Inayat was a Sufi teacher with a liberal outlook and Bulleh Shah's family opposed his decision because of Inayat's unorthodox views, more importantly because Inayat belonged to the Arais community, who were gardeners and Hindu converts to Islam, therefore, inferior to Muhammadans.

Inayat was a mystic with a scholarly disposition. He authored several books and even wrote commentaries on the works of some of the Sufi masters. In one of his books, he discussed various methods to attain salvation, and he claimed that this mystical knowledge and methods were from India and spread in Persia and then Greece when the soldiers of Alexander had carried the spiritual knowledge with them to their country. He was a genuine quester, whose belief in Prophet Mohammad did not prevent him from appreciating and learning from other spiritualties and even enunciating Hindu mysticism in his approach to salvation.

Despite serious opposition by the family and the threat of boycott by the Sayidi community, Bulleh accepted Inayat as his teacher. He was convinced that Inayat was his guru and would lead him to his salvation. It is said he was even beaten up by his family members and locked up in a room. But, finally, he managed to escape to the city of Lahore to be with his pir, Inayat. Under Inayat's influence and inspired by his syncretism, Bulleh started writing his kafis, rhymed verses composed in simple syllabic meters, in Punjabi. In some of his kafis, he did not mince words in criticizing, like Kabir, the irrelevance and futility of rituals and the stupidity of orthodoxy.

> Go to the mosque and tell the people,
> It is to no purpose your assembling there, if your heart
> does not bow in prayer.
> Outside purity is of no avail, if thy mind be impure.
> Even with the Perfect Teacher's guidance all thy
> prayers are of no avail.

Such prayers are like unto a bath in muddy water,
Such obeisance is like unto a dive in the oven and
Such repetition of Name is like painting with coal.
I found my Lord in myself,
So says Bulleh.

~

Going to Mecca is not the ultimate
Even if a hundred prayers are offered,
Going to River Ganges is not the ultimate
Even if you bathe in it a hundred times,
Unless the 'I' is removed from the heart!
So says Bulleh Shah.

(Behari, trans.,1962)

Such kafis disturbed, even annoyed Inayat. Such provocative utterances could get Bulleh killed. His own Sayidi community would certainly find him heretical. Many a Sufi saint had been done to death because of their utterances against the orthodoxy. They were living in dangerous times, under the rule of the fanatical King Aurangzeb, who had not only got a Maratha king and a Sikh guru brutally killed, but also had his elder brother Dara Shikoh and his teacher Sarmad, accused of heresy, executed. The story of Sarmad, a Sufi mystic, is in order here.

Sarmad Kashani was a Persian-speaking Armenian Jew who later converted to Islam. He came to India as a merchant from Armenia. At some stage, it is said, he gave up his trade, abandoned his wealth and turned into a wandering, naked fakir. In his compositions he was critical of all denominational religions and their bigotry, and talked of God as love and love as something that burned away all forms of identity and attachment to the world.

The dawn and sunset of the world I have seen.
My heart is cleansed of the hypocrisy and tarnish of the worldly
love.
I have watched the bud which when in its philanthropy,
Gave out its secret and smiled.

(Behari, trans.,1962)

Aurangzeb's brother Dara Shikoh became his disciple and, it is said,
Sarmad taught him the Upanishads and the Bhagavad Gita. Dara, the
rightful heir to the imperial throne, lost the war or succession against
Aurangzeb and was put to death in 1659. All those who had supported
Dara met the same fate, including Sarmad. Also, Sarmad was hated
by the Moulvis for his heretical verses, and to make matters worse,
he wandered about naked, which was supposed to be against the
mandates of the Holy Quran. Once, when he was asked the reason
for his strange behaviour by Aurangzeb, Sarmad replied:

He, who hath conferred on thee the crown of Kingship,
On me hath conferred the madness of Love.
He offered thee dress to hide thy faults,
But let me, the faultless one, pass naked.

(Behari, trans.,1962)

Sarmad was accused and convicted of atheism and heresy. He was
beheaded at the entrance of Jama Masjid in Delhi in 1661, where his
grave is located today, visited by both Hindus and Muslims.

Coming back to Bulleh Shah, Inayat forbade him from speaking
freely and openly against the conventional beliefs and practices of
Muslims. But when Bulleh showed no sign of restraining his critical
voice, Inayat asked him to leave. It was a very painful for Bulleh to leave
his master, but according to a legend, years later, the master repented,
forgave his disciple and the two were reunited.

Mystics such as Sarmad and Bulleh were not against society or people as such, but were critical of certain orthodox beliefs and practices that prevented the possibility of connecting with God and experiencing pure love. Besides, a mystic who has experienced such love that transcends all barriers and boundaries, cannot help speaking about it. Listen to Bulleh:

I know not who am I.
Neither I am a believer resting in the mosque nor a
Kafir seated in the temple,
I am neither pure nor a sinner,
Neither I am a Pharoah nor a Moses.
Nor can ye find me when ye seek me in Vedas.
Neither amidst the coterie of the intoxicants nor amongst
the drunkards ye can find me.
Neither I am amongst those asleep nor amongst those
who keep the vigil at nights.
Neither I woo mirth nor sadness.
Neither I perform virtuous deeds nor suffer from the
taint of evil ones.
Neither I am constituted of the elements — earth, air, water.
I belong to no country, India or any other.
Neither I dwell in the village nor in a city.
Neither I am a Mogul, a Hind, nor a Turk,
Neither I dwell in the centre nor at the circumference,
Neither I know the secret of spirituality, nor that Adam
or Eve gave birth to me.
Neither am I called by a name nor do I dwell in the
house nor in the wilderness.
I know only this that I am the beginning and the end.
I recognize none besides me.
None is cleverer than me.
Who then art thou, Bulleh?

I am who called himself Bulleh.
So says Bulleh.

(Behari, trans.,1962)

Unlike many a Sufi saint of the past, Bulleh was a unique mystic-poet akin to the nirguna poets of the bhakti movement. His Beloved was the Universal Soul, the Divine. Conversion from one religion to another was an anathema to him; in his words, it was enough to 'show love in perfect detachment, renounce all desires and hopes and cleanse your heart, the truth will surely shine therein'. He remained unmarried, and, it is said, his sister, who had supported him all along, also remained single and took care of him till his last days. He died in 1758. His songs remain popular to this day, some of which have been rendered by prominent singers in India and Pakistan.

He who suffers the pang of Love is lost to himself and
dances out of tune in the world.
Let none trouble them who suffer from the malady of Love.
They that love like to bear the pain themselves and tend
it too cheerfully.
Even the God of Death dare not root out the tree of
their pain.
They control their future which they foreknow.
Whosoever donned the garment of love, he obtained
the passport from the Lord.
Since I drank the cup that reached me from his Abode
I have no doubts and delusions left.
In whom the Lord makes His abode, he ever cries,
'O Lord! Where art thou?'
He needs no rhythm nor schooling in music.
He is ever drunk to the point of madness and knows
(Truth) as my Teacher did.

I discovered the Truth and thus the chaos of untruth
for me ceased.
I have told you the secret of that Truth.
So says Bulleh.

(Behari, trans., 1962)

I have got lost in the city of love,
I am being cleansed, withdrawing myself from my head, hands
   and feet.
I have got rid of my ego, and have attained my goal.
Thus it has all ended well.
O Bulleh, the Lord pervades both the worlds;
None now appears a stranger to me.

(Puri,trans., 1986)

Remove duality and do away with all disputes;
The Hindus and Muslims are not other than He.
Deem everyone virtuous, there are no thieves.
For, within everybody He himself resides.
How the Trickster has put on a mask.

(Puri, trans., 1986)

Ezhuthachan
(born c. 1700)

THUNCHATHTHU RAMANUJAN EZHUTHACHAN WAS A DEVOTIONAL POET
and an ingenious linguist. Some consider him to be the father of
modern Malayalam language, the principal language of the state of
Kerala. His *Adhyatma Ramayanam*, which is considered a landmark in

Malayalam and a great devotional text, is still recited in Hindu homes
and temples in Kerala during Kartikam, or what is called Ramayanam
masam, Ramayana month, from mid-July to mid-August every year.

Although he lived only about 400 years ago, we do not have
undisputable details of his background. It is said he was born sometime
around sixteenth century in Trikkandiyoor, close to the town of Tirur
in Malappuram. There is no consensus among scholars about his caste.
If some believe he was a brahmin, others think he was a nayar, a shudra,
and a few others suggest he could be a kaniyar by caste, traditional
astrologers well versed in Malayalam and Sanskrit yet considered
lower caste, currently listed under other backward communities
(OBC) by the Kerala Government. His name, 'Ezhuthachan', means
'father of letters', so is not indicative of a caste but only suggestive of
his profession, teaching. In his *Adhyatma Ramayanam*, Ezhuthachan
stated right at the beginning that he was 'the wise man among the
lowest Hindu varnas', although he did not mention the specific caste
he was born into.

It is said that he married young and had a daughter. After his
daughter came of age, he embraced sanyasa and went on a pilgrimage.
He travelled to Andhra Pradesh and Tamil Nadu, observed and
learnt much from different cultures, and also picked up Telugu and
Tamil. In due course, he settled down at Chittur (in Palakkad) with
his disciples. It was probably from here that he launched his literary
career that eventually transformed the Malayalam literary landscape.
At the site where he lived there is a traditional two-storied building
called Thunchan Gurumadam, now a memorial to Ezhuthachan,
where the Srichakra, sacred symbol of primordial energy, the idols of
deities he worshipped, the stylus and wooden slippers he used, and
old manuscripts are put on display.

Through his works, especially his translations of the Ramayana
and Mahabharata, he laid the foundation for the development of the
modern Malayalam language. It is said that he refined the style of
Malayalam and in the place of Vattezhutha, the old 30-letter script of

Malayalam, he created a 51 alphabet system corresponding to Sanskrit and shaped separate Malayalam letters. His *Adhyatma Ramayanam* marked the confluence of Sanskrit and Dravidian linguistic streams.

> This servant who has been working under their feet,
> Who is the wise man among the lowest Hindu Varnas,
> Am attempting to tell the old Ramayana which has been approved by Vedas,
> In such a way that even the ignorant would easily understand it,
> And I pray that the Vedas, vedangas and knowledge emanating from Vedas,
> Should become clear to my mind and I would try my best in my attempt.

> Let Lord Indra, the lord of Devas, Agni who is the Lord of Swaha,
> Lord Yama who is the lord of manes, Varuna, the Lord of water,
> The wind God, Kubhera the God of all wealth,
> The treasure of mercy Lord Shiva, Moon who is the Lord of stars,
> Lord Ganapathi who is the son of Lord Shiva,
> Lord Shiva who is the leader of Pramadhas,
> Lord Sun who is the soul of hearing and speech, the Lord of lands,
> All the beings of this world which move and do not move,
> Should bless me who does not have the support of any one,
> And I salute all of them through my innermost mind.
> My elder brother who is much greater in scholarship to me,
> My teacher who lives with very many disciples,
> Let Rama the teacher and all the chief elders who are my teachers,
> Should always live and bless me from my innermost self.

> (Ramachander, trans.)

Ezhuthachan begins the *Adhyatma Ramayanam* thus, introducing himself as one from the lowest Hindu varna and by invoking the gods and seeking their blessings. The whole text is in what is called Kilippattu format, that is, the narrator of Rama's story is a parrot. It is a literary device he probably adapted from the Old Tamil. Each chapter begins with invoking the archetypal parrot to start telling the story.

> Oh Parrot which is dear to Lakshmi, come here,
> Understand that it is not good to delay things,
> Please tell with interest and great joy,
> The story of Sri Rama further.

(Ramachander, trans.)

It is important to note here that *Adhyatma Ramayanam* is a translation of Ved Vyasa's *Adhyatma Ramayana*, a fourteenth century Sanskrit text that narrates the story of Rama in the Advaita Vedanta framework. These two Ramayanas, containing about 4,000 slokas, are different from the Valmiki's Ramayana, comprising 24,000 slokas, only in the treatment of the subject, but the storyline follows the original. The text portrays Rama as an avatar of Lord Vishnu and presents his every act as having spiritual significance. Sita is portrayed as Maya Shakti, and the Sita Ravana abducts is a shadow of the real one. After his death, Ravana's spirit enters into Rama and attains moksha, liberation. Importantly, throughout the narrative, Rama is shown as the Supreme Being and as the spiritual teacher who delivers sermons on jnana, knowledge, and bhakti, devotion, as the ways of liberation. *Rama Gita*, the song of Rama, which forms a philosophical part of the narrative, something like the Bhagavad Gita in Mahabharata, is a dialogue between Rama and Lakshman, wherein Rama expounds and explains the Advaita Vedanta, the philosophy of non-dualism.

Narsi Mehta
(1414–81)

IT WAS THE DAY NARSI MEHTA AND HIS BROTHER WERE PERFORMING their father's sraadh, a ceremony performed in honour of a dead ancestor. As the guests started arriving for the ceremony, it was discovered that there was a shortage of ghee required for the ritual. Narsi was told to quickly go and get ghee from the market. He went, but on the way saw a group of bhaktas singing bhajans, joined them and forgot all about sraadh and ghee.

This was not the first time he did this. Bhajans threw him into an ecstatic mood, and whatever the circumstance, he would join in without a second thought. The Lord, in whose praise he was singing now, smiled and knew that something had to be done to save his bhakta from trouble. After the bhajans, when Narsi returned home beaming in joy, his wife said, 'Why did you send ghee through your friend? Where were you all this time?'

'You surrender to God and God takes care of you' is a maxim that runs through the stories of all bhaktas. Narsi followed the principle to the letter and to his last days, it is said, he remained in the state of God-intoxication.

Narsi Mehta was born around 1414 to Krishnadas, who held an administrative post in a royal court. They belonged to Nagar brahmin community and lived in Junagadh district in Kathiyawad region of Gujarat. Krishnadas died when Narsi and his brother were very young. The brothers were brought up by their grandmother Jayakumari, a great devotee of Lord Krishna.

It is said Narsi was active and normal like any other child in every way except that he did not speak a word until he was seven. His grandmother was naturally worried about whether he would ever be able to speak. Once, at a temple she regularly visited, she saw a saint and sought his help. She told him about Narsi's problem.

The saint sprinkled holy water from his kamandal, water-pot, and whispered in Narsi's ears, 'Bolo Radhakrishna,' and instantly Narsi said, 'Radhakrishna'.

From a young age, Narsi loved to listen to songs of Krishna leela, the life of Lord Krishna, and participate in kirtans. The more his grandmother tried to distract his mind by giving him some tasks, the more he began to spend time in kirtans. Finally, she decided to get him married, hoping it would make him settle down to normal life. He married Manekbai and in course of time the couple had a son, Shyamaldas, and a daughter, Kunwarbai.

After the children were born, the family expected Narsi to take up a job, but he did not; instead, he continued to lose himself in his songs and kirtans, convinced that Lord Krishna would take care of his family. It was his brother, who was also married by then, who provided for the family. While his brother was indifferent to Narsi's religiosity, his sister-in-law, who believed Narsi was lazy and was taking advantage of his brother's goodness, grumbled and complained and, it is said, often taunted and ill-treated him.

One day, unable to bear the taunts of his sister-in-law, Narsi left home and went into the nearby jungle. In the jungle was an old Shiva temple where Narsi spent seven days in deep contemplation. It is said he had a vision of Shiva, who took him to Krishna, and Krishna told him that reciting his name would be the way out of all his problems. It is interesting to note here that both the Gods, Shiva and Krishna, icons of Shaivism and Vaishnavism respectively, came together to aid and bless Narsi.

The story goes that Narsi returned home and thanked his sister-in-law, because it was her insults that had driven him into the jungle and come upon the darshan of Lord Shiva and Krishna. Then he took his wife and children and walked out of the house. He had no specific plans, just that he had put his entire faith in the Lord. After walking the whole day, as the sun set behind trees, they luckily saw a dharmasala, or resting house, where they were allowed to stay for a night. They slept on empty stomachs and the next day morning his wife broke into a sob, worried about the fate of her children.

Just then, a man came there and recognized Narsi. Some days ago, he had seen Narsi leading a kirtan at a temple. Upon discovering the family's dire situation, he offered one of his houses for their stay. He said he was looking for a devotee who could narrate Hari-katha, the story of Vishnu's incarnations, and it would be a blessing if Narsi could stay at his place and perform the Hari-katha.

Thus, Narsi's family and his devotional pursuits were taken care of. Narsi was now invited by people living in surrounding places, including those from the lower strata of society, to sing kirtans and perform Hari-katha. Narsi was more than happy with these new developments. Though Narsi belonged to the Nagar Brahmin community, he did not believe in the notions of high and low, and cared little for caste rules. But the brahmin community, especially the Nagar Brahmins, took objection to his singing Hari kirtans in the colonies of the lower castes and barred him from their community.

According to another version, the Nagar brahmins despised him because, even though his family belonged to the Shaiva tradition, he took to Vaishnava tradition. Undeterred, Narsi carried on with his devotional service. Though unlettered, he composed hundreds of intense lyrics, which were later collected under the category of sringara, love and beauty, one of the nine rasas, emotional state of mind.

As the years rolled by and his daughter came of age, putting his faith in his Lord, he arranged her marriage. On the seventh day of his daughter's pregnancy, as per the custom known as Mameru, the parents were expected to give gifts and presents to the girl's in-laws. Yet again, it is said, Krishna came to his rescue in the guise of a friend and offered gifts to the family members and the girl's in-laws. Many such miracles mark Narsi's story. 'Mameru Na Pada', depicting how Krishna helped his beloved devotee, is a celebrated song sung to this day in Gujarat.

Years later, his wife and son died and he turned into a wandering poet-saint. He composed hundreds of songs, padas, but did not write them down; they were passed on orally and only written down after about 150 years. In Gujarat, he is known as Adi Kavi, the first poet, and his poetry has had a great impact on Gujarati literature. His song 'Vaishnava Janato Tene Kahiye', which was a favourite of Gandhiji and sung during his prayers, is hugely popular across the country, rendered by prominent singers such as Gangubai Hangal, Pandit Jasraj, Lata Mangeshkar and so on.

> One who is a true devotee of Vishnu
> feels the pain of others,
> does good to others
> without letting pride enter his mind.
> A Vaishnav respects everyone,
> does not speak ill of others,
> keeps his words, actions and thoughts pure,
> sees all equally, rejects greed and avarice,
> respects women as he respects his own mother.
> Though his tongue may tire he will utter no untruth
> and never touch the property of others.
> A Vaishnav is detached from worldly pleasures, lust and anger.
> The poet Narsi would love to meet such a great soul,
> by whose virtue the world is redeemed.

Mahima Dharma

MAHIMA DHARMA IS A UNIQUE SECT IN THAT IT HAS MANY PARALLELS with Jainism, Buddhism, Advaita Vedanta, Virashaivism, Sahajyana and Tantrayana, and yet it has its own indissoluble identity. There is a fine synthesis of Buddhist beliefs such as sunyata, emptiness or void, and rejection of idolatry and the authority of the Vedas; the Jain practice of non-violence and the tradition of fasting at night; the Vedantic notion of Parabrahma as one, formless, non-dual, and the universe as made of or created by Brahma, but without the subsequent idea of maya; and Virasahivism's critique of the caste system and the practice of equality between men and women.

It is not that Mahima Gosain, the founder of Mahima Dharma, and his disciple Bhima Bhois picked these notions from various sources and knitted them together to build a fine philosophy. It's most likely that these different schools of thought were living traditions and were part of the background of these two men, and they used some of these notions to communicate their vision of life. What is important to know, however, is how these two mystics creatively employed these notions, rather than trying to fit them into a particular branch of Indian thought. Let us say that Mahima Dharma is one of the innumerable branches of this great tree called Indian philosophy.

There were two other people who were the probable forerunners of Mahima Dharma. They were Chaitanya Das, who rejected the caste system and idol worship in his work *Nirguna Mahatmya*, and later, Chandramani Das, who further offered a philosophical argument as to why we need to discard the varnashrama dharma and idol worship. However, it was Mahima Gosain, and then Bhima Bhois, who gave it a definite form.

Mahima Gosain
(died 1876)

Gosain's story starts with his appearance on the streets of Puri in 1826. We know nothing about where he came from or his background. It is said he slept on sand and so people called him 'Dhulia Gosain'. People believed him to be a holy person and approached him for solutions to their problems. When his prophecies came true, word spread that there was a yogi in Puri whose blessings could benefit lives. He was invited by the Puri pandits to Mukti Mandap inside the Jagannath Temple for a discussion on spiritual matters. He took an uncompromising stance and talked about non-dual truth, meaning everything is interconnected, or all is one without a second, and the irrelevance of idol worship.

Later, he travelled to different places and lived in hill caves for 12 years. Legend has it that for all these years he survived on water alone, and so people called him 'Nirahari Gosain'. In 1838, he moved to Kapilash Hills in Dhenkanal, Odisha, and there in a cave he immersed himself in yoga samadhi, a state of intense meditation. This was probably when he came into the state of unitary consciousness, where the sense of separation between a person and the world dissolves. On the twenty-first day, a local happened to see him and instantly knew that the stranger in long hair and beard, clad meagrely with balkal, bark, of the kumbhi, a deciduous tree, his whole body aglow with a soothing light, could be none other than a sage. For the next 12 years, the locals served him and offered him fruits, and Gosain came to be called 'Phalahari Gosain'.

Spiritual questers sought him out, seeking his guidance, and gradually a considerable number of disciples grew around him. Sidha Govinda was his first disciple, and Bhima Bhoi, a mystic in his own right, took forward the guru's teaching and turned it into a distinctive sect which came to be called Satya Sanatana Mahima Dharma. After spending 12 years on Kapilash Hills, Gosain, who was now called Mahima Gosain, began to travel with his disciples in Odisha and the neighbouring regions, teaching people to shed their dependence on external aids and move beyond barriers of caste to reach alekha, formless, omnipresent, supreme reality.

After nearly 24 years of teaching this new dharma, he returned to Kapilash Hills. He was around 70 years old when he entered mahasamadhi in 1876. After his passing, Bhima Bhoi, through his writings and meetings with people, played a key role in Mahima Dharma spreading across Odisha and beyond.

Bhima Bhoi

(c. 1850–95)

Bhima Bhoi was a remarkable poet-philosopher who provided a philosophical foundation to Mahima Dharma and gave it a definite shape. His is one of the most significant voices in the history of Odisha's religious thought and literature.

Bhima Bhoi was a legend in his lifetime and several stories, some contradictory to each other, developed around him. As a result, there are different versions about his parents and the time and place of his birth. One thing that is certain is that he was born in a Khond tribe, people of the hills of Odisha state, sometime around 1845 and 1855. And all accounts agree that he had an unhappy childhood. It said that after his father's death, his mother remarried and he was left to fend for himself. In his autobiographical work, *Stuti Chintamoni*, Bhima Bhoi himself stated, 'I wandered in the woods everyday with the cattle. When I was overtaken by hunger and thirst, I drank water from the streams.'

He worked for Chaitanya Pradhan, a village landlord. Besides doing odd jobs, he tended his cattle and took them to the forest for grazing. Even as a young boy, he had a sharp and quick mind with a strong spiritual streak in him. One day, as usual, he took the cows out for grazing and the cows returned home at the fall of dusk, but he wasn't with them. Upon searching, the villagers found him fallen in a dry well. He refused offers of help and said that he would remain there until the Lord, who had caused his fall, himself came to rescue him. The legend recounts that the Lord came there in the form of Mahima Gosain, who lifted him out and then disappeared.

Perhaps this incident is indicative of some deep life-altering experience he underwent. For, after the incident, it is said, Chaitanya Pradhan and other villagers noticed a marked change in his behaviour. He was no ordinary boy, and the Pradhan let him completely free to do what he liked. The employer became his well-wisher and took charge of his well-being. Around this time began Bhoi's quest for truth and career as a poet. It is said he was initiated into Mahima Dharma by Mahima Gosain himself.

Initially, Bhima Bhoi's efforts to spread Mahima Dharma met with resistance and even opposition, since the faith challenged and critiqued many an existing norm, especially the caste hierarchy and idol worship. After Gosain's passing, Bhima Bhoi set up his own ashram at Khaliapali near Sonepur, Odisha. People were drawn to him in thousands by his charming personality and illuminating teaching. There was no distinction between men and women, between the so-called high and low castes. All were welcome to bathe in the glory of God.

He was a religious maverick and perhaps that aspect, too, appealed to many. He did not marry but had close relationships with four women of the ashram and had a son and a daughter from two of them. His spiritual consort, Annapurna, who ran and managed the ashram, was looked upon as a goddess. In fact, both Bhima Bhoi and Annapurna were worshipped as spiritual entities. This practice amounted to idolatry for some, and, along with the fact that he had fathered two children from two women, served to alienate Mahima Gosain's followers at Joranda, Gosain's first ashram.

However, most followers continued to be loyal to Bhima Bhoi and his position as the leader of Mahima Dharma grew from strength to strength, especially in western Odisha. And it is interesting to note here that the Christian missionaries, who planned to take advantage of the split within the followers of Mahima Dharma and woo the people into the Christian fold, could hardly make any headway as Bhima Bhoi's popularity as a new incarnation, as one who would free people from suffering and enable them to experience mahima, glory of God, grew everywhere.

> Boundless is the anguish and
> misery of the living,
> who can see it and tolerate?
> Let my soul be condemned to Hell,
> but let the Universe be redeemed.

It was Bhima Bhoi's rallying cry to free the world from the sorrows of life that appealed to the common people and greatly increased the number of his followers. The lines 'Let my soul be condemned to Hell, but let the Universe be redeemed,' were widely quoted and even displayed prominently in some of the reputed institutions in the country and abroad.

Bhima Bhoi died in 1895. He was 45 years old. After his passing Ma Annapurna became the head of the ashram. The ashram still exists, managed by a board of trustees. Bhima Bhoi Samadhi at Khaliapali is a pilgrim centre today. He was a great poet, composer and philosopher. His palm-leaf manuscripts in Odia were discovered at various places in Odisha and were put together in several volumes, though not all of them have been printed and translated.

As said earlier, Mahima Gosain did not produce any written work; it was Bhima Bhoi who shaped the doctrine of Mahima Dharma as a Yuga Dharma, Religion of the New Age, through his discourses and writings. Here are the salient features of Mahima Dharma:

God is the formless, omnipresent, omniscient Brahma who created the world out of his mahima, radiance, glory. But the absolute is beyond attributes, alekh, indescribable.

This spiritual being is the one and only Guru, accessible to all through bhakti. But this bhakti, or worshipping of the Guru, who is nowhere and everywhere, requires no idols or images, priests and temples. The divine is located in the body, pinda, and it is the replica of the brahmanda, universe.

The Mahima Dharma was against the varnashrama dharma based on caste hierarchy and raised its voice against the prevailing caste system in Odisha. It never distinguished between men and women, higher and lower caste, rich and poor. It believed in the principle of vasudhaivakutumbakam, the whole world as a single family.

Yoga and bhoga, meditation and pleasure, were seen as a unitary movement. There was no absolute difference, or antagonism

between bhakti, devotion, and jnana, knowledge, either. Bhima
Bhoi called it bhakti yukta gyana marga, that is, bhakti is to be
guided by jnana.

Selections from Bhima Bhoi's *Stuti Chintamoni*

My father is the beginningless Lord
My mother is the primal energy
From their union was I born
Gifted with the poetic arts.

~

We are under control of none
Except our Guru, on our heads
We never bear anyone else's command
We move only under the command of our Guru.
We are subject not to kings
Nor to moneylenders
We go wherever our Guru leads
None can stop us.

~

Oh sages and wise people, I speak harsh words,
Unless the woes of the world find some restraint
By the twenty-seventh anka
Listen to my vow.
Touching the waters of Mahanadi
As I sit on its bank, I swear
I will transgress all dharma, I will drink liquor.
I will elope with a Brahmin woman.

~

Endless are the agonies and sorrows of the living.
Who can bear to be witness?

Condemn my life to hell,
But let the world be uplifted.

(Mishra)

~~~~~

Sai Baba of Shirdi
(c. 1838–1918)

THE ELEVENTH CENTURY SAINT-POET OF KARNATAKA, DEVARA DASIMAYYA, once said: 'To the utterly at-one with Shiva... his front yard is the true Banaras.' Indeed, over the ages, sages have asserted that for the one pure at heart and devoted to God, everything is sacred and every place is pervaded with His presence and glory. However, millions of Hindus believe that by going on pilgrimages to holy places and a bath in a holy river, one obtains spiritual merit.

So, one day, Das Ganu, a devotee of Sai Baba, desired to go to the holy city of Prayag and take a dip at the Triveni Sangam, the confluence of the rivers Ganga, Yamuna and the mythical Saraswati. He sought Sai Baba's blessing and approval for doing so. Baba said, 'It is not necessary to go that far to earn your punya (merit). Our Prayag is here, trust me.' Realizing his mistake, Das Ganu prostrated at Baba's feet; Baba gently placed both his toes on Das Ganu's head and out flowed through his toes the holy waters.

Sai Baba himself was a miracle. Perhaps, as in the case of Anandamayi Ma, grace descended on him unasked and transformed him at an early age. Sai Baba was highly revered in his lifetime; he was like a wildflower that grew on the roadside, offering succour to the weary travellers and a glimpse into the mystery of life.

Despite being a well-known figure and living fairly recently, there is no definitive information about the time and place of his birth or his background. We do not even know his real name. Attempts were made to investigate his background and it was said that he was born to a brahmin couple in the village of Pathri, and when he was a little boy, his mother left him in the care of a fakir, who, some years later, put him under the care of a Hindu guru, with whom he stayed for 12 years.

Mhalsapati, the temple priest of Shirdi Khandoba Mandir and his first and close disciple, is believed to have reported that Sai Baba himself told him that he was born to Hindu parents and his mother gave him to a fakir. On another occasion, when asked about his parentage, Sai Baba is also believed to have said, 'I don't remember taking birth. I feel as if I am that which exists forever.' (Osborne, 1957). These words resonate well with what Kabir said once of himself: 'I did not take birth, nor did I dwell in a womb... I am beyond all body, the Infinite and Perfect One.' (Shah, 1977)

Sometime around 1854, Baba appeared at Shirdi, a village in the Ahmednagar district of Maharashtra. He was about 16 years old then. Nobody knew him and he was left to fend for himself. He stayed in Shirdi for three years and then disappeared for a year. He returned in 1858, a year after the Sepoy Mutiny. He did not move around much; rather, he just sat under a neem tree, lost in meditation for hours. At first, the people of the village thought he was a wanderer, perhaps an orphan without a home. But when they observed him sitting in padmasana under the tree day and night, they began to wonder if he was some kind of a religious saint.

One day, he went to the Khandoba Mandir in Shirdi. Mhalsapati saw the young man with flowing hair, clad in a knee-length robe, and welcomed him saying, 'Aao Sai', come Sai, and from then on, he came to be known as Sai Baba. There seemed something profound about the young man, the way he moved and his penetrating eyes. The priest took an instant liking to him. But, it is said, many Hindus of the village initially shunned him when he started wearing a cloth cap in the style of a typical Muslim fakir or a Sufi.

For about five years Sai Baba lived under a neem tree, braving cold, heat and rain. He ate whatever food he came by and remained mostly withdrawn and uncommunicative. At times, he went into the jungle for long hours and then returned to the spot. People did not interfere with his solitary life at first, but in due course persuaded him to take up residence in an old, dilapidated mosque. Gradually, when people were convinced he was a holy person, they started approaching him, seeking solutions to their problems in life.

Sai Baba maintained a dhuni, fire, from which he gave sacred ash and answered their questions pithily. It was found that the sacred ash, vibhuti, he offered, when smeared or sprinkled over the body, had miraculous powers. Soon, like a hakim, he started treating the sick with his ash, and occasionally talked on spiritual matters. He talked about the Ramayana and Bhagavad Gita to Hindus and the Quran to Muslims, and he spoke in parables and allegories and was full of wisecracks.

His fame as a saint with miraculous powers spread in the neighbouring villages and beyond, as far as Mumbai, and numerous people flocked to seek his blessings and solutions to their problems, both physical and spiritual. The old, ruined masjid now turned into an ashram, a spiritual centre, and then into a sacred place of pilgrimage.

Sai Baba was a compassionate saint as much as a harsh critic of religious orthodoxy and the artificial, denominational division between the Hindus and Muslims. He believed that the central message of both Hinduism and Islam was the same: love, service and freedom. Sai Baba himself acknowledged both religions; he chanted the name of Rama and often called out 'Allah Malik hai'.

He rejected the caste system, advising people to lead a moral life and love every living being without any discrimination. His teaching was simple and direct, often in the form of anecdotes and parables, although he could take on even sophisticated Vedantins by way of explaining things in the spirit of Advaita Vedanta. He shunned any kind of religious rituals around him, but loved listening to readings from the Quran, reciting the Al-Fatiha, a seven-verse prayer for the guidance and mercy of God, and listening to bhajans and qawwali accompanied by tabla and sarangi. Sometimes, sitting alone, he enjoyed smoking his hookah.

In his knee-length robe and cloth cap, he looked the picture of a mendicant. He shared food with dogs, which even some of his devotees found distasteful. He spoke in a soft, kind and loving voice, but at times, he would fly into a rage, use foul language and even chase people away. But there was a purpose behind every such act, which dawned upon people only later. There are many stories of him performing miracles such as bilocation, levitation, materialization of objects from nothing, curing the terminally sick, lighting lamps with water, appearing in the form of gods such as Rama, Vithoba, Shiva and so on, depending upon the faith of the devotees.

One story goes like this. One day, Sai Baba was eating with three of his devotees in a masjid when, all of a sudden, he looked up and shouted, 'Stop.' The devotees couldn't figure out why he shouted thus. However, since they were used to such sudden inexplicable outbursts from their pir, they continued with their meal. Lunch over, they cleared the dishes, and just as they all stepped out of the masjid, large chunks of the ceiling came crashing down on the very spot where they were having their meal only a few minutes earlier.

Sai Baba was fond of lights and come evening, he kept earthen lamps burning on the half-walls of the masjid. Once it so happened that upon the instigation of the village pandit, the oil seller told Sai Baba that there was not a drop of oil left in the shop to give him. Unperturbed, Baba returned to the masjid, took a tin box which contained a little oil and poured water into it. He took a few drops of it in his mouth and spat it out into the container. Then he took the tin and poured the contents into the little earthen bowls with dry wicks already in place, and lighted them all. The people around could not believe their eyes. Did Baba really turn water into oil? The lamps kept burning through the night!

The most common miracle he performed almost on a regular basis was with the ash he collected from the fire he kept burning in the masjid. This vibhuti is believed to have cured even incurable diseases. He gave pinches of vibhuti as prasad, divine offering, to people who came for his darshan, and sometimes demanded dakshina, donation or fee, in return. He would collect the money in a bowl and by evening, it is said, he would give it all away to fakirs and needy devotees. Once, a business man offered him a large sum of money. Quite curtly, Baba said, 'No, I want none of it. Go and give it to the woman you have kept at home, she needs it more than me.'

On another occasion, a rich man approached him and requested him for the divine knowledge that would keep him happy forever. Baba said, 'Yes, yes, why not? Nobody returns empty-handed from my door. But there is one condition, that is, one should be worthy enough to acquire it.' The man nodded, beaming with great hope. Baba turned to one of his disciples and asked him to go and get 100 rupees from one Moolji Seth. The order didn't make sense to the disciple, he nevertheless went and soon came back only to say that Moolji Seth was out of town.

So the disciple was sent out into the village but to no avail. Smiling, Baba sent him yet again to another person's house and he came back empty-handed yet again. It was lunchtime and Baba asked the man to share the meal with them. He said he had already eaten and he was now hungry for only spiritual knowledge. After lunch, the man repeated his request. Baba looked up and told him, 'Do you think divine knowledge is something like wealth, that you desire to acquire it now? You didn't want to sit with the people for lunch because you think you belong to a higher caste and it would pollute you. You didn't want to part with a mere hundred rupees when you have lots of it in your bag. Do you think I don't know? Without giving up these attachments to your caste and money, to name and fame, you think you are entitled to divine knowledge. You don't deserve that knowledge. Now get out of this place and never come back.'

Sai Baba was a kind-hearted guru, but he could turn into a fierce sage at times. However, devotees had no doubt that he was God, an avatar, incarnation of God in flesh and blood, who was omnipotent, omniscient and omnipresent. Even hundred years after his death in 1918, he remains one of the most widely revered and worshipped saints by millions of Hindus, Muslims, Zoroastrians, Sikhs and Christians across India today, an incredible figure among the saints and sages of India. There are innumerable Sai Baba temples across India, and in about 20 different countries the world over. The original temple in Shirdi is visited by an average of 25,000 pilgrims a day.

Sri Aurobindo
(1872–1950)

IN 1908, AUROBINDO GHOSE WAS ARRESTED FOR POLITICAL CONSPIRACY and lodged in Alipore Jail. The British government suspected he was the chief murderer of a British official as well as the initiator and secret leader of a group of young nationalist revolutionaries. However, for lack of evidence, the case fell through and he was acquitted and released on 6th May 1909.

In 1910, in a series of articles in the Bengali journal *Suprabhat*, he wrote about his time and the life-altering experience he had during his incarceration. He had thought that during his imprisonment, all bonds of a normal human life would be rent asunder and that for a whole year he would have to live like a caged animal. He had little idea then that his imprisonment would open the door to the higher realm of consciousness and that he would return to the field of action not as the revolutionary political activist Aurobindo Ghose but as a mystic. In his words: 'The British Government intended to cause harm but the result was its opposite. The British Government's wrath had but one significant outcome: I found God.' (Paranjape, 1999)

Here is a brief description of the experience he underwent in the prison that transformed his life forever. One day, while walking through the prison house, he felt a powerful energy enter him and there was a radical shift in his very perception of his surroundings. In his words: 'I looked at the jail that secluded me from men and it was no longer by its high walls that I was imprisoned; no, it was Vasudeva who surrounded me. I walked under the branches of the tree in front of my cell, but it was not the tree, I knew it was Vasudeva, it was Srikrishna whom I saw standing there and holding over me His shade. I looked at the bars of my cell, the very grating that did duty for a door and again I saw Vasudeva. It was Narayana who was guarding and standing sentry over me.' (Purani, 1978)

The profound and moving godly experience set Aurobindo up on the path to his eventual self-realization. Months later, he landed in Pondicherry and made his home there to pursue sadhana. He was a great spiritual empiricist of sorts, who, for about 23 years, probed, tested and experimented into the depths of his own body-mind to bring home what he called the 'Supramental Being'. According to him, the spiritualties of the various religions of the world, the lives and teachings of the ancient seers of India and sages such as the Buddha, Jesus Christ and others had opened up possibilities of attaining higher states of consciousness, building on which, it was time to surge ahead and transform the very human creature into a supramental being and thus create a new world.

Aurobindo Ghose was born in Calcutta (now Kolkata), to Krishna Dhun Ghose and Swarnalata Devi, on 15 August 1872. He studied at King's College, Cambridge, excelled in Classics, Literature and History and topped in Greek and Latin. His father was keen that he enter the Indian Civil Service (ICS) and serve the British Government. Aurobindo was not interested in serving the colonial power; nevertheless, to please his father, he passed the written ICS examination, but shrewdly skipped the horse-riding practical exam to get himself disqualified for the service.

Instead, he joined the Baroda State Service in 1893 and, after working in various departments, took to teaching and eventually became the vice-principal of Baroda College. During this period, he started taking an active interest in the politics of India's independence struggle against British rule, though he worked behind the scenes as his position in the college barred him from overt political activity. He linked up with radical political activists and helped people organize resistance groups in Bengal.

At age 28, he married Mrinalini, the 14-year-old daughter of Bhupal Chandra Bose, a senior official in government service. Double her age, Aurobindo was a man of firm ideas and strong inclination towards revolutionary politics and spirituality. For about 3-4 years they stayed together on and off and then began to drift apart, as Aurobindo became increasingly preoccupied with politics and in running the journals *Karmayogin* and *Dharma*. Between 1906 and 1908, he played an active role in the freedom struggle until he was arrested on charges of plotting and overseeing a bomb attack on a sitting British judge and sent to Alipore Jail. During his incarceration in Alipore Jail, he underwent deep mystical experiences that changed the course of his life forever.

After he was acquitted on all charges and released from jail in 1909, he quit political activism and turned his full attention to yoga. Two years later, he travelled to Pondicherry and settled in a house there to pursue his spiritual sadhana, founding one of the great spiritual movements of modern India. In December 1918, when Mrinalini was preparing to join him in Pondicherry, she succumbed to a severe attack of influenza.

Aurobindo was unique and innovative in his ideas and in the way he challenged some of the central notions of both Western and Indian philosophies. For instance, he reinterpreted the traditional notions of nirvana and moksha as not an end but as a forward movement towards supramental manifestation. He found Shankara's notion of maya problematic and interpreted maya not as something that is unreal or false, but as something that is incomplete, unfinished, and hence imperfect. What one needed therefore was a 'constant heightening and widening' (Sri Aurobindo, 1971) of one's understanding of life, truth and sadhana, which would, eventually, result in the manifestation of the Supramental Being on earth.

In other words, he maintained that it was not enough for individuals to move beyond the bonds of sorrow and become enlightened and perfect, rather they should move beyond individual perfection and work for the collective transformation of humanity. In effect, it was a bodhisattvic ideal to which he added the idea of evolution: according to Aurobindo, the state of a mystic, even a sage, is only a transitory phase and one should move beyond that to bring home the Supramental Being, who will be God, the end-product or fulfilment of evolution on earth.

In mid-1940, Aurobindo suffered from prostatitis and is believed have cured himself. A few years later, the old disease reappeared, and he developed other complications. His condition turned quite critical. On 5 December, 1950, frail of body, Aurobindo died of uraemia and kidney infection. He was 78 years old. The body was laid in a vault under a copper-pod tree, which is where the samadhi stands today.

Aurobindo's Major Works

The Life Divine
Savitri: A Legend and a Symbol
The Synthesis of Yoga
Essays on the Gita
The Ideal of Human Unity
The Human Cycle: The Psychology of Social Development
The Upanishads
Secret of the Veda
Hymns to the Mystic Fire

Teachings

It is true that the subliminal in man is the largest part of his nature and has in it the secret of the unseeen dynamisms which explain his surface activities. But the lower vital subconscious which is all that this psycho-analysis of Freud seems to know,—and of that it knows only a few ill-lit corners,—is no more than a restricted and very inferior portion of the subliminal whole... to begin by opening up the lower subconscious, risking to raise up all that is foul or obscure in it, is to go out of one's way to invite trouble.

~

The spiritual life (adhyatma-jivana), the religious life (dharma-jivana) and the ordinary human life of which morality is a part are three quite different things and one must know which one desires and not confuse the three together.

~

In the past the body has been regarded by spiritual seekers rather as an obstacle, as something to be overcome and discarded than as an instrument of spiritual perfection and a field of the spiritual change... The perfection of the body must be the ultimate aim of physical culture... If our seeking is for a perfection of the being, the physical part of it cannot be left aside; for the body is the material basis, the body is the instrument which we have to use. Sariram khalu dharma-sadhanam, says an old Sanskrit adage,—the body is the means of fulfilment of dharma, and dharma means every ideal which we can propose to ourselves and the law of its working out and its action. A total perfection is the ultimate aim which we set before us, for our ideal is the Divine Life... in the condition of the material universe.

~

True knowledge is not attained by thinking. It is what you are; it is what you become.

~

When mind is still, then truth gets her chance to be heard in the purity of the silence.

~

Life is life--whether in a cat, or dog or man. There is no difference there between a cat or a man. The idea of difference is a human conception for man's own advantage.

~

The existence of poverty is the proof of an unjust and ill-organised society, and our public charities are but the first tawdry awakening in the conscience of a robber.

~

The anarchic is the true divine state of man in the end as in the beginning; but in between it would lead us straight to the devil and his kingdom.

~

The whole world yearns after freedom, yet each creature is in love with his chains; this is the first paradox and inextricable knot of our nature.

~

In order to see, you have to stop being in the middle of the picture.

(Collated from Satprem, *Sri Aurobindo, or the Adventure of Consciousness*; Sri Aurobindo, *The Supramental Manifestation and Other Writings*; and Purani, *The Life of Sri Aurobindo*)

Ramana Maharshi
(1879–1950)

INSIDE THE SRI RAMANA MAHARSHI ASHRAM AT THIRUVANNAMALAI IN Tamil Nadu, adjacent to the Samadhi Hall, is the nearly 100-year-old rectangular room called the Old Hall, where Ramana used to give darshan. It was here that Ramana met and had discussions with countless people who came from the world over to see him, including famous personalities like the British writer and traveller Paul Brunton, the Hindu guru and teacher of yoga Paramahansa Yogananda, the English novelist and short story writer Somerset Maugham, the English writer on spirituality and biographer of Ramana Arthur Osborne, and the sage in rage U.G. Krishnamurti.

It was a place not just for profound discussions, but also a space where children felt free to sit on the couch and engage Ramana in pleasant little talks. Even animals, it is said, had the right to hop in and the birds to fly in and commune with the master. Peacocks felt free to come through the door right up to the couch where he rested, spread their beautiful tails and dance. Squirrels, dogs and monkeys, too, had free access. Many stories illustrate Ramana's love for and special bond with animals.

One day, Ramana read in the newspaper that certain people in vans were going to arrive in Thiruvannamalai the next day in order to catch monkeys for sale abroad for experiments. At the time, the alpha monkey happened to be there, clinging onto the bars of the window beside his couch. Ramana turned to the big fellow and said, 'Did you hear that? It isn't safe for monkeys here right now so you better take your tribe away.' When the vans came the next day, there wasn't a monkey in sight – not one in the whole ashram area or in the town – so no monkey was caught in the whole of Tiruvannamalai.

On another occasion, a group of monkeys from a nearby tamaraind tree grove came to Ramana, carrying a monkey corpse. The story goes that the tamaraind trees gave an unusually rich yield and the contractor took measures to protect the yield from the monkeys, driving them away by shooting stones at them from a catapult. That day, a stone from his catapult hit a monkey on its head so hard, it died on the spot. A large number of monkeys surrounded the corpse and began to wail and lament the death of their relative. Then they took the body to Ramana.

Ramana had been their friend and arbiter. It is said he even settled their internal disputes and acted as an honest broker when rival tribes were having territorial disputes. So, at this time of anger and grief, it was quite natural for the monkeys to bring both the corpse and their complaints to Ramana. As soon as they came near him, they burst into angry cries and tears. Ramana, whose heart registered and mirrored the emotions of those around him, responded to their anguish with tears of his own. Then he told them, 'Death is inevitable for everyone who is born. He at whose hands this monkey died will also meet with death one day. There is no need to grieve. Now go.' Pacified, the monkeys went away, carrying the corpse with them.

Ramana was a Maharshi, one who had come into the highest state of awareness and lived in the non-dual state of being, in tune with the world around him. He did not study any religious texts, let alone the Vedas or the Upanishads, nor did he perform any sadhana as per any religious tradition, yet 'grace' descended upon him and his life was transformed. His look, touch and words changed people. His utterances became the living scripture, the breathing, living Upanishad.

~

Born as Venkataraman Iyer, on 30 December, 1879, to Alagamma and Sundaram Iyer, in Tamil Nadu, Ramana had an ordinary childhood. He had his early schooling in his native town and then at Dindigul, a city situated on a tributary of the Cauvery River in Tamil Nadu. After the sudden death of his father in 1892, his uncle, Subba Iyer, took Venkataraman and his elder brother to his home in Madurai, where

Venkataraman joined the American Mission High School. Unlike his brother, he was not studious, and there was little to show that he was spiritually inclined either. He had probably read the *Periapuranam* (a hagiography on the lives of Nayanars, a group of 63 Shaivite poet-saints) by then, but we cannot be too sure.

However, on 17 July, 1896, a 16 year old Ramana underwent what is called a 'near-death' experience which altered him completely. One day, the young boy was seized with fear of death. He lay down on the floor, stretched his limbs and waited. 'Am I dead?' he asked himself but evidently he was not. In his words, 'It is silent and inert, but I feel the full force of the personality... All this was not dull thought; it flashed through me vividly as living truths which I perceived directly almost without thought process. I was something real, the only real thing about my present state, and all the conscious activity connected with the body was centred on that I. From that moment onwards, the "I" or Self focused attention on itself by a powerful fascination. Fear of death vanished once and for all.' (Osborne, 1970)

After this 'life-altering' experience, he completely lost interest in studies, friends and relations, and fell increasingly into fits of self-absorption. He turned meek and humble in his dealings with people and started visiting temples. One morning, just like that, he left home, took a train, and two days later, reached Thiruvannamalai. Straight he went to the Sri Arunachaleshwara temple, and, joining his palms, he stood before Lord Arunachaleshwara, a form of Lord Shiva. Tears running down his cheeks, he knew there was no going back, he had come *home*. He had his head shaven, threw away the sacred thread and clothes, and tore a strip off his dhoti to serve as kaupina, loincloth.

Absorbed in the Self, he stayed in the 1,000 pillared-hall of the temple for a few weeks before he took shelter in a vault, known as Patala Lingam, on the temple premises, where he spent days immersed in such deep samadhi that he was unaware of the bites of vermin and pests. He had to be carried out and forcibly fed. In 1899, he went up the Arunachala Hill, which is close to the temple, and took residence in

Virupaksha Cave, where he stayed for about 17 years. In 1922, he came down and settled at the foot of the hill – where the present ashram is situated – to live and teach.

Ramana's teaching may be considered as the path of knowledge, or jnana yoga, though he did not call it as such. He let seekers pursue whatever path suited them. However, like all Advaita Vedantins, he emphasized the importance of self-knowledge and awareness in the path to liberation. The teaching of the Upanishads too may be characterized as the way of knowledge aimed at the realization of the oneness of the individual self (Atman) and the supreme Self (Brahman). The Bhagavad Gita considers jnana yoga as the most difficult yet purest path to liberation, best suited for intellectually oriented seekers.

Ramana's teachings sought to answer the question 'Who am I?' which was different from the similar enquiry in the Upanishadic approach, wherein the seeker meditates on the oneness of Atman and Brahman and comes into the awareness that 'I am Brahman—ahama Brahmasmi'. Instead, Ramana suggested that as each thought arises, one should enquire with diligence, 'To whom has this thought arisen?' In his words, 'I rather emphasize *Self-Knowledge* [italics mine], for you are first concerned with yourself before you proceed to know the world or its Lord. The "I am He" or "I am Brahman" meditation is more or less mental, but the quest for the Self of which I speak is a direct method and is superior to it. For, the moment you get into the quest for the Self and begin to go deeper, the real Self is waiting there to receive you and then whatever is to be done is done by something else and you, as an individual, have no hand in it.' (Osborne, 2010)

In 1949, a small nodule appeared below the elbow of Ramana Maharshi's left arm and very soon it flared up and turned into cancer. He was 70 years old at the time. 'There is no cause for alarm,' Ramana said. 'The body itself is a disease; let it have its natural end.' (Cohen, 1998). Though Ramana was unruffled by his diagnosis, his disciples were not ready to see him go. He was subjected to radium therapy and other systems of medications. Nothing helped. Two days before his passing away, he refused all medication. On the evening of 14 April 1950, the devotees hung outside the room where he had been laid and started singing 'Arunachala-Siva'. Minutes after the singing began, outside the hall, from the hill, even down from the streets of the town, hundreds of people later reported to have seen a bright shooting star move across the sky and disappear behind the peak of Arunachala Hill, marking the passing away of Ramana Maharshi.

Teachings

The individual being which identifies its existence with that of the life in the physical body as 'I' is called the ego. The Self, which is pure Consciousness, has no ego-sense about it. Neither can the physical body, which is inert in itself, have this ego-sense. Between the two, that is between the Self or pure Consciousness and the inert physical body, there arises mysteriously the ego-sense or 'I' notion, the hybrid which is neither of them, and this flourishes as an individual being. This ego or individual being is at the root of all that is futile and undesirable in life. Therefore it is to be destroyed by any possible means; then That which ever is alone remains resplendent. This is Liberation or Enlightenment or Self-Realisation.

~

Self-enquiry, 'Who am I?' is a different technique from the meditation – 'I am Siva', or 'I am He'. I rather emphasise Self-Knowledge, for you are first concerned with yourself before you proceed to know the world or its Lord. The 'I am He' or 'I am Brahman', meditation is more or less mental, but the quest for the Self of which I speak is a direct method and is superior to it. For, the moment you get into the quest for the Self and begin to go deeper, the real Self is waiting there to receive you and then whatever is to be done is done by something else and you, as an individual, have no hand in it. In this process all doubts and discussions are automatically given up, just as one who sleeps forgets all his cares for the time being.

∼

There are no stages in Realisation or Mukti. There are no degrees of Liberation. So there cannot be one stage of Liberation with the body and another when the body has been shed. The Realised Man knows that he is the Self and that nothing, neither his body nor anything else, exists but the Self.

∼

It is impossible for you to be without effort. When you go deeper, it is impossible for you to make effort.

∼

Realisation or real awakening are all parts of the dream. When you attain realisation you will see there was neither the dream during sleep nor the waking state, but only yourself and your real state.

∼

Grace is not something outside you. In fact your very desire for grace is due to grace that is already working in you.

∼

Self-reform automatically results in social reform. Attend to self-reform and social reform will take care of itself.

∼

Why should you worry about the future? You don't even know the present properly. Take care of the present and the future will take care of itself.

∼

Preaching is simple communication of knowledge and can be done in silence too.

~

The charred ashes of a rope look like a rope but they are of no use to tie anything with.

(Collated from Osborne, *The Teachings of Ramana Maharshi in His own Words*; and Godman, ed., *Be As You Are: The Teachings of Sri Ramana Maharshi*)

❧

Nisargadatta Maharaj
(1897–1981)

VANAJA NARAYANASWAMI, A BRILLIANT MATHEMATICIAN AND A WELL travelled woman, met Nisargadatta Maharaj in 1978 and became his great admirer. She recorded his conversations in 500 audio tapes and contributed much to preserve and spread Nisargadatta Maharaj's teachings. One day, during a satsang with Nisargadatta, she thought to herself that there should be an ashram for Nisargadatta Maharaj, something similar to Sri Ramana Maharshi Ashram at Thiruvannamalai in Tamil Nadu. Her mother had land in Chennai, perhaps they could build an ashram or a temple dedicated to Maharaj there. Such were her thoughts. Suddenly, Maharaj looked at her and said, 'That is not the solution. There is no point in building an ashram. At the most you can build a temple with a golden statue of me in it. Do you think building it will bring an end to your desires? This will not lead you to the truth.'

Six months before his mahasamadhi, Nisargadatta Maharaj was experiencing severe breathing problems due to his throat cancer. Witnessing his suffering pained Vanaja, so she suggested to Maharaj that she could get an oxygen cylinder, which would help relieve his breathing problems.

Maharaj exploded in anger: 'This consciousness will stay as long it has to stay and go when it has to go. You know that I don't want to prolong this life even for one second. After hearing all my talks I am surprised you are saying this.'

Vanaja was in tears, and feeling bad, she went home. The next day when she went back to meet him, Maharaj exclaimed, 'Oh, you have come again! I thought after my angry outburst yesterday, you will never come back.' (Narayanaswami, 2020)

That was how Nisargadatta Maharaj lived and breathed and talked until his last days. He was a fiery sage of liberating wisdom. Living in the ever-burning present, in the vivid realization of the oneness of reality, he challenged, probed, goaded and guided all those who sought his spiritual advice. 'Consciousness is the same in all,' was his oft-repeated mantra. 'It is the same Consciousness in Lord Krishna, a human being, a donkey, or an ant... There is only one Consciousness... Discard all you are not and go ever deeper...You are Pure Awareness. You are that witness only.' (Maharaj, 1987)

~

Nisargadatta Maharaj, named Maruti Shivrampant Kambli, was born on 17 April 1897 in Bombay (now Mumbai). His parents, Shivrampant Kambli and Parvatibai, were deeply religious people. Shivrampant worked for a merchant at Colaba in Bombay. In 1896, when the plague broke out in Bombay, Shivrampant took his family to his village, Kandalgaon, in the Ratnagiri district of Maharashtra, and turned into a small-time farmer.

Maruti grew up with his two brothers and four sisters in Kandalgaon. He studied only up to class four at a local school and then dropped out. He loved tending cattle and working on the family's land. In 1915, his father died. The income from the land was hardly sufficient for the large, growing family. A year later, Maruti's elder brother left for Bombay in search of a job. Two years later, in 1918, Maruti joined him to support their family back home. He worked as a junior clerk at an office, but after a couple of months he left the job and turned to business, and opened a small general store. The business was good and within a year he had started eight retail shops.

At the age of 27, in 1924, he married Sumatibai and they had three daughters and a son. Outwardly, there was nothing extraordinary about his religious pursuit. Like most traditionalists, he read religious texts, followed the usual religious practices and learnt yogic exercises from a teacher.

In 1933, however, his life changed drastically when his friend introduced him to Siddharameshwar Maharaj, the head of the Inchagiri branch of the Navanath Sampradaya, the tradition of nine holy gurus, in Bijapur district of Karnataka. The Maharaj saw that Maruti was already adept in spiritual matters and initiated him into the path of the Navanath Sampradaya by giving him a 'nama mantra', a sacred utterance centred on the name of a particular god or diety. Thus began Maruti's self-enquiry and spiritual sadhana that eventually led him to the realization of the ultimate truth.

A year after his guru Siddharameshwar Maharaj's death in 1936, Maruti, now Nisargadatta, left Bombay and travelled across India. He gave up his expensive clothes, put on an ochre robe, and with just two small pieces of loin cloth and a coarse woollen robe, began the life of a jangama, wanderer. A year later, he returned a changed man to his family in Bombay. His zest for business having waned, he let go the tottering chain of shops he had maintained all these years, except the original shop, for it was necessary to sustain the family.

Now he followed a strict and regulated routine, spent several hours in meditation, observed religious practices, read spiritual texts such as *Yoga Vashista*, Bhagavad Gita, the Upanishads, *Amritanubhava*, *Dhyaneshwari* and so on.

At his small flat in Khetwadi, Bombay, a mezzanine floor was used for daily chanting, meditation sessions and talks. His instructions happened not so much through talks as through dialogues, through question and answer sessions, most of which were recorded and then later published as books.

He also witnessed the horrible violence and birth pangs of India's independence. He suffered two personal losses during the years 1942–48, first the death of his wife, followed by the death of his daughter, but, unruffled, he carried on with his routine. Soon, spiritual seekers started gathering around him. He gave talks and answered questions in a style plain, direct and uninhibited, which was all his own. In the words of Maurice Frydman, his long-time disciple and friend, he was 'warm-hearted, tender, shrewdly humorous, fearless and true; inspiring, guiding and supporting all who came to him'. (Godman, 2012)

To some, however, he seemed a 'tiger'! David Godman, a close associate, recalled the fiery yet cleansing days with Maharaj thus: 'We all got shouted at on various occasions, and we all got told off from time to time because of things we did or said. We were all a little fearful of him because we never knew when the next eruption would come. We had all come to have the dirt beaten out of us, in the same way that the dhobis [washer-folk] clean clothes by smashing them on rocks. Maharaj smashed our egos, our minds and our concepts on the immovable rock of the Self because he knew that in most cases that was the only way to help us.' (Godman, 2012)

Like Sri Ramana, Nisargadatta too emphasized the importance of self-enquiry, the path of knowledge or jnana yoga, but it was not the only approach to Truth. And so for many he suggested the path of devotion, the bhakti yoga: love of Guru and God, the practice of mantra repetition and singing devotional songs.

In 1951, after a personal revelation from his guru, Siddharameshwar Maharaj, he started to give initiations by way of giving nama mantra. During the course of these talks and conversations, on and off, he smoked beedis, a habit he did not give up until his last days. His words, fiery and cleansing, transformed hundreds of seekers, who now came from far-off places and even from outside the country. He dialogued with the seekers from different walks of life for 25 long years until his death on 8 September 1981, at the age of 84, of throat cancer.

The Teachings

People come here for knowledge. I talk because the words naturally come out. There is no intention behind my talk that you should get knowledge. Others come here because they are in difficulties. I make no determination that those difficulties should go away, but the fact remains that in many cases they do go away. I merely sit here, people come and go, I am not concerned. They come here from long distances because the consciousness feels the need to come here.

~

In the end you know that there is no sin, no guilt, no retribution, only life in its endless transformations. With the dissolution of the personal "I", personal suffering disappears. What remains is the great sadness of compassion, the horror of the unnecessary pain.

~

Realise that every mode of perception is subjective, that what is seen or heard, touched or smelt, felt or thought, expected or imagined, is in the mind and not in reality, and you will experience peace and freedom from fear.

~

You see yourself in the world, while I see the world in myself. To you, you get born and die, while to me the world appears and disappears. There is nothing wrong with the senses, it is your imagination that misleads you. It covers up the world as it is with what you imagine it to be – something existing independently of you and yet closely following your inherited or acquired patterns.

~

Once you realise that the world is your own projection, you are free of it. You need not free yourself of a world that does not exist, except in your own imagination! However is the picture, beautiful or ugly, you are painting it and you are not bound by it. Realise that there is nobody to force it on you, that it is due to the habit of taking the imaginary to be real. See the imaginary as imaginary and be free of fear.

~

Whatever has a form is only limitations imagined in my consciousness.

~

The world is but a show, a make-believe world.

~

Desire and fear come from seeing the world as separate from my-Self.

~

In reality there are no others, and by helping yourself you help everybody else.

~

Ultimately nothing is mine or yours, everything is ours. Just be one with yourself and you will be one with all, at home in the entire universe.

~

To act from desire and fear is bondage, to act from love is freedom.

~

I do not know bad people, I only know myself. I see no saints nor sinners, only living beings.

~

You will receive everything you need when you stop asking for what you do not need.

(Collated from Maharaj, *I am That*; and Powell, ed., *The Nectar of Immortality: Sri Nisargadatta Maharaj's Discourses on the Eternal*)

The Jains

ACCORDING TO THE *HARIVAMSA PURANA* COMPOSED BY ACHARYA Jinasena in 783 CE, king Ikshvaku was the founder of the Ikshvaku dynasty, otherwise called Suryavamsa or Solar dynasty. Interestingly, the lineage of not only Rishabanatha, the founder of Jainism, but also some of the greatest figures of India, such as Harishchandra, Lord Rama, Vashishta, Mahavira and Gautama Buddha are traced to the Ikshvaku dynasty.

Rishabanatha is known as Adinath, First Lord, the first of 24 Thirthankaras of Jainism. The term thirthankara literally means ford maker, since they were teachers who taught people the way to cross over the sea of samsara, escape the cycle of interminable births and deaths. According to some scholars, he lived about 3,000 years ago, say around 1000 BCE, though Jain tradition places him around 3000 BCE. These traditional statistics tend to be mythical; however, we can be fairly sure that Rishaba natha lived in the pre-Vedic period since one of the major Vedas, Yajurveda, mentions his name along with two other thirthankaras. Rishabanatha's son Bahubali is also a much-revered figure in Jainism.

The famous Mahavira, the last of the 24 thirthankaras, has been discussed earlier in the book. Here, we shall consider Bahubali, and two modern Jains, namely, Virchand R. Gandhi and Acharya Chandana.

Bahubali

According to the traditional account, Rishabanatha was born to King Nabhi and Queen Marudevi in the city of Ayodhya. He had two wives, Sunanda and Sumangala, from whom he had 100 sons, including Bharata and Bahubali, as well as two daughters. Legend has it that the news of the premature death of one of the court dancers reminded him of the impermanence of life and that filled with disgust, he gave up the royal life and power to become a monk.

Before renouncing his worldly ties and turning into a wandering monk, Rishaba is believed to have distributed his large kingdom among his 100 sons. Bharata got the kingdom of Ayodhya, Bahubali got Podanapur, Bodhan, a town in the present-day Nizamabad district in Telengana State, and the other 98 sons too got a kingdom each. Rishaba then wandered about for a year and, at Mount Asthapada, also known as Mount Kailash, close to the lake Manasarovar in Tibet, is believed to have attained nirvana. On Gopachal Hill, around the walls of the Gwalior Fort in Madhya Pradesh, are the statues of thirthankaras, among them is one of Rishaba, flanked by figures of yaksha and yakshi, guardian deities, with a bull and nyagrodha tree, banyan or peepal (ficus), as his emblem.

Legend recounts that Bharata desired to become a chakravartin, universal emperor, by extending the domain of his kingdom, which meant either he had to wage wars against and conquer the kingdoms ruled by his 99 brothers or the brothers had to willingly come under his suzerainty. All 98 brothers desisted from going to war with their eldest brother and submitted their kingdoms to him. But Bahubali dared to challenge Bharata, and Bharata had no choice but to declare war against Bahubali and defeat him if he truly wanted to be the emperor of the Indian subcontinent.

'Bahubali' literally means 'one with strong arms'. It is believed that the ancient warrior race was physically larger than people today, and that they lived for several hundred years. Legend has it that both Bahubali and Bharata were vajra-rsabhanaracasamhanana, endowed with such extraordinary physique and strength that no weapon could mortally wound them. Wishing to avoid unnecessary bloodshed, the elders advised the brothers that they should contest between themselves to settle the issue instead of involving their armies in the fight and sacrificing the lives of thousands of soldiers. The brothers agreed to three kinds of contests: eye-fight, which involved staring at each other without blinking, then jala-yuddha, water-fight, and finally, malla-yuddha, wrestling.

Bahubali won all three contests, but the victory gave him no joy. Instead, it filled him with disgust and disillusionment with his own life and the ways of the world. And so Bahubali decided to give it all up then and there. He abandoned his kingdom, severed all worldly ties, shed his clothes and turned into a Digambara monk. And he began to meditate with firm resolve to attain kevala jnana, omniscience.

Bharata was now proclaimed chakravartin, and according to both the Jain and Hindu Puranas, such as *Vishnu Purana*, *Brahmanda Purana* and so on, the Indian subcontinent came to be called Bharatavarsha or Bharata-bhumi after him.

Meanwhile, standing naked and motionless, Bahubali is said to have meditated for 12 years and attained kevala jnana, omniscience or supreme knowledge. According to another version, his sisters who came there to pay their respects noticed that Bahubali, despite attaining the great wisdom, was still not free of his pride. Without giving up his pride, or transcending his ego, there was no way he could enter kevala jnana, the final stage of liberation. 'Get off the elephant,' advised the sisters – comparing his pride to an elephant that everyone could see even though no one mentioned it – and that very instant, realizing his folly, Bahubali is believed to have overcome his pride and finally come into kevala jnana.

Kevala jnana is a state of being analogous to nirvana, where the individual is supposed to have been liberated from the fetters of samsara, of fear, conflict and sorrow. Interestingly, the Buddha sitting still under the bodhi tree, and Bahubali, who came to be known as Gommateshwara, standing absolutely naked, in what is called the kayotsarga pose, in a motionless, meditative state, are the two breathtaking images of nirvana or enlightenment celebrated across India and the world.

In Karnataka alone there are five monolithic statues of Gommateshwara, one each at Gommatagiri in Mysore district, built in the twelfth century CE; at Karkala in Udupi district, built in 1430; at Venur in Dakshina Kannada district in 1604; at Dharmasthala in Dakshina Kannada district in 1973. The tallest among them is the 57 feet Gommateshwara on Vindyagiri Hill at Shravanabelagola in Hassan District, built in 981 CE, by the scions of the Ganga dynasty, about 200 years before Akka Mahadevi, a mystic-poet of Karnataka, would walk naked.

Gommateshwara at Shravanabelagola is also one of the largest free-standing statues in the world. Gommata stands in motionless contemplation, kayotsarga, with vines climbing around his legs. The head sports curly hair ringlets, and large ears (similar to the Buddha's large ears), indicative of the physical changes that occur on attainment of nirvana. The eyes are slightly open, as if he is viewing the world with detachment, and there is a faint touch of a smile at the corner of the lips that express inner calm and intelligence. The shoulders are broad and the arms stretch straight down to the side of his thighs. The male genitals lie limp between the thighs, while the vines encircle both thighs and climb up around both arms. On either side of Gommata stand the nature spirits, yaksha and yakshi.

Once in 12 years, the period of time it took Bahubali to pass through rigorous tapas and attain nirvana, the Mahamastakabhisheka festival is held on the hills, when the Gommata statue is anointed with milk, saffron, ghee, sugarcane juice etc. Thousands of people from across the country and abroad, cutting across religions and sects, gather to witness and participate in the spectacular ceremony. It is, in bold contrast to the celebration of kings and political leaders occupying seats of power, the celebration not of power and glory, but of the act of relinquishing power and of one's awakening into the state of absolute freedom.

Virchand R. Gandhi
(1864–1901)

It is not hard to recall Swami Vivekananda's vibrant presence in turban and orange robes, his eloquent speech, his elucidation of the principles of Vedanta and of Hinduism at the World Parliament of Religions in Chicago in 1893, and the tremendous impact he made in the West.

But we hardly remember the remarkable contributions made by his fellow speakers, namely, Professor G.N. Chakravarti, Annie Besant, Dharmapala and Virchand Raghavji Gandhi. The American public, who had very little knowledge about India, were completely captivated by their profound discourses on the different spiritualties that existed in India. At that time, a thoroughly impressed Chicago editor even wrote, 'We have been for years spending millions of dollars in sending missionaries to convert these men, and have had very little success; they have sent over a few men, and have converted everybody.' (Olcott, 2011)

Just as Vivekananda stood out among the speakers as a fine exponent of Hinduism, Virchand stood out as an exponent of Jainism. The *New York Times* described him as, 'Wearing a turban of yellow, signifying knowledge, and a robe of purple, portraying purity and activity...' while *Buffalo Evening Times* wrote: 'Virchand Raghavji Gandhi preaches the universal brotherhood of man. He is much farther advanced in esoteric philosophy than the Western theosophists, and gives far more lucid explanations of the orient teachings. The Hindu is decidedly the lion of the season.' (Doshi and Hingarh, 2010)

Though Virchand represented Jainism at the World Parliament of Religions in Chicago, he also spoke eloquently on Hinduism and Buddhism and the catholicity of Indian culture in various other forums. In fact, when there were abusive comments on Hinduism and Indian culture, he dared to take on the misguided Christian missionaries who were presenting a distorted picture of India and its religions. Here is how he countered them:

> This platform is not a place for mutual recriminations, and I am heartily sorry that from time to time the most un-Christian spirit is allowed freely here, but I know how to take these recriminations at their proper value. I am glad that no one has dared to attack the religion I represent. It is well that they should not. But every attack has been directed to the abuses existing in our society. And I repeat now what I repeat every day, that these abuses are not from religion, but in spite of religion, as in every other country. Some men in their over-ambition, think that they are Pauls, and what they think they believe. These new Pauls go to vent their platitudes upon India. They go to India to convert the heathens in a mass, but when they find their dreams melting away, as dreams always do, they return and pass a whole life in abusing the Hindus. Abuses are not arguments against any religion, nor self-adulation, the proof of the truth of one's own. For such I have greatest pity.
>
> (Gandhi, 1964)

~

Virchand Raghavji Gandhi was born to Raghavji Tejpalji Gandhi and Mahuva Nagar Sheth, on 25 August, 1864, in Mahuva, near Bhavnagar, in the state of Gujarat. After completing his school education at Bhavnagar, he joined Elphinstone College of the University of Bombay and earned a bachelor's degree in Law with honours in 1884. He was a polyglot who spoke as many as 14 languages, including Gujarati,

Hindi, Bengali, English, Prakrit, Sanskrit and French. At the age of 21, he joined the Jain Association and successfully fought a case against a tax that had been levied on the pilgrims visiting Mount Shatrunjaya Palitana.

In 1893, Virchand's talk on Jainism at the first World Parliament of Religions and his later speeches on the religions of India were much appreciated and widely reported in the media, and he was invited by many institutions in the US to deliver more lectures. Vivekananda, who had become hugely popular for his electrifying speeches on Vedanta, deeply admired Virchand. Impressed by his delineation of Jain philosophy and Indian culture and his strict adherence to vegetarianism in Chicago, in a letter to the Diwan of Junagadh in India, he wrote: 'Now here is Virchand Gandhi, the Jain whom you knew well in Bombay. This man never takes anything but mere vegetables even in this terribly cold climate, and tooth and nail tries to defend his countrymen and the religion.' (Doshi and Hingarh, 2010)

Virchand stayed for two years in the US and one year in the UK. Altogether, he gave 535 lectures on Jainsim, Buddhism, Yoga, Indian systems of philosophy, Indian culture, occultism and spiritualism. His in-depth lectures on the Jain way of life, the Jain code of conduct, the Jain values of non-violence (ahimsa), science of eating and vegetarianism, and the respect for multiplicity of views (anekantvada), in particular, were much appreciated and covered by many newspapers and periodicals. It earned him a huge fan following, and he was felicitated in the US, England, France and Germany with many medals.

It is important to note here that in 1893, decades before India became free from the British rule, talking about economic and political freedom to the American public, this other Gandhi, Virchand Gandhi, declared: '...we are not an independent nation, but if we were a nation in all that that word implies, with our own government and our own rulers, with our laws and institutions controlled by us free and independent, I affirm that we should seek to establish and for ever maintain peaceful relations with all nations of the world.' (Gandhi,

1964) It was a bold declaration which came to pass five decades later. It is no wonder that he was much admired by the luminaries of the times, such as, to name a few, Mahatma Gandhi, Lokmanya Tilak, Mark Twain, Dr Paul Carus, Swami Vivekananda and Govind Ranade.

Virchand made two more visits to the West, in 1897 and 1899. He also founded various organizations, including the Gandhi Philosophical Society in Washington and the School of the Oriental Philosophy and the Jain Literature Society, both in London. In India, he established the Society for the Education of Women in India (SEWI) under whose aegis several Indian women went to the USA for higher studies.

Back home, he attended and participated in the activities of the Indian National Congress. He wrote many articles and books in Gujarati and English on topics such as the need for social and cultural reforms in India, on education of women and so on. He was a big proponent of women's education and rights, and wrote and spoke extensively on the subject. He was quite critical of the 'racism' of Christian missionaries in India and attacked them for misrepresenting Indian religions and the cultural lives of the natives.

It was truly a tragedy that Virchand Gandhi died prematurely of haemorrhaging of the lungs on 7 August 1901 at Mahuwar, near Mumbai. He was only 37 years of age. Years after his death, his admirers in the West mistook Mahatma Gandhi for Virchand Gandhi and wrote to him. To clear the confusion, Mahatma Gandhi had to reply to one such writer from America in 1931. He wrote: 'Madam, I have your letter for which I thank you. You are giving me credit of which I am wholly undeserving. You are thinking of another Mr. Gandhi my name-sake but in no way related to me.' Though sometimes referred to as 'the other Gandhi', Virchand had become famous much before M.K. Gandhi, but the latter would grow into a colossus and eclipse Virchand.

However, Virchand Gandhi and his good work haven't been forgotten. There exist memorials to this remarkable man. In the 1990s, statues of him were installed in Chicago and Mahuva. In 2009, the

Indian Postal Service honoured him by issuing a postal stamp with his image. In 2009, the play *Gandhi Before Gandhi*, based on Virchand Gandhi's life, written by Ashok Parmar and directed by Harin Thakkar, was performed in many parts of India and abroad.

Books by Virchand Gandhi

Jain Philosophy
Yoga Philosophy
The Unknown Life of Jesus Christ
The Life of Saint Iss
Religion and Philosophy of the Jainas
Speeches and Writings of Virchand R. Gandhi, collected and edited by Bhagu F. Karbhari

Quotes from Virchand Gandhi

To that man of high aim whose body, mind and soul act in correspondence, all secrets of nature become revealed to him. He feels within himself, as everywhere, that universal life wherein there is no distinction, no sense of separateness, but all around, all bliss, unity and peace.

∼

This is my country, that is your country, these are the conceptions of narrow souls, to the liberal minded the whole world is a family.

∼

The universe is not for man alone, but is a theatre of evolution for all living beings. Live and let live is its guiding principle. *Ahimsa Parmo Dharmah* – Non-injury is the highest religion.

∼

We preach and practice brotherhood not only of men but of all living beings, not on Sundays only but all the days of the week.

We believe in the law of universal justice. We believe that our present condition is the result of our past actions and that we are not bound by the freak of an irresponsible governor—Judge and Prosecutor at the same time. We depend for our salvation on our own acts and deeds and not on a constituted attorney.

~

In the history of a soul's evolution there is a critical point of the human incarnation that decides for us whether we stay there, go down or progress upwards. There is a knot of worldly desires impeding us; cut the knot by mastering desires and go forward. This done, progress is assured.

~

If a person's mind is controlled by forces of revenge and jealousy, it cannot express love and sympathy. And even if they show love and sympathy to others it will yield no good result. The thought will not be reflected in love but in hate.

(Collated from Doshi and Hingarh; and Gandhi, 1970)

Acharya Chandana (born 1937)

During the Upanishadic period (500–400 BCE), we come across women who, giving up the pleasure and security of married life, took to philosophical study and sadhana and a life of asceticism. They were called brahmavadinis. Gargi Vachaknavi, Vadava Pratitheyi, Sulabha Maitreyi, Romasa and Lopamudra were some of the notable brahmavadinis during the Upanishadic period, though all of them did not give up their family life, for they did not consider it antithetical to their spirituality.

However, this tradition of women taking to the path of spirituality gained considerable momentum when, during Mahavira's time

(599–527 BCE), large number of women walked into the spiritual fold by renouncing the worldly life to become nuns.

As mentioned earlier, Jainism eventually split into two sects, namely, Digambara (sky-clad) and Svetambara (white-clad). The Digambaras decreed that women could not attain Nirvana and so they barred women from the order. But the Svetambaras made no such distinction between men and women aspirants and admitted both into their order, a tradition that continues to this day. However, as in the Buddhist Orders, even in the Jain Orders, sadhvis, nuns, ranked below the monks. For over 2,600 years since the time of Mahavira, the position of acharyas, influential spiritual mentors, was always reserved for male monks, until the day in 1987, a Svetambara Jain sadhvi, a petite figure clad in white, was bestowed with the title 'Acharya Shri' by Pujya Rashtrasant Muniji and Shakuntala became Acharya Shri Chandana. Incidentally, Chandana was also the name of Mahavira's aunt, who was the first nun in Jain history.

Shakuntala was born to Manikchand and Prem Kuwar on 26 January 1937 in Chaskaman village of Maharashtra. She stopped going to school after class three because her maternal grandfather wanted her to become a nun and pursue religious learning instead of secular education. And so, at the age of 14, she was initiated into the Svetambara order of nuns by Jain Sadhvi Sumati Kuwar. Shakuntala took a 12-year vow of silence to study Jain scriptures. In her late twenties, however, in pursuance of knowledge she went on to earn the degrees of Darshanacharya from Bhartiya Vidya Bhavan, Sahitya Ratna from Prayag, and a master's degree from the Pathardi Dharmik Pariksha.

In 1974, at the age of 37, based on the principle of Jainism, she founded the organization Veerayatan – derived from two words – 'Veer' from Mahavira, and 'ayatan', which stands for a holy place. The organization was devoted to seva (service to humanity), shiksha (education) and sadhana (self-development). It was a first Jain organization of its kind, dedicated to promoting service to humanity.

Initially, there was some opposition to the organization from the orthodox sections of Jainism, for they believed that involvement in social work would not help in getting rid of kashayas, passions of anger, greed, ego, deceit and so on, which is necessary for the attainment of moksha.

But others believed that with engagement with society through mana yoga, activity of the mind, vachana yoga, activity of speech, and kaya yoga, activity of body, it is possible to get rid of kashayas and attain purity of mind. To Chandana, however, there was no such contradiction between nirvrutti, cessation of thoughts and action, and pravrutti, engagement with society. In fact, she interpreted the Jain notion of maitri, friendliness and compassion, as love and service of humankind.

In her words, 'Paryushan Parva [literally "abiding and coming together", an auspicious time when Jains fast and take on vows of study] neither belongs to nor is related to any one individual or religion. Two things are important in Bhagvan Mahavir's teachings: the first is protection of the environment and for that you have to accept maitri, friendliness. Only when you become a friend can you protect something or someone; Paryushan Parva is also called Maitri Parva. The second most important teaching is Parasparopagraho Jivanam, [souls render service to one another, or, all life is bound together by mutual support and dependence] — you need earth, water, air, plants and animals for your survival; you make use of everything that nature offers. But you have to remember, just like you take, you should also give back to the earth.'

Veerayatan has centres in Bihar, Kutch, Maharashtra, USA, UK, UAE, East Africa and Singapore. As said earlier, these centres focus on service, education and self-development activities. They run educational institutions, hospitals, and poverty alleviation programmes. Sri Chandana has been honoured for her great service to society and contributions to peace by several national and international institutions. She remains an epitome of compassion in action.

Inspiring Words from Acharya Sri Chandanaji

Religion accepts life in its entirety. To work towards getting rid of any physical or mental suffering is true religion. Service is no different from spirituality, service is spirituality.

~

Tirthankar Mahavir has said that if within a sangha (community) anyone gets unwell, then it is the responsibility of others to take care of the that person, even though it may disrupt their spiritual practices. Foremost is to do seva and this is sadhu's dharma. In the sangha, there are not just monks and nuns but also laymen and laywomen; we are all connected with each other. So if we extend what Tirthankar Mahavir said, then if a layperson is in need within the sangha, then is it not our duty as sadhus and sadhvis to help? Why should spirituality be an obstacle to seva at the time of need by saying that we have no connection with the lay people? If we are linked with the society, then every bit of the society is also ours.

~

When you get hurt in your foot, the hands will not say this is nothing to do with me. No, the pain and discomfort will affect the whole body. In the same way if someone in Society is in need and is in distress, then how can we say we have nothing to do with this? We are all linked together; such distress also affects us and therefore we should help and support. This is the reason for taking this path of seva.

~

Anukampa is that state when seeing pain and the suffering in others, we too feel and experience that pain and suffering, and in doing so our own eyes become moist and saddened. Not only this but just as that person wants to shed this pain and suffering, in the same way there arises within us an immense desire to help and support that person to achieve this. Another very important aspect of anukampa is to share in the happiness of others, to have a feeling of joy when we see or hear of something good that is happening to others, rather than being jealous. That is perhaps a more difficult aspect of anukampa to cultivate within us.

~

The fields of education, medicine, politics and armed forces should have more women. A woman will try to avoid war. Men should work in the fields, construct houses, and do whatever requires hard labour. Women, on the other hand, should take control of professions that require critical thinking... Take the example of Draupadi. When Ashwathama killed Draupadi's sons, Arjuna caught Ashwathama and presented him before Draupadi so that she could take her revenge by punishing him. But Draupadi said "I don't want his mother to cry like I am crying, having lost my children. A mother cannot be so cruel to others."

~

When I was working in Bihar, people would stop me, saying it is not safe to work among Naxalites and dacoits. But then many of them started working with me. They said, "Ma, we can be anything for the world, but we are powerless before your love; please teach our children."

Today our schools are among the best in Bihar, even in Naxal-hit areas. If women channel their power in the right direction, they can transform society. If you give jnana, then people might say that we have had enough, we don't need anymore. But, love is always required; at any stage in your life, you will not say that please don't love me. One attains liberation through selfless service of the less privileged and that is compassion in action.

(Collated from Veerayatan.org/Acharya-Sri-Chandanaji)

Subramania Bharati
(1882–1921)

ONE DAY, SUBRAMANIA BHARATI TOOK HIS FAMILY TO A ZOO AND THERE, in one of the enclosures where lions were kept, they came face to face with an adult lion. Gazing at the lion with wonder, Subramania Bharati is believed to have proudly said, 'Kaatuku raja nee, paatuku raja naan' (you are the king of the jungle all right, but I'm the king of poetry).

He was indeed the king of modern Tamil poetry. But the great irony is that when he died, leaving behind incredible volumes of extraordinary work, not many turned up at the funeral. Evidently, he was quite unpopular, perhaps because he had become an apbrahmana, one who had rebelled against Brahmanical traditions, and had won many enemies in an extremely orthodox society.

Being a staunch critic of the caste system, he threw away his sacred thread, but encouraged some of his Dalit friends to wear the sacred thread to challenge brahminism. He visited Muslim tea shops and spent time talking to the customers who came from all castes and religions, sometimes he went to their houses and ate with them. He broke every Brahmanical rule every single day and in every possible way.

What's more, he was a champion of women's rights and advocated widow remarriages. He was a revolutionary social reformer who stood firmly for an equitable and casteless society. During his lifetime he did not get the recognition he deserved, it was only much later that he was ranked high along with the greats such as Thiruvalluvar, Tholkappiyar, Agathiyar and Ilangovaddigal, and hailed as Mahakavi, a great poet, of Tamil Nadu.

Chinnaswami Subramania Bharati was born to Subramania Iyer and Lakshmi Ammal on 11 December 1882 in the village of Ettayapuram of Tirunelveli district in Tamil Nadu. He lost his mother at the age of five and was brought up by his father. It is said that from a young age, he was musically and poetically inclined, but his father wanted him to learn English, study mathematics and become an engineer. He did not; instead, pursuing his deep interests, he became a poet, journalist and freedom fighter.

But as regards his marriage, complying with his father's wish and the tradition during those days, as a young lad of 15, he married Chellamma, who was eight years younger to him. As his fate would have it, a year later his father too passed away, the family income dried up and he was faced with the prospect of poverty. He escaped the likely hardship by going to Varanasi, leaving Chellamma at her father's place.

There, he spent the next four years under the care of his aunt. He learned English, Sanskrit and Hindi and studied with great interest the texts on Hindu spirituality. Influenced by a Sikh friend, he grew a beard and wore a turban. In 1901, he returned home, beard and turban intact, and started working as the court poet of Raja Ettayapuram of Nayakar family, who were connoisseurs of art. He was not too happy serving the Raja and left the job two years later and started as a Tamil teacher in a school in Madurai. He was 22 years old and eager to explore new horizons of knowledge and experience. Also, by then, he had become a progressive nationalist and was keen to actively participate in the freedom struggle. But his wife, Chellamma, who now lived with him with their two growing daughters, wanted her husband to lead a normal life and take care of his family.

Bharati understood and empathised with his wife's expectation, but he wanted her to understand that life was not just about raising a family well. There was a larger life out there and a social responsibility, it was in fact a greater call, a sacred pledge he needed to fulfil. The conflict and quarrels between the couple at the time must have been exasperating. Giving expression to it, in a state of rage, he wrote:

Scriptures, rites and rituals,
signs, spells and the thali

with these, they murdered me,
fools of men who know no fairness.

(Bharati, 2013)

Bharati left the teaching job in the school and joined a Tamil daily, *Swadeshamitran*, as an assistant editor. In 1905, he attended the All India Congress session at Benaras. Much inspired by the deliberations on the demand for Swaraj, on his way back home, he happened to meet Sister Nivedita, a close associate and follower of Swami Vivekananda. Her views on the emancipation of women, woman as an emanation of Shakti and helpmate of man in building a new world, gave him a vision of a new India, where the nation would be liberated not only from the imperial rule of the British, but also from gender inequality and oppressive social beliefs and practices. He considered Nivedita as his guru and penned a couple of verses in her praise.

The next year, he attended the Congress session at Calcutta, and returning home, he plunged into active journalism with a nationalistic fervour. He edited the Tamil weekly *India* and the English newspaper *Bala Bharatham* and started to publish his poems regularly in the Tamil weekly. The poems ranged from the subject of nationalism and Russian and French revolutions to man-woman relationship and the spiritual relationship between God and man and so on.

In 1907, he attended the historic Surat Congress sessions, along with Chidambaram Pillai and Mandayam Srinivachariar. The radical and moderates within the party clashed in the very first session. While the moderates stuck to their stand on a constitutional approach to issues, the radicals, headed by Bal Gangadhar Tilak, wanted to intensify the struggle against the British rule. The moderates refused to compromise and there was near pandemonium, Tilak was booed and the meeting broke down. Subramania Bharati supported and favoured armed resistance against colonial rule. The British arrested many radical leaders of the Congress, including Tilak, on charges of sedition. In Madras, the proprietor of the weekly *India*, which Bharati edited, was arrested. Faced with the prospect of arrest, Bharati escaped to Pondicherry, which was under French rule.

From the safe environs of Pondicherry, Bharati continued to edit *India* and *Bala Bharatham*, along with a Tamil daily, *Vijaya*, and a local Tamil weekly, *Suryodayam*. During this period, he met many radical leaders, such as Lajpat Rai, V.V.S. Aiyar and Sri Aurobindo, who had all sought asylum under the French government. It was perhaps his association with Aurobindo that inspired him to take up the study of Vedic literature during this time.

This was his most creative period, too, considering the fact that three of his greatest works, *Kuyil Pattu*, *Panchali Sapatham* and *Kannan Pattu* were composed here. He also translated Vedic hymns, Patanjali's *Yoga Sutra* and the Bhagvad Gita from the Sanskrit into Tamil. And this was his most trying period as well. *India* and *Vijaya* were banned in India by the British government. The other journals did not do well either, and with almost no earning, Bharati's family lived in abject poverty.

He lived thus in exile for 10 years, producing great works, spending time with creative minds and suffering a life of extreme hardship. In 1918, he entered India near Cuddalore to meet with some friends and was arrested by the British force. For three weeks he was imprisoned in a jail in Cuddalore before he was released on the intervention of Annie Besant and C.P. Ramaswamy Aiyar, but the imprisonment took a heavy toll on his health. His illness upset his work and with no earnings for almost a year, he struggled with adversity.

In 1919, he began to travel, met M.K. Gandhi and then a year later, he resumed editing *Swadesimitran*. One day, in 1920, when a general amnesty order removed restrictions on his movements, he went to the famous Parthasarathy Temple dedicated to Lord Vishnu, in Triplicane, Madras, to seek the Lord's blessings. But as his fate would have it, he was struck by an elephant which, incidentally, he used to feed regularly at one time. He survived the attack, but his health deteriorated and he died on the morning of 11 September 1921. It was a colossal tragedy that a poet-activist of such intelligence and energy should die at the age of 38. Only a few days before, at the Karungaipalayam Library in Erode, he had delivered a lecture on the topic 'Man is Immortal'. He lived no more physically, but his works remain immortal.

Bharati could not publish his poems in book form during his lifetime. After his death, his wife, Chellamma, founded a publishing house called Bharati Ashramam and started publishing Bharati's poetry. Her elder brother, Appathurai Iyer, assisted her in this endeavour, by way of administering the financial, printing and practical side of publishing. They brought out two volumes of poetry but with no great success. C. Viswanatha Iyer, a close relative of the family, paid a paltry sum of 4,000 rupees and bought the copyright of Bharati's works from Chellamma.

Under a new publishing house, named Bharati Prachuralayam, Iyer published a few more volumes of Bharati's poetry. Three love poems of Bharati on Chellamma appeared for the first time in this new edition. But the name 'Chellamma' was replaced by 'Kannamma', allegedly by Appathurai Iyer. Perhaps he didn't want his sister's personal life to be so openly known to the public. Here are a few lines from one of the poems:

> She is queen among women
> Her beauty is magnificent
> She is the pupil of my eye
> She is the *rati* of my love
> Her words are sweet as music
> Her lips are a fount of nectar.

(Bharati, 2013)

Some of the other love poems tended to be more philosophical than romantic. Bharati believed woman to be a form of Para Shakti, the feminine half of Shiva's own body, worshipped as ardhanareeswar (androgynous form of Shiva and Parvati). To Bharati, love is the all-pervading force that unites all lives and woman is the Shakti that sustains and nurtures human existence. Bharati dreamt of a new world, which he called Kruta Yugam, that would be built and sustained on the cornerstone of love, service, freedom and respect for woman.

In 1949, the government of Madras bought the copyright from Viswanatha Iyer and began to publish Bharati's works. In 1954, the copyright was made public. Bharati's works were then published by many private publishers to huge success. Today, he is considered the father of modern Tamil literature and his revolutionary poetry and prose writings have inspired many a social reformer.

In Tamil Nadu, almost every district boasts of a street named after him, or a statue erected in his honour. In recognition of his contribution to Indian culture, he was considered as India's national poet and in 2004, a portrait of his was unveiled in India's Parliament Hall. His works have been translated into all major Indian languages, as well as a number of European languages, including French, German and Russian.

Bharati's Best-Known Works

Kaṇṇan Pattu (1917; Songs to Krishna)
Panchali Sapatham (1912; Panchali's Vow)
Kuyil Pattu (1912; Kuyil's Song)
Many of his English works were collected in *Agni and Other Poems* and *Translations and Essays and Other Prose Fragments* (1937).

A Selection from Bharati's Works

Rasa – The Key-Word of Indian Culture, that Rasa is the form of Shakti, the feminine aspect of the Supreme Being. For God is two-fold – Being and Energy, Masculine and Feminine, Absolute and Relative, Purusha and Shakti. In the unity of these two aspects, Existence becomes. And in the manifestations of Shakti, Existence moves and acts.

~

The loving wife is Shakti herself, and the state of godliness is attained through her…She is the daughter of Kali, she is the abode of Power (Shakti Nilayam), and she is the heroine of the poet's home! She transforms the meaningless events of everyday life – the empty grind of incidents which destroy the human spirit like thorns that grow in the barren desert – into life's fruitful experiences. She gives life to what is lifeless, shines light on what is dark, and beautifies each occurrence in life – making it meaningful.

~

There is no caste system. It is a sin to divide people on caste basis. The ones who are really of a superior class are the ones excelling in being just, wise, educated and loving. We shall not look at caste or religion. All human beings in this land — whether they be those who preach the Vedas or who belong to other castes — are one.

~

In ancient times, do you think that there was not the ignorant, and the shallow minded? And why after all should you embrace so fondly a carcass of dead thoughts. Live in the present and shape the future, do not be casting lingering looks to the distant past for the past has passed away, never again to return.

~

He who writes poetry is not a poet. He whose poetry has become his life, and who has made his life his poetry — it is he who is a poet.

(Collated from Bharati, *Subramania Bharati: Personality and Poetry;* and Nandakumar, *Bharati*)

~

Unbearable becomes the pain in my heart —
When I think of my people, broken down,
broken by disease in mind and limb.

On the edge of life they always linger;
For countless are the diseases
Of Ignorance and Hunger.
And on treacherous paths to Slavery
like children blind, they would walk behind
strangers from over the sea.
O, Divine Land, blessed by the gods!
O, ancient Mother of Culture and Art!
Thy children today are spineless hordes.

('When I Think Of My People Broken Down')

Jyotirao Phule
(1827–90)

and

Savitribai Phule
(1831–97)

THE LIVES OF JYOTIRAO PHULE AND SAVITRIBAI WERE SO DEEPLY intertwined that it would be impossible to speak about one without talking about the other. They were like two sides of the same coin. They were an ideal couple if there was one, perfect friends and partners in their pioneering educational activities and social work for the marginalized, oppressed women, Dalits and farmers. And at a time when even the shadow of untouchables was considered impure, the couple opened the well in their house for the use of 'untouchables'.

Jyotirao Phule was born in 1827 in Satara district of Maharashtra and belonged to the shudra caste of malis, gardeners. Phule's family specialized in growing and supplying flowers to the court of the

Peshwas. The business was good and the Phules were economically quite comfortable.

Jyotirao's mother passed away when he was hardly one year old and he was raised by his father, Govindrao. He studied in a Scottish missionary school, thanks to his enlightened aunt, Sagunabai, who was keen that he should get an English education. She was a child widow, and as a young woman, she had picked up some English while working as a domestic help in the house of a missionary and was also exposed to Western liberal values.

At age 13, he was married to nine-year old Savitribai.

Savitri was born in Naigaon, a village near Pune, Maharashtra, to Khandoji Nevshe Patil, a shudra by caste. Like most girls of her time, she had no chance of seeking education in a school. Being the eldest child in the family, she did the chores at home and helped her father in the fields. After her marriage and attainment of puberty, on coming to her husband's house, her life changed radically.

Post-marriage, Jyotirao, who was affectionately called Jyotiba, continued with his education. He was a bright and sensitive boy with a great thirst for knowledge. At the missionary school, he mixed with and befriended boys from other castes and developed a taste for books. He read widely on American democracy and the French Revolution and was strongly influenced by American writer Thomas Paine's book, *Rights of Man*. Three experiences revolutionized his outlook on life: his exposure to egalitarian ideas in the missionary school, the books he read, and his visit to a school run for girls by an American missionary in Ahmednagar.

Sometime during this period, he happened to attend the wedding of a brahmin friend, where he was insulted by the relatives of his friend because he belonged to a lower caste. This ugly incident awakened him to the absurdity and cruelty of the caste system.

He now belonged to the incrementally growing members of the English-educated middle class, who had begun to critically examine their religious beliefs and social practices with their newly acquired lens of Western liberal beliefs and values. If some came to believe that a fecund marriage between Western ideas and Eastern values was necessary for the growth and progress of the country, some were of the view that Western education and notions of equality, liberty and justice alone could liberate women and the downtrodden castes from the evils of the Brahmanical caste system and patriarchy.

Jyotiba was convinced that English education, especially for women and lower castes, was of critical importance to bringing about revolutionary changes in society. He encouraged his aunt Sagunabai as well as Savitribai to read and write, and personally coached them. Savitri even took to formal education in Ahmednagar, on completing which she underwent formal teacher's training in Pune.

In 1848, a hundred years before India would become politically independent and overhaul the education system, the young couple – Jyotiba in his twenties and Savitri barely 17 – started their first school for girls at Bhidewada in Pune. The first batch consisted of 25 girls drawn from different castes. Savitri, Fatima Sheikh (her classmate from the teacher's training school), Sagunabai, and a couple of male colleagues worked as teachers.

Over the next four years, they opened 18 schools for lower-caste girls, including children from Mahar and Mang castes, who were considered untouchables. The school's curriculum included science, mathematics and social studies, and did away with religious studies, which, incidentally, formed an important component of the curriculum in schools started by upper-caste groups. The three women teachers mentioned above were the first native women teachers of the country.

This noble task was seen as a provocative act by the upper castes, especially the brahmins, who had dominated the educational field. And these upper-caste people, conspiring to stop Jyotiba from meddling with the 'divinely' ordained caste order, convinced Jyotiba's father, Govindrao, that what his son and daughter-in-law were doing was in violation of Hindu dharma. When Govindrao told Jyotiba to choose between his schools and living in his house, the couple chose their schools and with a heavy heart moved out of the house. They took temporary shelter at Fatima's father, Usman Sheikh's house.

The couple, Savitri in particular, had to face stiff opposition, even torture from the upper castes. As Savitri walked through villages to reach her school, people, instigated by the upper castes, pelted stones and threw cow dung at her. Smiling, Savitri took it in her stride and called out that the stones were like 'flower petals showered' on her and that it only strengthened her resolve to rededicate herself to the education of girl children. Unruffled by the attempts to humiliate and intimidate her, she carried an extra saree with her to change into on reaching the school. One day, a ruffian tried to physically stop her from getting to school. Enraged, Savitri slapped the man and he took to his heels, leaving her alone. Later, a peon was employed to escort her to and from school.

Jyotiba and Savitri inspired and backed each other in their work. There's no doubt Jyotiba nurtured her intellect; however, there's also no doubt that Savitri was a fast learner and a woman of substance. In 1854, she came out with her first collection of poetry, *Kavyaphule*, which was a remarkable feat. In a revolting voice, she addressed the issues of women's oppression and education, casteism and so on. And in a celebratory poem on Jyotiba called 'Dialogue at Dawn', she hailed him as the messiah of the downtrodden.

Money was of utmost importance to run schools and their other social activities, and they could not entirely depend on funds from outside. Jyotiba went into the hardware business and also worked as a contractor for roadworks and bridges. The money he made from his business was used to support their various activities.

Jyotiba was in his forties now, and had become a prominent and influential person in Maharashtra. As a writer, too, he had become a powerful voice. By now, he had published several tracts on the condition of the peasantry, the hegemony of the upper castes, especially of the brahmins in the educational and political and spiritual realms, and how and why their dominance had to be challenged and their ideology questioned. He also wrote an important tract on the life and achievements of King Shivaji, giving subaltern view of history by highlighting the role of marginalized communities. He argued that Shivaji's great victories were possible because of the grit and loyalty of his 'peasant' armies, not because of the so-called ingenuity of his brahmin ministers and advisers, which had been the dominant narrative.

In the 1860s and 70s, the Phules turned their attention to the issue of child marriage and the plight of young widows. More often than not, young girls married to old men became child widows. They were treated as ritually impure and their very sight was a bad omen. Their heads were tonsured and they were forced to wear either white or saffron clothes, in an effort to quell their sexual appeal. However, they often fell prey to the lust of men within the family circle and faced disgrace if they happened to get pregnant as a result. And there were many instances of these child widows committing suicide.

The Phules once organized the barbers to refuse to shave the heads of widows and go on a strike against the inhuman custom. And they invited widows, even brahmin widows, into their home. Pregnant widows, too, were welcome to stay and deliver their child. And they were given the option to stay back or leave, with or without the child. Savitri personally tended to these young women and their little ones with care and love.

Jyotiba's commitment to equality for men and women extended into his personal life too. Even after years of marriage, Jyotiba and Savitri were childless. When Jyotiba was pressured to remarry, in hopes that a new bride might be able to bear him children, he refused, asking, 'What if I am medically responsible for this situation? Would you then allow Savitri to remarry?'

In 1874, it so happened that one evening, when Jyotiba went for a stroll by the river, he saw a woman about to throw herself into the waters. He rescued her and brought her home. She was a brahmin, six months pregnant and a victim of rape. Savitri accepted her with open arms and took care of her. In time, she delivered a male child. The Phules adopted the child, named him Yashwantrao and made him their legal heir.

At the time, there were many social organizations involved in serving the interests of upper-caste people, but none dedicated to the upliftment of the lower castes and women. Precisely for that reason, in 1873, the Phules founded the Satyashodak Samaj, the Society of Truth Seekers, which worked to create a just, caste-less society.

Some Salient Features of the Samaj

- Jyotiba coined the term 'Dalit', which means 'the broken', to apply to all people considered lower caste and untouchables by the brahmins.
- The samaj vehemently condemned the Vedas and other holy ancient texts that upheld varnashrama dharma. And the brahmins were held responsible for framing the exploitative and inhuman laws.
- The purpose of the Satyashodhak Samaj was to decontaminate the society from caste discrimination and liberate the oppressed lower-caste people from the stigmas inflicted by the brahmins.
- People from all religions and castes could become members of the Samaj, which worked to attain equal rights for both men and women from lower castes. Members from Phule's own community, who belonged to the Mali caste, proved to be the leading members and financial supporters for the organization.
- The Samaj opposed idolatry, rejected the need for priests in weddings and campaigned for the spread of rational thinking.
- The Samaj lobbied with the government to promote policies that would benefit farmers and labourers.
- *Deenabandhu*, a Pune-based newspaper, provided the voice for the views of the Samaj.

In 1876, Jyotiba was appointed as municipal council member to the then Poona municipality. He was bestowed with the title of 'Mahatma' on 11 May 1888 in recognition of his selfless services to humanity.

Jyotiba died on 28 November, 1890. He was 63 years old. It is ironical that a controversy should break out at the funeral rites of the man who had consistently fought against orthodoxy, against all forms of oppressive beliefs and practices. While some people wanted Jyotiba's adopted son, Yashwantrao, to light the funeral pyre, others insisted that a male blood relative should do it as per Hindu Law. And it is remarkable and instructive to know that Savitribai put an end to the unnecessary controversy by stepping forward and, bypassing convention, lit her husband's pyre herself.

After Jyotiba's death, Savitribai took over the reins of the Satyashodak Samaj and carried forward its work. In 1893, she presided over the annual session of the samaj. It was a remarkable feat for a woman to chair a session dominated by men. Men and women from the lower castes came out in large numbers when she visited villages in and around Pune. She was not a powerful speaker like Jyotiba, but in her own persuasive eloquence, she drew their attention to the social evils that kept them down and motivated them to educate themselves to improve their lives.

In 1892, her second collection of poems, *Bavan Kashi Subodh Ratnakar*, The Ocean of Pure Gems, was published. In 1897, a deadly bubonic plague spread in the already drought-stricken villages around Nalasopara, Maharashtra. Yashwantrao, now a medical doctor, set up a clinic on the outskirts of Pune. Savitribai worked hand to hand with other volunteers in caring for the patients at the clinic. While serving the plague patients, she was exposed to and contracted the disease herself and died from it on 10 March 1897. She was 68 years old.

The extraordinary lives of Jyotiba and Savitribai, their pioneering work in the field of education and their brave efforts to eradicate untouchability remain an inspirational story to Dalit leaders and public intellectuals and activists involved in the fight against the caste system and patriarchy. In point of fact, Dr Ambedkar's struggle for justice and

Dalit rights, and the social activist of Tamil Nadu E.V. Ramaswamy's Self-Respect Movement, marked a historical continuity of the justice and rights struggles the Phules initiated.

The work done by Jyotiba and Savitri was the first major attempt in Indian history to translate the centuries-old spiritual message of oneness of life into social equality in society. In that sense, it was a bodhisattvic ideal to work for the benefit of all, to create opportunities for all to live a life of dignity and freedom.

Jyotirao Phule's Published Works

Brahmanacha Kasab (1969). On the exploitation of the downtrodden by brahmin priests.

Gulamgiri (1873). A historical survey of the slavery of lower castes.

Shetkaryancha Asud (1883). On exploitation of peasants.

Sarvajanik Satyadharma Pustak (1891). On the need for a universal religion and eradication of blind faiths.

Asprushyanchi Kaifiyat (1893). On the crisis in agriculture and solutions to agrarian problems.

He also wrote plays and powerful articles that ranged from agrarian and labour issues to the politics of the caste system.

Quotes from Jyotirao Phule's Writings:

Without wisdom morals were lost; without morals development was lost; without development wealth was lost; without wealth the Shudras were ruined; So much has happened through lack of education.

~

The education which does not help the common mass of people to equip themselves for the struggle for life, which does not bring out strength of character, a spirit of philanthropy, and the courage of a lion is no education. The real education is that which enables one to stand on one's legs.

~

Both men and women are equally qualified to enjoy all human rights in equal measure. How can anyone then have one standard for women and quite another for lustful, adventurous men?

~

If holy women had written any scripture, then men would not have been able to ignore the due rights of women and they would also not have waxed so eloquent about their own rights. If women were learned enough, then men would never have been able to be so partial and deceitful.

~

In an ideal family, the woman of the house may embrace Buddhism, the man may embrace Christianity, the daughter may embrace Islam, and the son may embrace the Universal Religion of Truth... and all these members would never envy or hate the other persons' religion, rather they would live together in a spirit of love and understanding as the children of God.

(Collated from Keer, *Mahatma Jotirao Phooley: Father of the Indian Social Revolution*)

Excerpts from Savitribai's Poems

Jotiba fills my life with joy
As nectar does a flower...

~

Plentiful rains yield a bountiful harvest
In the garden near the well, fruits and flowers at their best...

~

The yellow champa flower
Of bright turmeric colour

This beauty stands apart
And silently steals my heart

~

Come dear children, it is a beautiful day
I am pleased to greet you all today
And welcome you on this very fine day
Come dear children, come...

~

Just one enemy do we have today
Let's thrash him and drive him away...
Ignorance!
Catch hold of him and thrash him blue
Drive him away from amongst you.

~

The woman from dawn to dusk doth labour
The man lives off her toil, the free-loader
Even birds and beasts labour together
Should these idlers still be called humans?
Rise my brethren, O outcasts, awake and arise!
To escape the bondage of tradition, rise!
O brethren, for knowledge arise!

(Mhatre, trans., 2012)

~

Bal Gangadhar Tilak
(1856–1920)

WRITING ABOUT THE KIND OF EDUCATION THE COUNTRY NEEDED, JYOTIBA
Phule once said that real education should bring out in students

strength of character, a spirit of philanthropy and the courage of a lion. It is amazing to note that Bal Gangadhar Tilak was not only a bright and talented student but also one who, even as a schoolboy, exhibited great character and courage, and these were not attributes instilled into him by school education.

A story goes that in the primary school where Tilak was studying, after the lunch break the teacher entered the classroom and found groundnut shells scattered on the floor. 'Who has thrown these groundnut shells like this?' he demanded, but no one spoke. This angered the teacher and he asked again, 'Speak up, who did this?' No one confessed. The teacher lost his temper and decided to punish the entire class. He began to give each boy two raps on the knuckles with his cane. When Bal's turn came, he did not hold out his hand; instead, he said to the teacher, 'I did not eat the groundnuts. So I will not receive the punishment.'

'Then tell me who ate the groundnuts?' asked the teacher. Bal replied, 'It is said that carrying tales is bad. So I'm sorry, I won't tell.' It was a pity that instead of appreciating the boy's truthfulness and courage, the teacher got extremely annoyed and sent him out of the class. The next day, on receiving a complaint against his son, Bal's father came to the school and clarified that what his son had said was true. Bal was not in the habit of eating anything outside his home and he, the father, never gave his son money to buy anything.

This story has been retold many times to highlight Bal Gangadhar Tilak's courage of conviction from his younger days and the fearless manner in which he lived and eventually became a bold and gritty revolutionary who gave his life for the country's freedom. He was, in fact, the first radical voice in the Indian National Congress, which had existed for only five years when he became an active member. The political struggles he initiated and led, such as the swadeshi movement (boycott of British goods) and demand for swarajya, self-rule, laid the foundation for the non-cooperation movement, swadeshi and Quit

India movement launched by the Congress Party under the leadership of Gandhiji years later.

Tilak was born on 23 July 1856, in a Marathi-speaking, Chitpavan brahmin family in Ratnagiri, Maharashtra. His father, Gangadhar Pant, was a schoolteacher. He lost his mother at an early age and was brought up by his paternal aunt. At the age of 16, Tilak married Tapibai but continued his studies at Deccan College in Pune. After obtaining his degrees in Mathematics and Law, he took to teaching in a private school. In 1880, along with his friends, he co-founded the New English School in Pune with the aim to improve the quality of education and impart nationalistic ideas. Four years later, they set up the Deccan Education Society and started the Fergusson College in Pune. For five years, Tilak taught Mathematics in this college before he took to active politics.

Together with Gopal Ganesh Agarkar, Tilak began to publish two weekly newspapers, one in Marathi, called *Kesari*, the other in English, called *The Maratha*, both geared towards awakening the political consciousness of the people.

He joined the Indian National Congress in 1890 and was not too happy with the soft approach of people like Gopal Krishna Gokhale, who would come to be known as the 'moderates'. The moderates pursued legal and constitutional methods to tackle knotty political issues with the British government and in their plea for self-rule. Tilak, however, wanted the party to adopt extra-constitutional methods in their fight for self-rule and wanted the members to be prepared to go to jail. He also sought to widen the base of the nationalist movement, which had been largely confined to the upper-class at the time. The political movement could gather momentum only if it expanded its base and reached the grassroots level. In view of that, he organized two major festivals in order to unite the people: a festival honouring Lord Ganesha in 1893 and another in 1895, celebrating Shivaji, the seventeenth century founder of the Maratha state. It was a masterstroke.

Ganesha, also known as Vinayaka, Ganapati and Binayak, is worshipped across India as the remover of obstacles, Vigneswara. But pujas and festivities were thus far confined to homes and temples. Tilak brought it out in the public space, and people in Maharashtra responded with great enthusiasm. Melas, cultural fairs, were held in most localities. Tilak arranged lectures on varied subjects touching upon Hinduism and nationalism and thus the festival turned into a platform to reach and organize people around crucial social and political issues. The idea soon caught up and people followed it up in many cities, and in the succeeding years it turned into a pan-Indian phenomenon.

Tilak was now popular as a man of action and this brought him in conflict with the British government. In 1897, an epidemic broke out in Poona, the same bubonic plague during which time, while serving patients, Savitribai Phule contracted the disease and died. In fact, several hundreds lost their lives to the disease. To counter the situation, the government entrusted work to Walter Charles Rand, an assistant collector. Rand used soldiers to vacate people and sanitize their homes. In the commotion that followed, the soldiers ill-treated women and children and acted carelessly by throwing away images and idols of gods.

Months later, the epidemic subsided. In June, Mr Rand and his military escort Lieutenant Ayerst were shot dead by unknown assailants for humiliating Hindu sentiments. Several arrests were made. Shortly before the murders, at the annual celebration of Shivaji Maharaj's ascension to the throne, Tilak had given a speech that recounted Shivaji killing Afzal Khan, the general who served Adil Shahi dynasty of Bijapur, saying: 'In killing Afzal Khan, Shivaji did not commit any sin, because he took his action not to further his own interest but to do public good.' (Pradhan, 1994). This remark was considered by the British government as being supportive of the murderers. Tilak wrote a series of articles in *Kesari*, defending himself and criticizing the government for its paranoia. Nevertheless, Tilak was arrested on the charges of sedition and sentenced to 18 months' rigorous imprisonment. His arrest aroused sympathy all over the country and earned him the title 'Lokamanya', beloved leader of the people. The Congress party members and political activists of every shade came out openly in support of him.

Out of jail after eleven months on conditional bail, Tilak resumed his political work with renewed vigour. He took a radical position in the struggle for swaraj, but he was a conservative when it came to social reforms, which were incongruous with his revolutionary politics. But he justified his stand on the ground that social reforms would distract and divert people's energy away from the political struggle for independence. There was a remarkable blend of the militant political activist and scholar in him. Amidst his political activism, continuing his study of the Vedas and other ancient Sanskrit texts, he wrote the book, *Orion, or, Researches into the Antiquity of the Vedas*. A decade later, in *The Arctic Home in the Vedas*, he argued that Hindus were the successors of the Vedic religion and that the Aryans came from the North Pole.

In 1905, Bengal was partitioned by the British government and Tilak supported and joined the struggle for the annulment of the act. He wrote fiery pieces in *Kesari* to expose the diabolic role of the British in India's economic exploitation. To counter the British power and its economic clout, he initiated what was called a four-point programme: swadeshi (self-reliance), which involved mobilization of manpower and other resources; boycott of British goods and ultimately the foreign rule; education, which entailed starting institutions to spread education among the masses; swarajya, the demand for self-government, which would eventually result in complete independence from the British. These techniques were later deployed by Gandhiji against the British with greater effect.

During this period, he came in direct clash with the moderates within the party, whose approach, he maintained, would take the edge off the political movement in the country. He argued for radical strategies and interacted actively with extremists, such as Aurobindo Ghose, who was then known for his militant political activism. But he did not approve of their approach, either. Aurobindo contended that freedom could be won only through revolution, but Tilak firmly believed that through the four-point programme they could build up a mass base which would play a crucial role in the last stage of their fight for freedom.

In 1907, disputes within the Congress Party reached a flashpoint in the session at Surat, which further widened the gulf between the radicals and the moderates. The government had decided to pass a law to curb the rights of the farmers in Punjab. Lala Lajpat Rai and other leaders of Punjab protested against the proposal and decided to launch an agitation. The government arrested Lala Lajpat Rai and Ajit Singh, the revolutionary nationalist, deported them to Burma and detained them at Mandalay. The moderates dubbed the government's repressive measures a reaction to the rash and reckless acts of the radicals, and they wanted the radicals to move out of the Congress. Tilak vehemently protested the decision. There were bound to be differences of opinion in a political party, and it was foolish to ask the radicals to move out and start their own party. They would never secede from the Congress, which offered a great platform for the struggle for freedom. Why should they?

Then, it so happened that Lala Lajpat Rai was released from Mandalay after five months and Tilak proposed his name for the post of Congress president. The moderates rejected it. They were not ready for a compromise on their constitutional approach to issues, while the radicals, headed by Tilak, deciding to stay within the party, wanted to intensify the struggle against the British rule. When Tilak started speaking at the Surat session, he was booed and a shoe was thrown at him, which narrowly missed the moderate leaders on the dais.

Tilak refused to secede from the Congress, refused to be the cause of the split in the party, and yet he also refused to tread the militant path advocated by the likes of Aurobindo. If they adopted the militant path and the government resorted to extreme repressive measures, the whole movement could get crushed, so he appealed for a middle path. 'Terrorist act would be suicidal,' he pleaded, 'it would do more harm to our struggle. Mangoes are not gathered before they are ripe and if you rush ahead, you get only sour mangoes to eat.' (Pradhan, 1994)

Around this time, the Bengal anti-partition protests flared up. Kingsford, a British judge, came down harshly on the protesters and many young activists were punished ruthlessly, even flogged in public. Two young revolutionaries, Khudiram Bose and Prafulla Kumar Chakravarti, sought revenge for this humiliation. They threw a bomb at a car, in which they mistakenly thought Kingsford was riding. Instead, it killed two English women. After the killing, Prafulla committed suicide, and Khudiram was arrested. Tilak wrote about the misfortune in *Kesari* and condemned the killing, but was equally critical of the repressive measures of the government.

Tilak was arrested on 24 July 1908, on charges of sedition. M.A. Jinnah offered his services as a lawyer, but Tilak decided to defend himself in the court. He spoke for 21 hours in his own defence, pleading innocence. He condemned violence and dubbed it a poisonous tree. He defended the freedom of the press and pleaded for a policy of conciliation, for giving more rights to people to air their views and carry on their fight for freedom, which was within the legal framework.

In spite of his spirited defence, Tilak was sentenced to six years' imprisonment at Mandalay in Burma. While serving his sentence, he lost his wife and worried about his two sons' health and education. He himself was not in good health, being diabetic and past 60, but he kept a strict, disciplined routine. He read books and planned to write books on the history of Hinduism, on nationality, on Ramayana, on the Hindu Law and so on, but could complete only one book, namely, *Gita Rahasya*. In his interpretation of the Bhagavad Gita, he laid emphasis on Karma yoga, or yoga of action, as its central message, over and above the paths of knowledge and devotion.

He was released in 1914, after five years of imprisonment. *Gita Rahasya* was published in 1915, and he plunged back into politics, determined to bring together the different political forces under the aegis of the Indian National Congress for the final battle for swarajya. Two tall cultural and political figures had entered the struggle now, namely, Annie Besant and Mohandas Karamchand Gandhi.

Tilak had lively interactions with both. He appreciated Gandhiji's Champaran Satyagraha to seek redressal for the grievances of the labourers working on indigo plantations. But he was not sure if the technique of Satyagraha could succeed on all fronts of the freedom struggle. Rather, he thought the time was ripe to press for home rule and launched the Home Rule League. It was during this time, that he made the famous, electrifying statement: 'Swarajya is my birthright and I shall have it.'

Through *Kesari*, he appealed to people to take up the good fight, to make a unanimous bid for swarajya. He joined hands with Annie Besant and went on a tour across India, taking the message of home rule to people. In 1918, he went to England to meet with political leaders, members of the Labour Party in particular, and apprise them of the situation in India and convince them of the just demand for self-government. The Labour Party members were sympathetic and promised to make earnest efforts to support India's cause.

During this time, the government passed the Rowlatt Act in India to restrict civil liberties. This evoked sharp reactions even in England, and the Labour Party condemned the act. At Cambridge and Oxford, Tilak spoke to the students about the Indian situation and the government's repressive measures. In India, Gandhiji was gearing up to launch Satyagraha against the despotic act. Returning home in 1919, Tilak plunged into work, organizing people to support and strengthen the Home Rule League, and decided to launch a Congress Democratic Party to intensify the struggle for swarajya. All of a sudden, however, Tilak caught a fever, which developed into pneumonia and turned worse. Prominent doctors of Bombay gathered around his bed in an effort to save him but could not. Tilak died on 1 August 1920. He was 64 years old.

Gandhiji was in Bombay at the time when Tilak was seriously ill. On the night of 31 July 1920, he was still awake in his room when he was informed about Tilak's condition. Mahadev Desai, his secretary, reported later that Gandhiji spent the whole night sitting on his bed, thinking, a lamp burning by his side. And Gandhiji is believed to have said, 'To whom shall I go for advice now in moments of difficulty? I have been working for Swaraj all along, but I have avoided uttering that word. But now it devolves upon me to keep Lokmanya's slogan alive and effective. It must not be allowed to sink into silence. The banner of Swaraj which this brave warrior raised must not be lowered for a moment' (Pradhan, 1994). Next morning, he participated in the funeral rites of the master. A couple of days later, he wrote in *Young India*: 'Lokamanya Bal Gangadhar Tilak is no more. The voice of the lion is hushed. His patriotism was a passion with him. He was a born democrat. For us he will go down for posterity as a maker of modern India.' (Pradhan, 1994)

Quotes from Bal Gangadhar Tilak

Religion and practical life are not different. To take sannyas, renunciation, is not to abandon life. The real spirit is to make the country, your family, work together instead of working only for your own. The step beyond is to serve humanity and the next step is to serve God.

~

The most practical teaching of the Gita, and one for which it is of abiding interest and value to the men of the world with whom life is a series of struggles, is not to give way to any morbid sentimentality when duty demands sternness and the boldness to face terrible things.

~

Progress is implied in independence. Without self-government neither industrial progress is possible, nor will the educational scheme be useful to the nation.

~

If God is put up with untouchability, I will not call him God.

~

You will never reach your destination if you stop and throw stones at every dog that barks…better, keep biscuits and move ahead.

~

Life is all about a card game. Choosing the right cards is not in our hand. But playing well with the cards in hand, determines our success.

(Collated from Pradhan, *Lokamanya Tilak*)

Rammohan Roy
(1772–1833)

SOMETIME IN 1811, RAMMOHAN'S OLDER BROTHER, JAGMOHAN, DIED and his young wife, Alakamanjari, was forced to commit sati. Rammohan was a witness to this horrible incident. The young girl was dressed in her fine wedding outfit, dragged and positioned on the funeral pyre, and, as the brahmin priests chanted their mantras, the pyre was lighted. The girl screamed, while people chanted, 'Maha Sati, Maha Sati,' meaning 'great wife', and she was burned alive with the corpse of her husband. She was hardly 17 years old.

The horrific event left a deep imprint on Rammohan and spurred him into taking up the cause of banning sati and of women's rights. It is said he regularly visited cremation grounds in Calcutta to persuade widows against immolation. He sought the support of prominent Bengalis and wrote articles to condemn the barbaric practice and to show that the Hindu scriptures did not approve of it. In 1818, he wrote a tract against the practice, titled *A Conference Between an Advocate for and an Opponent of the Practice of Burning Widows Alive*. The orthodox Hindu community did not take well his opposition to the practice of sati and rose against him.

He was not only abused in public but, it is said, there were even attempts made to silence him. Hard as it may be to believe today, between 1815 and 1818, the number of sati cases in Bengal doubled from 378 to 838, despite the strong opposition to it by the likes of Rammohan. Undeterred, Rammohan carried on his crusade against sati and the fight for social justice and women's rights. During this struggle he produced two important tracts, namely, *Brief Remarks Regarding Modern Encroachment on the Ancient Rights of Females According to Hindu Law of Inheritance* and *Essay on the Rights of the Hindoos over Ancestral Property According to the Law of Bengal*. In both these tracts he argued for equal rights for women, including the right to remarry and the right to hold property.

It must be remembered here that William Carey, a Christian evangelist, who also wrote a tract against sati, supported the cause of women and played a significant role in the abolition of sati by law. It was of course a long and bitter battle which started around 1814 and lasted fifteen years, till in 1829, the Governor-General of India, Lord William Bentick, passed the Bengal Sati Regulation, declaring the practice of burning or burying alive Hindu widows to be punishable by the criminal courts.

There is no doubt Rammohan was a pioneer of modern Indian renaissance, who not only succeeded in getting the inhuman practice of sati banned, but one who initiated and led the fight for women's rights in the country. The Brahmo Samaj he started in 1828, which was dedicated to social and religious reforms, was the most influential socio-religious movement of the time and it laid the foundation for many a socio-religious organization to emerge and make significant contributions to the making of modern India.

Rammohan Roy was born on 14 August 1772 in a wealthy brahmin family, to Ramakanta Roy, who was a Vaishnavite, and Tarini Devi, a Shaivite, in Radhanagar village of Hooghly district, Bengal Presidency. It is said that at the young age of 14, Rammohan wanted to be a sanyasi, but his mother refused to allow him to do so. His family life was not entirely a happy one. He was married at age nine but his wife died soon after the wedding. His second marriage at age ten lasted for 42 years and the couple had two sons. He married a third time when his second wife died in 1826.

Rammohan was a polyglot. Apart from his mother tongue, Bengali, in which he was well-versed, he learnt English at the age of 22, and then went on to master Sanskrit, Persian and Arabic. He was an Omnist who believed in all religions and studied scriptures of different religions like Hinduism, Islam, Christianity, Sufism and Buddhism.

He entered the services of the East India Company as a clerk in 1805, worked under the Collectorate of Ranpur and eventually became an officer entrusted with the duties of collecting revenues. As an officer visiting different villages, he saw up close the terrible poverty and social backwardness of Bengali society, burdened with beliefs and customs under which women suffered most, especially by practices such as child marriage, polygamy and sati. According to the sati custom, on losing her husband, a woman had to immolate herself at the husband's funeral pyre. This practice was prevalent largely among the brahmin and kshatriya families. Rammohan abhorred this cruel practice, for, more often than not, the women were forced to comply, failing which they were even drugged and dragged to the pyres.

Here is a broad list of the various social, religious and educational reforms he was involved in until his death.

- In 1817, along with David Hare, a philanthropist and educationist, he helped start Hindu College, which revolutionized the education system, and over the years, the college produced some of the best minds in India.

- He supported induction of Western learning into Indian education and in 1822, set up the Anglo-Hindu School, followed by the Vedanta College in 1826, where courses on Indian philosophical doctrines and Modern Western curriculum were offered.

- In 1828, along with like-minded reformists, Ramamohan set up Brahmo Sabha to challenge and fight against social evils, such as sati, polygamy, child marriage and caste system.

- For years, he crusaded vehemently against customs such as sati, child marriage and polygamy. In 1829, the Bengal Sati Regulation or the Bengal Code was passed that prohibited the practice of Sati Daha in Bengal Province, and any individual caught practicing it was liable to be punished.

- He championed the cause of women and fought for property inheritance rights for women.

- He published journals in English, Hindi, Persian and Bengali. *Sambad Kaumudi* (Moon of Intelligence) was the most popular and widely read journal, and covered subjects ranging from social evils to freedom of the press. Under the British rule, any item of news and articles had to be approved by the government. The journal took up the cause of free speech and expression, and rights of the vernacular press.

The Brahma Sabha he set up eventually became Brahmo Samaj and was later led by Devendranath Tagore. It was first conceived as a movement to reform the Bengali brahmin community and then expanded as a movement against social evils such as the caste system and the oppression of women in Hindu society. The society endorsed and propagated the unity of God and strove to revive the philosophical and ethical principles of the Vedanta as found in the Upanishads.

Salient Features of the Brahmo Samaj

- In the beginning, the one Supreme alone existed. He created the whole universe.
- He alone is the God of Truth, Infinite Wisdom, Goodness and Power, Eternal and All-pervading, the one without a second (Ekamevadvitiyam).
- Loving God and doing that which He loves constitute His worship.
- People of every caste or class have the right to worship God.
- There is no need of a symbol for devotion.
- Salvation is impossible without the mercy of God.
- The soul is immortal.
- To have love towards human beings is the supreme religion.
- There is no place for idol worship and animal sacrifice.

Rammohan's religio-philosophical and social outlook was deeply influenced by his study of different religions, especially by the ethical teaching of Christianity, deism of Sufism, liberal and rationalist doctrines of the West, not to mention the philosophy of the Vedas and the Upanishads. The ideals of Brahmo Samaj were in fact a creative blend of emancipatory ideals borrowed from these different streams of faith and philosophy. A great humanist, democrat and a man of action, he would be remembered as the man who laid the foundation for the reform of Indian society.

In 1830, Rammohan travelled to England as an ambassador of the Mughal Emperor, Akbar II, to plead for an increase in the royalty to the emperor and also to ensure the Sati Act would not be overturned. He stayed in England for almost three years and died of meningitis in Bristol before he could return to India. Years later, the British government named a street in Bristol as 'Raja Rammohan Roy Way' in his memory.

Aphorisms

I have now given up all worldly avocations, and am engaged in religious culture and in the investigation of truth.

~

The present system of Hindus is not well calculated to promote their political interests.

~

Truth and Virtue do not necessarily belong to Wealth and Power and Distinctions of Big Mansions.

~

...Women are in general inferior to men on bodily strength and energy; consequently the male part of the community, taking advantage of their corporeal weakness, have denied to them those excellent merits that they are entitled to by nature.

~

Despotic Governments naturally desire the suppression of any freedom of expression which might expose their acts to the obloquy.

~

Free Press is equally necessary for the sake of the Governors and the governed.

(Collated from Shashi and Ahluwalia, *Raja Rammohun Roy and the Indian Renaissance*)

Rabindranath Tagore
(1861–1941)

In 1929, Albert Einstein settled in a wooden villa upon a hill at Caputh, Germany, isolated from unwanted visitors and pestering media correspondents. And here, in the summer of 1930, Rabindranath Tagore came to see him. The conversation between the two Nobel laureates soon veered to the 'nature of reality', an authorized version of which was later published in the magazine *American Hebrew*. Their positions, in a sense, correspond to the three classic positions on the nature of reality: Reality exists independent of the human mind; reality is dependent on the mind; reality is only a construct of the mind.

To put it another way, their positions swung between three views: the dvaita (the world/atman and Brahman are completely distinct entities); visishtadvaita (Brahman is real, it's the ultimate cause; however, it manifests itself in multiple forms in the shape of the world/atman, knowing which we connect with Brahman); and advaita (Brahman is the only reality, and the phenomenal world, perceived by our senses, is illusory; atman and Brahman are essentially the same and it is indescribable).

Einstein: Do you believe in the divine isolated from the world?

Tagore: Not isolated. The infinite personality of man comprehends the universe. There cannot be anything that cannot be subsumed by the human personality, and this proves that the truth of the universe is human truth.

Einstein: There are two different conceptions about the nature of the universe – the world as a unity dependent on humanity, and the world as reality independent of the human factor.

Tagore: When our universe is in harmony with man, the eternal, we know it as truth, we feel it as beauty. The world is a human world – the scientific view of it is also that of the scientific man. Therefore, the world apart from us does not exist; it is a relative world, depending for its reality upon our consciousness.

Einstein: Truth, then, or beauty, is not independent of man?

Tagore: No, I do not say so.

Einstein: If there were no human beings any more, the Apollo Belvedere no longer would be beautiful?

Tagore: No!

Einstein: I agree with this conception of beauty, but not with regard to truth.

Tagore: Why not?

Einstein: I cannot prove, but I believe in the Pythagorean argument, that the truth is independent of human beings. It is the problem of the logic of continuity… The problem however is whether truth is independent of our consciousness.

(Tagore and Einstein, 1930)

Towards the end of this conversation, Tagore maintained that 'truth, which is one with the universal being, must be essentially human; otherwise, whatever we individuals realize as true, never can be called truth.' However, he proceeded to state that according to the Indian philosophy, 'there is Brahman, the absolute truth, which cannot be conceived by the isolation of the individual mind or described by words, but can be realized only by merging the individual in its infinity. But such a truth cannot belong to science. The nature of truth which we are discussing is an appearance; that is to say, what appears to be true to the human mind, and therefore is human, and may be called maya, or illusion.' (Tagore and Einstein, 1930)

It was a long conversation, where they also discussed music and other things too. However, Einstein was quite uncomfortable with the idea that we cannot know the ultimate cause or that the world and our notions of truth are mere mental constructs, although he later did move towards the position that perhaps we may not know the ultimate cause of the universe. Tagore's position was in many ways endorsed or affirmed by modern physics, quantum physics in particular, when some of its scientists, such as Niels Bohr, Martin Rees and so on, concurred that consciousness has an active role in determining what exists, or that the observer determines the physical reality.

Tagore was truly an Acharya, teacher, guide, mentor, who could hold forth about arts, culture, politics and philosophy. The only other person who was looked upon as an Acharya, perhaps even as a Paramacharya, supreme teacher, was Gandhiji. But Tagore was a multifaceted Acharya who could sing and play music, as well as compose songs, plays, short stories, novels; and in his philosophical and political reflections he was quite ahead of his times. It is said he reshaped Bengali literature and music. His writings, especially his poetic work, *Gitanjali*, for which he won the Nobel Prize, have had a remarkable impact on the literary landscape of modern India, and he remains one of the most widely known and appreciated figure in the literary world of all Indian languages across India. He is of course also remembered as the author of two national anthems: India's 'Jana Gana Mana' and Bangladesh's 'Amar Shonar Bangla'.

Rabindra was born in the wealthy and illustrious Tagore family on 7 May 1861 in Calcutta to Debendranath Tagore and Sarada Devi. Debendranath Tagore was a deeply religious man, a philosopher in his own right, and led the Brahmo Samaj after the death of its founder, Rammohan Roy. Debendranath and his wife, Sarada Devi, had 15 children, but not all of them survived. Rabindra was the youngest of 13 surviving children. After his birth, Sarada Devi fell ill and was bedridden, and his eldest sister Saudamini and the maidservants took care of him. Sarada Devi died when Rabindra was about 14 years old. He was old enough to feel the irreparable loss and, years later, in some of his short stories and novels, wrote movingly about mother's tender love.

Rabindra was a wunderkind; he started writing poetry at the age of eight and then eight years later, at 16, he came out with his first collection of poems under the pseudonym 'Bhanusimha', Sun Lion, that made the literary world sit up and take notice of the young talent. Before long, he had published short stories and plays, this time under his real name. He loathed formal education and was tutored by his brother Hemendranath.

It was through home education and travels that he learnt the arts and sciences and literatures and languages. The Tagore family often hosted literary activities, theatre and recitals of both Bengali and Western classical music. His elder brother, Dwijendranath, was a philosopher and poet; another brother, Jyotirindranath, a musician, composer and playwright; his sister, Swarnakumari, a poet and editor. Another brother, Satyendranath, was in the civil service and Rabindra enjoyed travelling with him outside Bengal.

In 1878, Tagore was sent to England to study law at University College, London. His father wanted him to become a barrister, but that was not to be. There, he developed an interest in Shakespeare's works and European musical traditions instead of the study of law. A couple of years later he dropped out of university, returned to Bengal and started publishing his poems, stories and novels. In 1883, at the age of 23, he was married to Mrinalini Devi, who was 12 years younger to him. She joined him in his house when she came of age. The couple had five children but only three survived.

From 1890, the family lived on their ancestral estate in Shelaidaha (presently a region of Bangladesh). It was a vast piece of verdant land and the family owned a luxurious boat. It was here for the first time that Rabindra saw, up close, people living in abject poverty. This was his most productive period too, and he produced around 40 stories, some of which mirrored the heartrending poverty that prevailed in rural Bengal. Many of his famous stories, such as 'The Post Master',

'Kabuliwala', 'Chitrangada', 'The Hungry Stones', 'The Home-Coming', were published during this time.

In 1901, the family shifted base to Shantiniketan, the abode of peace, a guesthouse built on a stretch of 20-acre land his father had bought years ago. With the funds Mrinalini Devi raised by selling most of her wedding jewellery, Tagore started an experimental school here, which followed the traditional gurukula method of teaching, where classes were held under trees rather than in classrooms. The response was heartening, especially from middle-class Bengalis. The school grew from strength to strength and, years later, with the money Tagore received with his Nobel Prize, the school was expanded and renamed Visva-Bharati University, which developed into one of India's most renowned places of higher learning.

Mrinalini Devi had come into the Tagore family without any formal education. Under Tagore and his elder brother, she learnt to read and write Bengali, English and Sanskrit. At Shantiniketan, according to her daughter, Mira, Mrinalini is believed to have translated the *Shanti Parva* of the Mahabharata and *Katha Upanishad* from the Sanskrit into Bengali. In 1902, just when she had started as a writer and translator, she fell seriously ill. Doctors at Calcutta failed to diagnose her disease and she died, leaving Tagore distraught. They had been married for 19 years, and she was barely 30 years old when she breathed her last. Three years later, Tagore's father died, at the age of 88, plunging him in deeper sorrow.

Tagore travelled outside Bengal frequently and was the most widely travelled Indian of his generation. Between 1878 and 1932, over 54 years, he made more than 30 trips to different countries over five continents, and his interactions with people of different cultures and persuasions, including artists, philosophers and scientists, truly deepened his understanding of humanity and its rich heritage. He was a shining example of a cosmopolitan. In 1912, he took his translated poems to England, where the poems were read by noted English poets such as William Butler Yeats, Ezra Pound, Robert Bridges and others.

The poems were published under the title *Gitanjali*, with a preface by Yeats. The book won him the Nobel Prize in 1913. He was Asia's first Nobel laureate and it gained him recognition all over the world.

Between 1916 and 1917, he travelled in Japan and the USA, giving talks and interacting with artists and writers. His talks on nationalism in the West, in Japan and in India, were both scorned and praised. His critique of nationalism, which was foregrounded in his novels such as *Gora*, *Char Adhyay* and *Ghare Baire*, as an 'epidemic of evil', as 'brotherhood of hooliganism' that threaten the growth of 'higher humanity' remains a profound warning against the dangers of the exclusive, faith- and identity-centric nationalism spreading across India today. And his alternative vision of inclusive nationalism, of peace, harmony and spiritual unity of humankind, is more relevant today than ever before.

Gandhi and Tagore shared a certain spiritual affinity, yet they differed from each other and argued over a variety of issues. If Gandhi considered the modern Western civilization driven by greed 'an evil', Tagore thought Western nationalism as a divisive force that led to destructive conflict between people. Both were against centralized political power and believed in individual freedom as something sacred. There were many areas of agreement between them; however, Tagore was quite suspicious of the passion released by the ideas of swaraj, non-cooperation and civil disobedience that seemed like 'pugnacious nationalism' (Tagore, 1961), which could eventually turn destructive. To Tagore, swaraj was not the objective; rather, the fight, he argued, should be for the emancipation of man from the constricted idea of nationalism, winning for all humanity.

But Gandhi did not think of the non-cooperation movement as a threat to universalist values as Tagore feared; rather, he saw it as a step towards the political and moral liberation of India. 'If India is ever to attain the Swaraj of the poet's dream,' he argued, 'she will do so only by non-violent, non-cooperation.' And he assured Tagore that

'Indian nationalism is not exclusive, nor aggressive, nor destructive. It is health giving, religious and therefore humanitarian.' (Tagore, 1961)

It was a great debate between a poet who dreamt of one humanity and an activist who saw India's freedom only as a necessary step towards the attainment of greater freedom and peace for humanity. Spiritually, they were co-workers, but politically, they were rivals, though ones who respected each other deeply. Tagore called Gandhi 'Mahatma', the great soul, the one whose heart bleeds for the poor, and in turn, Gandhi called Tagore 'Gurudev', revered teacher, luminous spiritual guide.

Gandhi and Tagore met for the first time in 1915 at Shantiniketan. Gandhi in his skimpy dhoti, simple kurta and a Kashmiri cap looked a comical contrast to the tall figure with silvery hair and long beard and striking choga, gown, but they struck up a lasting friendship straightaway. The meeting was followed by many others over the next several years. They maintained a regular correspondence through letters, and like good old friends, frankly debated several topics, including truth, freedom, democracy and education.

In 1940, Gandhi and his wife Kasturba visited Shantiniketan. It was the last meeting between the poet and the yogi. At one point during this meeting, Tagore is believed to have asked Gandhi if he would take Shantiniketan under his wing, and Gandhi is believed to have replied, 'Who am I to take this institution under my protection? It carries God's protection because it is the creation of an earnest soul.' (mkgandhi.org)

Tagore's last five years were marked by chronic illnesses. He suffered pain and discomfort from severe uraemia and other complications so much that he could not write. He had lived his dream and become a master of letters, though one other art he very much desired to master but could not was painting. He died on 7 August 1941, aged 80, in the same mansion in which he was brought up. A week before his death, on 30 July 1941, he had summoned his young friend A.K. Sen and dictated his last poem to him:

I'm lost in the middle of my birthday. I want my friends, their touch, with the earth's last love. I will take life's final offering, I will take the human's last blessing. Today my sack is empty. I have given completely whatever I had to give. In return if I receive anything—some love, some forgiveness—then I will take it with me when I step on the boat that crosses to the festival of the wordless end.

(Tagore, 1952)

Selected Quotes and a Poem from Tagore

The idea of the Nation is one of the most powerful anaesthetics that Man has invented. Under the influence of its fumes the whole people can carry out its systematic programme of the most virulent self-seeking without being in the least aware of its moral perversion.

~

According to the Upanishads, the complete aspect of Truth is in the reconciliation on the finite and the infinite, of ever-changing things and the eternal spirit of perfection. When in our life and work the harmony between these two is broken, then either our life is thinned into a shadow, or it becomes gross with accumulations.

~

When old words die out on the tongue, new melodies break forth from the heart; and where the old tracks are lost, new country is revealed with its wonders.

~

All the great utterances of man have to be judged not by the letter but by the spirit — the spirit which unfolds itself with the growth of life in history.

~

Of course man is useful to man, because his body is a marvellous machine and his mind an organ of wonderful efficiency. But he is a spirit as well, and this spirit is truly known only by love.

～

Man is not entirely an animal. He aspires to a spiritual vision, which is the vision of the whole truth. This gives him the highest delight, because it reveals to him the deepest harmony that exists between him and his surroundings.

～

The fish in the water is silent, the animal on the earth is noisy, the bird in the air is singing, but Man has in him the silence of the sea, the noise of the earth and the music of the air.

～

If you shed tears when you miss the sun, you also miss the stars.

～

Life is given to us, we earn it by giving it.

～

We read the world wrong and say that it deceives us.

～

If you shut your door to all errors truth will be shut out.

～

The roots below the earth claim no rewards for making the branches fruitful.

～

He who is too busy doing good finds no time to be good.

～

You can't cross the sea merely by standing and staring at the water.

～

Death is not extinguishing the light; it is only putting out the lamp because the dawn has come.

~

I slept and dreamt that life was joy. I awoke and saw that life was service. I acted and behold, service was joy.

~

Don't limit a child to your own learning, for he was born in another time.

~

Love does not claim possession, but gives freedom.

~

Ekla Chalo Re

If they heed not your call,
walk alone, friend.
If they speak not and are afraid,
If they turn and walk away
O unlucky one, do not be afraid,
trample the thorns under thy tread
and along the blood-lined track
walk alone, friend.
If they do not hold up the light
and the night is long and dark,
do not be afraid, friend.
With thunder flame of pain
ignite thy own heart and let it burn alone.

(Collated from Tagore, *A Tagore Reader*; and Tagore, *The English Writings of Rabindranath Tagore*)

Mohandas Karamchand Gandhi
(1869–1948)

A YEAR BEFORE THE PARTITION OF THE INDIAN SUBCONTINENT, THE Muslim League declared 16 August 1946 as Direct Action Day to assert its demand for a separate Muslim homeland. Jinnah warned, 'We will either have a divided India or a destroyed India', and Calcutta erupted in flames. Within 72 hours more than 4,000 Hindus and Muslims lay dead and over one lakh people were rendered homeless. It was only the beginning of a series of bloody riots that would soon engulf the nation. On 10 October 1946, in Noakhali (in the Chittagong division of Bengal, now in Bangladesh), there was unabated mayhem for about a week. More than 5,000 people were killed, women were abducted and raped, and thousands were forcibly converted.

Gandhi arrived in Noakhali in November and set up his base in a half-burnt house in the village of Srirampur. The route to Srirampur had been deliberately littered with human excrement, shards of glass and brambles, and he had been greeted with shouts and boos and demands for Pakistan. He had never been treated so badly, never before witnessed such a gory riot or heard of forced religious conversions on such a large scale. He was in agony for he knew too well that the massacres in Noakhali could trigger riots in other parts and convert the country into a slaughterhouse, unless they strained every nerve to stem the violence.

It was the moment of truth both for him and the nation at large. And he was on trial, his ideas of truth and ahimsa were on trial. He decided to keep only Nirmal Kumar Bose, a Bengal University professor, and Parasuram as his assistants, while his other associates, including Dr Sushila Nayar, Pyarelal and Mira Behn, were strictly told that they should each stay in different villages, work to stop the killings and conversions, strive to build peace and harmony between the communities and be prepared to die for the cause; they could return home if they didn't find themselves equal to the task.

As for himself, like the male bhaktas all through the ages, who renounced their caste identity, wealth, family pleasure, even their masculinity, to cleanse themselves of any vestigial 'ahamkara', egoism, to make themselves pure and fit for their Lord, he would launch his last and final experiment with truth. It would be a trial through fire that would burn to ashes the last vestiges of his desire and pride, and enable him to become woman – rather, move beyond gender ('god-eunuch' is the term he used), purified and thus worthy of coming face to face with God.

Some biographers would say that there were different Gandhis in the Mahatma: England Gandhi, South African Gandhi, the rebel Gandhi of the 1920s, the revolutionary Gandhi of the 1930s and 40s, and lastly the Noakhali Gandhi who prevented the subcontinent from destroying itself. But at the core of his being was just one Mohan, the ardent seeker of truth, the devoted bhakta who constantly yearned to come face to face with God, and the modern Acharya, who reinterpreted Indian culture and philosophy in the lab of his own body-mind and in the light of the ideals or aspirations of the people of the country and the world at large.

Almost all of Gandhi's biographers have largely focussed on the political Gandhi and depicted his life story as a political saga. The political side of him was naturally the most visible one, and the way he forged the weapon of Satyagraha to fight against British imperialism and social evils was one of a kind and remains an inspiration. However, this narrative, though brief and pointed, will focus on Mohandas Gandhi as one of the questers after truth, in the long line of questers from the time of the Buddha.

Way back in the 1922, when he was arrested on charges of sedition and imprisoned in Yerwada Jail in Pune for six years, Gandhi had started writing his autobiography, *The Story of My Experiments with Truth*. At the very beginning of his story, he declared, 'What I want to achieve, what I have been striving and pining to achieve these 30 years, is self-realisation, to see God face to face, to attain Moksha.' And the only way to find God was to see him in His creation and be one with it. So, leading a religious life, for Gandhi, meant identifying himself with the whole of humankind, which, in other words, meant there was no option of not taking part in politics.

Moksha to Gandhi did not entail disengagement or cutting oneself off from society; rather, the quest for moksha involved constructive engagement with society. A true karmayogi would not renounce society but only the fruits of one's actions. A genuine search for and realization of truth and ahimsa cannot be transacted outside society but within society, in the thick of samsara. For outside society individuals cannot be good and realize the truth; rather, within the praxis of a continuous, tireless search for truth, individual and social health and happiness are made possible.

In effect, his theory of liberation, so to say, entailed liberation from not only historical, political and social oppression and injustice but also from all forms of violence within and without. Once all traces of violence are cleansed, the individual attains moksha and spiritual power, which the likes of Mohammad, Christ and the Buddha possessed. *Patanjali Yoga Sutra* stated that a realized person would have the spiritual power to tame even the wildest animals, let alone win over the most implacable enemies. Gandhi believed it was possible to attain such spiritual power, and with it, he could make Jinnah and Nehru listen to the voice of sanity and prevent Partition.

That was not to be. As a reaction to the killings of Hindus in Noakhali, bloody riots broke out in Bihar towards the end of 1946, and large-scale massacre of Muslims there and in Patna and Bhagalpur brought Partition closer to inevitability. Abandoning his mission in Noakhali, Gandhi went to Bihar to douse the communal flames. Months later, what was regarded as Bharata Khanda, the land of Bharata, was partitioned into India and Pakistan. About a million Hindus, Muslims and Sikhs died in the maddening riots that swept across the borders of the newly born nations.

When Jawaharlal Nehru delivered his famous 'Tryst with Destiny' speech on the eve of India's independence, and while Indians rejoiced in their new-found freedom, Gandhi, who had camped in Calcutta in an attempt to stem the carnage, after spending the day fasting and praying and appealing for peace and harmony between communities, was fast asleep. In the following turbulent months, he focussed all his energy in infusing some sanity in an otherwise maddening house of distrust, deceit, hate, rage and violence.

There had been five failed attempts to assassinate him and he had, in a matter-of-fact tone, talked about his impending death a few times before. He was ready to die for the cause he had lived for and upheld all his life. On the morning of 30 January 1948, he handed over the final draft of his future plan for the Indian National Congress to his aide Pyarelal; in the afternoon, listened to a Gujarati bhajan: *Whether tired or not, O man do not take rest, stop not your struggle...* Nothing would stop him except bullets from an assassin's pistol, he had said once. And so it happened; after the work for the day was done, at the fall of dusk, just as he started for a scheduled prayer meeting, Nathuram Godse fired three bullets into his chest at point-blank range and Gandhi died with the name of 'Ram' on his lips.

~

Mohandas Karamchand Gandhi was born on 2 October 1869 in a Hindu Modh Baniya family in Porbandar, a coastal town in Gujarat. His father served as the diwan (chief minister) of Porbandar state. His first two wives died young, his third wife was childless, and so with her permission, he married Putlibai from a Pranami Vaishnava family. The couple had three sons and a daughter, Mohandas was their last child.

Mohandas went to a local school at Rajkot. Even as a little boy, it is said, he was as 'restless as mercury' and quite mischievous. Perhaps that could be said of many children. There was nothing so extraordinary about his early years to indicate his future greatness. However, we may identify a few incidents, experiences and influences from his early years that probably shaped him into what he became later.

For instance, his childhood fear of darkness and ghosts, against which he wrestled to grow into a fearless person. The classic stories of Shravana, and his unalloyed love and devotion to his parents, and of king Harishchandra, and his absolute commitment to truth even at the cost of his life, made a deep impression on young Mohandas. His mother's fasting and piety, by his own admission, had a hand in forging Satyagraha and fasting as tools of active resistance. His mother was a follower of the Pranami sampradaya, a religious tradition within Vaishnavism, which taught him to respect all religions at an early age. At the Krishna temple where his mother went to offer puja, the priest, in Gandhi's own words, 'used to read from the Muslim Koran and the Hindu Gita, moving from one to the other as if it mattered not which book was being read, as long as God was being worshipped'. (Gandhi, 1927)

In 1883, at the young age of 13, he was married to Kasturba, who was a year older to him. Two years after his marriage, his father died. Many years later, writing about his father's passing in his autobiography, he described with regret the lustful feelings he felt for his young wife, and how he came to abandon his terminally ill father to be with her. For many years, the memory haunted him with terrible guilt, before it turned into a kind of metaphor for man's destructive lust, greed, aggressiveness and violence that had to be transcended in order to build a new Yugadharma nurtured by maternal principle, and in order to attain his own moksha.

In 1888, he went to England for higher studies. He was not a bright student but a serious seeker who exhibited steady learning and tremendous growth. For a brief while he fancied becoming an English man and took lessons in music and dancing, then changed track, joined the London Vegetarian Society, came in contact with members of the

Theosophical Society and was introduced to the study of Christian, Buddhist and Hindu literatures. This is when he read the Bhagavad Gita for the first time and became its ardent follower.

After completion of his course in law, he returned to India and at age 23, tried to establish a law practice in Bombay but failed to perform at the court. Back in his home town, Rajkot, he tried to make a modest career by drafting petitions for litigants only to run afoul of a British officer and discontinue his job. Fortuitous circumstances led him to one Dada Abdullah, a successful businessman in South Africa, who wanted Mohandas to fight a case for his cousin in Johannesburg, and his life changed forever.

Arriving in South Africa in 1893, from an economically comfortable family and respectable Baniya caste, and as a qualified lawyer from London, Gandhi was devastated by the racial discrimination he experienced there. He was thrown out of a train at Pietermaritzburg, kicked and spat at by policemen on streets because he had trespassed on spaces meant for white people. He felt both humiliated and angry and wondered if he should fight for his rights or go back to India. He decided to stay. Gandhi the rebel was born that moment.

The discrimination he faced was a symptom of the deep disease of racial prejudice. He decided he should root out the disease and he suffered hardships in the process. The Abdullah case concluded in May 1894, but he decided to stay on. He helped found the Natal Indian Congress to fight for the rights of immigrant Indians and oppose the newly introduced bill that denied them the right to vote.

Out of his own pain and indignation and the suffering of injustices by the people, he forged Satyagraha, truth force, to fight for the rights of Indians in South Africa. This was an utterly new form of active resistance – which involved defying the black laws through non-violent means and suffering the punishment for doing so. He had, in effect, transposed the passive soul force that women and the marginalized used against injustice into the social and political realms, with far-reaching consequences for both victims and perpetrators of injustice.

This was only the beginning; Gandhi's method of protest was to evolve and take different forms when he organized protests against the British rule in India. In the beginning, however, Gandhi focussed on racial persecution of Indians and ignored the brutal oppression of native Africans. In fact, he objected to Indians being classed with the natives of South Africa. Only years later, seeing through his own racial prejudices, did he begin to sympathize with the cause of the Black people. He supported their struggle but did not take up their issues himself.

He knew John L. Dube, the first president of the South African Native National Congress (1912), whose school was only a mile away from his own rural settlement in Phoenix. They interacted and visited each other on a few occasions and Gandhi introduced Dube to readers of *Indian Opinion*, the newspaper Gandhi had started to build resistance movement against racial discrimination and fight for civil rights for the Indians. Once, he even took Gopala Krishna Gokhale, and Rev. W.W. Pearson, pastor and educator from Britain, to his place in Ohlange, when they both visited South Africa. And Rev. W.W. Pearson is believed to have urged Dube to adopt Satyagraha in their struggle.

In fact, in an interview to *Natal Mercury* in 1909, Gandhi himself had appealed to the Black people and had invited them to 'adopt our methods, and replace physical violence by passive resistance, it would be a positive gain for South Africa. Passive resisters, when they are in the wrong, do mischief only to themselves. When they are right, they succeed in spite of any odds.' (Hunt)

Dube admired Gandhi, and the fearlessness and self-suffering of the satyagrahis in their fight against the black laws, but he chose not to adopt the method of satyagraha, afraid that if the natives ever acted in self-defence and hit back, the British government would completely crush them.

To this day, many believe that the reason Gandhi did not take up the cause of Black people in South Africa and fight for their dignity and rights the way he did for immigrant Indians was because he was a racist. While this was true in the beginning, he did change later, as he matured his thoughts. In his essay 'Gandhi and the Black People of South Africa', the American professor of philosophy James D. Hunt explains it well: 'Gandhi began as a perfectly ordinary intelligent lawyer trying to establish a career. In time he transformed himself into something else. It is that transformation which should interest us. He did fail to change South Africa very much, but in the attempt he learned a great deal, grew in personal stature, and left behind a legacy of resistance to injustice.'

Gandhi was 23 years old when he left India for South Africa, and 44 when he returned in 1915, with a huge reputation as a successful leader. His South African experience would certainly stand him in good stead when he had to lead the freedom struggle in India. However, before that could happen, he needed to understand the ground reality that had changed much during his 21 year absence. So, upon the advice of Gokhale, he went on a long study tour through the length and breadth of the country and returned a changed man.

There is no doubt Gandhi was inspired by Gokhale's philosophy, Tilak's radical politics and the works of Thoreau and Ruskin. His correspondences with Leo Tolstoy and the reading of the Sermon on the Mount influenced him enormously. The image of Jesus on the cross came to symbolize in his mind a satyagrahi's sacrifice and suffering for truth. In his words, 'Of all things I read what remained with me forever was that Jesus came almost to give a new law.' (Gandhi, 1959)

And it was left to him to complete the task by forging that new law, namely, Satyagraha, active resistance against all forms of violence and proven wrongs in society. However, it must be pointed out that he approached these influences creatively from within the crucible of Indian spiritualty, of which he saw himself as both a student and exemplar. He accepted no scripture as ultimate authority, no person as his guru. He walked alone, guided by his own evolving philosophy of satya and ahimsa, and his inner voice, which he regarded as the voice of truth, became his satguru, true guru.

The way he conducted his life in the open, articulated his philosophy and redefined and renewed political ideas, especially some of the classical Hindu concepts (almost turning some of them on their heads), and projected them on to the social and political realms was something unique and his own. His work marked at once both a departure and continuity of Indian philosophy and spirituality.

For instance, the notion of ahimsa, which traditionally meant avoidance of violence or refusal to inflict violence on others, in the hands of Gandhi, gained an activist's meaning: it meant intervention in or engagement with the world to free society from all forms of violence. By introducing ahimsa into the political struggle, he offered an extra-constitutional and extra-legal approach to the struggle that had been stuck in legal and constitutional strategies to win swaraj. Ahimsa appealed to the spiritual psyche of Indians, especially women, and the freedom movement, that had been confined to the Western educated elite in the Congress party, was transformed into a mass movement of enormous scale.

Crucially, ahimsa as a way of conflict resolution provided 'the basis of a respect for the inalienable freedom and the fundamental equality of all citizens united in their concern for truth and peace' (Iyer, 1986). At a deeper level, ahimsa put existence before essence and goodness before truth; further, and more importantly, ahimsa accepted the sacredness of 'the other', indeed, the other as oneself.

Before Gandhi entered the freedom struggle, Tilak and others had identified the concept of swaraj exclusively with political or national independence. Under Gandhi, the term was inflated to encompass social, economic and spiritual freedom as well. Gandhi did not reject tradition but radicalized it by lifting it out of its caste, religious and personal moorings and giving it a larger, liberating purpose and direction. For instance, under him, ashram became a space within society where one not only led an austere life of study, prayer and contemplation, but learnt and developed the art of confronting personal and social evils and engaged in reconstruction of society.

Tapasya, an ancient sadhana for self-realization, which was a self-centred practice, was turned inside out by 'de-centring' the self. Tagore's 'Ekla Cholo Re' and Narsi Mehata's 'Vaishnava Janato' became marching songs, while the Upanishadic notion of abhayam Brahman – Brahman is fearless – became the mantra and armour of a satyagrahi. To the ancient vratas – the disciplines of Patanjali's *Yoga Sutra*, such as satya, ahimsa, asteya, brahmacharya and so on – which had to be practised for self-realization, he added four niyamas, rules, namely, abolition of untouchability, bread labour – that man must earn his bread from his own labour – swadeshi, and respect for all religions.

Gandhi's Rama was not a mythical Rama, and his notion of Ramarajya was not some golden period in the past, nor a a utopia, say, something like the stateless state, but an immanent human potential realizable here and *now*, with ahimsa as yugadharma. Once, expressing the ideal differently, he said: 'I want Khudai Raj [a divine state], which is the same thing as the Kingdom of God on earth, the establishment of such a rajya [state] would not only mean welfare of the Indian people but of the whole world.' (Schouten, 2008)

Gandhi was called a Mahatma, a great soul, but he saw himself as an alpatma, lesser soul. He certainly was not without faults and weaknesses. He himself admitted to having committed Himalayan blunders. He could be harsh and even cruel at times, and expressed his anger and disapproval without reservation. In his ashram dealings on issues of diet, clothing, spinning and brahmacharya or practice of celibacy, he was almost a tyrant.

His relationship with his eldest son, Harilal, remained turbulent till his last days. Harilal never forgave his father for preventing him from going to England for higher studies. By his strict adherence to his ideals, which were not always shared by others, one might argue, he was blind to the feelings, desires and expectations of his near and dear ones, including his co-workers. However, Gandhi never made a fetish of consistency. 'I am a votary of Truth,' he said, 'and I must say what I feel and think at a given moment on the question, without regard to what I may have said before on it. ... As my vision gets clearer, my views must grow clearer with daily practice. Where I have deliberately altered an opinion, the change should be obvious.' (Guha, 2018)

Gandhi was not without critics even during his lifetime. Ambedkar found Gandhi's interpretation of the varnadharma reactionary and alleged that Gandhi never wanted the total abolition of the caste system. If he was really committed to the cause, why did he never keep any fast to end untouchability? The Left dubbed him a crafty politician who favoured the interests of the capitalists and the bourgeois, his non-violence only a crafty means to wean the masses away from the revolutionary path.

Christian missionaries considered him a thorn in their flesh, for he disapproved of religious conversions. He believed in sarvadharma-samabhav, equal respect to all religions, and condemned forcible conversions and conversions of the poor by offering them material benefits. He was critical of Muslim women wearing burkhas, just as he opposed the practice of child marriage, dowry and sati among the Hindus. When some Muslims objected to his comments on Islam and Islamic Law, he said he considered himself to be a good Muslim as he was a good Hindu and equally a good Christian and Parsi and therefore had every right to study and interpret the message of Islam and other religions.

If Muslims who were in favour of Partition viewed him as a shrewd Hindu and a veiled enemy of Islam, the Hindu Right despised him as an apostate who sided with Muslims. Nathuram Godse, who killed Gandhi, stated in his trial that he had to kill him because he had betrayed his Hindu religion and culture, exploited the feelings of tolerant Hindus and made too many concessions to Muslims. By feminizing politics through his ideals of truth and non-violence, Godse believed Gandhi had emasculated India's kshatra dharma, strength, disciplined unity and will to resist evil, and so he had to be put away if

India had to reclaim its past glory. On the day Gandhi was assassinated, sweets were distributed at RSS headquarters and in religious centres run by upper-caste Hindu leaders.

Gandhi was capable of taking instant decisions on crucial issues at crucial times; at the same time, he was slow to change his mind on certain matters, perhaps because he was afraid that if certain issues were not handled carefully, one would divide people and cause conflict and violence. But he did evolve and change over the years and towards the end of his life in particular, his views on certain critical issues took a radical turn.

For instance, till the 1920s he held a rather romantic view of the caste system or varnashrama dharma. He considered it was a form of social classification which was purely functional and did not have any hierarchical connotations, and that untouchability was an aberration, a contemptible abnormal outgrowth in the Hindu social structure. Varnadharma bereft of untouchability, he believed, could promote social harmony and even egalitarian values; unfortunately, the prevalent caste system was a corrupt form of the Vedic system, and the pristine law fell into disrepute and became distorted by rigidity in its observance by the high-caste, orthodox Hindus.

In 1946, however, there was a radical shift in his stance on the caste system. It is important to note here that his interactions and debates with Ambedkar and Ramachandra Rao, a champion of inter-caste dining and marriage, eventually awakened him to the horrors of the caste system. His turning away from the caste system is evident in small but significant episodes. To Ramachandra Rao's prospective son-in-law, Arjuna Rao, a Dalit by birth, he advised, 'You should become like Ambedkar. You should work for the removal of untouchability and caste.' In the mid 1940s, in his weekly *Harijan*, he increasingly wrote about inter-caste marriages, especially between upper caste girls and harijan boys, as the way out of the evils of the caste system: 'If... castes and sub-castes as we know them disappear – as they should – we should [then] unhesitatingly accord the highest importance to marriages between ati-shudras and caste-Hindus.' (Lindley, 1997)

As historian Ramachandra Guha (2018) rightly points out, 'Gandhi is impossible to classify in terms of conventional political categories. Was he a socialist, conservative, liberal or all of these? He was a true original.' Perhaps the best we could say about him is that he was non-modern, non-traditional critical insider, a serious quester after truth, who led an absolutely open life and was open to self-correction. Who knows, he might well have evolved further, especially with regard to critical issues such as the trusteeship theory and capitalist economy, Hindu-Muslim unity, religious conversions, the feudal structures in villages and the problem of the peasantry, if he had not been assassinated in 1948.

Gandhi's life and work have inspired and continue to inspire millions across the world today. Perhaps his equation of satya and ahimsa, truth and non-violence, and his doctrine of Satyagraha were his most original contributions to the world of thought, the relevance of which in the realm of both politics and religion, and in a world that seems to be drifting towards religious fundamentalism and political fascism, has become more important and urgent than ever before.

❧

Ram Manohar Lohia
(1910–67)

The Quit India movement was launched by the Congress Party, led by Gandhi, on 8 August 1942, demanding complete Independence and an end to British Rule. However, the Muslim League, Hindu Mahasabha, Rashtriya Swayamsevak Sangh, Communist Party of India and the princely states opposed the move and kept themselves outside the movement. Gandhi and other Congress leaders were arrested on 9 August 1942. Ram Manohar Lohia and Jayaprakash Narayan went underground, and in hiding, moved from place to place to build support for the movement. However, two years later, on 20 May 1944, both were arrested in Bombay and imprisoned in a dark cell in the Lahore Fort. In 1945, Lohia was sent to Agra Jail. Gandhi and other Congress leaders were released when World War II ended, but not Lohia and Narayan.

During this period Lohia's father, Hiralal, died. Lohia was not allowed to go to his father's funeral. Friends appealed to the British government to release Lohia at least on parole. Lohia did not anticipate this and asked his friends why they had to petition the government for his parole. 'So that you could go and pay tribute to your father,' they said. Lohia, however, did not expect any mercy from the despotic government. He considered it an honour to be imprisoned in the fight for India's independence, and reminded his friends that his late father, himself a freedom fighter, would have thought so too. 'Do not name tribute as an escape from duty. I do not want anyone's favour. My father kept fighting for his ideals all his life. How can I pay tribute to his ideals by rejecting them, by escaping from duty? No. I will pay homage to my father from here while following my ideals. It is not acceptable for me to seek sympathy from a government that has to end its tyranny and quit India.' (Kelkar, 2009)

That was Ram Manohar Lohia, a heretic among radicals. A political activist and a public intellectual of the highest order, who inspired and drew thousands of young writers, activists and artists into the struggle for a just and equal society. He principally spoke in Hindi, but knew English, French and German very well and was quite proficient in Bengali. A man of incisive logic and sharp intellect, fearless and thorough in whatever task he performed, a votary of absolute equality and a socialist to the core. Next only to Gandhi, Lohia has left an indelible mark on the politics, arts and culture of the country.

~

Ram Manohar Lohia was born on 23 March 1910, in a Marwari family in Faizabad, Uttar Pradesh, to Hiralal and Chandri. There was no trace of the typical Marwari talent for business in him, although his opponents in political circles uncharitably joked about him as 'the son of a moneylender Marwari'. He lost his mother at quite a young age and Hiralal, who never married again, brought him up.

The family had been in the hardware trade for generations, but Lohia had no appetite for business. Perhaps, this was the influence of his father, Hiralal, who lent support to the Congress in the freedom struggle and eventually left the family business and turned into an active freedom fighter.

Even as a school-going boy, Lohia was interested in political issues and attended the Congress political meetings. In 1930, when Gandhiji launched his Salt Satyagraha, Lohia was 20 years old and was so inspired by the novel form of the non-violent protest that, on joining Humboldt University of Berlin, Germany, he wrote his Ph.D on 'Salt Laws and Satyagraha'.

On securing his Ph.D and returning to India from Germany, he was expected to take up the family business or a job and help Hiralal tide over financial difficulties, but instead, Lohia decided take the plunge into national politics. He had had the first taste of political activism in Germany, where, as a student, he had participated in an anti-British boycott demonstration. Now back in India, he started his political work first among students of Calcutta, then joined the Congress, helped set up the Congress Socialist group and was appointed member of the All-India Working Committee (AIWC). A great admirer of Gandhiji and the doctrine of non-violence, he now came under his direct influence, as well as Nehru's, with whom he worked side by side for some years.

Lohia's philosophy and political activism was mainly inspired and shaped by Karl Marx and Mahatma Gandhi, but he was neither a Marxist nor a Gandhian. He accepted the inevitability of class struggle but not the inescapability of violence as a valid means to bring about revolutionary changes. He was bold and honest and openly differed from both Marx and Gandhi on many issues. For instance, he agreed with Gandhi in the supreme efficacy of non-violence for changing India's social and political structures and solving its many problems, but not in the context of conflict between nations. And he had doubts about the effectiveness of gram-swaraj, village self-rule, and was critical of the notion of trusteeship, the Gandhian socio-economic philosophy, which proposed that the wealthy should hold wealth/property/ means of production as trustees for the welfare of the people. Unlike his socialist friends, he disapproved of the way Marxism functioned in Soviet Union at the time. He believed it was possible to creatively combine Marxist ideology with Gandhian concerns and methods of struggle, to develop what he called a 'Third Force', an indigenous model of socialism suitable for the Indian condition.

Here is a list of some of the major activities he was involved in, in his 30-year long political life:

- In 1936, the Congress had no foreign policy, so he prompted the then president, Nehru, to start a Foreign Policy Department, worked as its secretary for three years, and penned four significant booklets – 'Civil Liberties', 'Indian Foreign Policy', 'China and India', and 'Plunder by Foreign Monopolies'.

- In 1942, during the Quit India movement, along with Jayaprakash Narayan, Achyut Patwardhan and Aruna Asaf Ali, he went underground to run Congress radio centres, produce revolutionary leaflets and pamphlets, and organize political protests.

- Together with Jayaprakash Narayan, he strongly opposed Partition. In 1946–47, during Hindu-Muslim riots, he worked with Gandhiji in Calcutta, Delhi and Noakhali.

- In 1948, he resigned from the Congress Party but chose to stay with the Congress Socialist Party and worked closely with the likes of Jayaprakash Narayan, Narendra Dev, Minoo Masani, Achyut Patwardhan and Kamaladevi Chattopadhya.

- In 1950, he founded and presided over the first conference of the Hind Kisan Panchayat at Rewa in Madhya Pradesh. Two of the major demands of the panchayat were abolition of landlordism and the distribution of land, with holdings being a minimum 12 acre and maximum of 30 acre.

- In 1952, along with Jayaprakash Narayan and Acharya Kripalani, he set up the Praja Socialist Party (PSP). But when the Congress swept the polls yet again in the 1952 general election and his fellow party workers, Ashok Mehta, Acharya Kripalani and Jayaprakash Narayan, wanted to cooperate and work closely with the Congress, Lohia broke away from PSP and, in 1955, formed his own Socialist Party.

- He was arrested and imprisoned more than 15 times in independent India for leading protests on issues of social justice against the Indian government. He was an uncompromising critic of the policies of the government headed by Pandit Nehru, who had been his idol during the freedom struggle. He raged that Nehru's government was dominated by the English-speaking, wealthy, upper castes, funded by the rich and blindly supported and elected by the poor.

- In 1967, in order to take forward the socialist concerns and break the Congress Party's monopoly, which he believed was not good for a truly democratic system, Lohia helped opposition parties unite and defeat the Congress in the general elections. For the first time, several states came under the rule of non-Congress parties. However, Lohia was deeply disappointed and outraged when the opposition parties that captured power in these states failed to implement socialist programmes. The government had changed in name only.

In the third general election in 1962, Lohia had fought against Nehru in Phulpur constituency of Uttar Pradesh and lost. But in 1967, Lohia contested and won as a Socialist Party candidate in a by-election in the Farrukhabad constituency in Uttar Pradesh. In a nod to his usual anti-government stance, an English daily described his presence in Lok Sabha as 'a bull in a china-shop' (Kelkar, 2009). In one of his interventions in the parliament, he thundered: '... Here government and members sit chewing cud like animals. Parliament has to become the mirror of national reality' (Kelkar, 2009). True enough, along with able, quick-witted parliamentarians like Acharya Kripalani, Madhu Limaye, Kishan Pattnaik and so on, he succeeded in transforming the Loka Sabha into a place where the problems, hopes and aspirations of the people were brought to the table.

Short, dark, with a broad forehead and penetrating eyes behind glasses, persistent and impatient, Ram Manohar Lohia was a restless soul. An ardent socialist, he bristled with rage against all forms of injustice. He was poetic, quite an eccentric and a committed vegetarian. He was an atheist, but not a hater of religion; rather, he believed that certain aspects of religion could serve as an effective instrument of change.

He remained unmarried, wholly committed to his socialist mission, but he joked: 'Man desires two things, God and woman. Of these two, I have never met God nor did I ever meet a woman who could accept me' (Kelkar, 2009). However, it was a well-known fact that Lohia had a relationship with Rama Mitra, a lecturer at Delhi University, and the two lived together without marriage.

Always a champion of women's rights, Lohia was ahead of his time in arguing for preferential treatment and demanded 60 per cent reservation of seats for women in the public sector and in the state legislatures and Lok Sabha. In the 1962 elections, he supported Sukho, a Dalit woman, in contesting the election against the Maharani of Gwalior, Vijaya Raje Scindia, and campaigned for her. Sukho lost the election, but it was necessary to show that in a democracy even a Dalit woman could oppose a hugely popular Maharani.

During his last years, he immersed himself in a variety of political tasks. He saw corruption and power-hungry politicians all around, and he was upset. His sharp tongue and self-righteousness won him many enemies in political circles, although he had many friends, too, who supported him. He was a man burning inside with anger. One day, a friend told him, 'Control your anger…it may become the hindrance in your path.' Lohia is believed to have laughed and replied, 'My life is short.' (Kelkar, 2009)

And it came to pass. The idealist in a hurry had somewhat managed to control high blood pressure over the years, but to it was now added serious urinary trouble. It was a result of the enlargement of his prostate gland, and so doctors advised surgery. He was admitted to Willingdon (now Rammanohar Lohia) Hospital in Delhi. It was a bad operation, it is said, conducted by a junior doctor, instead of the head surgeon as promised. The wound turned septic. Friends and top cabinet ministers intervened and brought in expert doctors. But it was too late, and Lohia died on 12 October 1967, at the age of 57. Later, reports of two probes into the cause of death revealed that all the necessary precautions and use of germicides were neglected during the surgery.

Veteran leaders such as Kripalani, Jayaprakash Narayan, Morarji Desai, Y.B. Chavan and others were among the coffin bearers. Shortly after Lohia's passing, the famous artist M.F. Hussain, who had been much inspired by Lohia's reading of the epics and myths, painted his legendry series on Ramayana and Mahabharata.

~

Lohia had a great impact on a whole generation of activists, writers and artists who were all, like their guru, a creative mix of Marx and Gandhi, a new brand of Indian socialists. The people he influenced included U.R. Ananthamurthy, Raghuvir Sahay, Pahaniswaranath Renu, Raghuvansh and so on. He also had considerable influence on literary and social movements in the country. To give examples from Karnataka, theatre person K.V. Subbanna, poet Gopalakrishna Adiga, writers such as Devanoor Mahadeva, and the farmer's leader M.D. Nanjundaswamy were all inspired by Lohia's activism and ideas.

Aphorisms

The inequality between men and women is perhaps the foundation of all other inequalities.

~

There is no greater virtue today than to smash these abominable segregation of caste and sex that are inter-related and sustain each other.

~

Caste restricts opportunity. Restricted opportunity constricts ability. Constricted ability further restricts opportunity. Where caste prevails, opportunity and ability are restricted to ever-narrowing circles of the people.

~

Live communities don't wait for five years to make the change. A Government which has misruled the country and lost faith of its citizens should be thrown out by the people before the completion of its term of 5 years.

~

With faith in the great crucible of the human race and equal faith in the vigour of all Indian people, let the high-caste choose to mingle tradition with mass. Simultaneously, a great burden rests on the youth of the lower castes. Not the aping of the high-caste in all its traditions and manners, not dislike of manual labour, not individual self-advancement, not bitter jealousy, but the staffing of the nation's leadership as though it were a sacred work should now be the supreme concern of women, Sudras, Harijans, Muslims and Adivasis.

~

God is not in high heavens but in the hearts of common folk and attempt should be made to discover him there.

~

Religion should eschew conflict and the tendency to support status quo in prevailing social and economic systems and that which refuses to do so should be the object of contempt.

~

Ram and Krishna and Siva are India's three great dreams of perfection. They go, each his own way. Ram is the perfection of the limited personality. Krishna of the exuberant personality and Siva of the non-dimensional personality, but each is perfect.

(Collated from Kelkar, *Dr. Ram Manohar Lohia, His Life and Philosophy*)

Lohia's major writings in English

Collected Works of Dr Lohia. Edited by Mastram Kapoor. Nine volumes. New Delhi: Anamika Publications, 2011.

Fragments of World Mind. Allahabad: Maitrayani Publishers and Booksellers, 1949.

Fundamentals of a World Mind. Edited by K.S. Karanth. Bombay: Sindhu Publications, 1987.

Guilty Men of India's Partition. Hyderabad: Lohia Samata Vidyalaya Nyas, Publication Department, 1970.

India, China, and Northern Frontiers. Hyderabad: Navahind, 1963.

Interval During Politics. Hyderabad: Navahind, 1965.

Marx, Gandhi and Socialism. Hyderabad: Navahind, 1963.

The Caste System. Hyderabad: Navahind, 1964.

Sarojini Naidu
(1879–1949)

AT THE BEHEST OF GOKHALE, IN 1914, GANDHI BRIEFLY STOPPED OVER in England on his way from South Africa to India. Sarojini Naidu happened to be in London at that time and visited him at his lodging in the Kensington area. It marked the start of a glorious relationship between the two as master and disciple, father and daughter and as two mature friends who could joke about each other and have a bellyful of laughter.

Remembering her first meeting with the hero from South Africa, Naidu wrote: 'I went wandering around in search of his lodging in an obscure part of Kensington and climbed up the steep stairs of an old, unfashionable house, to find an open door framing a living picture of a little man with a shaven head seated on the floor on a blank prison blow. Around him were ranged some battered tine of parched groundnut and tasteless biscuits of dried plantain flour. I burst instinctively into happy laughter at the amusing and unexpected vision of a famous leader, whose name had already become a household word in our country' (Mathur, 1989).

Gandhi lifted his eyes and laughed back at her saying: 'Ah, you must be Mrs. Naidu! Who else dare be so irreverent. Come in and share my meal.'

'No thanks,' she replied, sniffing, 'what an abominable mess it is!'

Thus began their lifelong friendship, laughingly. Both were endowed with great wit and wisdom. In his letters, he addressed her variously as 'Dear Old Singer', 'My dear Bulbul', 'Dear Sweet Singer' and on a couple of occasions, 'My dear Ammajan'. In return, she always addressed him as 'My little man' or 'My beloved little man'. She revered him as her guru, but that did not prevent her from teasing him and joking about him. She famously called him 'Mickey Mouse', and once, commenting on his frugal lifestyle, she quipped, 'If only he knew how much it costs us to keep him in poverty' (Mathur, 1989).

~

Sarojini Naidu was born on 13 February 1879 in Hyderabad, to an illustrious family of Kulin brahmins. Her father, Agorenath Chattopadhya, was a doctor of science from Edinburgh University, and founded the Hyderabad College, which later became the Nizam's College; her mother, Barada Sundari Devi, was a Bengali poet. Sarojini was the eldest of eight siblings. Among her brothers, Birendranath was a political revolutionary, and Harindranath was a well-known poet, dramatist and actor.

Sarojini was a prodigy. She was proficient in multiple languages, including English, Bengali, Urdu, Telugu and Persian. She topped the matriculation examination at Madras University, and wrote her first poem at age 11, when she took a break from working on a knotty algebra problem. Once, recalling her career as a poet, she said: 'One day when I was eleven I was sighing over a sum in Algebra, it wouldn't come right; but instead a whole poem came to me suddenly' (Naidu, 2010). Two years later, she wrote a 1,300 lines-long poem, 'The Lady of the Lake', on the spur of a moment, without forethought, just to spite her doctor, who said she was very ill and must not touch a book. This talent was like a revelation, a bewildering self-discovery for one who was training to be a mathematician. Thus, a poet was born!

At the age of 16, she travelled to England to study first at King's College, London, and later at Girton College, Cambridge. There she met many famous writers, took Edmond Gosse's advice seriously to stick to Indian themes in her poetry. And it was while studying here, at the age of 19, she met and fell in love with Muthyala Govindarajulu Naidu, a South Indian, non-brahmin physician. Returning to India, the couple got married by the Brahmo Marriage Act (1872), in Madras in 1898, at a time when inter-caste marriages were opposed; however, both their families approved the marriage. Later, the couple settled down in Hyderabad. They had four children in quick succession, from 1898 to 1904. Sarojini is supposed to have celebrated their advent into the world by writing a poem dedicated to each new arrival.

Her anthologies of poems, namely, *The Golden Threshold* (1905), *The Bird of Time* (1912), *The Broken Wing* (1917), *The Sceptred Flute* (1928) and *The Feather of the Dawn* (1961), earned her the sobriquet 'The Nightingale of India'. Her poems, dealing with love and death, separation and longing, and the mystery of life, were featured in English textbooks both at the high school and college levels across independent India and Sarojini Naidu became a household name for decades thereafter, and an inspiration to budding poets.

Sarojini Naidu also wrote on women's and political issues and played an active role in the freedom struggle. She worked along with Gopal Krishna Gokhale, Jawaharlal Nehru, Gandhi and other Congress leaders. Here is a brief summary of her cultural and political activism:

- In 1916, along with Nehru, she worked for the welfare of indigo workers of Champaran, Bihar, and fought for their rights.
- She travelled all over India and delivered speeches on the welfare of youth, dignity of labour, women's emancipation and nationalism.
- In 1917, along with Annie Besant and other prominent leaders, she helped found the Women's India Association.
- Opposing the Rowlatt Act in 1919, which severely curtailed civil liberties, Sarojini joined the non-cooperation movement led by Mahatma Gandhi.
- She travelled to Kenya, South Africa and southern Rhodesia, where she spread her message against indentured labour.
- In 1925, Naidu was appointed the President of the National Congress, making her the first Indian woman to hold the post.
- In 1927, she took part in the Pan Pacific Women's Conference at Honolulu and worked for the National Council for Women in India and the International Council for Women.

- In 1928–29, she travelled extensively in the United States of America and many European countries as the flagbearer of the Indian nationalist struggle.
- In 1931, she accompanied Gandhi to London for the second session of the Round Table Conference for Indian–British cooperation (1931). Again, in 1932, she was at the Round Table Conference in London as the representative of Indian women.
- In 1936, she helped the Women's Indian Association (WIA) draw up 'The Women's Manifesto'. Established in 1917, the WIA was a multi-ethnic feminist group that took up the cause of women's rights and fought against oppressive social customs. The manifesto centred on promotion of women's education, widow remarriage, abolition of child marriage and raising marriageable age of girls to sixteen, women's equality and participation in public life, and female suffrage on par with men in the provincial legislatures.
- She was arrested several times for taking part in the freedom struggle and incarcerated for short periods of time in 1930, 1932 and 1942–43.
- Sarojini addressed the Patna Session of the Women's Conference, where the campaign against purdah was debated. Sarojini argued against the custom of purdah and seclusion of women from the public life.
- In independent India, she was the first woman governor of Uttar Pradesh.

Sarojini Naidu was sharp, witty, courageous and committed to her ideals. She related with the giants of the time with ease and on equal footing. She worked relentlessly for the upliftment of women from economic insecurity, for their political rights, the right to divorce and right to shed purdah. She played a prominent role in the Salt Satyagraha led by Gandhiji and was a role model for women who were keen to work for India's cultural progress and political freedom.

She believed, despite her modern sensibility, that Indian women could look back to their precolonial heritage, wherein they enjoyed equal rights with men, to find a solution and the inspiration for their social and political struggles. She was celebrated as the 'Nightingale of India', though the modern poets were quite critical of her art, which they found to be sentimental and her language 'decorative' and indulgent. However, Sarojini was a woman of substance, and, in both her private and public life, she was a living example of an intelligent, emancipated woman.

While she was still the governor of Uttar Pradesh, Sarojini Naidu died of cardiac arrest on 2 March 1949, marking the end to a glorious life lived entirely on her own terms. Sushila Nayar, a noted general physician and Gandhian, echoed thoughts of many an admirer of Sarojini Naidu when she said: 'She was a scintillating personality, bright and intelligent, full of ready wit and humour, courteous, hospitable and ever ready to help.' (Baig, 1985)

Extracts from Some of Sarojini Naidu's Poems

Bird of Time
Songs of the glory and gladness of life
Of poignant sorrow and passionate strife,
And the lilting joy of the spring
Of hope that sows for the years unborn.
And faith that dreams of a tarrying mom.
The fragrant peace of the twilight's breath.
And the mystic silence that men call death.
Hark to the ageless,
divine invocation!

Autumn Song
Like a joy on the heart of a sorrow,
The sunset hangs on a cloud;
A golden storm of glittering sheaves,

Of fair and frail and fluttering leaves,
The wild wind blows in a cloud.

Hark to a voice that is calling
To my heart in the voice of the wind:
My heart is weary and sad and alone,
For its dreams like the fluttering leaves have gone,
And why should I stay behind?

Indian Weavers

Weavers, weaving at break of day,
Why do you weave a garment so gay?
Blue as the wing of a halcyon wild,
We weave the robes of a new-born child.
Weavers, weaving at fall of night,
Why do you weave a garment so bright?
Like the plumes of a peacock, purple and green,
We weave the marriage-veils of a queen.
Weavers, weaving solemn and still,
What do you weave in the moonlight chill?
White as a feather and white as a cloud,
We weave a dead man's funeral shroud.

(Extracted from Naidu, *Sarojini Naidu: Selected Poetry and Prose*)

Birsa Munda
(1875–1900)

SOMETIME IN MAY–JUNE 1895, BIRSA MUNDA IS SAID TO HAVE COME
upon the experience of the Supreme God of the Munda tribe, that
transformed him and turned him into their messiah. Mundas are one
of the largest scheduled tribes scattered across the states of Jharkhand,
Odisha and West Bengal.

The story goes that one night, Birsa dreamt of a grey-haired old man, who was none other than Singhbonga, the Supreme God Himself, accompanied by a bong (spirit), a raja (king), a judge (representing British rule) and Birsa himself. The old man planted a mahua tree, smeared it with oil and butter, and placed a sacred object on top of it. Then he called the raja, bong, judge and Birsa to climb the tree and bring down the sacred object. The bong, the raja and the judge tried to climb the tree one after the other, but all three slipped and fell down. Birsa went up and retrieved the sacred object, at which point Birsa woke up.

To him the dream was a clear message that he had been chosen to be the messenger of God, the messiah of the Mundas, who would recover the lost kingdom for his people. It is said that his transformation was drastic, he uttered words he had never known before and healed a sick child to prove his divine power.

Birsa was born on 15 Novemeber 1875 at Ulihatu in the then Bengal Presidency, now in the Khunti district of Jharkhand. He was the fourth child of his parents Sugana Munda and Karmi Hatu. After Birsa's birth, the family moved from place to place in search of employment and finally settled at Chalkad in Khunti district of Jharkand, where Sugana Munda worked as a labourer on a farmland. The tribal agrarian system had turned into a feudal state when the government had invited landlords from outside to settle and cultivate lands in the tribal belt of Jharkand. In 1856, there were about 600 landlords, who controlled over 150 villages. Over the years, the Mundas, along with the Oraon and Kharia tribes, came to lose their proprietary rights and were reduced to the position of farm labourers.

Legend recounts that Birsa was a bright and mischievous child. As a young boy, he learnt to play the flute and became an expert, and he went round with the tuila, the one-stringed-instrument, in one hand and the flute strung to his waist. After his primary education at a local school, his father wanted him to continue his higher studies in a school run by a Christian missionary. But converting to Christianity was obligatory to obtain a seat in the German Mission School. The father gave his consent and Birsa was duly converted to Christianity and renamed Birsa David. He studied at the school for three years and left in 1890, when the Sardar agitation against the government – started when restrictions were imposed on the traditional rights of the Mundas in the protected forest – turned against the German Mission. He ceased to be a Christian and reverted to his old tribal faith.

Around this time, when he was about 15 years of age, Birsa came in contact with Anand Panre, who was a Vaishnavite and a guru of sorts. Birsa stayed with him for three years at Patpur village in Jharkand and came under the influence of Vaishnavism. He wore the sandal mark, a sacred thread and took to worshipping the tulsi plant. Years later, Birsa's disciples claimed that at Patpur their master had a vision of Mahaprabhu Vishnu Bhagwan.

Although he was intensely religious in his outlook and lifestyle, he did not keep himself out of the Sardar agitation. In fact, he led a number of protests, and was jailed a couple of times. He was now looked upon as the leader among the Mundas. He was young, tall and handsome. Two women, including his brother's wife, desired to be his wives, but he declined their offers. Instead, he lived with a woman by name Sali of Burudih.

At the age of 20, he had the life-altering dream mentioned above. According to another version, the radical change came about when one day, in the early monsoon of May-July, a lightning struck him and he was transfigured. He became a healer, preacher and the messiah of the Mundas. He wore the sacred thread, a pair of wooden sandals and dhotis of different colours: yellow in the morning, white in the afternoon and blue in the evening.

Not only the Mundas, but even Oraons and Kharias, as well as people cutting across the lines of caste and tribe, including Muslims and recent converts to Christianity, came to see and listen to him, and many among them turned into his disciples. He was now regarded as Dharti Aba, Father of the Earth, Singhbonga, the Sun God, the Bhagwan himself. On special occasions, six to seven thousand people from all over the land turned up for his darshan and to participate in prayers.

Thus the healer and preacher grew to be a messiah, and his unorthodox religion gradually turned into a large-scale politico-religious movement. The religion he preached was a mix of Vaishnava piety and Christian missionary zeal for radical change. His idea of apocalypse was derived straight from Christian theology, though he interpreted it as the end of Kaliyuga, which would be caused by water, fire, war or agrarian disorder, famine and starvation.

The idea of the golden age was inspired by the Hindu concept of creation and four epochs, namely, Satyayuga, Tretayuga, Dwaparayuga and Kaliyuga, and he translated the concept as transition from Kaliyuga to Satyayuga, which in effect meant recovery of the lost Munda Raj. The Sardars, tribal chiefs, saw an opportunity in the new religion to strengthen their agitation under Birsa's leadership.

Consequently, their involvement turned Birsa's religious movement into a political battle against the landlords, the government forces and the Christian missionaries, who were now seen as usurpers of the tribal land and freedom. The idea of asuras, powerful demigods from Hindu mythology, would lend itself well to justify their attack on the British rule and Christian missionaries, also on Sarnaism, the indigenous religion of the tribals in and around Jharkhand, its priesthood, worship of the spirits, bongas, and the practice of drinking rice beer. Until then, the Sardars had lacked a clear plan of action to tackle their issues; now, with Birsa's support, they were emboldened to surge forward. They accepted him as their Prophet and Bhagwan.

The new religion came to be called Birsaism and its followers Birsaites. The heavy political content embodying the aspirations of the tribal people was inevitable. After all, Birsa had participated in the Sardar political agitations only recently and from a young age he knew intimately the enormous troubles his community had faced over the years. Their liberation lay in establishing the Munda Raj, which meant driving out all foreigners and reclaiming their lost lands. The followers went back to their respective villages to collect weapons such as balaws, barrel axes, tangis, ordinary axe, and bows and arrows. The plan was to collect the weapons and meet at Chalkad, Birsa's house, and then on the appointed day launch their attack. A few of the zamindars, missionaries and government officials were marked in their first plan of attack.

The missionaries had by then turned against Birsa, who now threatened their power and their evangelical mission. Alarmed by the new development, the deputy commissioner of Ranchi summoned Birsa, but Birsa did not care to meet him. He told the police officer, 'I am preaching a new religion, how can the government stop it? People by themselves are coming in large numbers, how can the government stop them?' (Singh, 2002). The government officials smelt trouble and when the zamindars reported Birsa's growing power and that Birsaites were planning to kill not only the saheb log, the government officials, but also all those who did not honour and have faith in Birsa, they decided to arrest him.

The police swooped down on Birsa's house and arrested him. Birsa and a number of his followers were convicted on 19 November 1895 on the charge of rioting and sentenced to a rigorous imprisonment of two years. His imprisonment reinforced the anti-government bias of the people but the movement suffered a setback. To make things worse, the widespread famine in the tribal belt as a result of the neglect of farming and complete failure of the rains dealt almost a death blow to the movement.

However, Birsa remained a formidable force even inside the jail. The Christian missionaries tried to negotiate with him and win him over to their side but with no success. He was released after two years and the preparation for the revolt began yet again. It is said that Birsa offered two options to his followers: either they adopt the religious method or the violent one to win back their kingdom. He himself preferred the peaceful religious approach to achieve their goal, but when his followers argued that the violent method was the right way to deal with a government run by a foreign power, he is believed to have agreed, however reluctantly.

The arrest warrant was once again out for Birsa, but he kept moving from place to place, eluding arrest. It is said that there were as many as 16 secret meetings, where Birsa and his followers deliberated on strategies. His disciples danced and sang in praise of him, and Birsa himself sang his revolutionary hymns. And the British were likened to Ravana and a plantain effigy, symbolizing the British Empire, was burnt.

The first phase of the uprising began in December 1899, on the eve of Christmas, with attacks on government officials. At some places, when even Christian missionaries were targeted, Birsa instructed his followers not to harm a person of Munda origin, whether Christian or not, their real enemies were the white leaders, the saheb log. Ranchi was in the grip of fear. Large contingents of the police and the army patrolled the nearly 400 square kilometres of the district to prevent the attacks and catch the Birsaites.

A few government houses were burnt, four constables were killed and a government official was wounded. Their arrow-shooting and outdated weapons were no match to the sophisticated weapons of the police. The uprising, which was sudden but sporadic in different regions of the hilly country, died down in a couple of months.

Hundreds of Birsaites were arrested, their properties were seized and they were tortured and interrogated by the police. On 3 February 1900, Birsa was arrested and was incarcerated along with 400 Birsaites in a Ranchi jail. Birsa told a Munda visiting him in the jail: 'I had told you earlier that if we fought with the weapon of religion, we would not experience any difficulty and would accomplish our purpose. You did not accept it. We left our family, our children and wives... Let us not lose heart, let us wait patiently. I will return one day and win my kingdom.' (Singh, 2002)

But that was not to be. He never came out of the jail. He died, it was reported, of cholera on 9 June 1900. He was hardly 25 years old.

He was cremated by the jail sweeper on the banks of Harmu River at Kadru in Ranchi. Out of the 482 accused Birsaites, 98 were convicted and the rest were acquitted and discharged.

The Munda uprising became national news, there were debates on it in the newspapers and once the issue was raised in the Legislative Council. A study in the early 1960s revealed that there were about 10,000 Birsaites, spread over 100 villages in the Porahat region of Singhbhum in Ranchi district (Singh, 2002). They considered themselves the practitioners of a distinct religion, different from Sarnaism – the original religion of the Mundas centred on the worship of nature. These followers worship Birsa as their god, and practice abstention from alcohol and meat.

The Chota Nagpur Tenancy Act of 1908 ended the century-old agrarian strife by recognizing the rights of the tribals to reclaimed lands. The act also prohibited the transfer of tribal land to non-tribals. It is interesting to note that the state of Jharkhand was formed in November 2000, on the 15th, which happens to be Birsa's birthday. In recognition of Birsa Munda as an 'exemplary son of India', as the first adivasi freedom fighter and advocate and exponent of tribal rights, his portrait was unveiled on 16 October 1989 in the precincts of the Parliament House.

Bhimrao Ramji Ambedkar
(1891–1956)

ON 4 AUGUST, 1923, RAO BAHADUR S.K. BOLE, A FAMOUS SOCIAL WORKER, moved a resolution in the Bombay Legislature to the effect that the Depressed Classes (all the socially marginalized and economically weaker castes, including Dalits; later to be known as scheduled castes) be allowed access to all public watercourses, wells, public schools, courts, offices and dispensaries maintained out of public funds and administered by government bodies. The Bombay Legislative Council issued a directive to give effect to the resolution, but it remained a mere gesture, a directive on paper, until Ambedkar, four years later, decided to take up the cause.

It was time for direct action. On 19 and 20 March, 1927, a huge conference of the Depressed Classes was held at Mahad, in Raigad district of Maharashtra state, under the leadership of Ambedkar. About 10,000 people from the Depressed Classes, including Dalits, from many districts of Maharashtra and Gujarat, attended the conference. Ambedkar spoke to them about the absolute necessity of rooting out ideas of high and low and raise themselves through self-help, self-respect and self-knowledge. He urged them to develop mastery over language, to renounce eating carrion, to do away with humiliating and enslaving traditions, to abandon demeaning occupations and become agriculturists instead, or educate themselves and enter government services. After the conference, with Ambedkar in the lead, the 10,000 people marched in a procession to the Chowda Tank, a public tank, to assert their right to drink and take water from it, something that had been denied to them until then. Ambedkar drew water from the tank and drank it. Soon, the vast crowd followed suit and vindicated their right.

Within hours of this historic event, a rumour spread that the untouchables were planning to enter the local Veereshwar Temple. Gangs of caste Hindus, armed with sticks, attacked some delegates. There would have been a bloody riot but for Ambedkar, who appealed to his people for peace and discipline. A bitter controversy raged. Opinions clashed, and despite the criticism, caste Hindus went ahead with their plan and 'purified' the tank: to the chanting of Sanskrit mantras by brahmin priests, 108 pitchers filled with mixtures of cow's dung and urine, curd and water were poured into the tank and the tank was declared free of 'pollution'.

On 25 December 1927, six months after the first march, under the stewardship of Ambedkar, the lower caste people gathered yet again to intensify their struggle for their rights, although the Mahad Tank case was still under judicial enquiry and consideration. The District Magistrate intervened to stop their march towards the tank. Ambedkar did not wish to antagonize the government and yet did not want to disappoint and fail his people, either. It was a tricky situation. Ambedkar decided to suspend the satyagraha; nevertheless, he led the conference in burning copies of the *Manusmriti*, Laws of Manu, the ancient Hindu text that was the source of the belief in and practice of the varnadharma, caste system.

The depressed class had to wait for another ten years for the Bombay High Court to decide the case in their favour and throw open the Mahad Tank to them. The Mahad Tank march was the first large scale protest and direct action against caste discrimination; more importantly, it was a satyagraha, a *non-violent* struggle to claim the civic rights of the Dalits. But we have failed to recognize and appreciate the social struggles of the downtrodden as a non-violent one. Therefore, it is imperative to recognize and assert that not only the freedom struggle led by Gandhi, but also the socio-political struggles led by Ambedkar for the freedom, equality and dignity of the Dalits has been a non-violent struggle, involving immense suffering and sacrifice on the part of the Dalits.

~

Bhimrao Ramji Ambedkar was born on 14 April 1891 to Ramji Maloji Sakpal and Bhimabai Sakpal in the town of Mhow, present-day Ambedkar Nagar in Indore district of Madhya Pradesh. Ramji and Bhimabai had 14 children, of which only three daughters and two sons survived. Bhim was the fourteenth child. Ramji Maloji Sakpal belonged to the Marathi-speaking Mahar caste, who were treated as untouchables. However, Mahars had served in various armies over centuries, including the army of Maratha king Shivaji in the seventeenth century, and were considered brave and virile. Ambedkar's grandfather had served in and retired from the British army, while his father held the rank of a Subedar in the Mahar Regiment. Economically, Mahars were well above most other untouchable groups, but still they could not escape social discrimination.

Ramji retired from military service in 1894, and two years later, the family moved to Dapoli in Konkan where, at the age of five, Bhim started his primary school education along with his elder brother. A year later, when the family moved to Satara, where his father took up a job, his mother passed away. The children were cared for by their father and aunt. Of his brothers and sisters, only Bhim went to high school. His surname was Sakpal, but his father got his name registered as Ambavadekar, after his native village, Ambavade. Bhim's teacher Krishna Keshav Ambedkar, who liked him very much, changed Bhim's surname to 'Ambedkar' after his own surname.

Bhim did well in his studies and enjoyed the extra care given to him at home and the little pocket money he received regularly. Ramji married again, breaking his promise made to Bhim that he would never bring home a stepmother. Bhim resented the woman taking his mother's place and wearing his mother's jewels. It was a difficult period for him and he even thought of leaving home, finding a job in Bombay Mills and living independently. Soon, he realized it would be foolish of him to act impulsively, and he decided to 'study hard and get through my examinations as fast as possible, so that I might earn my own livelihood and be independent of my father' (Keer, 1961). To be fair to his father, he often went out of his way to support his son's education. He knew Bhim's passion for books and ungrudgingly gave him money for books, even if it meant borrowing from his married daughters.

In 1897, the family moved to Bombay and Bhim joined Elphinstone High School, which, at the time, was one of the leading schools in the city. Bhim lived with the family in a one-room tenement that served as a kitchen, a drawing-cum-study-cum-sleeping room, often noisy and smoky, with a tethered goat bleating away. He would wake up at two in the morning and study under a kerosene lamp until the break of dawn. Thus he studied hard and was the first Mahar to pass the matriculation exams in 1907 from Elphinstone High School. The occasion was celebrated in the presence of S.K. Bole, the famous social reformer, and K.A. Keluskar, Marathi writer and teacher, who presented his favourite student with a copy of his new book, *Life of Gautama Buddha*. Four decades later, Ambedkar was to go back to the life and teaching of the Buddha to find a new hope, a new calling and refuge for himself and his people.

In 1906, when he was about 15 years old and still at school, he was married to a nine-year old girl, Ramabai. Ambedkar did not let this early marriage affect his education. After his matriculation, he joined Elphinstone College. Those were difficult days for Ramji and he could not support Ambedkar's education. Keluskar intervened in time and took Ambedkar to the progressive ruler, Maharaja Sayaji Rao, who granted him a scholarship of 25 rupees per month. Despite troubles on the home front and the caste discrimination he had to suffer in college, undeterred, Ambedkar concentrated his energies on his studies and passed his B.A. Examination in 1912, with English and Persian as his subjects.

After his graduation, Ambedkar joined the Baroda State Service. But the condition in the office, manned by orthodox caste Hindus, was so oppressive and humiliating that he was left with no alternative but to resign from his post. To make things worse, his father died, plunging him in deep sorrow. But soon, there emerged a new hope: a great opportunity to pursue higher studies abroad. In 1913, gaining the Baroda State Scholarship, he went to study at the prestigious Columbia University in New York City. He had just turned 22 and broken out of the limitation his birth had imposed on him. It was to be a historic event.

He studied for 18 hours a day. The open and free environment in the university helped his concentration and resolve. None here would look down upon him because he was a Mahar, or even care to know to which caste he belonged to. He studied Political Science, Moral Philosophy, Anthropology, Sociology and Economics for his course, under the stewardship of Professor Seligman, a well-known economist. He presented his thesis on *Ancient Indian Commerce* and completed his post-graduation in 1915, majoring in Economics, and for his Ph.D, submitted his thesis on *National Dividend of India—A Historic and Analytical Study.* The thesis was accepted and Columbia University awarded him the degree of Doctor of Philosophy. From then on he was always referred to as 'Doctor'. During this period, he also produced a seminar paper, *Castes in India, Their Mechanism, Genesis and Development,* which marked the beginning of his lifelong critical engagement with the caste system in India.

The foreign degree and doctorate only whetted his appetite for more knowledge and degrees. In 1916, having decided to become a lawyer, he moved to London, enrolled for the Bar Course at Gray's Inn and began work on another doctorate at the London School of Economics. But soon he had to return to India because his scholarship ended. In 1920, he went back to London on another scholarship, resumed his studies, passed the Bar Course at Gray's Inn, and a year later, completed his M.Sc. in Economics. In 1923, he completed a DSc in Economics from the London School of Economics, where his thesis on *Problem of the Rupee* was accepted. He was a different man now: grown in knowledge, experience and stature. He was a barrister with double doctorates. He was mature and ready to inaugurate his struggle for the emancipation of the downtrodden. India awaited him.

Ambedkar, of course, did not plunge into politics straightaway. He had to earn his living and take care of his family before he would storm the political arena with trenchant critiques of orthodox Hinduism and its oppressive caste system, and launch his anti-caste movement – a movement that would change the contours of Indian social politics and rouse Gandhi to commit himself more urgently and deeply to the removal of untouchability.

Ambedkar made humble beginnings as a barrister at the Indian courts in Bombay. He worked with whatever cases came his way in the mofussil centres before forging his own path to the front benches of the High Court. He won several remarkable and weighty cases, most of them in favour of the non-brahmin community, and grew into a lawyer to be reckoned with. His deep understanding of law and its sociopolitical implications would earn him the position of a leader of the labour class, later that of the Law Minister and eventually the Chairman of the Constitution Drafting Committee.

The 1920s was a decade of great political ferment, as sociopolitical movements, including Dalit movements with far-reaching consequences, began to develop, including Adi-Dharm in Punjab, Adi-Hindu in Uttar Pradesh and Hyderabad, and Adi-Andhra and Adi-Karnataka in South India. Adi-Dravida in Madras, also called the Self-respect Movement, was spearheaded by E.V. Ramasamy Naicker. Ambedkar was somewhat cynical about the socio-political movements started by non-Dalits. For he suspected, not without reason, that these movements were not geared to bring about changes in the power structures of the Hindu society, which should put a Dalit on equal footing with a caste Hindu.

Saints and sages through ages had propounded philosophies and notions of bhakti according to which all human beings were equal before God, but that remained a mere sentiment and could not lead to the creation of an egalitarian society. Mahatmas had raised lots of dust but not raised the level of the Dalits. And history had taught Ambedkar that, ultimately, injustice could not be removed until the victim himself did away with it by his own exertions and actions. So long as the conscience of a slave did not burn with hatred for his victimhood and slavery, there was no hope for his salvation. Self-help, self-elevation and self-respect were the mantras Ambedkar offered to his people to goad them into action.

His activism began in 1919, when he argued for creating separate electorates and reservations for Dalits in his speech before the Southborough Franchise Committee in London. In 1920, he started a weekly paper *Mooknayak*, Leader of the Voiceless, to highlight and champion the cause of Dalits. In 1924, along with his co-workers, he founded Bahishkrit Hitakarini Sabha, Organization for the Welfare of the Excluded, with the objectives:

- To promote the spread of education and culture among Dalits by opening hostels, libraries, study circles and so on;
- To advance and improve the economic condition of Dalits by starting industrial and agricultural schools;
- To represent the grievances of the Depressed Classes.

In 1927, the Mahad Tank Satyagraha, as discussed earlier, was the first large-scale non-violent struggle that was both a protest against caste discrimination as well as a struggle to claim civic rights of the Dalits. This was followed by burning of pages of the Manusmriti that imposed and perpetuated the social, economic and political slavery of the shudras and ati-shudras. Ambedkar compared the burning of the Manusmriti to the burning of foreign clothes, in Gandhi's campaign against British goods. At that time, Ambedkar believed it was possible to abolish varnadharma and transform the Hindu society. He said, '…though I do not accept the authority of the Vedas, I consider myself to be a Sanatan Hindu' (Keer, 1961).

Three years later, on 2 March 1930, he organized the largest and longest Satyagraha for Dalit entry to the famous Kala Ram Temple at Nasik. Around 15,000 Mahars and Chamars, including women and children, marched to the temple only to see its doors firmly shut. After a month-long struggle, a compromise was reached between the caste Hindus and the Dalits. It was agreed that both the caste Hindus and untouchables would draw the chariot of Lord Ram on public roads on the day of Ram Navami. But the agreement was broken by the caste Hindus and the temple was closed for about a year to keep the Dalits from entering it. The Dalits had to carry on the agitation for almost five years before the doors of the temple were finally thrown open to them.

Ambedkar began to lose faith in the possibility of cleansing Hinduism of its pernicious caste system and eventually, in 1956, he would leave Hinduism to become a Buddhist. After the Mahad Tank and temple entry agitations, however, he became a force to reckon with and was considered the most influential and articulate leader of the Depressed Classes. In September 1930, Ambedkar, as the representative of the Depressed Classes, was invited by the British Government to attend the First Round Table Conference in London, to discuss constitutional reforms in India.

At the conference, Ambedkar drew the attention of the world to the terrible condition of Dalits, comparable to that of the Blacks in America. By his graphic description of the plights of Dalits, he made the British government become acutely aware of and recognize the problems of the Depressed Classes and prepared the ground for securing the rights of Dalits and their representation in the Legislatures, Cabinet and government services.

In 1931, he attended the Second Round Table Conference, with the likes of Gandhi, Sarojini Naidu and Pandit Mohan Malaviya. Three years ago, Ambedkar had been against the introduction of separate electorates for minorities, but now he rooted for it, arguing that it would further the political empowerment of the Depressed Classes and ensure they were not at the mercy of the dominant parties. Gandhi was against the proposal, and it marked the beginning of a long feud between Gandhi and Ambedkar over the subject of the caste system in particular, and Hinduism in general.

In 1932, the British announced what was called the Communal Award. The scheme offered separate electorates to Muslims, Sikhs and the Depressed Classes. Gandhi, who was imprisoned in Yerwada Jail at the time, went on an indefinite fast for the abrogation of the separate electorate for the Depressed Classes. To him, the scheme was nothing less than a disaster, for he believed it would tear apart and disrupt the nation without doing any good. Meetings were organized all over the country by the Congress party, demanding withdrawal of the Communal Award and appeals were sent to Ambedkar to resolve the deadlock and save Gandhi's life.

Despite the appeals and threats, Ambedkar did not budge from his stance until Gandhi's health began to fail and the situation reached a boiling point. After hectic negotiations, at last, Ambedkar met Gandhi in Yerwada Jail. Ambedkar agreed to suspend his demand for separate electorate to the Depressed Classes, but as compensation demanded 197 seats, instead of the 71 seats promised by the Communal Award. Eventually, it was agreed that 148 seats would be reserved for the Depressed Classes, and Ambedkar signed what famously came to be known as the Poona Pact.

Perhaps, if the separate electorate scheme for the Depressed Classes had been implemented for 10 years, as Ambedkar had demanded, it would have emboldened the Depressed Classes to effect substantial changes, to gain political ascendancy and the power to safeguard their interests. Or, according to Gandhi, it would have divided Hindu society, condemned the untouchables to remain untouchables in perpetuity and proved to be counterproductive to their interests and growth. While we do not know how things could have been different, it is a well known fact that, in later years, Ambedkar regretted his decision to sign the Poona Pact. He felt betrayed when he realized that the reformist measures such as inter-caste dining, enabling the lower caste people to access temples, schools, roads, water resources and so on had not led to any substantial improvement in the condition of the Depressed Classes, not to speak of their political empowerment, and attributed the political failure of his party and his own defeat in the provincial elections held in 1936-37 to the Poona Pact.

Ambedkar moved away from his previous attempts to cleanse Hinduism and exhorted the Dalits to stop depending on gods and saints to liberate them from slavery. Their salvation lay in gaining political power and not in making pilgrimages and observing fasts. What they needed were education, higher employment and better ways of earning a living.

In 1935, alongside his hectic political activism, Ambedkar became the Principal of the Government Law College, Bombay. At last, after living in a two-room chawl for 20 years, he himself designed and built a house in Dadar, Bombay, and called it Rajagriha, after the name of the hill in Bihar where the Buddha had delivered his major discourses. He now had a personal library, which held about 50,000 books collected over the years, including books he had picked from second-hand bookshops. After a long wait, Ramabai was happy to have a house of her own, where her children would be secure. She had lived the major portion of her married life in pinching poverty, taking care of the growing children without much support from her husband, who spent most of his time abroad, pursuing his higher studies, and once back home, working tirelessly for the welfare of the Dalits.

Hardly a couple of months had passed in the new house when the cruel hand of fate struck Ambedkar. Ramabai died on 27 May 1935. As an act of love and respect for his wife, Ambedkar let his son perform the funeral obsequies according to Hindu tradition, which was, incidentally, presided over by a Mahar priest, Sambhoo More, his friend since schooldays. Ambedkar was 42 years old then.

For some time now Ambedkar had been dropping hints that he would change his religion. At the Yeola Conference on 13 October 1935, which was attended by about 10,000 people from the Depressed Classes, he famously declared that though he was born a Hindu, he would not die a Hindu. He finally converted to Buddhism 20 years later; meanwhile, religious leaders from both Islam and Christianity began to woo him and try to win him over to their faith. During this period, he wrote a series of critical pieces on the roots of the caste system, as well as on Gandhism and the Congress. His tract, *Annihilation of Caste*, which was actually the text of his speech prepared for the 1936 Annual Conference of the Jat Pat Todak Mandal of Lahore, which he was not allowed to deliver, elicited sharp reactions. It was an incisive critique of the caste system, and his thesis was that the caste system was not merely a division of labour but a division of labourers.

According to Ambedkar, there was no hope for Hinduism unless its followers 'cleanse their minds of the pernicious notions founded on the shastras'. Gandhi called the thesis 'Ambedkar's Indictment' and admitted it was a challenge to Hinduism; however, he later argued that the caste system had nothing to do with religion, that every religion would fail if judged by Ambedkar's standards.

Meanwhile, Ambedkar decided to take his political commitment further, by standing in the election. For the first time in the history of British India, general elections were to be held in 1937, with a view to initiate provincial autonomy under the Government of India Act, 1935. The Depressed Classes had no party of their own to fight for their cause. In 1936, Ambedkar formed the Independent Labour Party (ILP) to fight the elections in the old Bombay Presidency. Out of the 17 candidates put up by the ILP, 15 won the election, including Ambedkar. In 1942, he was nominated to the Viceroy's Executive Council. On 15 August 1947, India became politically independent and Nehru invited Ambedkar to join the new cabinet as Law Minister. It came as a great surprise, however, that Ambedkar accepted the job and served as the first 'untouchable' minister for four years, before resigning in September 1951.

On 29 August 1947, Ambedkar was appointed as the Chairman of the Constitution Drafting Committee. It was the crowning glory of his political career. The other members of the committee were legal luminaries such as Gopalswami Ayyangar, Alladi Krishnaswami, K.M. Munshi, Muhammad Sadulla, B.L. Mitter and D.P. Khaitan. It so happened that a few months later, D.P. Khaitan passed away, and several other members, for one reason or the other, could not attend the meetings regularly. The burden of drafting the Constitution largely fell on Ambedkar and he responded magnificently.

The Constitution of India was passed and adopted by the Assembly in 1949, and it came into force on 26 January 1950. Born in a poor Mahar family, harassed and humiliated by caste Hindus, Ambedkar had risen to become a great political leader, jurist and a writer with penetrating insights. He had fought, struggled and struck back, not with vengeance but with sensitivity and concern, sometimes with indignation and rectitude, to become the chief architect of the Constitution that would inaugurate a new era in the history of this ancient land.

Ambedkar's political party, now called Republican Party of India, did not do well in the 1952 general elections. The long hours of work over the years ultimately took its toll on his health. He was in his sixties now and was diabetic. In need of a companion and a caretaker, he had married Dr Sharada Kabir on 15 April 1948, his personal doctor and a Saraswath brahmin, who later adopted the name Savita Ambedkar. He was now deeply attracted to the life and teachings of the Buddha and started working on his magnum opus *The Buddha and His Dhamma*, also on other works, namely, *Revolution and Counter Revolution* and *Buddha and Karl Marx*.

But the book of his life had reached its last chapter. On 14 October 1956, along with 500,000 Dalits, most of them from the Mahar community, he formally embraced Buddhism, accepting the traditional three refuges and five precepts from a Buddhist monk, Mahasthavir Chandramani. Explaining his decision to the press, he said, 'I prefer Buddhism because it gives three principles in combination which no other religion does. Buddhism teaches Prajna (understanding as against superstition and Supernaturalism), Karuna (love) and Samata (equality). This is what man wants for a good and happy life on earth.' (Keer, 1961)

Then, remembering Gandhi, he told the reporters that though he differed radically from Gandhi on the issue of untouchability and chaturvarna, he had assured Gandhi that when the time came for him to renounce Hinduism, he would 'choose only the least harmful way for the country.' Clearly, Ambedkar was mindful of the effect his conversion would have on the nation, and considered his embrace of Buddhism 'the greatest benefit [he was] conferring on the country', adding, 'Buddhism is a part and parcel of Bharathiya Culture. I have taken care that my conversion will not harm the tradition of the culture and history of this land' (Keer, 1961). Fifty-one days later, after completing his work *Buddha and Karl Marx*, Ambedkar died in his sleep on 6 December 1956, at his home in Delhi. He was 65 years old.

Ambedkar was not only an inspiring leader of the lower castes but a national leader of the highest order. His picture adorns the walls of the homes of millions of Dalits across India and he continues to inspire their struggle for equality, dignity and justice. His sociopolitical thought has transformed the way we look at socio-economic policies, education and language issues, federalism and constitutionalism in India today; though, it must be admitted, the political and legal activism he initiated in favour of the downtrodden and the marginalized remains unfinished.

❧

E.V. Ramasamy
(1879–1973)

E.V. RAMASAMY WAS A PUBLIC INTELLECTUAL, SOCIAL REFORMER AND zealous advocate of rationality. Almost 50 years after Jyotiba Phule and 20 years before Dr Ambedkar, he launched in southern India the fight against the evils of the caste system and championed the cause of women. Like Basavanna 800 years before him, he saw temples as the seat of Brahmanical religious and political power, and tried to dismantle the power structure, sometimes adopting extreme measures.

Erode Venkata Naicker Ramasamy was born on 17 September 1879 at Erode, to Thiru Venkata Naicker and Thirumathi Chinnathayamma. Theirs was a fairly rich, Kannada-speaking family, and with deep religious faith, followed customs and rituals like any other Hindu family.

E.V.R.'s formal schooling was brief, lasting about five years. At the young age of 12, he joined his father's business. In 1898, aged 19, he was married to 13-year-old Nagammal. Two years later, a daughter was born but the child died after five months and they had no children thereafter. As a social and human rights activist, Nagammal led the women in protests during the anti-caste Vaikom Satyagraha, and supported E.V.R. in his Self-Respect Movement. Theirs was an ideal marriage and lasted till Nagammal's death in 1933, at age 48.

As a young man, E.V.R. was a restless soul. Not too happy with his father's business and the goings-on in the family, at age 25, E.V.R. left home and went on a pilgrimage to Kashi. At Kashi, otherwise called Varanasi, he was in for a rude shock. At a choultry, resting house, where free meals were served, he was denied entry because the place – incidentally built and sponsored by a non-brahmin South Indian – was reserved for brahmins. He was starving and had to eat. Pretending to be a brahmin, he tried to enter another choultry, but his moustache betrayed his non-brahmin origin and he was pushed out. Extreme hunger drove him to feed himself on the leftovers on the street. This painful experience radically changed his view on Hinduism.

After Kashi, E.V.R. headed to Hyderabad. However, his father succeeded in locating him there, brought him back home and entrusted full responsibility of the business to him. This time around, E.V.R. earnestly took care of the business and did well. And soon, he grew to be a man of some importance in the town. He became the chairman of the district temple committee, chairman of the Erode Municipal Council, honorary magistrate – in all, he held about two dozen offices of importance for some years. It was the time of consolidation of his powers before he would plunge into politics.

In 1919, he resigned from public offices and joined the Congress Party, thus entering active public life. He threw himself into the party's various activities with unswerving dedication and was the President of the Madras Presidency Congress Committee during 1922–24. He was for total prohibition in the state and industriously promoted the khadi programme. However, when it came to eradication of caste, which, according to him, was of critical importance if one wanted to create a just society with equal opportunities, he found the party members not sufficiently determined to go the whole hog to bring in the required changes. To his great disappointment, he found many Congressmen, including Gandhi, were not for the total abolition of caste, although they spoke and worked conscientiously for the removal of untouchability. The Vaikom Satyagraha (1924-25) for temple entry – where he thought the Congress party soft-peddled the agitation – was one of the reasons he turned his back on the party.

As per the caste system, Dalits were denied access to knowledge, especially spiritual knowledge, and entry into temples. In Vaikom, a small town in Travancore, Dalits could not even use the streets in and around the temple, let alone enter the temple. In 1924, with the support of Gandhi and Narayana Guru, and under the leadership of T.K. Madhavan, a Satyagraha was launched to seek the rights for Dalits to use the public roads around the temple and also enter and offer pujas at the Sri Mahadeva Temple.

As the struggle gathered support from all over the country, and from people of other faiths as well, Gandhi thought it would be better if only the local people participated in the satyagraha. So people from other faiths and other states were discouraged from participating. Dismayed by this decision, nevertheless very keen to be a part of such an historical struggle against the caste system, along with his wife Nagammal, E.V.R. went to Vaikom. He was arrested and imprisoned for a short period. Once out of prison, he plunged into the struggle again and yet again he was arrested.

Eventually, the streets in and around the temple area were opened to Dalits, but it was only after 12 years, in 1936, that they were allowed to enter the temple. In recognition of his contribution to the struggle, the Madras Presidency Congress hailed E.V.R. as Vaikom Veerar, Vaikom Hero. E.V.R., however, was quite disappointed and upset with the method the Congress Party had adopted in the struggle.

The other issue on which he differed with the Congress was that its members did not care much for the principle of communal representation in education and employment, about which he had passed a resolution in one of the annual conferences of the party.

Finally, in 1925, he left the Congress Party and started his Self-Respect Movement. One of the often-quoted mottos of the movement was 'We are fit to think of "self-respect" only when the notion of "superior" and "inferior" caste is banished from our land.'

E.V.R. was convinced that self-respect was of cardinal importance if one were to develop a sense of individuality and dignity. To him, only self-respect enabled genuine freedom, without which the struggle for political freedom spearheaded by leaders such as Gandhi and Nehru would be hollow and meaningless. Thus, the Self-Respect Movement was conceived as parallel to the political freedom movement led by the Congress Party.

Some of the salient features of the movement were:

- To do away with such social structure of the society where one class of people were seen as superior to others.
- To achieve equal opportunities for all people, irrespective of their caste or class, and secure equal status for women in society.
- To completely eradicate untouchability and to establish a united society based on brotherhood and sisterhood.
- To establish and maintain homes for orphans and widows and to run educational institutions.
- To remove practices of using caste marks, caste costumes and caste names, and do away with needless customs, meaningless ceremonies, and blind superstitious beliefs that perpetuated caste discrimination and inequality.
- To stop employing brahmin priests to officiate at marriages and other ceremonies of society.
- To simplify laws relating to divorce, widow remarriage and inter-caste marriage.

E.V.R. held brahmins and their brahminism responsible for both direct and indirect oppression of the lower castes. Of the Shastras, Vedas, Puranas, Ithihasas, Manusmriti and other Hindu texts, he believed they only served as a mask for the exploitation of the lower castes and women. But he held *Tirukkural*, the fifth century text composed by Thiruvalluvar, in high esteem. This text alone, which, E.V.R. believed, upheld high ethical values, was enough to educate the people of India. Sometimes his critique of brahminism and gods and scriptures took a militant form when idols of gods were broken and their pictures defaced and burnt.

He travelled widely in India and met with several leaders, including Dr Ambedkar. From 1929 to 1932, he went on tour to Europe, as well as the Soviet Union, Malaya and Singapore, to study the history and politics of different countries. He ran a series of journals to reach out to people across the Madras Presidency. In 1938, when Hindi was introduced as a compulsory language of study in schools by the then Chief Minister of Madras Presidency, Rajagopalachari, E.V.R. made common cause with the Justice Party and opposed the move. The fight sometimes took a racial connotation and was seen as a North–South, Aryan–Dravidian conflict. In fact, it was during this fight that E.V.R. raised the slogan 'Tamil Nadu for Tamilians'. The fight later grew into what came to be called Dravidian Movement. The anti-Hindi agitations, cutting across party lines, were to recur in 1948, 1952 and 1965.

E.V.R. became the president of the Justice Party in 1939 and five years later, in 1944, he changed the name of the party to Dravidar Kazhagam. With C.N. Annadurai as his able lieutenant, he had the party intensify its social reformist work, with particular focus on the abolition of the practice of untouchability, promotion of women's rights and education, widow remarriages and so on. Notably, he was the first to advocate the abolition of the devadasi system, which had reduced devadasis to the status of temple prostitutes.

In 1948, however, cracks began to appear in the party when there was a difference of opinion about whether to demand a separate Dravidian or Tamil State, and when E.V.R., who was 70 years of age, married the 32-year old Maniammai, his long-time caretaker, nurse and assistant. Many party workers pleaded with him not to marry, even Rajagopalachari advised him to desist from it as it would spoil his image and adversely affect his 50 years of selfless work. E.V.R., however, remained unmoved and said that his life was an open book and there was no hypocrisy in what he was doing. At his age, he needed someone to take care of him both physically and emotionally. Also, he needed to transfer his huge properties and bequeath the good work to someone he trusted.

Because of these controversies, C.N. Annadurai, split from E.V.R. and Dravidar Kazhagam, formed his own party under the name Dravidar Munnetra Kazhagam. However, he remained faithful to the ideals of his mentor. E.V.R. remained active until his last days; he never gave up the fight against the imposition of Hindi and died in 1973, at the ripe age of 94. There is no doubt that the trajectory of Tamil Nadu politics, especially regarding issues concerning the caste system and rights of women, was largely shaped by E.V.R., and his legacy continues to influence Tamil society today. He remains one of the major icons in India's history of struggle against caste discrimination and the fight for the rights of Dalits and women.

Aphorisms

If god is the root cause for our degradation, destroy that god. If it is religion, destroy it. If it is Manu Dharma, Gita, or any other Mythology or Purana, burn them to ashes. If it is temple, tank, or festival, boycott them.

~

There should be no differentiation amongst the people. All should be treated as equals. On this basis the Brahmin must give up his false prestige. In the interest of the society, I say that the blind beliefs should be given up.

~

I have not talked of anything to despise the Brahmins, just because they are born as Brahmins.

~

Brahmins cannot hope to claim a high and superior status forever. Times are changing. They have to come down. Then only they could survive with dignity. Otherwise they will one day be forfeiting their high status. It will not be by force. It will be just laws of the land and the people.

~

Man treats woman as his own property and not as being capable of feelings, like himself. The way man treats women is much worse than the way landlords treat servants and the high-caste treat the low-caste.

~

Money lending is a horrible profession. If we are to call it otherwise it is lawful plundering.

~

Wisdom lies in thinking. The spear-head of thinking is rationalism.

~

You cannot expect any rational thought from a religious man. He is like a rocking log in water.

~

The Brahmins are making you fools in the name of god. He makes you have faith in superstitions. He leads a very comfortable life condemning you as untouchable. He bargains with you to offer prayers to god on your behalf. I strongly condemn this brokerage business and warn you not to believe such Brahmins anymore.

(Collated from Veeramani, *Collected Works of Periyar E.V.R.*)

Asghar Ali Engineer
(1939–2013)

AN 18-YEAR-OLD, UNMARRIED HINDU GIRL, LIVING WITH HER PARENTS in Jabalpur, committed suicide on 3 February 1961. A local Hindi daily alleged that the girl was raped by a Muslim boy when she was alone at home and later the helpless girl burnt herself. The news spread through the town and the two religious communities came to a clash. About 15 people were killed in the clash and police firing, nearly a hundred injured and more than 200 houses were damaged. The Muslims suffered the most.

Asghar Ali was only 22 years old then. He was an engineering student at the time and was so disturbed by the news of the riots that he visited Jabalpur to investigate and identify the likely cause. As an eight-year-old boy living in Wardha, Maharashtra, at the time of Partition, he had heard many 'horrible stories of people being killed and trains full of dead bodies' (Engineer, 2012) and had begun wondering, even at that young age, why people killed each other in the name of religion. Now, his visit to Jabalpur marked the beginning of his lifelong fight against communalism and endeavours to create inter-religious harmony.

Born on 10 March 1939, in a Bohra Muslim family in Rajasthan, as a young boy, Asghar Ali learned Arabic language and studied the Quran, the Hadith and the Prophet's sayings. After his schooling, he graduated with a degree in civil engineering from Vikram University in Ujjain, Madhya Pradesh. He served for 20 years as an engineer in the Bombay Municipal Corporation. He was generally referred to as Asghar Ali Engineer, after his profession, and the name stuck.

In 1972, he took voluntary retirement from service at the young age of 33 to work for the progress and welfare of the Bohra community and create a platform for progressive Muslims in India and elsewhere. The reformist movement he initiated came to be known as 'liberation theology in Islam' after the liberation theology of Latin America.

Liberation theology, as a synthesis of Christian theology and Marxian socio-economic analyses with its social concern for the poor and liberation of the oppressed, first emerged in the 1960s in Latin America and then spread to Brazil, Uruguay and Spain. Basically, it was a reinterpretation of the life and teachings of Jesus Christ from the perspective of the downtrodden, with emphasis on action and agency of the oppressed. Inspired by this new politico-religious philosophy, new forms of theologies of liberation developed in other parts of the world, such as Black theology in the USA and South Africa, Palestinian liberation theology in Palestine, and Dalit theology in India.

Challenging the regressive beliefs and practices propagated by the clergymen, Asghar Ali Engineer deployed liberation theology to show that the teachings of the Quran and Prophet Muhammad are compatible with the principles of economic, social and gender equality, and with pluralism and democracy. Besides, he took up study of communal and ethnic violence in India and South Asia and worked tirelessly for communal harmony. He wrote more than 50 books and lectured extensively on the tenets of Islam in light of liberation theology, on Hindu-Muslim relations and the urgent need for developing intra-religious and interfaith dialogues.

He was a great advocate for the modernization of madrasas, abolition of burkha and the practice of triple talaq, and pleaded for developing a liberal and modernist version of Islam. Defending his stance, he often reiterated all religious scriptures have, what he called, 'contextual and normative parts'. The values of the scripture, which are normative, remain constant and universal. But the contextual part of scriptures is subject to interpretations and change in the light of present-day knowledge, aspirations and ideals. Religious thinking and its abiding values, he argued, ought not to be confused with culture or cultural practices that keep changing from time to time.

He was elected as General Secretary of the Central Board of Dawoodi Bohra Community in 1977 but was expelled in 2004 due to his criticism of authoritarianism in the Bohra priesthood. His writings and lectures not only challenged Bohra priesthood but also the orthodox, retrogressive interpretation of the Quran by the priestly class in general, because of which there were even a few attempts on his life, in an effort to silence him.

In 1980, he set up the Institute of Islamic Studies in Mumbai, under which he produced numerous booklets offering radical interpretations of Islam for modern times. And he started the Centre for Study of Society and Secularism in 1993 for promoting interfaith dialogues and communal harmony. Recognized as a distinguished scholar of Islam, he was invited to lecture at many universities and institutions in USA, Canada, UK, Germany, France, Malaysia, Pakistan, Egypt and Moscow. He was given several awards during his lifetime, including the international award the Right Livelihood Award in 2004 for his strong commitment to promote values of co-existence and tolerance.

Some of Asghar Ali Engineer's Important Works

Origin and Development of Islam: An Essay on Its Socio-Economic Growth. South Asia Books, 1980.

The Islamic State. New Delhi: Vikas Publishing House, 1980.

Islam and Its Relevance to Our Age. Mumbai1: Institute of Islamic Studies, 1984.

Islam and Revolution. New Delhi: Ajanta Publications, 1984.

Indian Muslims: A Study of Minority Problems in India. New Delhi: Ajanta Publications, 1985.

Status of Women in Islam. New Delhi: Ajanta Publications, 1987.

Religion and Liberation. New Delhi: Ajanta Publications, 1989.

Secular Crown on Fire: the Kashmir Problem. New Delhi: Ajanta Publications, 1991.

Rights of Women in Islam. New Delhi: Sterling Publishers, 1992.

Lifting the Veil: Communal Violence and Communal Harmony in Contemporary India. Hyderabad: Sangam Books, 1995.

Problems of Muslim Women in India. Mumbai: Institute of Islamic Studies, 1995.

Rethinking Issues in Islam. Mumbai: Sangam Books, 1998.

The Gujarat Carnage. Hyderabad: Orient Longman, 2003.

The Quran, Women, and Modern Society. Elgin, Illinois: New Dawn Press Group, 2005.

Islam in Post-Modern World. Gurgaon: Hope India Publications, 2009.

A Living Faith: My Quest for Peace, Harmony and Social Change. New Delhi: Orient Blackswan, 2012.

Selected Quotes from His Writings

Religion helps you relate with the universe. Buddha was indifferent to the concept of god yet he gave us values.

~

History is full of instances of people who challenged the mighty forces of evil and they were not only fighting a lonely battle but were left alone to die.

~

Jihad is nothing but making efforts to realise goodness in life.

~

Quran says do not abuse others' gods, they will abuse Allah. But most people do not believe in this... they feel their way is the only right one. This is to maintain religious hegemony.

~

Real 'imaan' is faith in humanity, so those who deny goodness are kafirs.

~

Women's position includes so many pre-Islamic customs that have become an integral part of the Shariat. I am fighting that. Triple talaq is not mentioned in the Quran. Of course, there is a controversy; some maintain that the Prophet approved of it. Even if he did, maybe he had social constraints.

~

I am not an individualist in the Western sense. Collectivism can become oppressive when it tries to dictate; the rights of the two should not clash.

~

Atheists blame religion when priests do wrong. Anything can be misused, whether it is nuclear power or a matchstick. So, how can I blame religion? Patriotism too can be misused, by misinforming others and eliminating people, so do we start hating the country?

~

The Sufi saint Mazhar Jaan Jana of eighteenth century Delhi believed that the Quran condemns bowing before deities because in pre-Islamic idol worship stones were considered god. But Hindus pray to god through that idol, which is a reflection of god. In Vedas god is nirguna and nirakara, that is, he has no attributes and no shape, that is the real belief of Hindus. As Muslims visit graves, so Hindus worship idols.

~

My personal belief is we should not bow to any object. But Islam was aware of this human weakness and fulfilled that need through Haj to kiss a stone. A stone is a stone but the vacuum was filled and it became the holiest object. I have performed Haj and seen the devotion of people braving stampedes only to kiss that stone.

~

Many people asked me to convert. I said my religious convictions remain. I am fighting the wrongs within my own community. And if I decide to convert I will lose the right to fight.

(Collated from Engineer, *A Living Faith: My Quest for Peace, Harmony and Social Change*.)

৩৩৩৩

Gopi Krishna
(1903–84)

ONE DAY, AS WAS HIS PRACTICE FOR THE PAST 17 YEARS, GOPI KRISHNA sat in a corner of a room in his house for his meditation. Over these years, he had developed the art of sitting in padmasana for hours at a time without the least discomfort. It had been his desire to attain the state of consciousness, said to be the ultimate goal of yoga, where one came into the state of supreme happiness or bliss, beyond the spheres of opposites, where one was released from the desire for life and fear of death.

For 17 years, he had yearned to be in that state of being but nothing tangible had happened, and he had begun to despair and to doubt if the method he had adopted was right. However, he had carried on with the rigorous discipline without fail. Now, he sat down on the mat, breathing slowly and rhythmically, his attention drawn towards the crown of his head, 'contemplating an imaginary lotus in full bloom, radiating light'. What happened next changed him forever. In his words:

Suddenly, with a roar like that of a waterfall, I felt a stream of liquid light entering my brain through the spinal cord. The illumination grew brighter and brighter, the roaring louder, I experienced a rocking sensation and then felt myself slipping out of my body, enveloped in a halo of light. I felt the point of consciousness that was myself growing wider surrounded by waves of light. It grew wider and wider, spreading outward... I was now all consciousness without any outline, without any idea of corporeal appendage, without any feeling or sensation coming from the senses, immersed in a sea of light simultaneously conscious and aware at every point, spread out, as it were, in all directions without any barrier or material obstruction. I was no longer myself, or a small point of awareness confined to a body, but instead was a vast circle of consciousness in which the body was but a point, bathed in light and in a state of exultation and happiness impossible to describe.

(Krishna, 1993)

It was only the beginning of an incredible journey into an uncharted, turbulent sea with no shore in sight. He had no clue what was happening to him. He had yearned for a state of permanent bliss but now was tossed around over gigantic waves of sensations he could not comprehend. He did not know then that he was being prepared to enter the state 'beyond the spheres of opposites', but not in the sense he had imagined it. It was a torturous, mind-boggling journey, but worth the sacrifice of even 'the kingdom of God'. (Krishna, 1993)

～

Gopi Krishna was born in 1903 in a small village called Gairoo, on the outskirts of Srinagar. There was nothing very unusual about his childhood, except perhaps a very strange dream he had at the age of eight, wherein he saw in a diffused, ethereal world, celestial beings and his own self transfigured in a gloriously bright world, in stark contrast to the shabby, noisy surroundings in which he lived. Perhaps the dream was indicative of things that would happen in the future.

Gopi Krishna's ancestors were among the refugees who had fled the massacre of Kashmiri Pandits in Kashmir and settled in Lahore, though for jobs and other domestic reasons the family moved between Srinagar and Lahore. His mother's family lived in Srinagar. Past his prime, his father had moved from Amritsar to Srinagar, joined the Public Works Department there and married late, at the age of 38.

His father was a deeply spiritual person and a seeker in his own right. He spent most of his free time either with sadhus and yogis, or his books on spirituality. After 12 years of marriage and three children, he took voluntary retirement from the lucrative government job before he was even 50. It is said he immersed himself in his spiritual pursuits and led a recluse's life, leaving the entire responsibility of managing the household and the task of bringing up their two daughters and a son entirely on the shoulders of his young wife, who was barely 28 years old.

It is interesting to note here that their relatives and the family members, including the wife, held him in awe. He carried an aura with his clairvoyant and prophetic gifts. Perhaps, the son would speculate later, his father had experienced the arousal of the Kundalini, spiritual energy or life force, had gained extraordinary occult powers, but not the bliss and tranquillity of liberated consciousness. However, if, on the one hand, Gopi Krishna inherited the deep spiritual vein from his father, for which he was grateful; on the other, seeing his father's negligence of the family he resolved never to abandon his familial responsibilities.

The family lived poorly, but Gopi's mother did not complain; instead, she resigned to the Divine Will and carried on the best way possible. With some help from her side of the family, she managed the household and saw the children through their education. Gopi Krishna completed his high school education and joined a college in Srinagar for his graduation. He took to reading books, starting with *The Arabian Nights*, then progressing from easy stories to literary works, and moving from Kashmiri to Urdu to English. He devoured books that came into his hands. And he turned into an 'agnostic, full of doubts and questions' about religious beliefs and ideas. He 'thirsted for rationality in religion, for the worship of the truth'.

As a youngster in search of his identity and looking for a bright future, he found himself at the crossroads when, as a result of neglecting his studies, he failed in his exams. He felt he had betrayed his mother's trust in him and was struck with remorse. It seemed there was no way for him to go back and repair the damage. He did not confess his failure, nor did he share his agony with his mother. Instead, he decided to live a life of self-restraint and took to meditation. From meditation it was but a step to yoga and spiritual studies. Recalling this difficult phase in his life, Gopi Krishna wrote, 'At this time of acute conflict, the sublime message of the *Bhagavad Gita* had a most profound and salutary effect on me' (Krishna, 1976).

Giving up his studies, he applied for a job and luckily found a post in the Public Works Department at Srinagar, the same department from where his father had taken voluntary retirement. He continued with his spiritual pursuits but the thought of giving up his family never occurred to him. In fact, he was revolted by the idea of becoming a homeless ascetic, depending on the labour of others for his sustenance. He married a 15-year-old Kashmiri girl and decided to live a simple and clean life, 'free from the fever of social rivalry and display', and pursue calmly the path he had chosen for himself. A few years later, he was transferred to the Education Department, where his work was not as demanding as it used to be in the Public Works Department, and it was certainly free of corrupt practices.

In 1937, at the age of 37, he experienced the first stirrings of Kundalini power. It was something he had least expected, and it came upon him like a tidal wave at sea. The experience was not one of absolute peace and ecstasy; rather, it was often terrifying and torturous. The few brief intervals of mental elation – the expansion of his consciousness, a radiant current flowing through his body – were followed by fits of depression so acute that he had to muster all his strength and willpower to keep himself from succumbing to their influence. Repeatedly, he felt he was dying, and his body burned as if the scorching sun had risen inside it. He felt like a 'terror-stricken stranger in [his] own flesh'.

Despite suffering these terrible physiological conditions, he did not seek help from any physician, let alone consult a psychiatrist. He did not share the 'life-and-death struggle' he was going through with his wife either. He tried to seek guidance from sadhus and mystics but they were of no help. None could give him accurate information on the mysterious power and its enigmatic ways. More importantly, in his words, 'Even the advocates of kundalini yoga, starting with the discipline and purification of internal organs, failed to give the corporeal frame the status it deserved' (Krishna, 1976). In other words, they had no understanding of the biological basis of this tremendous phenomenon. It could be because of the absence of adequate physiological information. So he had to be his own guide and paddle the canoe all by himself and hope to reach the other shore.

Gopi Krishna had to endure these terrible pains and the other side effects of the physiological changes taking place within his body for 15 years before the state of 'cosmic consciousness' stabilized. Then, given his sceptical bent of mind, he took another 20 years before he went public with his experiences.

It was a case of radical transformation in the microbiology of every cell, tissue and fibre of the organism. The arousal of Kundalini implied the activation of a hitherto sleeping force, and the start of 'a new activity in the whole system to adapt it to a new pattern of consciousness by changing the composition of the bio-energy or subtle life force permeating the whole body' (Krishna, 1976). The terrible discomfort he had to endure was due to the process of purgation, the internal purification of the organs and nerves; it was Kundalini Shakti 'hammering and pounding them into a certain shape'. It was a terrific journey that put him in a state of higher consciousness, yet he never equated himself with sages like the Buddha or Ramana Maharshi.

He said, 'I do not claim to be illuminated in the sense we ascribe illumination to Buddha ... I am still very much entrenched in the world and have not completely risen above it. I feel more at home in calling myself a normal human being, like millions of others who inhabit the earth.

'All I claim is that for more than forty years, I have been undergoing a most extraordinary experience which is now a constant source of wonder and joy to me ... I am always conscious of a luminous glow, not only in my interior but pervading the whole field of my vision during the hours of my wakefulness ... In other words, I have gained a new power of perception that was not present before. The luminosity does not end with my waking time. It persists even in my dreams ... In every state of being—eating, drinking, talking, working, laughing, grieving, walking or sleeping—I always dwell in a rapturous world of light.' (Krishna, 1993)

Given this state of being, Gopi Krishna could have easily become a guru, but he did not. He was an extraordinarily honest mystic, the likes of whom are hard to find today. He was truly a living example of the liberating powers of Kundalini, of the cellular revolution within the body that lifts one out of that which is limited, the 'I' consciousness. And he never tired of reiterating that it is false and delusional to think that 'the human mind can win entry to supersensory realms without affecting the body in any way'.

He died in 1984 at the age of 81 after a severe lung disease. Until then, he worked tirelessly to correct the false perception of the body as a mere mechanical, corporeal frame and to persuade scientists to investigate the phenomenon of Kundalini. He believed such research would ultimately lead to the discovery of the biological factors responsible for higher states of consciousness and it could, in the course of time, also put an end to the rivalry between science and religion and the needless controversies and conflicts among the various religions.

Unfortunately, no scientific group evinced sufficient interest in his proposal during his lifetime. Only years later, research organizations came to be established in New York, Canada and Switzerland to collate information on the subject of Kundalini and to collect case histories of individuals and promote scientific and medical research. However, it is important to remember here that it was most notably Gopi Krishna, followed by the Mother of Pondicherry and U.G. Krishnamurti, who drew the attention of scientists, scholars and spiritual questers engaged in the study of consciousness to investigate the physiological basis of the mystical or higher states of consciousness.

◈

The Mother of Pondicherry
(1878–1973)

ONCE, SPEAKING TO A GATHERING OF THE TEACHERS AT THE AUROBINDO Ashram in Pondicherry, the Mother said, 'Basically, the only thing you should do assiduously is to teach them to know themselves and to choose their own destinies... Teach them to examine themselves, to understand themselves, and to want themselves. It's far more important than teaching the past history of the earth, or even how the earth is made...'

Then, addressing the students, she said, 'You are here to become the representatives of the new race. Everything depends on your will and your sincerity. If you no longer want to belong to the ordinary humanity, if you no longer want to be only evolved animals, if you want to become the new human, if you want to live a new and higher life upon a renewed earth, then you will find here all the help needed to succeed... Humanity is not the last rung of terrestrial creation. Evolution continues and the human will be surpassed. It is for each one to decide whether he or she wants to participate in the adventure of the new species.' (Satprem, 2005)

The Mother was regarded as the forerunner of a new species on earth by many of her followers. The Mother was born as Mirra Alfassa on 21 Febraury 1878 in Paris to a Turkish Jewish father, Moise Maurice Alfassa, and an Egyptian Jewish mother, Mathilde Ismalun. Months before Mirra was born, the couple separated and Mirra grew up with her maternal grandmother, Mira Ismalum.

From a young age, Mirra was fond of reading books, and it is said that by the age of 14, she had read most of the books in her father's library. Later, after studying art, she became an accomplished painter and in 1897, married Henri Morisset, also an artist. Mirra was not a particularly religious person, not a believer in God; yet, even as a girl, she had various 'occult' experiences. She recalled later that she knew nothing of the subject or its significance and yet she continued to have these experiences which seemed to come over her spontaneously.

It is only in her late twenties that she developed an urge to know the significance of such 'mystical' happenings. She read Swami Vivekananda's *Raja Yoga* and the Bhagavad Gita in French, and got involved with the Cosmic Movement, founded by Max Theon around 1900 and aimed at the spiritual advancement of humanity. This eventually led her to meet with Buddhists and other spiritually oriented people.

Her marriage to Henri had ended in 1908. In 1911, she married her second husband, Paul Richard, and three years later, in 1914, along with Richard, she travelled to India and visited Pondicherry, then a French colony. The husband and wife met Aurobindo, who had by then settled in Pondicherry. At their very first meeting, Mirra at once recognized him as the master who had appeared in her dreams several times over the years and had inwardly been guiding her spiritual development, and her life changed that day.

A year later, Mirra joined Aurobindo in his sadhana. Initially, she encountered a general feeling of resistance from the other residents of Aurobindo House. But once Aurobindo, who considered her to be of equal yogic stature, called her the 'Mother', the resistance melted away and the members looked upon her as a gifted yogini.

For about 10 years, Aurobindo worked with the Mother and other members in developing the 'ashram' as a kind of spiritual laboratory, where fullness and prosperity, equality of the sexes and a life-affirming attitude were cultivated, where, more importantly, the new integral, divine life was tried on a much larger scale than had ever been attempted before.

In 1926, when Aurobindo withdrew from all activities to concentrate on his Integral Yoga, the Mother took charge of the ashram. Under her guidance, which extended nearly 50 years, the ashram grew into a large, multi-faceted community. She founded the Sri Aurobindo International Centre of Education in 1951, and the international township Auroville in 1968. It was the Mother's dream that 'there should be somewhere on earth a place where no nation could claim as its own... a place of peace, concord and harmony... In this ideal place money would no longer be the sovereign lord; individual worth would have a far greater importance than that of material wealth and social standing' (Das, 1978).

After Sri Aurobindo's passing away in 1950, the Mother carried on the work with unexpected but revealing discoveries. Satprem, her close associate for 19 years, recorded these discoveries. These recordings were later published under the title *Mother's Agenda*, a massive 13 volume, 6,000 page journal. In these pages, the Mother described in detail the changes, in particular the physical changes she underwent – or what she called 'cellular changes' – from 1962 onwards until her passing in 1973. *The Mind of the Cells* by Satprem is a distilled but more cohesive account of these very same changes.

It was a great discovery in the sense that the mother realized that the 'I' or the individual had no role to play in this process of change. It was the body with its innate intelligence *taking over and doing what had to be done*. And the Mother wondered why the spiritual teachers of the past sought liberation by abandoning their body, and why they spoke of nirvana as something outside the body. Why did they not know this, instead going after 'religions, gods, and all those sorts of things?'

'Salvation is physical,' she declared in unequivocal terms and went on to explain that it is not the mind but the body, the physical, that is capable of receiving and manifesting 'the Superior Light, the

Truth, the true consciousness' (Satprem, 1982). It is instructive to note here that her illustrious contemporaries, namely, Gopi Krishna and U.G. Krishnamurti, following different trajectories, arrived at the same conclusion, that is, the body is the field of light and energy, the source and ground of intelligence and enlightenment.

And yet, we cannot say that this was entirely a new discovery, for, in varied ways, texts such as Kundalini Yoga and Tantra Yoga, poet-saints and sages such as Abhinavagupta and Lalleshwari, to name a few, reveal in clear terms the physiological basis of the mystical or higher states of consciousness. However, we could still claim that in modern times, the Mother, along with Gopi Krishna and U.G. Krishnamurti, was one of the first people to have articulated in a plain and definitive language the biological foundation of nirvana.

The Teachings

For me everything in human life is mixed, nothing is completely good, nothing completely bad. I cannot give my entire and exclusive support to this idea or that idea, to one cause or another. The only important thing for me, in action, is Sri Aurobindo's work, automatically my conscious support is with all that helps that work and in proportion to the help. And for the work to be carried on as it must be I need all collaborations and all helps, I cannot accept only this one or that one and reject the others. I cannot belong to this party or that party. I belong to the Divine alone and my action upon earth is and will always be for the triumph of the Divine, irrespective of all sects and parties.

∼

What you must know is exactly the thing you want to do in life. The time needed to learn it does not matter at all. For those who wish to live according to Truth, there is always something to learn and some progress to make.

∼

The true aim of life is to find the Divine's Presence deep inside oneself and to surrender to It so that It takes the lead of the life, all the feelings and all the actions of the body. This gives a true and luminous aim to existence.

~

Never forget that you are not alone. The Divine is with you helping and guiding you. He is the companion who never fails, the friend whose love comforts and strengthens. Have faith and He will do everything for you.

~

The intellectual attitude comes first and practice follows little by little. What is very important is to maintain very alert the will to live and to be what one knows to be the truth. Then it is impossible to stop and even more to fall back.

~

Our human consciousness has windows that open on the Infinite but generally men keep these windows carefully shut. They have to be opened wide and allow the Infinite freely to enter into us and transform us.

~

When you sit in meditation you must be as candid and simple as a child, not interfering by your external mind, expecting nothing, insisting on nothing. Once this condition is there, all the rest depends upon the aspiration deep within you. And if you call upon Divinity, then too you will have the answer.

~

Sex seems rather to be more of the body. It is only when you pass from the lower to the higher hemisphere that you can completely erase the thing. Sex belongs to Nature in her lower working and as long as you belong to that Nature, her working will be there automatically in you.

~

You should not confuse a calm mind with a silent mind. You can calm your mind and stop its ordinary activity, but it may still be open to ideas coming from outside and that too disturbs the calm. And for the mind to be completely silent, you must not only stop its own activity but shut out all that comes from other minds.

(Collated from *Words of the Mother I, II and III*, 2004)

❦

Jiddu Krishnamurti
(1895–1986)

JIDDU KRISHNAMURTI WAS SCHEDULED TO VISIT INDIA FOR A SERIES OF talks in October 1976. The state of Emergency that Prime Minister Indira Gandhi had declared the previous year, on 25 June 1975, was still in force, and so J.K. was not sure if he should visit a country where freedom of speech had been severely curtailed. His talks usually focussed on freedom at all levels and on fearless and honest enquiry into problems of living. Would he be jailed if he questioned the political authority? He could not allow himself to be put in prison or prevented from leaving the country, and he would not seek special favours either.

Pupul Jayakar, one of his close associates and a friend of Indira Gandhi, assured him that he could not be jailed for speaking freely, for the culture of India always looked upon religious teachers as 'a light that could not be extinguished'. Pupul added that the prime minister herself had assured unequivocally that Krishnaji was welcome and could speak freely.

He arrived in October, when, due to the Emergency, many leaders had been jailed. On 27 October, Indira Gandhi had her first meeting with J.K. and his associates over dinner. No serious talk took place then, only a few humorous tales were exchanged, which lessened the tension. The next morning, Indira Gandhi came back and had a private meeting with J.K. for over an hour.

She was different, J.K. told Pupul later, attentive to his every word. She had admitted that she was riding the back of a tiger and did not know how to get off it. J.K. had said that if she was more intelligent than the tiger she would know how to deal with it, and had advised her to 'act rightly, without fear of consequence' (Jayakar, 1986).

Less than three months later, on 18 January 1977, Prime Minister Indira Gandhi called fresh general elections and released all political prisoners. The state of Emergency officially ended on 23 March 1977. Ten years later, in 1986, Pupul published her book *Krishnamurti: A Biography* (1986), in which she wrote about a chance meeting she had had with Indira Gandhi, a month after the lifting of the Emergency. Indira Gandhi had apparently admitted to Pupul that, in her second meeting with J.K., on October 28, 1976, 'a frail movement had awakened in her, suggesting an end to emergency, whatever the consequences. She had mulled over this feeling, talked to a few people close to her, and finally took the decision to call for elections.' (Jayakar, 1986)

~

Jiddu Krishnamurti was born in a Telugu-speaking brahmin family on 12 May 1895, in the small town of Madanapalle in Andhra Pradesh. He was the eighth child of Jiddu Narayaniah and Sanjeevamma, and was named after the Hindu god Krishna. His mother died when he was 10 and he and his siblings were brought up by their father.

After his retirement from the government service in 1909, Jiddu Narayaniah sought employment in the Theosophical Society at Adyar and the family moved to Madras. The Theosophical Society had completed 34 years by then and its philosophy was seen as one of the spiritual alternatives that could unite people of all races in a war-torn world. However, at this point in time, the society was on the lookout for a World Teacher, or, what they called 'Lord Maitreya', an advanced spiritual entity, who would lead them and guide the evolution of humankind.

In April 1909, the long search for the likely 'Lord Maitreya' came to fruition when Charles Webster Leadbeater, a prominent member of the society, spotted the 14-year-old Jiddu Krishnamurti, with rather vacant eyes, squatted on the sands of the Adyar beach and saw in him the future world teacher. Along with his brother Nityananda, Krishnamurti was adopted by Annie Besant and was taken to England, to be groomed as the head of the 'Order of the Star', a special society of Theosophists that had been already established to facilitate the coming of the World Teacher.

In 1922, during a stay at Ojai, California, J.K. underwent an intense, 'life-changing' experience while he sat beneath an old pepper tree. Later, talking about the experience in a letter to a close associate, J.K. wrote: 'Nothing could ever be the same... I have seen the Light. I have touched compassion... I have drunk at the fountain of Joy and eternal Beauty. I am God-intoxicated' (Lutyens, 1983). This 'life-altering' experience was followed by what was then called the 'process', a series of mystical experiences, which would recur, at frequent intervals and with varying intensity, until his last days. In his notebooks, J.K. described these experiences interchangeably as the 'presence', 'immensity', 'sacredness', 'vastness' and 'otherness'.

As news of his mystical experiences spread, the belief concerning his messianic status was further strengthened. But all that came to naught when in 1925, his brother, Nitya, died at Ojai from complications of influenza and tuberculosis. He was only 27 years old. J.K. received the terrible news while he was on his way to Adyar to attend the Theosophical Society's Jubilee Convention in Madras. Nitya's premature death shook J.K.'s belief in theosophy and his faith in the masters and the leaders of the Theosophical Society. The masters had promised to protect Nityananda against all danger and work with him in his career as the World Teacher, but that was not to be.

Over the next few years, J.K. began to seriously question and re-examine the ideology and practices of the society and his own role as its World Teacher. There was indeed a radical shift in his outlook and it showed in the new concepts that appeared in his talks, discussions and correspondences. It seemed to him that spiritual authority of any kind was wrong, and suddenly he was not sure if he should play the role of the World Teacher the way it had been projected by the Theosophical Society.

In 1927, in a gathering of theosophists, he declared: 'I hold that doubt is essential for the discovery and the understanding of the Truth...' And he reprimanded his followers for their blind beliefs and invited them to reject all spiritual authorities, including his own. Two years later, on 3 August 1929, he dissolved the Order of the Star and severed all his connections with the society. He said:

> I maintain that truth is a pathless land, and you cannot approach
> it by any path whatsoever, by any religion, by any sect. That is my
> point of view, and I adhere to that absolutely and unconditionally.
> ...And I desire to free him from all cages, from all fears, and not
> to found religions, new sects, nor to establish new theories and
> new philosophies.

(Lutyens, 1983)

He resigned from the various trusts and other organizations that were affiliated with the now defunct Order of the Star and returned the donated monies and properties of the order to their donors. From then on J.K. was on his own, holding dialogues and giving public talks around the world. Many theosophists were hurt and disappointed; some felt that he hadn't been fit to be the world teacher, while a few remained his ardent admirers and followed him in his new path.

In his talks now, he questioned, doubted, probed, tested and negated the established and sacred beliefs and ideas of religious traditions of the East and West. For over 60 years, he travelled the world, and with doubt as his method, he spoke on the nature of belief, truth, sorrow, freedom, death and the quest for a spiritually fulfilled life. In every talk and discussion, he reiterated that what he was trying to do was not teaching, but 'sharing', 'merely acting as a mirror' in which others could see themselves clearly and then discard the mirror.

J.K.'s teaching marked a major departure in religious thinking and the philosophy of religion in modern times. It was a voice utterly new and revolutionary, that changed the way people regarded religious discourses. And it wouldn't be an exaggeration to state that he was the first 'deconstructionist', so to speak, who dissected and analysed words to discover their true significance and blaze a scorching new path to analyse the intriguing nature and functioning of the human mind, much before the postmodernist thinkers, such as Jacques Derrida, Gilles Deleuze, Michel Foucault and others appeared on the world scene. His epic career as a teacher came to a dramatic end when he fell seriously ill and was diagnosed with cancer of the pancreas. He died on 17 February 1986, at the age of 90.

Today, there are four Krishnamurti Foundations in the UK, USA, India and Spain, actively engaged in publishing and translating J.K.'s books, most of which are transcriptions of his talks. A significant number of these books have been translated into over 30 languages of the world, including most Indian languages.

Some of these foundations also run Krishnamurti Study Centres, where interested seekers watch videos of his talks and engage in discussions of his teachings. Rishi Valley School at Madanapalle, Andhra Pradesh, was the first school he founded in 1926. Thereafter seven more schools were started, one each in UK and USA, and five in different parts of India. The schools follow a holistic approach to education, where an informal, Montessori method of teaching is followed with curricula that includes developing an appreciation for the environment, art, music and athletics, in addition to traditional subjects, such as science and humanities.

The Teachings

You and the world are not two different entities with separate problems; you and the world are one. You may be the result of certain tendencies, on environmental influences, but you are not different fundamentally from another. Inwardly we are very much alike; we are all driven by greed, ill will, fear, ambition, and so on.

~

If we would bring about a sane and happy society we must begin with ourselves and not with another, not outside of ourselves, but with ourselves. As we are—the world is. That is, if we are greedy, envious, competitive, our society will be competitive, envious, greedy, which brings misery and war. The State is what we are. To bring about order and peace, we must begin with ourselves and not with society, not with the State, for the world is ourselves.

~

Organized religion separates man from man. You are a Muslim, I am a Hindu, another is a Christian or a Buddhist—and we are wrangling, butchering each other. Is there any truth in that?

~

Truth is not of the past or the present, it is timeless; the man who quotes the truth of the Buddha, of Shankara, of Christ, or who merely repeats what I am saying, will not find truth, because repetition is not truth. Repetition is a lie.

~

To die every day to every problem, every pleasure, and not

carry over any problem at all so the mind remains tremendously attentive, active, clear.

~

People need to be awakened, not instructed.

~

When all authority of every kind is put aside, denied, then you can find out for yourself.

~

To be vulnerable is to live. To withdraw is to die.

~

Beware of the man who offers you a reward in this world or the next.

~

The state of the mind that questions is much more important than the question itself.

~

Truth is an eternal movement, and so cannot be measured in words or in time.

~

When our hearts are empty, we collect things.

~

Freedom from desire for an answer is essential to the understanding of a problem.

~

Knowledge prevents listening.

~

The ideal is always what is not.

(Collated from the books: *Total Freedom*, *The Essential Krishnamurti*, Krishnamurti Foundation India, 2002; and *The Awakening of Intelligence*, Penguin Books India, 2000)

❦

U.G. Krishnamurti
(1918–2007)

THIS INCIDENT TOOK PLACE SOMETIME IN 1969. ONE EVENING, WHEN his friends had gone out and U.G. Krishnamurti was alone in a coffee estate near Chickmangaluru, Karnataka, he heard a wild wailing of a child coming from the backyard and was drawn to the outhouse there. He went in and saw a woman beating her child. She hit the child so hard that the child almost turned blue. He could not intervene, because he simply could not move. There was no way he could stop the mother, for he felt a continuous movement inside of him, which embodied both the anger and frustration of the mother and the pain and suffering of the child.

Later that evening, when his friends returned and he told them about the incident, one of them asked why he did not intervene to stop the mother from beating the child. He showed them the marks of the beating on his back and said:

You are the child and you are the mother, which one you are and for which one the heart is beating, you do not know. There is one continuous movement here. Anything that is happening there is affecting you. This is affection, compassion. To bear and suffer; sorrow and pity excited by the misfortunes of another. You are affected by everything that is happening there. There is a flow of compassion both towards the child and to the mother. The one who is beating the child is me, and the child who is receiving the beatings is also myself. It is very difficult to communicate this to you.

(Rao, 2005)

A similar incident took place sometime in the mid-seventies, when Krishnamurti, Valentine, his close associate, and a few other friends were staying in a hill station in North Goa. One morning, Krishnamurti and his friends climbed down a hill and sat at its foot, chatting. Valentine, who found the path down the hill too steep and slippery for her, decided against joining the group. It seemed like a wise decision, for it had been quite risky coming down the slippery path. The men now got to talking about what each one would have done if Valentine had decided to come with them and slipped and fallen. Krishnamurti said nothing.

After a while, Valentine came out of her cottage and ventured down the treacherous path, and indeed slipped and fell. Even the man who happened to be just behind her could not help her, let alone the ones sitting down. A stunned silence fell over the group as Valentine got up and limped down and joined the group. With a bemused smile U.G. Krishnamurti pointed out to the men that they did nothing even though each of them had said they would help her.

One of the members of the group asked him, 'How come you yourself did nothing to help then?' He said quietly, 'I never said that I would give her a helping hand. If, however, you want to see for yourself how I myself was involved in that event...' and he rolled up the leg of his trouser. They found scratches upon his knee similar to those found on Valentine's knee. (Rao, 2005)

His friends and admirers lovingly called him 'U.G'. The media dubbed him a sage in rage, a cosmic Naxalite, anti-guru and so on. Sometimes, he jokingly called himself a 'useless guy', and seriously as an 'unconverted member of the human race', meaning he absolutely did not belong to or endorse any religion, any philosophy, any political ideology, or any -ism whatsoever. During his career as an 'anti-guru',

U.G. dismantled all spiritual discourses and teachings, and refused to erect or construct anything new in its place. In his negation of all approaches to truth, he insisted that his teaching, if it could be called a teaching at all, implied no method and so it could not be made into yet another approach. He was a tremendous force, truthful and cleansing. A fiery embodiment of the non-dual state of being.

~

Uppaluri Gopala Krishnamurti was born on 9 July 1918 in Masulipatnam, a town in coastal Andhra Pradesh, India. His mother died seven days after he was born and he was brought up by his maternal grandparents. He grew up in a peculiar milieu of both theosophy and Hindu religious beliefs and practices. He completed his primary education in a school at Gudivada in Krishna district of Andhra Pradesh and then went to Madras for higher studies. During his three-year degree course in Philosophy and Psychology at Madras University, he spent summer days in the Himalaya, studying yoga and practising meditation.

At this time, he came upon certain mystical experiences, yet deep within him, he realized, there was no fundamental change. He felt he was going nowhere either in his spiritual pursuits or academic studies and so in utter frustration he left the university. He had just stepped into his twenties and already he had started feeling utterly lost. However, one day, upon his friend's suggestion, he went to meet Ramana Maharshi. He asked Ramana:

'Is there anything like moksha? Can you give it to me?'

Ramana said, 'I can give it, but can you take it?'

No guru before had given him such an answer. They had only advised him to do more sadhana, more of what he had already done and finished with. But here was a guru, an enlightened being, asking, 'Can you take it?' The counter-question struck U.G. like a thunderbolt and he realized that nobody could really give that state to him, he had to find the truth for himself.

In 1943, at 25 years of age, he married and started working for the Theosophical Society, Madras. He travelled extensively in India and Europe and gave talks on theosophy. At the end of his seventh year with the society, he quit the post. Between 1947 and 1953, he listened to J. Krishnamurti's talks and interacted with him at a personal level. It was during this period that he underwent what he called a 'near-death experience' that altered his perception of life and eventually lead him up to a 'final death' and awakening in 1967.

In brief, he went to the USA to get medical treatment for his polio-stricken son, took to lecturing to earn a living, and, after his wife and sons went back to India, visited parts of Europe on work and then began to drift aimlessly in London, like a dry leaf blown hither and thither. Eventually he landed up in Saanen, Switzerland, and let go of everything. The search for truth had ceased by then. Nonetheless, as fate would have it, on 13 August 1967, on the completion of his forty-ninth year, he experienced biological changes begin to manifest in him. For the next seven days, seven bewildering changes took place and catapulted him into what he called the 'Natural State'.

In seven days, the whole chemistry of his body, including the five senses, was transformed. His eyes stopped blinking, his skin turned soft, and when he rubbed any part of his body with his palm, it produced a sort of ash. His senses started functioning independently and at peak sensitivity. The hitherto dormant ductless glands, such as the thymus, the pituitary, the pineal, which Kundalini Yoga calls the chakras or energy centres, were activated. And on the eighth day, he went through a 'death' experience, only to be reborn in the state of 'undivided consciousness'.

For about 40 odd years until his death, U.G. travelled the world, and, wherever he stayed, people came to see him and to listen to his 'anti-teaching'. He talked openly of the Natural State and responded to people's queries and answered their questions candidly, holding nothing back, 'revealing all the secrets' (Arms, 1982).

He gave his first and only public talk at the Indian Institute of World Culture in Bangalore, in May 1972. He usually stayed with friends or in small, rented apartments. He gave no lectures or discourses. He had no organization, no office, no secretary and no fixed address.

He often insisted on using the term 'Natural State' rather than 'Enlightenment', for he asserted that whatever transformation he had gone through was within the structure of the human body and not in the mind at all. And, avoiding religious terms, he described the Natural State as a pure and simple physical and physiological state of being. It is the 'undivided state of consciousness', where all desires and fear, and the search for happiness and pleasure, God and truth, have come to an end. In addition, he never tired of pointing out that 'this is the way you, stripped of the machinations of thought, are also functioning' (Arms, 1982).

If, on the one hand, U.G. marked a creative continuity of the enlightenment traditions of the Buddha, the Upanishadic and the later sages of India, on the other hand, he marked a radical departure from the enlightenment traditions in the way he de-psychologized and demystified the notion of enlightenment and redefined it as the Natural State in physical and physiological terms. More importantly, by knocking off all grand narratives and systems of knowledge, he offered not only release from the tyranny of sacred symbols and ideas, gods and goals, but also a foretaste of the vast emptiness.

U.G. often said, 'Life and death cannot be separated. When what you call clinical death takes place, the body breaks itself into its constituent elements and that provides the basis for the continuity of life. In that sense the body is immortal.' He died on 22 March 2007 in Vallecrosia, Italy, on the Mediterranean coast close to the French border. He was 89 years old (Bhatt, 2009).

Anti-Teachings

There is no teaching of mine, and never shall be one. 'Teaching' is not the word for it. A teaching implies a method or a system, a technique or a new way of thinking to be applied in order to bring about a transformation in your way of life. What I am saying is outside the field of teachability; it is simply a description of the way I am functioning. It is just a description of the *natural state* of man – this is the way you, stripped of the machinations of thought, are also functioning.

~

The natural state is not the state of a self-realised, God-realised man, it is not a thing to be achieved or attained, it is not a thing to be willed into existence; it is *there* – it is the living state. This state is just the functional activity of life. By 'life' I do not mean something abstract; it is the life of the senses, functioning naturally without the interference of thought. Thought is an interloper, which thrusts itself into the affairs of the senses. It has a profit motive: thought directs the activity of the senses to get something out of them, and uses them to give continuity to itself.

~

The separation between mind and body must come to an end. Actually, there is no separation. I have no objection to the word mind but it is not in one particular location or area. Every cell in your system has a mind of its own and its functioning or working is quite different from that of the other cells.

~

Mind or thought is not yours or mine. It is our common inheritance. There is no such thing as your mind and my mind (it is in that sense mind is a myth). There is only mind, the totality of all that has been known, felt and experienced by man, handed down from generation to generation. We are all thinking and functioning in that thought sphere just as we all share the same atmosphere for breathing.

~

The body which is immortal. The moment you die, the body begins to decay, returning back to other, differently organized forms of life, putting an end to nothing. Life has no beginning and no end. A dead and dying body feeds the hungry ants there in the grave, and rotting corpses give off soil-enriching chemicals, which in turn nourish other life forms. You cannot put an end to your life, it is impossible. The body is immortal and never asks silly questions like, 'Is there immortality?' It knows that it will come to an end in that particular form, only to continue on in others. Questions about life after death are always asked out of fear.

Aphorisms

The plain fact is that if you don't have a problem, you create one. If you don't have a problem you don't feel that you are living.

~

A messiah is the one who leaves a mess behind him in this world.

~

Religions have promised roses but you end up with only thorns.

~

Anything you want to be free from for whatever reason is the very thing that can free you.

~

God and sex go together. If God goes sex goes, too.

~

When you know nothing, you say a lot. When you know something, there is nothing to say.

~

It is mortality that creates immortality. It is the known that creates the unknown. It is the time that has created the timeless. It is thought that has created the thoughtless.

~

All experiences however extraordinary they may be are in the area of sensuality.

~

Man cannot be anything other than what he is. Whatever he is, he will create a society that mirrors him.

~

Inspiration is a meaningless thing. Lost, desperate people create a market for inspiration. All inspired action will eventually destroy you and your kind.

~

Love and hate are not opposite ends of the same spectrum; they are one and the same thing. They are much closer than kissing cousins.

~

Hinduism is not a religion in the usual sense. It is a combination and confusion of many things. It is like a street with hundreds of shops.

~

Gurus play a social role, so do prostitutes.

~

Society, which has created all these sociopaths, has invented morality to protect itself from them. Society has created the 'saints' and 'sinners'. I don't accept them as such.

~

By using the models of Jesus, Buddha, or Krishna we have destroyed the possibility of nature throwing up unique individuals.

~

As long as you are doing something to be selfless, you will be a self-centred individual.

~

Society is built on a foundation of conflict, and you are society. Therefore you must always be in conflict with society.

~

It would be more interesting to learn from children, than try to teach them how to behave, how to live and how to function.

~

Food, clothing and shelter- these are the basic needs. Beyond that, if you want anything, it is the beginning of self-deception.

~

Man eats for pleasure. Your food orgies are not different from your sex orgies. Everything that man does is for pleasure.

~

Anything you experience based on knowledge is an illusion.

~

You eat not food but ideas. What you wear are not clothes, but labels and names.

~

If you do not know what happiness is, you will never be unhappy.

~

Cause and effect are not two different things, they are one. It is the mind that separates the two.

~

You formulate questions from the answers you already have.

~

You are not at peace with yourself and how can you create peace in the world.

~

All moral absolutes, all moral abstractions are falsifying you.

~

To become somebody else you need time, to be yourself it doesn't need time.

(Collated from Arms, ed., *The Mystique of Enlightenment*; and
Rao, ed., *The Biology of Enlightenment*)

❧

The Vaswanis

THE SINDHIS ARE AN ETHNOLINGUISTIC GROUP NATIVE TO THE SINDH province which came under Pakistan after Partition. After the subcontinent was partitioned in 1947, Sindhi Hindus and Sindhi Sikhs migrated to India. Ethnic Sindhi Hindus have spread themselves in many parts of India and around the world, but mainly inhabit the states of Gujarat, Maharashtra, Rajasthan and Madhya Pradesh. And they have a noteworthy presence in Indonesia, Singapore, United States,

Canada and the United Kingdom. The Vaswanis are a group of Sindhi Hindus who belong to the Lohana Kshatriya caste and were natives of Multan, a city situated on the bank of the Chenab River in Pakistan.

Sadhu Vaswani

(1879–1966)

Sadhu Vaswani was born Thanwardas Lilaram on 25 November 1879, to Lilaram and Varandevi, in Hyderabad, Sindh, a part of Pakistan today. His father was a zamindar fallen on bad times, but the family lived in relative comfort. Even as a young boy, it is said, Vaswani exhibited a spiritual bent of mind. The word 'Thanwar' means 'steadfast', one who is absorbed in the Eternal, who is calm, and the young Vaswani displayed a resoluteness which was rare among children.

One day, a story goes, on the way to Bakasrai Primary School where he studied, he and his friends happened to pass by a butcher's shop. He could not figure out the red carcasses that were hanging outside the shop. His friends laughed at his ignorance and said they were slaughtered and skinned lambs and goat, and the meat he ate at home was obtained from such carcasses. He was shocked and resolved never to eat meat again.

According to another story, one day his father took him to a Kali temple. After the puja, the priest distributed 'prasad', devotional offering. Vaswani knew a goat had been sacrificed to the Goddess and the 'prasad' was the goat meat. He shuddered at the sight of the chops of meat and refused to touch it. And he is believed to have told his father, 'Kali is the Mother of the Universe. How can the Goddess be pleased when you slaughter one of Her children and offer its flesh to Her?' Neither the father nor the priest of the temple had any answer to the question (Vaswani, 2002).

Vaswani was an extraordinarily sensitive lad, and intelligent too, who noticed early on the huge contradictions between people's beliefs and their practices. While he was at school, he was introduced to the study of the Upanishads by Brahmabandhab Upadhyay, a brahmin from Bengal, who had converted to Christianity and called himself a Hindu Catholic.

Vaswani went on to complete his BA and MA degrees from the University of Bombay in 1902 with excellent credentials. After completing his studies, he wanted to devote the rest of his life in the service of God and society, but his mother disapproved. Instead, she wanted him to take up a job, get married and settle down in life like all young people did. Not wanting to disappoint his mother, Vaswani took up a teaching job at Sindh College in Karachi, but refused to get married. A year later, he accepted a position as Professor of History and Philosophy at the famous Metropolitan College in Calcutta. He soon proved to be an excellent teacher and was admired and respected by his students. He led a frugal life and sent most of the salary he received to his mother back home.

His spiritual quest, however, continued unabated, which eventually led him to Sri Promotholal Sen, affectionately called 'Naluda'. Naluda was a nephew of the great Sri Keshab Chandra Sen, founder of the Navavidhan Brahmo Samaj. He was an unusual master with great spiritual depth. Vaswani was deeply drawn to him and came to accept him as his guru. Meanwhile, the post of Professor of Philosophy in D.J. College, Karachi, fell vacant and the members of the Collegiate Board wanted him to take up the job. He returned to Karachi and took up the post in 1908.

His reputation as a powerful teacher grew very quickly and he was invited by several organizations as a guest lecturer. In 1910, he received an invitation to participate in the World Congress of Religions to be held in Berlin, Germany. It is said he was reluctant to accept the offer, but on Naluda's advice, he agreed to go. It was indeed an opportunity to take the message of India's spirituality to lands across the seas.

Seventeen years before, in 1893, speaking at the World Parliament of Religions in Chicago, USA, Swami Vivekananda had made a great impact on Western minds. During those years, Vivekananda's and Virchand Gandhi's talks and interactions with people in USA and later in Europe had marked the beginning of the spread of Indian philosophy and its different spiritualties in the West.

In his thirties, mature in thought and brilliant in his articulation of ideas, Vaswani's speech at the World Congress of Religions in Berlin carried forward the message of the atman and oneness of life and aroused deep interest in Indian thought and culture.

Vaswani had moved out of Sindh College and was working as the Principal of Mahendra College in Patiala when his mother fell seriously ill. Plague had broken out in Sindh and his mother had fallen a victim to the dreadful disease and was taken to Karachi for treatment. It was reported later that to offer her some solace and comfort in her final hours, after she sipped some water from a glass, Vaswani took the glass from her and drank the remaining water, exposing himself to the possible infection. Such was his love to his mother. He was sorry, he told his mother, for not getting married as per her wish. But his mother reassured him that he shouldn't regret his decision, that in fact he did well in remaining a brahmachari and that she had no grief on that account.

His mother's death devastated Vaswani, but it also released him from family responsibilities. He was now free to dedicate himself to God and the service of His children. He was 40 years old then. In 1920, the Congress Party launched the non-cooperation movement and he supported it and took part in passing a resolution supporting the movement at the Sindh Political Conference of the National Congress. During that time he even wrote multiple books, including *India Arisen*, *My Motherland*, *Builders of Tomorrow* and *Apostles of Freedom*.

Later, however, he withdrew from active politics in order to concentrate on educational, cultural and spiritual activities that were the need of the hour for the revitalization of the young. He started Bharat Yuvak Sanghas and youth ashrams for training and channelizing the energies of young people. His early morning satsangs, where he gave long discourses on the Gita, the Upanishads and so on, were a great success.

In 1931, he started Sakhi Satsang for women and girls. But there was more to be done, for there was a crying need for proper educational institutions that would offer value-based education and a sense of direction to the young girls. In 1933, Vaswani resolved to attend to this urgent task by starting what later came to be called the Mira Movement, offering value-based, inclusive education to millions.

The first St. Mira's School for Girls was inaugurated in rented premises in Sindh, with just seven girls. After the Partition, in 1948, Vaswani moved out of Sindh to Pune and set up the headquarters there. The first St. Mira's High School for Girls was started in 1950, and then a college in 1962. Over the next few years, institutes offering post-graduate studies, management studies and teacher's training were also set up.

Sadhu Vaswani died on 16 January 1966. He was 86 years old. The Mira Movement and satsangs he started all over the world were his great contributions. He is revered by millions all over the world as a pure soul and an embodiment of love. He viewed different religions as different paths to one God. 'There are so many,' he said, 'who can believe in only one thing at a time. I am so made as to rejoice in the many and behold the beauty of the One in the many. Hence my affinity with many religions. In them all I see revelations of the One Spirit. And deep in my heart is the conviction that I am a servant of all prophets' (Vaswani, 2002).

His heart bled at the cruelties inflicted upon animals. 'Take my head,' he pleaded, 'but pray stop all slaughter!' This deep awareness of the need for reverence for all life and respect for all religions were central to his teachings. His devotees all over the world observe November 25, which happens to be Sadhu Vaswani's birthday, as Meatless Day and Animal Rights Day, expressing their shared commitment to the ideal of reverence for all life.

The Teachings

There is no death! Death is very much like sunset. It is only an appearance. For, when the sun sets here, it rises elsewhere. In reality, the sun never sets. Likewise, death is only an illusion, an appearance. For, what is death here is birth elsewhere. For life is endless.

~

Whenever you have taken up work in hand, you must see it to the finish. That is the ultimate secret of success. Never, never, never give up!

~

When we begin to understand the concept of Karma we will never ever blame God for anything that happens to us. We will realise that we are responsible for all that happens to us. As we sow, so shall we reap. Rich or poor, saint or sinner, miser or philanthropist, learned or illiterate... This is the Universal Law that applies to individuals, to whole communities, societies, nations and races. As we sow, so shall we reap.

~

How long will you wait for the right time to come? The right time is now and the right place is here.

~

We cannot separate ourselves from those whom we call the 'lower' animals. They are lower in the scale of evolution, but they, like us, are members of the One Family. We must not take away the life of any creature. Indeed, we must never take away that which we cannot give. And as we cannot restore a dead creature to life, we have no right to take away its life.

~

Empathy is forgetting oneself in the joys and sorrows of another, so much so that you actually feel that the joy or sorrow experienced by another is your own joy and sorrow. Empathy involves complete identification with another.

~

Are you in quest of truth? Don't go the ways of multitudes. They follow custom. Custom and tradition must you set aside and tread the lonely path, if you would be a student and a servant of truth.

~

Everything we have, our time and talents, our energy and experience, our wealth and wisdom, our knowledge and influence, our life itself is a loan given to us to be passed on to those whose need is greater than ours.

~

Within you, within every one of you, is a power of the Eternal. Have faith in yourselves. Unfold, release, set free the divine within you, and you will be able to make the impossible possible.

(Collated from Vaswani, *Sadhu Vaswani: His Life and Teachings*)

Dada Vaswani
(1918–2018)

Jashan Pahlajrai Vaswani came under the influence of Sadhu Vaswani at quite a young age and became his disciple, later rising to be a prominent player in the educational and spiritual activities started by the Sadhu Vaswani Mission. And after the master's death, J.P. Vaswani became the spiritual head of the mission, a non-profit organization headquartered in Pune, with centres around the world. In fact, it was through his efforts that the mission's activities, including its educational programmes, spread far and wide.

He was born on 2 August 1918 to Pahlajrai Vaswani and Krishnadevi, in Hyderabad, Sindh. His father worked in the educational sector and his mother was one of the few women of her generation who had had

English education. J.P. Vaswani was an extraordinarily brilliant child and started his primary education at the age of three. He received a double promotion at the primary school level and triple promotion at high school, and completed his schooling much earlier than boys of his age. He finished his graduation at 17 and earned a fellowship to do his post-graduation in Science at Karachi University. It is said that his M.Sc. thesis on X-rays was examined by the Nobel-laureate C.V. Raman, who was impressed by the originality of his views.

He was only 21 years of age, and when with such brilliant academic qualifications he could have taken up any well-paid job or pursued a bright career in the field of Science, he gave it all up to follow his guru, Sadhu Vaswani. From 1939, for over 27 years he travelled and worked closely with his master, carrying the message of love and compassion, peace and brotherhood.

A man of endearing simplicity, humility and compassion, he was a gifted speaker and writer. He authored about 150 books on meditation, karma, prophets and patriots, and many on self-help techniques, including a biography on Sadhu Vaswani. He spoke at many renowned global forums, including the UNO and the Parliament of Religions, Chicago. Like his master, he stood up for animal rights and followed an all-encompassing approach to various belief systems of the world. He believed in the possibility of creating a new world order grounded in reverence to all forms of life, respect for all religions and unconditional love and compassion.

He died on 12 July 2018, three weeks shy of his 100th birthday. His birthday, which falls on August 2, is celebrated as Forgiveness Day by his devotees all over the world. His books are widely read and he remains an inspirational figure in the field of education and spirituality.

Aphorisms

Let us not curse the darkness. Let us kindle little lights.

~

There is no such thing as emotional incompatibility. There are only misunderstandings and mistakes which can easily be set right if we have the will to do so.

~

Sincere practice, makes the impossible possible.

~

Enthusiasm is the greatest asset you can possess, for it can take you further than money, power or influence.

~

Philosophy and theology have so much to tell us about God, but people today want to experience God. There is a difference between eating dinner and merely reading the menu.

~

People need to know that they are not alone, that they have not been abandoned; but that there is One Who loves them for what they are, who cares about them.

~

From compassion springs humility. The ego is verily a gateway to hell. The person who is egoistic is far from being religious.

~

The farthest place on earth is the hour that is just over. Make the best use of the hour that has just begun.

~

It's wise to burn anger, before anger itself burns your peace and happiness.

~

Whenever you feel tension mounting up, just smile: you will break the force of tension.

~

When you eliminate the ego, you will grow in the realization that all of us are equal in the eyes of God.

~

Anger becomes righteous when you use it to defend the rights of another, without nursing any selfish motive.

~

If you wait for the right time to come it will never come. Begin where you are and with what you have.

~

The mind alone is the cause of man's bondage: the mind is also an instrument of man's liberation.

~

Forgiveness works like a miracle. It takes away the ill-feelings which gnaw at our own mind.

(Collated from *Sadhu Vaswani Mission*; and Rajendran,
'Dada J.P. Vaswani Quotes')

Jesus in India

JESUS WAS INTRODUCED INTO INDIA THROUGH CHRISTIAN FAITH IN THE Malabar coast of Kerala by Saint Thomas, one of his 12 apostles, sometime in the first century CE. Local rulers offered Thomas lands and various rights to establish churches and preach the Christian faith. According to another tradition, more or less at the same time, Bartholomew, another apostle, brought Christianity into the Bombay region, along the Konkan coast. Considerable number of people in both the regions became Christians, and by the sixth century, Christian communities were firmly established in India.

Their slow and steady growth accelerated appreciably between thirteenth and sixteenth centuries when waves of Catholic and Protestant missionaries arrived in India. Under the influence of the French Dominican missionary Jordanus Catalani in Gujarat, and Saint Francis Xavier in Goa, thousands of Indians, especially from the lower classes and castes, including the adivasis, took to Christianity.

In time, missionaries of different orders, such as Franciscans, Dominicans, Jesuits, Augustinians, Baptists and so on, came one after the other and established their respective churches across the Indian subcontinent. The establishment of the colonial regimes of the Dutch, Danish, French and English gave further impetus for missionaries to carry out their evangelical activities in different parts of India. English education was introduced by Protestant missionaries, and they also produced early translations of the Holy Bible in Indian languages.

Henrique de Henrique (1520–1600), a Jesuit missionary, established the first printing press in Goa in 1556; and many years later, printing presses started in Bombay (1670) and Tamil Nadu (1714). Besides the Bible, the life story of Jesus and his gospels were published in regional languages, and that helped spread information and disseminate the Christian faith and knowledge widely across the subcontinent.

Indigenization of Christianity, that is, the process of making Christianity more native, or indigenous, required the missionaries to study local languages and culture, which they did with remarkable discipline and rigour. It is interesting to note here that in due course, some of them began to read, write and research in the regional languages and went on to make significant contributions in the fields of language, literature and journalism.

As a matter of fact, missionaries were early translators of some of the notable regional works into English. This they did with dedication despite rebukes and even punishments from their respective orders. For instance, Reverend Ferdinand Kittel (1832–1903) undertook an exhaustive study of the Kannada language and produced the first Kannada-English dictionary of about 70,000 words in 1894. He also translated the work of Nagavarma, scholar and grammarian of old-Kannada language, into English. Constanzio Beschi (1680–1747) produced a fourfold Tamil dictionary, Bishop Robert Caldwell (1815–91) brought out in English three classical works of Tamil literature, including *Tirukkural*, besides the *Comparative Grammar of the Dravidian Languages*, and Reverend S.H. Kellogg produced in 1893 *A Grammar of the Hindi Language*.

The year 1885, when the Indian National Congress was founded, may be seen as the organized beginning of the struggle for India's freedom, but it would take a couple of decades for the freedom struggle to gather momentum and develop into a mass movement. However, interestingly, almost all the freedom fighters were English educated. Missionary work, especially in the field of education, both vernacular and English, played a crucial role in the emergence of revolutionary thought.

Furthermore, critical writings produced by missionaries on traditional beliefs and practices such as sati, treatment of widows, child marriage, infanticide, devadasi system, caste system and so on kindled not only serious interrogation of the social beliefs and structures of society, but also motivated people to study forms of social oppression and injustice, and deploy the new knowledge in their anti-colonial, socio-economic and politico-cultural struggles.

Jesus as Sage

There are 27.8 million Christians in India, as per the 2011 census, constituting about 2.3 per cent of the total population. A significant number of these Christians, although they profess Christianity as their faith and believe in Jesus as the Divine Being, do not belong to any traditional and institutionalized Christianity. Nor are they associated with any church. More significantly, millions of non-Christians have had no problem in accepting Jesus as a sage and even as one of God's messengers. And they rejoice in celebrating Christmas as one of their own festivals, and even visit churches, as they would darghas, to worship and pray for their well-being.

The belief that there is one God but this God may be called by different names, worshipped in different forms or approached by different paths, is something deeply ingrained in the Hindu mind. The Buddha is regarded as one of the avatars, alongside Rama and Krishna, and adding Jesus in the list is no big deal for Hindus, given their catholic outlook.

Orthodox Christians may not accept such a position with regard to their belief in Jesus. For them, Jesus is the only Son of God, the only Messiah, and only through Him would one find salvation. Hindus would find such a view quite problematic. In the early nineteenth century, it was notably Rammohan Roy who, in the public realm, spoke of Jesus as one of many messiahs and sages, engaged in debates with missionaries and even wrote extensively on what he considered the essential teachings of Jesus.

Rammohan Roy (1772–1833), considered by many as the father of modern India, was a philosopher and social reformer in his own right. His extensive study of Hinduism, Islam and Christianity led him to believe that essentially the teachings of all religions centred round the idea of one Divine Being. He was friends with missionaries in Bengal, participated in the church services and supported them in their fight against the practice of sati – playing a decisive role in getting the evil custom banned.

In the 1820s, he wrote several tracts on *The Precepts of Jesus*, where he offered his own interpretations on the *Sermon on the Mount* in the New Testament of the Bible, and the gospel according to Matthew, Luke and others. His missionary friends fell out over his interpretation of the personality and teaching of Jesus and his dismissal of the apostles as unessential to understanding Jesus. In effect, Roy viewed and wrote about Jesus as a teacher of wisdom, a true gurudev, a divine guru. And those who followed the teaching of Jesus – even if they did not believe in the idea of his divine birth, the Holy Spirit and so on – could call themselves Christian; in that sense, he saw himself as a Christian as much as a Hindu.

The Vaishnava saint Sri Ramakrishna too studied Christianity. In the 1870s, in his late thirties, Ramakrishna went through rigorous sadhana in Vaishnava bhakti, Tantra and Vedanta, and he is believed to have explored all the well-known modes of spiritual practices and experienced the Divinity in all its forms and manifestations, including in Islam and Christianity. For a period of time, he turned into a Muslim devotee. He lived outside the temple complex, dressed like an Arab Muslim, chanted the name of Allah, recited the namaz five times daily and immersed himself in Islamic practices. Three days into this sadhana, he had a vision of a '...radiant personage with grave countenance and white beard resembling the Prophet and merging with his body' (Nikhilananda, 2008).

In 1874, he learned about Jesus' life and teaching and took to Christianity. And he is believed to have had a vision of the Madonna and Child, and then of Jesus Christ, who, too, is supposed to have embraced him and merged into him. He remained under the spell of this vision for three days and was convinced Jesus Christ was a sage and a way to God. His disciples, including Vivekananda, did not have any difficulty in accepting Ramakrishna's vision of Jesus as the gift of true spirituality that went beyond all boundaries, and they accepted Jesus as a yogi and a self-realized sage (Nikhilananda, 2008).

That was the position of Advaita Vedanta. A sage is one who has realized the oneness of reality, in that sense he is a messenger of God. Vivekananda believed Jesus Christ was such a free, self-realized human being. His life indicated that it is possible for every human being, cutting across creed, race and religion, to attain such a state of enlightenment, but the church had locked him up in the image of an exclusive Messiah, who would deliver people only if they believed in him and the tenets of Christianity. Jesus' statement 'I and my Father are one' (John 10:30), according to Vivekananda, was not something that revealed Christ's unique relationship with God; rather, it expressed the unity of all that exists, including human beings.

Mohandas Karamchand Gandhi (1869–1948), during his England days as a student studying law, studied the Bhagavad Gita and the Bible for the first time. The Gita became his lifelong companion, rather a 'mother' to whom he turned to when in doubt. He was more impressed by the New Testament than the Old Testament, and the Sermon on the Mount went straight to his heart.

He did not care much for Christian theology and refused to accept Jesus as the only incarnation of God but believed in Jesus as one of the greatest teachers of the world, whose suffering and passive resistance to evil was an example to follow. The message of the kingdom of God being within you came close to his own notion of Ramarajya, and the image of Jesus suffering on the cross was a sort of a symbol for the sacrifice and suffering of a satyagrahi in his active resistance to the proven wrongs in society. During his lifetime, many saw Gandhi as an unbaptized, exemplary Christian.

It would take a separate book to write about all the Indians who were drawn to Jesus as a sage and guru but did not become Christians, another one to write about those who, inspired by Jesus, became Christians and turned into apostles of Christ.

Nilakantha Goreh, who lived in the holy city of Varanasi, was one such person. He came from a prominent brahmin family and was well educated in Sanskrit and Hindu scriptures, and became known as a pandit. Those were the days when Christian missionaries preached the faith on street corners. Nilakantha confronted one such Anglican missionary – William Smith. It is said Nilakantha disputed Smith's claims and even wrote a tract criticizing Christian theology. In response, Smith gave him a copy of the New Testament and a Sanskrit work called *Matapariksha*, An Investigation into the Religions, written by John Muir, a British civil servant who was well versed in Sanskrit.

Nilakantha read *Matapariksha*, and refuting Muir's arguments, he wrote a long reply in the form of a poem in Sanskrit. Defending Hinduism, he called the Bible a deceitful work and Christ a false prophet. A year later, he is believed to have resumed his arguments with Smith and, as he became more and more acquainted with the life of Jesus and Christian tenets, Nilakantha underwent a complete change of heart and three years later, in 1848, became a Christian.

Now, like a born-again Christian (the phenomenon of gaining faith in Jesus Christ through experience), Father Nehemiah Goreh argued and wrote about the superiority of the Christian faith, with as much passion and rigour as he had once defended Hinduism. His work in Hindi, *Sha-darshana-darpana*, on the problematics of the six classical Hindu philosophical systems, translated into English under the title *Mirror of the Six Schools*, later retitled as *A Rational Refutation of the Hindu Philosophical Systems*, followed by *Proofs of the Divinity of our Lord*, made him one of the most famous proponents of Christianity in India.

Ramabai was Goreh's contemporary, and like him, she too turned to Christianity and came to be recognized as the social face of Christian faith.

Pandita Ramabai
(1858–1922)

Ramabai was born as Rama Dongre on 23 April 1858 in a Marathi speaking family. Her father, Shastri Dongre, was a Sanskrit scholar, and unlike orthodox brahmins of his community, taught Sanskrit to his wife, who in turn taught Ramabai the language and literature. The family lived an itinerant life. They travelled by foot to pilgrimage centres. At temples, Shastri Dongre recited sacred texts in Sanskrit for devotees, and in turn received gifts of money.

When the great famine of 1876–78 that killed millions spread over the whole of South India, offers from temples and religious institutions to recite the sacred texts completely dried up. Dongre, being a brahmin pandit, would not bring himself to do manual work. Dongre and his wife succumbed to hunger and died one after the other.

Ramabai was 16 years old at the time and by then had mastered Sanskrit and knew the *Bhagavata Purana* by heart. Left with no choice, she and her elder brother travelled the country and managed to survive by reciting the sacred texts for a fee. At Kolkata, their lives changed when invitations came from different quarters to display their remarkable talent. In 1878, after testing her knowledge of Sanskrit by a team of eminent scholars, Ramabai was given the honorary title Sarasvati, the name of the goddess of wisdom, and the right to call herself 'Pandita', one who is learned in Sanskrit and Hindu philosophy and religion.

She was now in demand to give lectures and even instruct higher caste women on the rules of conduct as found in the Puranas. For the first time, as a Pandita, she studied the Vedas and other Shastras, access to which were generally denied to women. And she became acutely aware of how the Brahmanical tradition that oppressed women derived its authority from the Shastras. In her travels over these years, she had seen up close women, especially among the higher castes, suffer under the laws derived from these texts. There was, sadly, no base for equality between men and women in the Shastras.

At a time when her fame and prosperity were on the rise, tragedy struck again, and she lost her brother who had been ill for some time. All her family members gone, feeling utterly alone, she sought a companion. She married Babu Bipin Beharidas Medhavi, a successful lawyer. Bipin was from the shudra caste and they were married in a civil court in 1880. The couple had a daughter whom they named Manorama. Through Bipin, who was a member of the Brahmo Samaj, Ramabai came in contact with the samaj members and subscribed to its monotheism. She also came in touch with Christian groups in Kolkata and even attended their prayer meetings and was much taken in by the fairness and parity among the members, irrespective of the caste they came from.

After nearly two years of married life, in 1882, Bipin died of cholera. Ramabai was only 23 years old then, and she left Kolkata with her daughter and went back to her native place, Pune, where she resumed reciting the Puranas at temples and at religious events. With the money she had saved up, and funds from people, she founded the Arya Mahila Samaj to promote women's education and provide health facilities and shelter to widows.

A few years before, not far from where Ramabai lived in Pune, the Phules – Jyotiba and Savitri – had started schools for lower-caste girls and then later shelter homes for widows. Ramabai had witnessed the hardship, harassment and suffering women went through, especially child widows who were shaved bald, forced to wear white clothing and live in wretched conditions. Eventually, it became her lifelong mission to work for the amelioration of unfortunate Indian women.

Around this time, she became seriously interested in the Christian faith. She studied the Bible and met with missionaries. Nehemiah Goreh, who had 30 years earlier converted to Christianity, exercised a great influence on her. Both were, incidentally, Sanskrit scholars and Chitpavan brahmins. Like Goreh, she found Christianity superior to Hinduism; Jesus Christ and his teaching were accessible to everyone, irrespective of caste and gender. Christianity was good news, especially to women like her, who had suffered the discriminatory Hindu laws.

A year later, she went to England to do a course in the English language and natural sciences. Her contact and conversations with the sisters of the Anglican religious community there deepened her understanding of the Christian faith, and she and her daughter Manorama converted to Christianity in September 1883. After completing her studies in England, she visited the United States and here she found great support for her cause of Indian women from different quarters.

Her two-and-a-half-year stay changed her significantly. Her book, *The High Caste Hindu Woman*, in which she described and analysed the problems of high-caste women, was published in Philadelphia in 1887. The book won her many hearts and enormous support for the project she would soon start in India.

Back home in February 1889, she founded Sharada Sadan, House of Wisdom, to promote education of women and offer training to young girls and women to become teachers. Both she and her daughter lived among the students and led a simple life of austerity and learning. Gradually, as she delved deeper into Christian theology, she began to see herself as a born-again Christian and that gave a new direction to her faith and mission.

Hitherto, education and training in Sharada Sadan had been kept secular; now, she changed its name to Mukti Sadan, House of Salvation, preached Christian faith and invited conversions. Further, the doors of the sadan were thrown open to girls and women from the lower castes as well. Talking about her source of inspiration, in her autobiographical book *A Testimony of Our Inexhaustible Treasure*, she wrote about how she was enormously influenced by the service aspect of Christianity: 'I realized, after reading the 4th Chapter of St. John's Gospel, that Christ was truly the Divine Saviour He claimed to be, and no one but He could transform and uplift the downtrodden womanhood of India, and of every land.'

The way she reached out to women in distress runs parallel to the great work done by the Phules. It is said, whenever reports of distressful cases reached her, she would travel disguised as a lower-caste woman in order to rescue girls and women in trouble. Many girls in distress found refuge in Mukti Sadan, which eventually grew into a large institution that could accommodate 2,000 girls and women. In 1896, when famine broke out in the Central Province, she travelled widely in the area and rescued about 300 girls and women.

Ramabai was a unique woman in many ways. When she was baptized, she refused to take the new Christian name 'Mary' and kept the name given to her by her parents. She wore Indian clothing, followed a strict vegetarian diet and refused to touch alcohol. She studied Greek and Hebrew and, working over several years, translated the Bible into Marathi from the original Hebrew and Greek. In her way of life, she combined traditional Indian customs with Christianity, although, as years passed, she completely distanced herself from Hinduism and turned into a zealous votary of Christian faith as the only way to salvation.

Ramabai's daughter, Manorama Bai, did her B.A. at Bombay University, went to the US for higher studies and returned to India to take over the ministry of Mukti Mission. But, as fate would have it, she died in 1921, at the age of 42. Nine months later, Ramabai died from septic bronchitis in 1922, a few weeks before her 64th birthday. The Mukti Sadan was renamed Pandita Ramabai Mukti Sadan and it continues to serve many needy groups, including widows, orphans and the blind, by providing them housing, education, vocational training and so on. On 26 October 1989, in recognition of her contribution to the advancement of Indian women, the Government of India issued a commemorative stamp in her honour.

Mother Teresa
(1910–97)

Seven years after Ramabai's passing away, a 19-year-old Teresa, a Roman Catholic nun, arrived in India as a novice and later began her career as a teacher at St. Teresa's School near her convent in Darjeeling, in the lower Himalaya. She worked for 20 years as a teacher and then went on to dedicate the rest of her life to serving the poor and destitute around the world.

Teresa was born Agnes Gonxha Bojaxhiu on 26 August 1910 into a Kosovar Albanian family in Skopje (now the capital of North Macedonia). Early in life, Teresa was fascinated by the stories of the lives of missionaries and wanted to lead a religious life. At 18, she joined the Sisters of Loreto and learnt English to prepare herself for the life of a missionary. A year later, she left her family and went to India and became a teacher, first at St. Teresa's School, then at the Loreto Convent at Kolkata.

In 1937, she took her Solemn Vows (of poverty, chastity and obedience) and chose the name Teresa. The killing poverty in the villages and towns around Kolkata during the Bengal famine in 1943, then three years later the bloody Partition riots that killed millions and caused immense suffering, changed her life. She felt what she later called, 'that call within the call' and left the convent to help and live among the poor and distressed. 'It was an order. To fail would have been to break the faith' (Clucas, 1988). Thus, Sister Teresa was transformed into Mother Teresa to succour the poor and the dying.

In 1948, she adopted Indian citizenship, trained herself as a nurse at Holy Family Hospital in Patna and then started working for the 'poorest among the poor' in the slums of Kolkata. She wore a white Indian cotton sari with blue border, and with a small band of nuns, survived on minimal income and food, often having to beg for funds. It was not an easy life and at times she was not sure if she was equal to the task, troubled by self-doubt and the temptation to return to the comfort of her convent life. However, undeterred, she egged on, '...of free choice, my God, and out of love for you. I desire to remain and do whatever be your Holy will in my regard. I did not let a single tear come' (Clucas, 1988).

She was joined in her efforts by a group of young women and, in 1950, they founded the Missionaries of Charity. Two years later, they started the first hospice and then the Home of the Pure Heart, a home for the dying, in an old, abandoned temple. They cared for the hungry, the homeless, the blind and lepers, and victims of floods and famine.

People abandoned and on the verge of death were brought to the home to die loved, wanted and with dignity. However, the home was criticised for not providing medical care and analgesics for those in pain; instead, allowing them to die. Teresa, who was now known as Mother Teresa, responded saying these people were terminally ill, in the throes of dying, like Christ on the cross, and had to suffer for their redemption. However, Teresa never sought to convert those of another faith to Christianity, and the dying, whether Hindu, Muslim or Christian, received the services or religious rites in accordance with their faith.

Support and donations for the Missionaries of Charity began

pouring in from all quarters. The mission opened a separate hospice for those with leprosy and an independent, full-fledged home for homeless children, named Nirmala Shishu Bhavan. By the 1960s several hospices, orphanages and leper houses were opened throughout India. Further, Mother Teresa opened houses in Italy, Tanzania, Austria and the United States. By 2013, the Missionaries of Charity numbered about 5,000 sisters and 450 brothers worldwide, operating 700 missions, schools and shelters in 130 countries.

Mother Teresa declared: 'By blood, I am Albanian. By citizenship, an Indian. By faith, I am a Catholic nun. As to my calling, I belong to the world. As to my heart, I belong entirely to the Heart of Jesus.' Towards the end of her life, however, like a bhakta who agonizes over her not-yet-bridged separation from God, Teresa, by her own admission, felt a spiritual 'emptiness and darkness' (Chawla, 1996).

In one of her letters to her spiritual confidant, Michael van der Peet, she wrote, 'Jesus has a very special love for you. [But] as for me, the silence and the emptiness is so great, that I look and do not see— listen and do not hear—the tongue moves [in prayer] but does not speak ... I want you to pray for me—that I let Him have [a] free hand.' Nonetheless, her confession of 'emptiness' came to be interpreted as the 'Dark Night of the Soul', and similar to the experience of Jesus, who is believed to have said when he was crucified: 'My God, why have you forsaken me?' (Chawla, 1996).

Mother Teresa became a symbol of charitable, selfless work and, in recognition of her work, she received several national and international awards during her lifetime, including the Nobel Peace Prize in 1979. Despite a heart attack in 1989, she remained active and travelled around the world. Eight years later, she passed away due to cardiac arrest on September 5, 1997. She was 87 years old.

Six years later, she was beatified and, on September 4, 2016, was formally canonized as Saint Teresa by the Pope Francis I in St. Peter's Square in Vatican City. Today, she remains an inspiration to millions all over the world, and while Catholic Christians recognize and revere her as a saint, there are many Hindus in Kolkata and elsewhere who worship her as a deity.

The Christian Ashram

Roberto de Nobili (1577–1656) was a very imaginative, bold and clever Italian Jesuit missionary. He arrived in Goa in 1605, then stayed in Cochin, Kerala, for a short period of time before taking residence in Madurai in Tamil Nadu. In a sense, he was the first one to initiate Christian inculturation, or indigenization of Christianity in India. Inculturation is a theological concept used by many theologians and scholars to mean the inclusion of local cultural elements, including art forms such as music, architecture, dance and dress, into various aspects of Christian life and liturgy. Simply put, it is an attempt by which Christian faith is understood and expressed through the symbols and language of one's own culture.

Located amidst the colony of orthodox Hindus, the 15-year-old Christian Mission in Madurai had succeeded in converting a mere 60 Hindus to Christian faith. Roberto de Nobili changed it all. Clothed as a sanyasi, staff in hand, he decided to travel widely and 'win their innumerable peoples for Christ Our Lord' (Pillai, 2019). He learnt Sanskrit, Telugu and Tamil languages, and adopted the lifestyle of a Hindu sanyasi. He shaved his head, keeping only a tiny tuft, and wore an ochre robe and wooden sandals.

A three-stringed thread across his chest, however, represented the Holy Trinity. And he expounded the Christian doctrine in Hindu terms. He was the first one to use the terms 'guru' and 'avatar' to refer to Jesus, apply Tamil words such as 'kovil' for a place of worship, 'arul' and 'prasadam' for grace, 'guru' for priest or teacher and 'Vedam' for the Bible. Fellow Jesuit missionaries objected to his method and complained to higher authorities, which ultimately came to nothing.

Until then, conversion of Hindus had taken place within a European philosophical framework, both in spirit and content, and Roberto de Nobili showed that the noble work of conversion could be done more successfully within the Indian/Hindu philosophical framework. By the time he died at the age of 79, he had converted 4,000 people, most of them from the lower castes. He of course deployed as strategy the Indian elements 'to become a Hindu to save Hindus', to impress and convert; however, the inculturation process he set in motion was to take root and grow into a genuine effort to bring Christian faith closer to Indian ethos, on the one hand, and on the other, to develop a spirituality transcending religious denomination, to see and experience Jesus as a guru, as jagadguru, world teacher, an avatar, a cosmic spirit.

The actual inculturation, however, began effectively only in the beginning of the twentieth century. Ramabai refused to adopt European clothing and food habits and chose Indian forms for the church services at her Mukti Sadan. People sat cross-legged down on the floor instead of on pews, celebrated communion with chapatis and grapes instead of bread, and sang bhajans accompanied by Indian musical instruments.

Brahmabandhab Upadhyay (1861–1907), like Ramabai, came from a Hindu brahmin family. He was born Bhavani Charan Bandyopadhyay. On his conversion to Christianity at the age of 30, he chose the name Brahmabandhab Upadhyay instead of a European one. He wore saffron clothes and an ebony cross around his neck, walked barefoot and called himself a Hindu Catholic. Defending his sanyasi lifestyle, he argued, 'By birth we are Hindu and shall remain Hindu till death... We are Hindus so far as our physical and mental constitution is concerned, but in regard to our immortal souls we are Catholic. We are Hindu Catholic' (Lipner, 1999). He envisioned the Indian church clothed in Indian features. But this burning zeal to convert Christianity into Hindu form did not last long. Towards the end of his life, he reverted to Hinduism and died prematurely at the age of 46.

Down South, Chakkarai's was a successful and more significant story. Vengal Chakkarai (1880–1958) was born in a Hindu Chettiar family in Madras. Educated at the Scottish Mission School and then at Madras Christian College and later at Madras Law College, he was naturally drawn to Christianity. He was attracted to Gandhi's philosophy as well and participated in the Indian independence movement. In 1913, he joined the Danish Mission and worked as a missionary for 20 years.

He strived to understand and explain the Christian faith in the framework of Hindu concepts. He interpreted sin as pasa, the chain that prevents the human soul from reaching God, yet it is sin that drives one to find 'the mystery of the forbidden mystery' (Schouten, 2008). He considered Jesus as truly human, sat purusa, also as an avatar, a divine being similar to Krishna and Rama. The knowledge of God was only jnana, an intellectual thing, and that was not enough, he maintained; rather, one needed to put effort for anubhava, personal experience of God. In 1926, he published the book *Jesus the Avatar*, wherein he argued and demonstrated how Christianity could be Indianized by taking it out of the European philosophical framework in which it had been trapped for centuries.

Alongside Chakkarai and a few others, Aiyadurai Jesudasen Appasamy (1891–1980), a theologian and bishop of the Church of South India, was a prominent member of what came to be called the 'Rethinking Christianity Group'. His father had been a Shaivite before he turned to Christianity. In quest of God experience, his father learnt yoga from a Hindu guru and began practising dhyana, meditation, regularly and is believed to have come upon mystical experiences. Profoundly influenced by his father, Appasamy took to the study of philosophy and Hinduism, with particular focus on Ramanuja's Vishishtadvaita, and neo-Hindu movements such as Brahmo Samaj and Ramakrishna Mission. And he tried to construct Christian theology as essentially a bhakti marg.

This new Christology to make Jesus an Indian guru and Christianity an Indian wisdom and a path of bhakti were met with both success and resistance. However, and more interestingly, the new image of Jesus as guru, cosmic spirit, avatar and so on, opened a debate among the missionaries and theologians. For instance, the notion of avatar as periodical descent of divinity was at odds with the uniqueness of Christ as the only Son of God. While some tried to resolve the issue by calling Christ the *only* avatar, others had no difficulty in considering Christ as one of the avatars by dropping all claims to universal truth. Dalit groups, however, found the historical Christ, who stood by the poor and women, more agreeable and inspiring.

Paintings, murals, works in bronze, stone and other art forms during this period boldly reflected the various new interpretations of Christ and Christian faith from within the framework of the Indian spiritual landscape. Both non-Christian and Christian artists contributed significantly to this new art form and some of them were revolutionary in their approach. While the work of non-Christian artists reflected their own relation to the person of Christ, the Christian artists tried to frame Christ in Indian landscape.

For instance, Abanindranath Tagore depicted white Christ in a white halo, holding a stick and with a dove; Nandlal Bose portrayed Christ carrying the cross, with a crown of thorns framed in a halo and a woman helping Christ lift the cross; Alfred Thomas, an Anglican artist, depicted Christ as an exalted sanyasi, clothed in ochre robe and bearing a strong resemblance to the Buddha and Krishna; Angelo da Fonseca, a Goan artist, painted Mary in an Indian sari; K.C.S. Paniker showed Christ as one among the Indian peasants, while Solomon Raj depicted Christ as a poor Dalit. Jyoti Sahi, an Indian artist born to an Indian father and a British mother, produced many works of painting and woodcuts, also works in batik and stained glass windows, on Christ and Christian themes using Indian symbols. More interestingly, many of these artists typically portrayed Christ as brown skinned and represented the suffering Christ, which was in stark contrast to the images of Hindu gods and goddesses that are always depicted with happy, peaceful visages.

Although initially the idea of the Christian Ashram in India drew inspiration from Gandhi's ashrams, Brahmo Samaj and Ramakrishna Mission, eventually the idea developed into a movement within Christianity in order to combine the Christian faith with the Hindu ashram model and sanyasa tradition. Brahmabandhab Upadhyay was a disciple of the famous Keshab Chandra Sen and was a close acquaintance of Ramakrishna, Vivekananda and Rabindranath Tagore. He was one of the first important theologians among the Roman Catholic Indians who interpreted Christian faith in Hindu terms. As mentioned earlier, he wore saffron clothes and called himself a Christian sanyasi and a Hindu Catholic.

Upadhyay established Kasthalika Math, a Catholic monastery, founded on Thomism and Sankara's Vedanta. He declared that the math would '...be conducted on strictly Hindu lines. There should not be the least trace of Europeanism in the mode of life and living of the Hindu Catholic monks. The parivrajakas (itinerants) should be well versed in the Vedanta philosophy as well as in the philosophy of St. Thomas' (Lipner, 1999). But it was a short-lived attempt since he could not carry on the experiment without funds and support from the Catholic institutions. However, in 1898, he started a weekly journal, *Sophia*, and through various articles, tried to explore the possibilities of using Vedantic categories to expound Christian faith.

A year later, he started a school in Kolkata in 1901, where students were offered modern education, besides courses in Vedic and Vedantic ideas. Rabindranath Tagore was attracted to this new pedagogy initiated by Brahmabandhab Upadhyay and went on to found Shantinekatan in his father's estate. Towards the end of his life, however, Brahmabandhab Upadhyay became more of a Vedantin than a Hindu Catholic, then he drifted into the political struggle for Indian independence and was arrested on charges of sedition. His life was cut short at 46, and one could only wonder what more he would have done in the fields of politics and religion. However, his was the first attempt to indigenize and Indianize the Christian faith.

After Upadhyay's failure, several Christian ashrams were established, particularly after India became Independent, by both Catholic and Protestant groups. In the 1880s there were about 100 ashrams spread across the Indian subcontinent. These ashrams may be broadly arranged into two categories: khadi (hand spun rough cotton material representing social service and activism) and bhakti marg, led by and large by the Protestant groups, and kaavi (ochre robe, representing sanyasa tradition) and jnana marg by Catholic groups. Christakula Ashram in Tirupattur, founded in 1921 by Ernest Forrester Paton and S. Jesudasan; Christa Prema Seva Ashram in Bangalore, founded in 1927 by Anglican Jack Winslow; Sat Tal Ashram in 1930, founded by E. Stanley Jones; Saccidananda Ashram founded in 1950 by French priest Jules Monchanin and French Benedictine monk Le Saux were some of the trailblazing ashrams.

Remarkably, Saccidananda Ashram, more popularly known as Shantivanam, Woods of Peace, was the home of many a founder and member of ashrams that emerged later. It was Jules Monchanin (1895–1957), a French Catholic priest, who first came up with the idea of integrating Benedictine monasticism with the Hindu ashram tradition. He first called his ashram Bhakti Ashram, then later, borrowing the Sanskrit term Sat-Chit-Ananda, meaning Being-Consciousness-Bliss, he chose the name Saccidananda to mean the Christian Holy Trinity. Monchanin adopted the Hindu name Param Arubi Ananda, Man of the Supreme Joy.

Sat-Chit-Ananda is an epithet and description of the ultimate reality or state of being, and all three are considered inseparable from the nature of Brahman, while the doctrine of the Trinity is a triad: the Father, the Son and the Holy Spirit; all three are distinct, yet are one 'substance, essence or nature' (Schouten, 2008). Monchanin did not seek to identify Brahman with the Trinity, and yet he believed it was possible to reconcile the two mystical traditions on several grounds. In effect, he sought to Christianize Hindu concepts, while Dom Henri Le Saux (1910–73), a French monk, who joined him later and took the name Abhishiktananda, the Blessing of the Anointed, believed that

Indian, including Buddhist, mysticism could transform Christianity.

Dom Henri Le Saux, unlike Monchanin, was drawn deeply to Advaita Vedanta. His study of Indian philosophy and meetings with sages such as Ramakrishna and Poonja and then Swami Gnanananda Giri are believed to have finally led him to realize the oneness of reality. To him, it was not a mere philosophical or advaitic concept but lived experience of reality. He wrote in depth about his stay and experiences at Arunachala in *The Secret of Arunachal*, and about his meeting with and teachings of Swami Gnanananda in his *Guru and His Disciple*.

Monchanin died in 1957 and Le Saux-Abhishiktananda continued with the ashram tradition. Increasingly drawn to a life of contemplation, he moved out of Shantivanam and settled into a life of a true sanyasi in a small cottage in Uttarakashi in 1968. He died on 7 December 1973 in Indore. In his posthumous book, *The Further Shore*, he described his spiritual awakening thus: 'O I have found the Grail ... The quest for the Grail is basically nothing else than the quest for the Self ... It is yourself that you are seeking through everything. And in this quest you are running about everywhere, whereas the Grail is here, close at hand, you only have to open your eyes ... There is only the Awakening.'

Bede Griffiths
(1906–93)

Swami Abhishiktananda passed on the leadership of Shantivanam to Bede Griffiths, a Benedictine monk, before he left the ashram for Uttarakashi. Under Bede Griffiths's guidance, Shantivanam grew to be a centre of contemplative life and a space for inter-religious dialogue and exploration of the 'indescribable mystery behind all religions' (Schouten, 2008).

Alan Richard Griffiths was born in 1906 in a middle-class British family. He ranked first in his exams at school and received a scholarship for further studies at Oxford. He studied English literature and philosophy and in his third year at Oxford, under the influence of C.S. Lewis, a British teacher-writer and lay theologian, became deeply engrossed in faith and study of wisdom literature of other religions. Gifted with a strong spiritual bent of mind, he longed to be a monk. At the age of 25, he converted to the Roman Catholic Church and became a Benedictine monk and received the name of Bede. He studied Thomism (doctrines attributed to Thomas Aquinas) and found its philosophy to be almost identical with that of Shankara's Advaita Vedanta.

In 1955, at the age of 49, he came to India. Before leaving for India, in a letter to a friend, he wrote, 'I am going to discover the other half of my soul.' After two years of stay in a Benedictine Order in Bangalore, he went to Kerala and, together with a Cistercian monk, Francis Mahieu, established a small ashram in Kottayam. The ashram was called Kurishumala, Hill of the Cross, modelled after Shantivanam, and the inmates wore saffron clothes and followed the Hindu sanyasi tradition. They sported a Christian cross bearing the Hindu symbol of Om. Bede Griffiths took the Hindu name Swami Dayananda, the Blessing of Compassion. He learnt Sanskrit and studied not only Hinduism but also Taoism, Gnosticism, and was well acquainted with modern physics and the New Age thinking that grew in the Western world during the 1970s.

In 1968, he gladly took over the leadership of Shantivanam. Under his leadership, Shantivanam became a meeting place for East and West in an effort to go beyond all binaries. He said, 'We cannot return to the past forms of Catholicism or Buddhism or Confucianism or Hindu or Islamic orthodoxy. Each religion has to return to its source in the eternal religion' (Griffiths, 1981). And it did not matter whether that source or the mystery is called Nirvana, Brahman, Tao or simply God. He identified God the Father with the concept of Nirguna Brahman, equated the Trinity with sat-chit-ananda, being-consciousness-bliss, and described the Son as the 'Self-manifestation of the unmanifest God'. In effect, he espoused and embraced not the historical Christ, or asserted the Hindu Brahman, but the One that is deep and ineffable, behind every mysticism.

In 1990s, Bede Griffiths suffered a stroke. He soon recovered well
and wrote about an intense mystical experience he had while his life
swung on the edge of death. Later, he travelled the world, giving
roving lectures on his exegesis, syncretic philosophy and the mystical
state he had experienced. In January 1993, he had a series of strokes
and died on May 13, aged 86.

Bede Griffiths was brilliant in describing interconnections and
relationships between passages from different spiritual texts. One
of the passages he often quoted was from the *Chandogya Upanishad*
(8,3), which reflected his own mystical awareness: 'There is this city
of Brahman (the human body) and in it there is a small shrine in the
form of a lotus, and within it can be found a small space. This little
space within the heart is as great as this vast universe. The heavens and
the earth are there, and the sun and the moon and the stars; fire and
lightening and wind are there, and all that now is and is not yet – all
that is contained within it.'

~

Orthodox groups within Christianity were highly critical of Bede
Griffiths's exegetical work and his syncretism because they thought it
trivialized the historical Christ. They alleged that Bede Griffiths used
Christian language to interpret Hindu concepts and vice versa, only
to produce a brand of Christology which was neither here nor there.
In effect, it only obscured genuine efforts to create an Indian Christian
theology. One may say this was a case of misplaced expectation. In
one's spiritual journey one cannot know beforehand what one may
come to experience and become. Initially, Bede Griffiths may have
wanted to develop an Indian Christian theology, but soon he moved
out of such an agenda and turned a quester, yearning to understand
and experience the mystery behind all religions. For, finally, religion
is not a theology but something to be experienced and lived.

Not surprisingly, even Hindu orthodox groups launched a long diatribe against him, Swami Abhishiktananda and other such monks. These Hindu groups considered white monks who wore ochre robes and took Hindu names as wolves in sheep's clothing, come to Christianize Hinduism. They alleged that these experimentalists projected the Virgin Mary as a Hindu goddess, Christian saints as rishis, Jesus as an avatar, Bible as a Veda, donned ochre robes and adopted ascetic practices – even vegetarianism and puja-like rituals – not to Hinduize Christianity but to Christianize Hinduism.

This strictly denominational point of view, however, is ultimately counterproductive to a fair and sensible understanding of the different *spiritualities* practised the world over. The word 'religion' is derived from the Latin 're-ligio', which means 'to link back, to bind', to return to the source, to our natural state. Hindus have more or less the same meaning for Yoga too. The one in quest of 'the source', or the 'indescribable mystery behind all religions' as Bede Griffiths put it, may be drawn to the teachings in different religions and work out his or her own path to self-realization. In fact, a significantly large number of people the world over today, drawing on both Eastern and Western spiritual and philosophical traditions, besides transpersonal, integral and parapsychology, Consciousness research and so on, have given expression to what is popularly called the New Age spirituality, which is a spirituality without borders and without the need for a religious identity.

In this context, it should be instructive to know that no religion is 'pure', in the sense that no religion grew independently. In fact, all religions have not only borrowed ideas, insights and symbols from each other, but also from the religious beliefs and practices of 'primitive' societies, and borrowed deeply at that. A study of the myths and religious beliefs of the world would reveal how Zoroastrianism was influenced by ancient cultures, Judaism by Zoroastrianism, Christianity by Judaism, Islam by Judaism and Christianity, Buddhism by the Upanishads and Sankhya philosophy, and Hinduism, especially Advaita Vedanta, by Buddhist thought. It is, in fact, impossible to establish one's religious identity in exclusive terms. We can, however, appreciate and learn from all these various religions, and the enlightened minds who have lived before us.

~

Some of the important books Griffiths authored were: *Christ in India, Vedanta and Christian Faith, Return to the Centre, The Marriage of East and West, The Cosmic Revelation* and *River of Compassion: A Christian Reading of the Bhagavad Gita.*

Aphorisms

God had brought me to my knees and made me acknowledge my own nothingness, and out of that knowledge I had been reborn. I was no longer the centre of my life and therefore I could see God in everything.

~

I suddenly saw that all the time it was not I who had been seeking God, but God who had been seeking me. I had made myself the centre of my own existence and had my back turned to God.

~

Atheism and agnosticism signify the rejection of certain images and concepts of God or of truth, which are historically conditioned and therefore inadequate. Atheism is a challenge to religion to purifiy its images and concepts and come nearer to the truth of divine mystery.

~

Above all we have to go beyond words and images and concepts. No imaginative vision or conceptual framework is adequate to the great reality.

~

It is no longer a question of a Christian going about to convert others to the faith, but of each one being ready to listen to the other and so to grow together in mutual understanding.

~

The resurrection does not consist merely of the appearances of Jesus to his disciples after his death. Many think that these appearances in Galilee and Jerusalem are the resurrection. But they are simply to confirm the faith of the disciples. The real resurrection is the passing beyond the world altogether. It is Jesus' passage from this world to the Father. It was not an event in space and time, but the passage beyond space and time to the eternal, to reality. Jesus passed into reality. That is our starting point.

It is into that world that we are invited to enter by meditation. We do not have to wait for physical death, but we can enter now into that eternal world. We have to go beyond the outer appearances of the senses and beyond the concepts of the mind, and open ourselves to the reality of Christ within, the Christ of the resurrection.

~

When we approach the Upanishads for an understanding of the Cosmic Mystery, we are coming to the very heart of the Hindu experience of God. This is what we want to try to understand, not with our minds, but with our hearts: to enter into the heart and continually remind ourselves that the Upanishads are intended to lead us to the heart. The Greek fathers of the Church used to say, 'Lead the thoughts from the head into the heart and keep them there.' This is to open to the Cosmic Mystery.

~

Stillness within one individual can affect society beyond measure.

~

God has graced every tradition with insight into the divine mystery, from the most primitive to the most sophisticated—each has a gift to bring to the world.

~

This is criterion by which the Church is to be judged, not by the forms of its doctrine or ritual, but by the reality of the reality of the love which it manifests.

~

The main theme of the Bible is the restoration of humanity and, through humanity, of the whole of creation to its original harmony.

(Collated from Griffiths, *Bede Griffiths: Essential Writings*)

Raimundo Panikkar
(1918–2010)

Raimundo Panikkar, a friend of Bede Griffiths, had much in common with him in his view of Christianity and the Hindu tradition, and, like Bede Griffiths, he too went beyond developing an Indian Christian theology. However, the trajectory of his career as a quester and philosopher was quite different from that of Bede Griffiths. He held a unique position in the world of thought. Conversant with a dozen or so languages and fluent in at least six, trained in Catholic theology and Thomism, with in-depth knowledge of the Western philosophical tradition and exceptional knowledge of Indian philosophical and spiritual traditions, and having written 50 books, in Catalan, Italian and English, translated into several languages of the world, Raimundo Panikkar was undoubtedly one of the great minds of twentieth-century.

Raimon Panikkar Alemany, more popularly known as Raimundo Panikkar (1918–2010) was born in Barcelona to a Spanish Roman Catholic mother and a Hindu father from a Malabar Nair family. He completed his schooling in a Jesuit school in Barcelona, then studied philosophy and chemistry at the universities of Barcelona and Madrid. In 1946, at age 33, he became a Catholic priest, earned a doctorate in Philosophy at the University of Madrid and joined the same university as a teacher of Philosophy.

In 1954, he made his first trip to India where he studied Indian philosophy and spiritual traditions at the University of Mysore and Banaras Hindu University. It was during this time that he became acquainted with the Christian ashram movement and met with several experimentalist Western monks, such as Swami Abhisktananda and Bede Griffiths. He felt as if he was on a familiar ground. His doctoral thesis had been on a comparative study of St. Thomas Aquinas's philosophy and Shankara's interpretation of the Brahma Sutras. So it seemed but natural that, after being trained in his mother's religious tradition, he should visit India and study the religion of his father.

In 1964, his book *The Unknown Christ of Hinduism* drew the attention of people from both Hindu and Christian worlds. It was an original work where he tried to prove the presence of Christ in the sacred Hindu texts: not the historical Jesus but Christ the divine being. He used the term 'theandrism' to mean union of the divine and the human in Christ, akin to Isvara, the manifested form of the Brahman.

On the one hand, Brahman is unknowable and immutable; on the other, Brahman in its manifested form is Isvara: 'that from which this world comes forth and to which it returns and by which it is sustained'. According to Panikkar, that enigma, called Isvara, is Christ. It was a radical interpretation of Christ that sought to synthesize Christianity with Hindu philosophy.

Christian theologians had problems with Panikkar's Cosmic Christ, for it seemed to downplay Jesus' life, the related historical events and the development of the Christian faith. In effect, Panikkar's view came closer to the view of many Indian spiritual leaders who looked upon Jesus as a sage, a guru, a realized soul or as an aspect of God.

Combining the spiritualties of East and West and reinterpreting their central concerns, Panikkar hoped to open new possibilities for understanding the real or the truth. The human being cannot be reduced to the 'logos', derived from a Greek word meaning word, reason or discourse; nor could human consciousness be reduced to reflective knowledge. Inspired by the principle of Advaita Vedanta, he endeavoured to discover the 'human invariant' (common factors) in all religions, Hinduism, Christianity and Buddhism in particular, which all aim at the realization of the individual in a continuing process of creation and recreation. 'The more we have the courage to walk new paths,' he said, 'the more we must remain rooted in our own tradition, open to others who let us know that we are not alone and permit us to acquire a wider vision of reality.' 'My aspiration,' he stated, 'does not consist so much in defending my truth but rather to live it out' (Terricabras, 2008).

Over the course of his life, Panikkar received numerous prizes and international awards, and was invited by universities and prestigious institutions around the world to give lectures. The most prestigious invite came from the University of Edinburgh, where Panikkar delivered the Gifford Lectures in 1989, about his own lifetime effort to connect worlds of religion, philosophy and science and the light they shed on the mystery of cosmic life. This was later published as a book entitled *The Rhythm of Being*.

Panikkar was not only a great scholar but also an unconventional priest. At the age of 70, he violated Church law and married his close associate in a civil ceremony. It is said that Panikkar and the woman never actually lived together, or lived together only briefly. When one of his friends asked about his marriage, he replied that at his age, it was not a question of sex but a protest against the tradition of combining priesthood with celibacy. It was, in effect, 'an experiment with truth' that would symbolize new possibilities, both for himself and others.

Talking about himself in his middle age, Panikkar had said: 'I left Europe [for India] as a Christian, I discovered I was a Hindu and returned as a Buddhist without ever having ceased to be a Christian' (Terricabras, 2008). However, to the end of his life, he was faithful to his ideals, to the mystic truth he had discovered, and achieved a depth of spirituality that transcended borders. He remained, to use his words, the 'universalist monk'. He died at his home in Tavertet, near Barcelona, Spain, on August 26, 2010. He was 91.

~

Panikkar authored around 50 books and 900 articles. Some of Panikkar's well-known and widely discussed books are *The Vedic Experience*; *The Intrareligious Dialogue*; *Myth, Faith, and Hermeneutics*; *The Silence of God*; *The Cosmotheandric Experience*; and *The Invisible Harmony*. *The Vedic Experience*, which was written over 10 years of research and contemplation and first published in 1977, remains his masterpiece. The work reads like a postmodern narrative on the deep, complex and illuminating stream of thoughts and experiences of the human, gleaned from the Vedas, Upanishads and Bhagavad Gita.

Selected Passages from Raimundo Panikkar's Interviews and Writings

Philosophy is but the conscious and critical accompaniment of Man's journeying towards his destiny. This journeying is called religion in many cultures.

~

Interculturality is problematic. The very moment that I open my mouth to speak, I am obliged to use a concrete language, and thus I am completely in a particular culture: I am on a land which already belongs to someone. I am in my culture, cultivating my land, speaking my language. And if I must, moreover, be understood by my readers, I must necessarily enter a land which is common to all.

This is the great challenge of pluralism and one of the cements of interculturality.

~

We have already suggested that we initially and provisionally understand by philosophy, that human activity which asks questions about the very foundations of human life under the heavens and on earth.

∼

Culture is not simply an object, since we are constitutively immersed in it as subjects. It is the one that makes it possible for us to see the world as objects, since self-consciousness, i.e. subjectivity, essentially belongs to the human being.

∼

Cultural respect requires that we respect those ways of life that we disapprove, or even those that we consider as pernicious. We may be obliged to go as far as to combat these cultures, but we cannot elevate our own to the rank of universal paradigm in order to judge the other ones.

∼

Human reality does not exhaust itself in history, nor human history in the history of ideas.

∼

All cultures are the result of a continuous mutual fecundation.

∼

Each philosophy is a human effort to move out of its own myth, an attempt to move out of the horizon of one's own world, as represented in miniatures of the late renaissance, which show man piercing the heavens, and glimpsing into an infinite universe which was then starting to dawn before his very eyes.

∼

The dialogue between cultures requires not only mutual respect but also a minimum of mutual understanding, which is impossible without sympathy and love.

~

When man breaks his connection with Earth, wanting to fulfill himself, he becomes a monster who destroys himself. When man breaks his connection with heaven, wanting to lead himself on his own, he becomes an automaton that destroys others.

~

Religion is not an experiment, it is an experience of life through which one is part of the cosmic adventure.

~

Without purity of heart, not only can one not 'see' God, but it is equally impossible to have any idea of what is involved in doing so. Without the silence of the intellect and the will, without the silence of the senses, without the openness of what some call 'the third eye' (spoken of not only by Tibetans but also by the disciples of Richard of Saint Victor), it is not possible to approach the sphere in which the word God can have a meaning.

~

To look for a purpose in Life outside Life itself amounts to killing Life. Reason is given by Life, not vice versa. Life is prior to meaning... Human life is joyful interrogation.

~

Love is not split into service of God and concern for our fellow-beings. The 'Presence of God' is not an act of the memory or the will.

~

We are Divine as much as the Divine is Human - without confusion and division.

~

If the church wishes to live, it should not be afraid of assimilating elements that come from other religious traditions, whose existence it can today no longer ignore.

~

There are not three realities: God, Man, and the World; but neither is there one, whether God, Man or World. Reality is cosmotheandric. It is our way of looking that makes reality appear to us at times under one aspect, at times under another. God, Man, and World are, so to speak, in an intimate and constitutive collaboration to construct Reality, to make history advance, to continue creation.

~

If there have been divine manifestations before, we cannot assume that they will never again occur. Moreover, the present situation of the world, new in the history of mankind, could be the right time for a new revelation – I don't know if through Masters who came before or new ones, I don't think that's very important. But it might well be that this revelation has not much to do with, or it does not resemble, the ones we have known until now. Reality is always new.

~

The concepts of physics – energy, force, mass, number – are as mysterious as the word God. But in physics, even though in many ways we do not know what physical reality is, we nevertheless devise or affirm parameters that permit us to measure regularity or to formulate possible laws in regard to the functioning of physical reality. Such an operation is not possible in regard to God. There are no adequate parameters that would permit us to speak of the 'functioning' of that reality we call God.

(Collated from 'Interview on Religion, Philosophy and Culture')

Acknowledgements

I am deeply indebted to the innumerable authors whose books provided me with valuable material to work on a book of this magnitude. I am grateful to my friends Vidya Ramachandran and Rajeshwara Rao for their valuable criticism of the early drafts, and to Sai Samarth and Swaha Das for helping me with data for some chapters. I owe many thanks to Rukmini Kumar Chawla for the idea of the book, advice and feedback; to Neelima P. Aryan for the lovely cover; Rosemary Sebastian for her editorial assistance; and Shyama Warner and Sneha Gusain for their diligent proofreading. My special thanks to Sonali Jindal for her meticulous work on the final copy which has enriched the book in many ways. I am sincerely grateful to Poulomi Chatterjee, editor and publisher, for her support and enthusiasm for the book, and for producing it so well.

Bibliography

Introduction

Ambedkar, B.R. *Annihilation of Caste*. Chawani: Anand Sahityasadan, 1989.

Dhawan, R.K. *Henry David Thoreau: A Study in Indian Influence*. New Delhi: Classical Publishing, 1985.

Gandhi, Mahatma. *What is Hinduism?* New Delhi: National Book Trust, 1994.

Mueller, Max. *What can India teach us?*, 1883. Gutenberg.org

Nikhilananda, Swami. *Vivekananda: A Biography*. New York: Ramakrishna-Vivekananda Center, 1953.

Rao, Mukunda. *Belief and Beyond: Adventures in Consciousness from the Upanishads to Modern Times*. New Delhi: HarperCollins Publishers, 2019.

Ratcliffe, Susan. *Oxford Essential Quotations*. Oxford University Press. Published online: 2017.

Twain, Mark. *Following the Equator: A Journey Around the World*, 1897. Gutenberg.org

Kapila

Dasgupta, Surendranath. *A History of Indian Philosophy*, Volume III. New Delhi: Motilal Banarsidass, 2015.

Founders of Philosophy. New Delhi: Publications Division, 1981.

Harshananda, Swami. *The Concise Encyclopaedia of Hinduism*. Bangalore: Ramakrishna Math, 2008.

Hiriyanna, M. *The Essentials of Indian Philosophy*. New Delhi: Motilal Banarsidass, 1995.

Radhakrishnan, Sarvepalli and Charles A. Moore, eds. *A Sourcebook in Indian Philosophy*. Princeton, NJ: Princeton University Press, 1973.

Radhakrishnan, Sarvepalli. *Indian Philosophy*, Volumes I and II. New Delhi: Oxford University Press, 1989.

Sharma, Chandrahar. *A Critical Survey of Indian Philosophy*. New Delhi: Motilal Banarsidass, 2003.

Zimmer, Heinrich Robert and Joseph Campbell. *Philosophies of India*. Bollingen Series, 26. New York: Pantheon Books, 1951.

Kanada

Founders of Philosophy. New Delhi: Publications Division, 1981.

Fowler, Jeaneane D. *Perspectives of Reality: An Introduction to the Philosophy of Hinduism*. Eastbourne: Sussex Academic Press, 2002.

Harshananda, Swami. *The Concise Encyclopaedia of Hinduism*. Bangalore: Ramakrishna Math, 2008.

Hiriyanna, M. *The Essentials of Indian Philosophy*. New Delhi: Motilal Banarsidass, 1995.

Matilal, Bimal Krishna. *Nyaya-Vaisesika*. Wiesbaden: Otto Harrassowitz Verlag, 1977.

Radhakrishnan, Sarvepalli. *Indian Philosophy*, Volumes I and II. New Delhi: Oxford University Press, 1989.

Sharma, Chandradhar. *A Critical Survey of Indian Philosophy*. New Delhi: Motilal Banarsidass, 2003.

Patanjali

Akhilananda, Swami. *Hindu Psychology: Its Meaning for the West*. London: Routledge, 2001.

Feuerstein, Georg and Ken Wilber. 'The Wheel of Yoga'. *The Yoga Tradition*. New Delhi: Motilal Banarsidass, 2001.

Maehle, Gregor. *Ashtanga Yoga: Practice and Philosophy*. Novato: New World Library, 2006.

Michaels, Axel. *Hinduism, Past and Present*. Princeton, NJ: Princeton University Press, 2004.

Sen, Amiya P., ed. 'Raja Yoga: The Science of Self-Realization'. *The Indispensable Vivekananda*. New Delhi: Orient Blackswan, 2006.

Sri Aurobindo. *The Supramental Manifestation and Other Writings*. Puducherry: Aurobindo Ashram Trust, 1989.

Tola, Fernando and Carmen Dragonetti. *The Yogasu-tras of Patañjali on Concentration of Mind*. Translated by K.D. Prithipaul. New Delhi: Motilal Banarsidass, 2001.

Vivekananda, Swami. *Raja Yoga*. New York: Ramakrishna-Vivekananda Center, 1982.

White, David Gordon. *The Yoga Sutra of Patanjali: A Biography*. Princeton, NJ: Princeton University Press, 2014.

Mahavira

Dundas, Paul. *The Jains*. London: Routledge, 1992.

Eliade, Mircea and Colette Caillat, eds. 'Mahavira'. *The Encyclopedia of Religion*. London: Macmillan, 1987.

Hemacandra. *The Lives of the Jain Elders*. Translated by R.C.C. Fynes. Oxford: Oxford University Press, 1998.

Hiriyanna, M. *An Introduction to Indian Philosophy*. New Delhi: Oxford University Press, 1978.

Radhakrishnan, Sarvepalli. *Indian Philosophy*, Volumes I and II. New Delhi: Oxford University Press, 1989.

Upadhye, A.N., ed. *Mahavira and His Teachings*. Bombay: Shree Vallabhsuri Smarak Nidhi, 1977.

The Buddha

Anguttara Nikaya, Tika Nipata, Mahavagga, Sutta No. III, 65. In *The Teachings of the Compassionate Buddha*, edited by E.A. Burtt. New York: Signet, 1955.

Armstrong, Karen. *Buddha*. London: Phoenix, 2006.

Carus, Paul. *Gospel of the Buddha*. Varanasi: Pilgrims Publishing, 2003.

Coward, Harold G., ed. *Studies in Indian Thought: Collected Papers of Prof. T.R.V. Murti*. New Delhi: Motilal Banarsidass, 1983.

Hanh, Thich Nhat. *Old Path White Clouds: Walking in the Footsteps of the Buddha*. New Delhi: Full Circle, 2007.

Majjhima Nikaya 36 and *Samyutta Nikaya 56, 11*. Translated from the Pali by Thanissaro Bhikkhu; Pali Text Society. www.accesstoinsight.org.

Murti, T.R.V. *The Central Philosophy of Buddhism. A Study of Madhyamika System*. New Delhi: Munshiram Manoharlal Publishers Pvt. Ltd, 2010.

Oldenberg, Hermann. *Buddha: His Life, His Doctrine, His Order*. Translated by William Hoey. London: Williams and Norgate, 1882.

Radhakrishnan, Sarvepalli. *Indian Philosophy*, Volume. I. New Delhi: Oxford University Press, 1989.

Rahula, Walpola Sri. *What the Buddha Taught*. Oxford: Oneworld Publications, 2007.

Rao, Mukunda. *The Buddha: An Alternative Narrative of His Life and Teaching*. New Delhi: HarperCollins Publishers, 2018.

Sangharakshita. *A Survey of Buddhism: Its Doctrines and Methods through the Ages*. London: Tharpa Publications, 1987.

Singh, Iqbal. 'Gautama Buddha'. In *The Buddhism Omnibus*, edited by Matthew T. Kapstein. New Delhi: Oxford University Press, 2008.

The Teachings of the Compassionate Buddha. Translated by Edward Conze, edited by Edwin A. Burtt. New York: Mentor Books, 1955.

Women Savants in Ancient Times

Brihada-ranyaka Upanis.ad 4.5.1. Translated by Swami Madhavananda. Kolkata: Advaita Ashram, 1960.

Harshananda, Swami. 'Brahmavadinis'. In *The Concise Encyclopedia of Hinduism*. Bangalore: Ramakrishna Math, 2008.

Rajapakse, Vijitha. *The Therigatha: A Revaluation*. Kandy: Buddhist Publication Society, 2000. BPS online edition, 2008. https://www.bps.lk/olib/wh/wh436_RajaPakse_The-Therigatha--A-Revaluation.pdf.

'Chapter VI–Yajnavalkya and Gargi (I)' in Brihadaranyaka Upanishad, in *The Upanishads*. Translated by Swami Nikhilananda. New York: Ramakrishna-Vivekananda Center, 1987. http://www.vivekananda.net/PDFBooks/upanishads_ nikhilananda.pdf.

Therigatha: Poems of the First Buddhist Women. Translated by Charles Hallisey. Murty Classical Library of India. Cambridge, MA: Harvard University Press, 2015.

Therigathapali: Verses of the Elder Bhikkhunis. Translated by Anagarika Mahendra. Roslindale, MA: Dhamma Publishers, 2017.

Verses of the Senior Nuns. Translated by Bhikkhu Sujato and Jessica Walton. SuttaCentral (website), 2019.

Sarahapada

Guenther, Herbert V. *The Royal Song of Saraha: A Study in the History of Buddhist Thought*. New paperback edition. Boulder: Shambhala Publications, 1973.

Jackson, Roger R. *Tantric Treasures: Three Collections of Mystical Verse from Buddhist India*. New York: Oxford University Press, 2004.

Osho. *The Tantra Experience: Discourses on the Royal Song of Saraha*. Cologne: Osho Media International, 1978.

A Song for the King: Saraha on Mahamudra Meditation. Edited by Michele Martin and commentary by Khenchen Thrangu Rinpoche. Boston: Wisdom Publications, 2006.

Saraha's Royal Son. Translated by Kunzang Tenzin. Keith Dowman (website). http://keithdowman.net/index.html.

Schaeffer, Kurtis R. *Dreaming the Great Brahmin: Tibetan Traditions of the Buddhist Poet-Saint Saraha*. New York: Oxford University Press, 2005.

The Mystic Songs of Kanha and Saraha: The Doha-Kosa and the Carya. Translated from the French by Pranabesh Sinha Ray. Kolkata: The Asiatic Society, 2007.

Nagarjuna

Batchelor, Stephen. *Verses from the Centre: A Buddhist Vision of the Sublime*. New York: Riverhead, 2000.

Burton, David. *Emptiness Appraised: A Critical Study of Nagarjuna's Philosophy*. New Delhi: Motilal Banarsidass, 2001.

Garfield, J.L. *Empty Words: Buddhist Philosophy and Cross-Cultural Interpretation*. New York: Oxford University Press, 2002.

Kalupahana, David. *Mulamadhyamakakarika of Nagarjuna: The Philosophy of the Middle Way*. New Delhi: Motilal Banarsidass, 2005.

Murti, T.R.V. *The Central Philosophy of Buddhism: A Study of Madhyamika System*. New Delhi: Munshiram Manoharlal Publishers Pvt. Ltd, 2010.

Murty, K. Satchidananda. *Nagarjuna*. New Delhi: National Book Trust, 1971.

Ramanan, K. Venkata. *Nagarjuna's Philosophy*. New Delhi: Motilal Banarsidass, 1978.

Bhartrihari

Coward, Harold G. *The Sphota Theory of Language: A Philosophical Analysis*. New Delh: Motilal Banarsidass, 1997.

Houben, Jan E.M., *The Sambandha-samuddeśa and Bhartrihari's Philosophy of Language*. Gonda Indological Series, 2. Groningen: Egbert Forsten, 1995.

Matilal, B.K. *The Word and the World: India's Contribution to the Study of Language*. New Delhi: Oxford University Press, 1990.

Patnaik, Tandra. *Śabda: A Study of Bhartrihari's Philosophy of Language*. New Delhi: D.K. Printworld, 1994.

Poems from the Sanskrit. Translated with an Introduction by John Brough. London: Penguin Books, 1977.

Sarukkai, Sundar. *Indian Philosophy and Philosophy of Science*. New Delhi: Centre for Studies in Civilizations, 2005.

The Century of Life: The Nitishataka of Bhartrihari. Translated by Sri Aurobindo. Puducherry: Sri Aurobindo Ashram, 1969.

Gaudapada

Cole, Colin A. *Apsara-Yoga: A Study of Gaudapada's Mandukya Karika*. New Delhi: Motilal Banarsidass, 2004.

Gaudapada: Mandukya Karika. Translated by Swami Gambhirananda. Trichur: Ramakrishna Math, 1987.

Mahadevan, T.M.P. *Gaudapada: A Study in Early Vedanta*. Madras: University of Madras, 1960.

Mandukya Upanishad with Gaudapada's Karika. Translated by Swami Nikhilananda. Chennai: Sri Ramakrishna Math, 2002.

Adi Shankara

Dasgupta, Surendranath. *A History of Indian Philosophy*, Volume I. New Delhi: Motilal Banarsidass, 2015.

Hiriyanna, M. *An Introduction to Indian Philosophy*. New Delhi: Oxford University Press, 1978.

Madhava-Vidyaranya. *Sankara Digvijaya: The Traditional Life of Sri Sankaracharya*. Translated by Swami Tapasyananda. Madras: Sri Ramakrishna Math, 1980.

Radhakrishnan, Sarvepalli. *Indian Philosophy*, Volumes I and II. New Delhi: Oxford University Press, 1989.

Sankara the Missionary. Mumbai: Central Chinmaya Mission Trust, 1978.

Upadeshasahasri: A Thousand Teachings of Sri Sankaracharya. Translated into English with explanatory notes by Swami Jagadananda. Madras: Sri Ramakrishna Math, 1949.

Abhinavagupta

Abhinavagupta and Jaideva Singh. *A Trident of Wisdom*. SUNY Series in Tantric Studies. Albany: State University of New York Press, 1989.

Dupuche, John R. *Abhinavagupta: The Kula Ritual*. New Delhi: Shri Jainendra Press, 2003.

Gerow, Edwin. 'Abhinavagupta's Aesthetics as a Speculative Paradigm'. *Journal of the American Oriental Society*, Volume 114 (1994): 186–208.

Isayeva, Natalia. *From Early Vedanta to Kashmir Shaivism*. Albany: State University of New York Press, 1995.

Lidke, Jeffrey S. *A Thousand Years of Abhinavagupta*. 2016. http://www.sutrajournal.com/a-thousand-years-of-abhinavagupta-by-jeffrey-lidke.

Marjanovic, Boris. *Gitartha-samgraha: Abhinavagupta's Commentary on the Bhagavad Gita*. Varanasi: Indica Books, 2003.

Muller-Ortega, Paul E. *The Triadic Heart of Siva*. New Delhi: Sri Satguru Publications, 1989.

Sanderson, Alexis. 'A Commentary on the Opening Verses of the Tantrasara of Abhinavagupta'. In *Samarasya: Studies in Indian Arts, Philosophy, and Interreligious Dialogue*, edited by Sadananda Das and Ernst Furlinger. Delhi: D.K. Printworld, 2005.

Singh, Jaideva. *Abhinavagupta: A Tradition of Wisdom*. Albany: State University of New York Press, 1988.

Singh, Jaideva. *Para-Trisika-Vivarana by Abhinavagupta: The Secret of Tantric Mysticism*. New Delhi: Motilal Banarsidass, 2014.

Wallis, Christopher. 'The Descent of Power: Possession, Mysticism, and Initiation in the Saiva Theology of Abhinavagupta'. *Journal of Indian Philosophy*, Volume 36, Issue 2 (2007): 247–295.

Basavanna

Somanatha, Palkuriki. *Basava Puranam*, a thirteenth century Telugu biographical epic poem.

Desai, P.B. *Basaveshwara and His Times*. Bangalore: Basava Samithi, Basava Bhavan, 1968.

Murthy, M. Chidananda. *Vachana Sahitya*. Mysore: Prasaranga, Mysore University, 1975.

Nandimath, S.C. *A Handbook of Virasaivism*. New Delhi: Motilal Banarsidass, 1979.

Ramanujan, A.K. *Speaking of Siva*. New Delhi: Penguin Books, 1973.

Rao, Mukunda. *In Search of Shiva: A Novel*. Bangalore: Dronequill Publishers Pvt. Ltd, 2010.

Siva's Warriors: The Basava Purana of Palkuriki Somanatha. Translated by Velcheru Narayana Rao and Gene H. Roghair. Princeton, NJ: Princeton University Press, 1990. Rendered into Kannada more elaborately as *Basava Purana* by Bhima Kavi, 1369.

Sunya Sampadane, by Gummalapurada Siddalingadevaru. Edited by R.C. Hiremath. Dharwad: Kannada Study Centre, Karnataka University, 1972.

Allama Prabhu

Allamana Vachanagalu: Selected Vachanas of Allama Prabhu. Edited by Dr L. Basavaraju. Mysore: Geetha Book House, 1997.

Murthy, M. Chidananda. *Vachana Sahitya*. Mysore: Prasaranga, Mysore University, 1975.

Nagaraj, D.R. *Allama Prabhu Mattu Shaiva Pratibhe: A Critical Study of Allama Prabhu and the Shaiva Imagination*. Heggodu, Sagar: Akshara Prakashana, 1999.

Nandimath, S.C. *A Handbook of Virasaivism*. New Delhi: Motilal Banarsidass, 1979.

Ramanujan, A.K. *Speaking of Siva*. New Delhi: Penguin Books, 1973.

Rao, Basrur Subba. *Allama Prabhu: A Study in Philosophy with Translation of Poems*. Bangalore: Shri Mangesh Publishers, 2007.

Rao, Mukunda. *In Search of Shiva: A Novel*. Bangalore: Dronequill Publishers Pvt. Ltd, 2010.

Akka Mahadevi

Channabasavanka's Mahadeviyakkana Purana. Edited by B.N. Chandraiah. Mysore: Sharath Prakashana, 1967.

Menezes, Armando. *Songs from the Saranas and Other Poems*. Dharwar: Karnataka University, 1973.

Nandimath, S.C. *A Handbook of Virasaivism*. New Delhi: Motilal Banarsidass, 1979.

Ramanujan, A.K. *Speaking of Siva*. New Delhi: Penguin Books, 1973.

Ramaswamy, Vijaya. *Walking Naked: Women, Society, Spirituality in South India*. Shimla: Indian Institute of Advanced Study, 2007.

Rao, Mukunda. *In Search of Shiva: A Novel*. Bangalore: Dronequill Publishers Pvt. Ltd, 2010.

Rao, Mukunda. *Sky-Clad: The Extraordinary Life and Times of Akka Mahadevi*. New Delhi: Westland, 2018.

Sreekantaiya, T.N. 'On Akka Mahadevi'. In *Women Saints: East and West*, edited by Swami Ghanananda and John Stewart Wallace. Hollywood: Vedanta Press, 1979.

Sunya Sampadane, Gummalapurada Siddalingadevaru. Edited by R.C. Hiremath. Dharwad: Kannada Study Centre, Karnataka University, 1972.

Thiruvalluvar

Ambrosia of Thirukkural. Translated by Swamiji Iraianban. New Delhi: Abhinav Publications, 1997.

Rajagopalachari, C. *Kural: The Great Book of Tiru-Valluvar*. Mumbai: Bharatiya Vidya Bhavan, 1996.

Robinson, Edward Jewitt. *Tamil Wisdom: Traditions Concerning Hindu Sages and Selections from Their Writings*. New Delhi: Asian Educational Services, 2001.

Sarma, Shuddhananda A. *Tamil Siddhas: A Study from Historical, Socio-cultural and Religio-philosophical Perspectives*. New Delhi: Munshiram Manoharlal, 2007.

Nandanar

Basu, Raj Sekhar. *Nandanar's Children: The Paraiyans' Tryst with Destiny, Tamil Nadu 1850–1956*. New Delhi: Sage Publications, 2011.

Bharathi, Gopalakrishna. *Nandanar Charithram: The Musical drama of the story of Nandanar*. Translated by P.R. Ramachander. 2013. http://translationsofsomesongsofcarnticmusic.blogspot.com/2013/01/nandanar-charithram-of-gopala-krishna_1266.html. Accessed 23 September 2020.

Peterson, Indira Viswanathan. *Poems to Siva: The Hymns of the Tamil Saints*. New Delhi: Motilal Banarsidass, 1991.

Sivananda, Swami. *Sixty-three Nayanar Saints*. Sivanandanagar: The Divine Life Society, 1999.

Andal

Bailey, Greg and Ian Kesarcodi-Watson. *Bhakti Studies*. New Delhi: Sterling Publishers, 1992.

Chakravarty, Uma. 'The World of the Bhaktin in South Indian Traditions: The Body and Beyond' (PDF). *Manushi*, Volume 10, Nos. 50–52 (1989).

Chari, S.M. Srinivasa. *Philosophy and Theistic Mysticism of the Alvars*. New Delhi: Motilal Banarsidass, 1997.

Dehejia, Vidya. *The Body Adorned: Sacred and Profane in Indian Art*. New York: Columbia University Press, 2008.

Kandasamy, Meena. *Ms Militancy*. New Delhi: Navayana, 2010.

Mulchandani, Sandhya. 'Divine Love'. *Indian Quarterly*, 2014.

Sarukkai, Priya and Ravi Shankar. *Andal: The Autobiography of a Goddess*. New Delhi: Zubaan, 2016.

Thiruppavai. Translated by P.R. Ramachander. http://ibiblio.org/sripedia/ebooks/ramachander/ thiruppavai.doc. Accessed 23 September 2020.

Dalrymple, William. 'In Search of Tamil Nadu's Poet-preachers'. *Financial Times*, 10 July 2015.

Ramanuja

Aiyangar, S. Krishnaswami; Rajagopala Chariar and M. Rangacharya. *Sri Ramanujacharya: A Sketch of His Life and Times and His Philosophical System*. Madras: G.A. Natesan, 1911.

Dasgupta, Surendranath. *A History of Indian Philosophy*, Volume II. New Delhi: Motilal Banarsidass, 2015.

Gaudiya History: Ramanujacharya. https://gaudiyahistory.iskcondesiretree.com/ramanujacarya/

Hiriyanna, M. *An Introduction to Indian Philosophy*. New Delhi: Oxford University Press, 1978.

Radhakrishnan, Sarvepalli. *Indian Philosophy*, Volumes I and II. New Delhi: Oxford University Press, 1989.

Ramakrishnananda, Swami. *The Life of Sri Ramanuja*. Madras: Sri Ramakrishna Math, 1965.

Rangachari, Dewan Bahadur. *The Sri Vaishnava Brahmans*. New Delhi: Gian Publishing House, 1986.

Srinivasa Chari, S.M. *Visistadvaita Vedanta*. New Delhi: Motilal Banarsidass, 1998.

Srinivasa Chari, S.M. *Vaisnavism: Its Philosophy, Theology and Religious Discipline*. New Delhi: Motilal Banarsidass, 2017.

Madhvacharya

Rao, Vasudeva. *Living Traditions in Contemporary Context: The Madhva Matha of Udupi*. London: Sangam Books, 2002.

Sarma, Deepak. *An Introduction to Madhva Vedanta*. Burlington, VT: Ashgate Publishing, 2003.

Sarma, Deepak. *Epistemologies and the Limitations of Philosophical Inquiry: Doctrine in Madhva Vedanta*. New York: Routledge, 2005.

Sharma, B.N.K. *Philosophy of Sri Madhvacarya*. New Delhi: Motilal Banarsidass, 1986.

'Madhvacharya'. *Hindupedia*. www.hindupedia.com/en/Madhvacarya. Accessed 23 September 2020.

Tapasyananda. *Bhakti Schools of Vedanta*. Madras: Sri Ramakrishna Math, 1991.

Lalleshwari

Ghanananda, Swami and John Stewart Wallace, eds. *Women Saints: East and West*. Hollywood: Vedanta Press, 1979.

I, Lalla: The Poems of Lal Ded. Translated with Introduction and Notes by Ranjit Hoskote. New Delhi: Penguin Books India, 2013.

Kaul, Jayalal. *Lal Ded*. New Delhi: Sahitya Akademi, 1972.

'Lalleshwari'. *Saints and Sages of Kashmir*. Accessed 26 September 2020. https://koausa.org/site/wp-content/uploads/2017/02/saints.pdf

Parimoo, B.N. *The Ascent of Self: A Reinterpretation of the Mystical Poetry of Lalla-Ded*. New Delhi: Motilal Banarsidass, 2013.

Rao, Mukunda. *Sky-Clad: The Extraordinary Life and Times of Akka Mahadevi*. Chennai: Westland Publications Pvt. Ltd, 2018.

Razdan, P.N. (Mahanori). *Gems of Kasmiri Literature and Kashmiriyat, The Trio of Saint Poets*. New Delhi: Smakaleen Prakashan, 1998.

Kabir

Dharwadker, Vinay, trans. *Kabir: The Weaver's Songs*. New Delhi: Penguin Books India, 2003.

Songs of Kabir. Translated by Rabindranath Tagore. New York: Macmillan Co. Ltd, 1915.

The Bijak of Kabir. Translated by Ahmad Shah. New Delhi: Asian Publication Services, 1977.

The Collected Essays of A.K. Ramanujan. Edited by Vinay Dharwadker. New Delhi: Oxford University Press, 2001.

Varkaris

Deleury, G.A. *The Cult of Vithoba*. Poona: Deccan College, 1960.

Pande, Suruchi. 'The Vithoba of Pandharpur'. *Prabuddha Bharata*, September 2008. https://advaitaashrama.org/pb/2008/092008.pdf.

Ranade, Ramchandra Dattatraya. *Indian Mysticism: Mysticism in Maharashtra*. Volume VII of *History of Indian Philosophy*, edited by S.K. Belvalkar and R.D. Ranade. Poona: Aryabhushan Press, 1933.

Jnaneshwar

Bobde, P.V. *Garland of Divine Flowers: Selected Devotional Lyrics of Saint Jnanesvara*. New Delhi: Motilal Banarsidass, 1987.

Jnaneshvari: Written by Shri Jnyaneshvar. Translated by Vitthal G. Pradhan and edited by Hester M. Lambert. Albany: SUNY Press, 1987.

Mokashi, Digambar Balkrishna. *Palkhi: An Indian Pilgrimage*. Albany: SUNY Press, 1987.

Ranade, Ramchandra Dattatraya. *Mysticism in India: The Poet-Saints of Maharashtra*. Albany: SUNY Press, 1933.

Namdev

Dass, Nirmal. *Songs of the Saints from the Adi Granth*. Albany: SUNY, 2000.

Maurya, R.N. *Namdev, His Mind and Art: A Linguistic Analysis of Namdev's Poetry*. New Delhi: Bahri Publications, 1988.

Namdev. 'He is the One in Many'. Translated by Nirmal Dass. Poetry Chaikhana: Sacred Poetry from Around the World (website). http://www.poetry-chaikhana.com/Poets/N/Namdev/HeisOnein/index.html. Accessed 26 September 2020.

Prill, Susan. 'Representing Sainthood in India: Sikh and Hindu Visions of Namdev'. Material Religion, Volume 5, No. 2 (2009): 156–79.

Puri, J.R. and V.K. Sethi. *Saint Namdev*. Punjab: Radha Soami Satsang Beas, 1978.

'Sant Jnaneshwar Visits Namdev'. *Aumamen*. http://aumamen.com/story/sant-jnaneshwar-visits-namdev. Accessed 26 September 2020.

Chokhamela

Mokashi-Punekar, Rohini. *Bhakti as Protest*. New Delhi: Book Review Literary Trust, 2002.

Nimavat, B.S. 'Chokhamela: The Pioneer of Untouchable Movement in Maharashtra'. In *Dalit Literature: A Critical Exploration*, edited by Amar Nath Prasad and M.B. Gaija, 9-16. New Delhi: Sarup and Sons, 2007.

On the Threshold: Songs of Chokhamela. Translated by Rohini Mokashi-Punekar. New Delhi: Book Review Literary Trust, 2002.

Zelliot, Eleanor. 'Chokhamela and Eknath: Two Modes of Legitimacy for Modern Change'. *Journal of Asian and African Studies*, Volume 15, No. 1–2 (January 1980): 136–56.

Tukaram

Bhandarkar, R.G. *Vaisnavism, Saivism and Minor Religious Systems*. London: Routledge, 2014.

Chattopadhyaya, Harindranath. *Tukaram*. New Delhi: Rupa Publications, 2002.

Chitre, Dilip. *Says Tuka: Selected Poetry of Tukaram*. New Delhi: Penguin Books India, 1991.

'Prevailing Political, Social and Religious Situation'. *Tukaram*. http://

tukaram.com/english/biography/more/bio_2.htm. Accessed 26 September 2020.

Ranade, Ramchandra D. *Tukaram*. New York: State University of New York Press, 1994.

'Tukaram'. *IndiaDivine*. https://www. indiadivine.org/content/ topic/1344019-tukaram/. Accessed 26 September 2020.

Tukaram. 'Saintliness is Not to be Purchased in Shops'. Translated by M.K. Gandhi.

Bahinabai

Feldhaus, Anne. 'Bahina Bai: Wife and Saint'. *Journal of the American Academy of Religion*, Volume 50, No. 4 (December 1982): 591–604.

Pandharipande, Rajeshwari V. 'Janabai: A Woman Saint of India'. In *Women Saints in World Religions*, edited by Arvind Sharma. Albany: SUNY Press, 2000, pp.145–79.

Women Writing in India: 600 B.C. to the Present, Volume 1. Edited by Susie J. Tharu and K. Lalita. New York: City University of New York, 1991.

Sankardev

Barman, Sivnath. *An Unsung Colossus: An Introduction to the Life and Works of Sankardev*. Guwahati: Forum for Sankaradeva Studies, North Eastern Hill University, 1999.

Bhuyan, Abhijit. *Sankardeva and Neo-Vaishnavism in Assam*. https://www. scribd.com/document397232570/ Sankardeva-and-NVM. Accessed 26 September 2020.

Borkakoti, Sanjib Kumar. *Mahapurusha Srimanta Sankaradeva*. Guwahati: Bani Mandir, 2005.

Rajkhowa, Jyoti Prasad. *Sankardeva, His Life, Preachings, and Practices: A Historical Biography*, 2003.

Sarma, S.N. *The Neo-Vaisnavite Movement and the Satra Institution of Assam*. Guwahati: Gauhati University, 1966.

Krishna Chaitanya

Banerji, Chitrita. *Chaitanya Mahaprabhu: The Story of Bengal's Greatest Bhakti Saint*. New Delhi: Juggernaut Books, 2018.

Das, Khudiram. *Sri Chaitanya and Gaudiya Vaishnava Dharma*. E-book. 2017.

Prabhupada, A.C. Bhaktivedanta Swami. *Teachings of Lord Chaitanya*. 1968.

Rosen, Steven. *India's Spiritual Renaissance: The Life and Times of Lord Chaitanya*. Columbia: Folk Books, 1988.

'Sri Krishna Chaitanya Mahaprabhu'. *Hindupedia*. http://hindupedia.com/en/Sri_Krishna_Chaitanya_Mahaprabhu. Accessed 26 September 2020.

Thakur, Srila Bhaktivinoda. *Sri Chaitanya: His Life and Precepts*. E-book. 1896.

Ravidas

Amritabani Satguru Ravidas Maharaj Ji. Translated by Sri Ram Arsh. http://www.shrigururavidasji.com/site/ articles_books/ravidasji/ravidas_a_b_amritabani.php. Accessed 26 September 2020.

Callewaert, W.M. and P.G. Friedlander. *The Life and Works of Raidas*. New Delhi: Manohar Publications, 1992.

'Concept of Begampura'. Ravidassiadharam.in. http://www.ravidassiadharam.in/concept-of-begampura/. Accessed 26 September 2020.

Khare, Ravindra S. *The Untouchable as Himself: Ideology, Identity, and Pragmatism among the Lucknow Chamars*. Cambridge: Cambridge University Press, 1985.

Kumar, Manish. *Saint Ravidas*. New Delhi: Prabhat Prakashan, 2015.

Lorenzen, David. *Bhakti Religion in North India: Community Identity and Political Action*. Albany: State University of New York Press, 1995.

Sharma, Arvind. *The Study of Hinduism*. Columbia: University of South Carolina Press, 2003.

Guru Nanak

Grewal, J.S. *The Sikhs of the Punjab*. Cambridge: Cambridge University Press, 1998.

'Guru Nanak'. Sikhwiki (website). https://www. sikhiwiki.org/index.php/Guru_Nanak. Accessed 12 October 2020.

'Guru Nanak's Message of Equality'. Worldsikh. https://www.worldsikh.org/celebrating_guru_nanak_s_message_of_equality. Accessed 12 October 2020.

Khalsa, Gurutej Singh. 'Nanak's Talk with the Yogis'. Sikh Dharma International (website). https://www.sikhdharma.org/nanaks-talk-with-the-yogis/.

McLeod, W.H. *Sikhs and Sikhism*. New Delhi: Oxford University Press, 2004.

Prasoon, Shrikant. *Knowing Guru Nanak*. Bangalore: Pustak Mahal, 2007.

Singh, Kartar. *Life Story of Guru Nanak*. New Delhi: Hemkunt Press, 1984.

Singh, Khushwant. *The Illustrated History of the Sikhs*. New Delhi: Oxford University Press, 2006.

'The First Master Guru Nanak (1469–1539)'. Sikhs (website). https://www.sikhs.org/guru1.htm. Accessed 12 October 2020.

The Guru Granth Sahib. One Little Angel: A Spiritual and Interfaith Dialogue (website). onelittleangel.com. Accessed 6 October 2020.

Meera Bai

Behari, Bankey. *The Story of Mira Bai*. Gorakhpur: Gita Press, 1935.

Bly, Robert and Jane Hirschfield. *Mirabai: Ecstatic Poems*. Boston: Beacon Press, 2004.

Goetz, Hermann. *Mira Bai: Her Life and Times*. Bombay: Bharatiya Vidya Bhavan, 1966.

Hawley, John Stratton. *The Bhakti Voices: Mirbai, Surdas, and Kabir in Their Times and Ours*. New York: Oxford University Press, 2005.

Levi, Louise Landes. *Sweet on My Lips: The Love Poems of Mira Bai*. Brooklyn: Cool Grove Press, 2017.

Sethi, V.K. *Mira: The Divine Lover*. Punjab: Radha Soami Satsang Beas, 1988.

Shekhawat, B.S. *Translations of Meera's Poems*. 2019.

Kanaka Dasa

Ayyappapanicker, ed. *Medieval Indian Literature: An Anthology*. New Delhi: Sahitya Akademi, 1997.

Basavaraj, M. *Karnatakada Mahasant Kanakadasa*. New Delhi: Publications Division, 2007.

Naikar, Basavaraj. *Kanakadasa: The Golden Servant of Lord Hari*. New Delhi: National Book Trust, 2016.

Ravikumar, C.P. *An English Mirror for Kannada Poetry*. cp-ravikumar-kannadapoems2english.blogspot.com/. Accessed 6 October 2020.

Tulsidas

Growse, Frederic Salmon. *The Ramayana of Tulsi Das*. Allahabad: Ram Narain Lal Publisher and Bookseller, 1914.

Handoo, Chandra Kumari. *Tulsidasa: Poet, Saint and Philosopher of the Sixteenth Century*. Bombay: Orient Longman, 1964.

Lutgendorf, Philip. *Hanuman's Tale: The Messages of a Divine Monkey*. New York: Oxford University Press, 2007.

Macfie, J.M. *The Ramayana of Tulsidas or the Bible of Northern India*. Whitefish, Montana: Kessinger Publishing, LLC, 2004.

Sri Ramacharitamanasa or The Manasa Lake Brimming Over with the Exploits of Sri Rama (with Hindi text and English translation). Gorakhpur: Gita Press, 1968.

Vemana

Brown, C.P. *Verses of Vemana*. Madras: V. Ramaswamy Sastrulu, 1911.

Moorty, J.S. R.L. Narayana and Elliot Roberts. *Selected Verses of Vemana*. New Delhi: Sahitya Akademi, 1995.

Narla, V.R. *Vemana*. New Delhi: Sahitya Akademi, 1969.

Narla, V.R. *Vemana Through Western Eyes*. Machilipatnam: Seshachalam & Co., 1969.

Shishunala Sharifa

Bhatt, Lakshminarayan. *Santakavi Shishunala Sharif Saheb*. New Delhi: National Book Trust India, 2011.

Gubbannavar, Shivananda. *Shishunala Sharif Sahebaru*. New Delhi: Sahitya Akademi, 1992.

Nagabharana, T.S., dir. *Santha Shishunala Sharifa*. 1990.

Unpublished translations of Sharifa's tattvapadas by H.S. Shivaprakash, 2019.

Sri Ramakrishna

Ghanananda, Swami. *Sri Ramakrishna and His Unique Message*, third edition. London: Ramakrishna Vedanta Centre, 1970.

Gupta, Mahendranath. *The Gospel of Sri Ramakrishna*. Translated by Swami Nikhilananda. Chennai: Sri Ramakrishna Math, 2002.

Isherwood, Christopher. *Ramakrishna and His Disciples*. Hollywood: Vedanta Press, 1965.

Nikhilananda, Swami. *Life of Sri Ramakrishna*. Khat Khutam, Uttarakhand: Advaita Ashrama, 2008.

Ramakrishna as We Saw Him. Edited and translated by Swami Chetanananda. Kolkata: Advaita Ashram, 1999.

Vivekananda

Burke, Marie Louise. *Swami Vivekananda in the West: New Discoveries*, 6 Volumes. Kolkata: Advaita Ashrama, 1985.

Chetanananda, Swami. *Various Facets of Vivekananda*. Vedanta Society of St. Louis. https://vedantastl.org/wp-content/uploads/2018/04/VariousFacetsofVivekananda.pdf Accessed 15 October 2020.

Dhar, Shailendra Nath. *A Comprehensive Biography of Swami Vivekananda*. Madras: Vivekananda Prakashan Kendra, 1975.

Ghosh, Gautam. *The Prophet of Modern India: A Biography of Swami Vivekananda*. New Delhi: Rupa Publications, 2003.

Mukherji, Mani Shankar. *The Monk as Man: The Unknown Life of Swami Vivekananda*. New Delhi: Penguin Books India, 2011.

Nikhilananda, Swami. *Vivekananda: A Biography*. New York: Ramakrishna-Vivekananda Center, 1953.

Nikhilananda, Swami. *Life of Sri Ramakrishna*. Khat Khutam, Uttarakhand: Advaita Ashrama, 2008.

Paranjape, Makarand. *Penguin Swami Vivekananda Reader*. New Delhi: Penguin Books India, 2005.

Ramakrishna as We Saw Him. Edited and translated by Swami Chetanananda. Kolkata: Advaita Ashram, 1999.

Rolland, Romain. *The Life of Vivekananda and the Universal Gospel*. 1931. http://archive.org/details/in.ernet.dli.2015.64304. Accessed 15 October 2020.

Virajananda, Swami, ed. *The Life of Swami Vivekananda by his Eastern and Western Disciples*, Volumes I and II. Kolkata: Advaita Ashrama, 2006.

Vivekananda, Swami. *Complete Works of Swami Vivekananda*, 9 Volumes. Kolkata: Advaita Ashrama, 1907, 2001.

Narayana Guru

Bhaskaran, T. *Brahmarshi Sree Narayana Guru*. New Delhi: Sahitya Akademi, 2009.

Guru, Nataraja. *The Word of the Guru: The Life and Teaching of Guru Narayana*. New Delhi: D.K. Printworld, 2003.

Kunhappa, Murkot. *Sree Narayana Guru*. New Delhi: National Book Trust, 1982.

Prasad, Swami Muni Narayana. *The Philosophy of Narayana Guru*. New Delhi: D.K. Printworld, 2003.

Sanu, M.K. *Sree Narayana Guru: Life and Times*. Edited by O.V. Usha and translated by P.R. Mukundan. Kochi: Open Door Media, 2017.

Sasidharan, G.K. *Sree Narayana Gurudev: The Maharshi who made Advaita a Science*. Kollam: Many Worlds Publications, 2014.

Srinarayana Guruvinte Sampoorna Kruthikal (The Complete Works of Sri Narayana Guru). Kozhikode: Mathrubhoomi Publishers, 2005.

Teachings of Narayana Guru. 2017. www. sevenamuk.com/teachings-of-narayana-guru/. Accessed 19 October 2020.

Yati, Nityachaitanya. *Narayana Guru*. New Delhi: Indian Council of Philosophical Research, 2005.

Anandamayi Ma

Chaudhuri, Narayan. *That Compassionate Touch of Ma Anandamayee*. New Delhi: Motilal Banarsidass, 2006.

Ghanananda, Swami and John Stewart Wallace, eds. *Women Saints: East and West*. Hollywood: Vedanta Press, 1979.

Lipski, Alexander. *Life and Teaching of Sri Anandamayi Ma*. New Delhi: Motilal Banarsidass, 2000.

Mangalananda, Swami. *A Goddess Among Us: The Divine Life of Anandamayi Ma*. Mumbai: Yogi Impressions Books Pvt. Ltd, 2016.

McDaniel, June. *The Madness of the Saints: Ecstatic Religion in Bengal*. Illinois: University of Chicago Press, 1989.

Mother, as Seen by Her Devotees. Shree Shree Anandamayee Sangha, 1995.

Sufism and the Illustrious Indian Sufis

'Amir Khusro'. *All Poetry*. https://www. allpoetry.com/Amir-Khusro. Accessed 16 October 2020.

Anjum, Tanvir. *Chishti Sufis in the Sultanate of Delhi 1190–1400: From Restrained Indifference to Calculated Defiance*. Karachi: Oxford University Press, 2011.

Behari, Bankey. *Sufis, Mystics and Yogis of India*. Bombay: Bharatiya Vidya Bhavan, 1991.

Bhattacharjya, Dhritiabrata. 'Hazrat Nizamuddin Auliya: People's Saint'. *New Age Islam*. 2011. http://newageislam. com/islam-and-spiritualism/ dhritiabrata-bhattacharjya-tato/hazrat- nizamuddin-auliya-peoples-saint/d/5020. Accessed 16 October 2020.

Chopra, R.M. *Great Sufi Poets of the Punjab*. Kolkata: Iran Society, 1999.

Chopra, R.M. *The Rise, Growth and Decline of Indo-Persian Literature*. New Delhi, Kolkata: Iran Culture House and Iran Society, 2012.

'Excerpts from Khusrau's Persian Poetry'. *Amir Khusrau* (website). http:// www.angelfire.com/sd/urdumedia/love.html. Accessed 15 October 2020.

Jafri, Saiyid Zaheer Husain and Helmut Reifeld, eds. *The Islamic Path: Sufism, Politics, and Society in India*. New Delhi: Konrad Adenauer Foundation, 2006.

Karishna, Lajwanti Rama. 'Bullhe Shah'. http://www.wichaar.com/ news/239/ARTICLE/7115/2008-05-18.html. Quoted in Malik, Jamal. *Islam in South Asia: A Short History*. Leiden: Brill, 2008.

Malik, Anas Ibn. Hadith I. Islamweb. http:// www.islamweb.net/en/ article/76856/the-prophets-way-in-correcting- peoples-mistakes. Accessed 15 October 2020.

Nizami, Khaliq Ahmad. *Sheikh Nizamuddin Auliya*. New Delhi: National Book Trust, 2004.

Puri, J.R. and Tilaka Raj Shangri. *Bulleh Shah: The Love-Intoxicated Iconoclast*. Punjab: Radha Soami Satsang Beas, 1986.

Schimmel, Annemarie. 'Sufi Orders and Fraternities' in *Mystical Dimensions of Islam*. Chapel Hill: University of North Carolina Press, 1975.

Sharma, Sunil. *Amir Khusraw: Poets of Sultans and Sufis*. Oxford: Oneworld Press, 2005.

Singh, Harbhajan. *Sheikh Farid*. New Delhi: Hindi Pocket Books, 2015.

Ezhuthachan

Ezhuthachan, Thunchath. *Adhyathma Ramayanam*. Thiruvananthapuram: Authentic Books, 2008.

Ezhuthachan, Thunchath. *Adhyathma Ramayanam*. Translated by P.R. Ramachander and edited by T.N. Sethumadhavan. https://www. esamskriti.com/e/Spirituality/Philosophy/ Adhyatma-Ramayan/. Accessed 16 October 2020.

'Preface to Adhyatma Ramayanam of Thunjathu Ezhuthachan'. *Thunchathu Ezhuthachan's Adhyathma Ramayanam*. rajathathas.blogspot. com/2012/05/preface-to-adhyatma- ramayanam-of.html. Accessed 11 October 2020.

Narsi Mehta

Devotional Songs of Narsi Mehta. Varanasi. Translated by Swami Mahadevananda. New Delhi: Motilal Banarsidass, 1985.

Munshi, K.M. *Gujarat and Its Literature: A Survey from the Earliest Times.* Bombay: Longman Green and Co. Ltd, 1935.

Shukla-Bhatt, Neelima. *Narasinha Mehta of Gujarat: A Legacy of Bhakti in Songs and Stories*. New Delhi: Oxford University Press, 2015.

Tripathi, Govardhanram. *Poets of Gujarat and Their Influence on Society and Morals*. Mumbai: Forbes Gujarati Sabha, 1958.

Zhaveri, Mansukhlal. *History of Gujarati Literature*. New Delhi: Sahitya Akademi, 1978.

Mahima Dharma

Banerjee-Dube, Ishita and Johannes Beltz eds. *Popular Religion and Ascetic Practices. New Studies on Mahima Dharma*. New Delhi: Manohar Publishers, 2008.

Eschmann, A., H. Kulke and C.G. Tripathi, eds. *The Cult of Jagannath and the Regional Tradition of Orissa*. New Delhi: Manohar, 1978.

Mishra, Kedar. *Bhima Bhoi's Poetry: A Weapon to Defend and a Balm to Heal*. https://www.academia.edu/2946086/ Bhima_Bhois_poetry_A_ weapon_to_defend_and_balm_to_heal. Accessed 16 October 2020.

Nepak, Bhagirathi. 'Mahima Dharma, Bhima Bhoi and Biswanathbaba'. *Orissa Review*, May 2005. http://magazines.odisha.gov.in/Orissareview/may2005/engpdf/mahima_dharma_bhima_bhoi_biswanathbaba.pdf.

Sai Baba of Shirdi

Arulneyam, Dura. *The Gospel of Shri Shirdi Sai Baba: A Holy Spiritual Path*. New Delhi: Sterling Publishers, 2008.

Kamath, M.V. and V.B. Kher. *Sai Baba of Shirdi: A Unique Saint, India*. New Delhi: Jaico Publishing House, 1997.

Osborne, Arthur. *The Incredible Sai Baba: The Life and Miracles of a Modern-day Saint*. Hyderabad: Orient Longman, 1957.

Panday, Balkrishna. *Sai Baba's 261 Leelas: A Treasure House of Miracles*. New Delhi. Sterling Publishers, 2004.

Parthasarathy, Rangaswami. *God Who Walked on Earth: The Life and Times of Shirdi Sai Baba*. New Delhi: Sterling Publishers, 1996.

Venkataraman, Krishnaswamy. *Shirdi Stories*. New Delhi: Srishti Publishers, 2002.

White, Charles S.J. *The Sai Baba Movement: Study of a Unique Contemporary Moral and Spiritual Movement*. New Delhi: Arnold-Heinemann, 1985.

The Bijak of Kabir. Translated by Ahmad Shah. New Delhi: Asian Publication Services,1977.

Sri Aurobindo

Heehs, Peter. *The Lives of Sri Aurobindo*. New York: Columbia University Press, 2008.

Nirodbaran. *Twelve Years with Sri Aurobindo*, Puducherry: Sri Aurobindo Ashram, 1973.

Paranjape, Makarand, ed. *The Penguin Sri Aurobindo Reader*. New Delhi: Penguin Books India, 1999.

Purani, A.B. *The Life of Sri Aurobindo*. Puducherry: Sri Aurobindo Ashram, 1978.

Purani, A.B. *Evening Talks with Sri Aurobindo (1938–50)*. Puducherry: Sri Aurobindo Ashram, 1987.

Satprem. *Sri Aurobindo, or the Adventure of Consciousness*. Puducherry: Sri Aurobindo Ashram, 1968.

Sri Aurobindo. *The Life Divine*. Puducherry: Sri Aurobindo Ashram, 1971.

Sri Aurobindo. *The Supramental Manifestation AND Other Writings*. Puducherry: Sri Aurobindo Ashram, 1971.

Ramana Maharshi

Brunton, Paul. *The Maharshi and His Message*. Tiruvannamalai: Sri Ramanasramam, 2007.

Cohen, S.S. *Guru Ramana*. Tiruvannamalai: Sri Ramanasramam, 1998.

Godman, David, ed. *Be As You Are: The Teachings of Sri Ramana Maharshi*. New Delhi: Penguin Books India, 1992.

Godman, David, ed. *Living by the Words of Bhagvan*. Tiruvannamalai: Sri Ramanasramam, 1999.

Osborne, Arthur. *The Teachings of Ramana Maharshi in His Own Words*. Tiruvannamalai: Sri Ramanasramam, 2010.

Osborne, Arthur. *Ramana Maharshi and the Path of Self-knowledge*. Tiruvannamalai: Sri Ramanasramam, 1970.

Nisargadatta Maharaj

Dunn, Jean, ed. *Consciousness and the Absolute: The Final Talks of Sri Nisargadatta Maharaj*. Mumbai: Chetana. Published in arrangement with Acorn Press, Durham, 1994.

Godman, David. 'Remembering Nisargadatta Maharaj'. David Godman (website), 2012. https://www.davidgodman.org/remembering-nisargadatta-maharaj/. Accessed 16 October 2020.

Gogate, Shrikant and P.T. Phadol. 'Meet the Sage: Sri Nisargadatta'. Sri Nisargadatta Maharaj (website). http://sri-nisargadatta-maharaj.blogspot.com/2014/11/meet-sage-sri-nisargadatta.html. Accessed 16 October 2020.

Maharaj, Sri Nisargadatta. *I Am That*. Translated by Maurice Frydman. Mumbai: Chetana, 1987.

Narayanaswami, Vanaja. *Experiences with Nisargadatta Maharaj*. https://innerspiritualawakening.com/nisargadatta-maharaj/vanaja-stories-experiences. Accessed 30 October 2020.

Powell, Robert, ed. *The Nectar of Immortality: Sri Nisargadatta Maharaj's Discourses on the Eternal*. New Delhi: Motilal Banarsidass, 2008.

The Jains

'Acharya Shri Chandanaji'. Veerayatan (website). https:// veerayatan.org/ acharya-sri-chandanaji. Accessed 21 October 2020.

Chapple, Christopher Key. *Jainism and Ecology: Non-violence in the Web of Life*. New Delhi: Motilal Banarsidass, 2006.

Doshi, Bipin and Pankaz Hingarh. *Virchand Gandhi, a Gandhi before Gandhi*. https://jainelibrary.org/elib_master/article/230000_article_gujarati/ Virchand_R_Gandhi_A_Gandhi_before_Gandhi_249055_std.pdf. Accessed 21 October 2020.

Dundas, Paul. *The Jains*. London and New York: Routledge, 2002.

Gandhi, Virchand Raghavji. *Selected Speeches of Shri Virchand Raghavji Gandhi*. https:// www.jaina.org/resource/resmgr/vrg_documents/z_ gandhi_vr_-_selected_speec.doc. Accessed 21 October 2020.

Gandhi, Virchand Raghavji. *The Systems of Indian Philosophy: Speeches and Writings of Virchand R. Gandhi*. Edited by K.K. Dixit. Mumbai: Shri Mahavir Jain Vidyalaya Bombay, 1970.

Olcott, Henry Steel. *Old Diary Leaves 1893–96: The Only Authentic History of the Theosophical Society*. New York: Cambridge University Press, 2011.

Sangave, Vilas Adinath. *Sravana-Belagola*. New Delhi: Bharatiya Jnanpith,1981.

Shah, Natubhai. *Jainism: The World of Conquerors*. New Delhi: Motilal Banarsidass, 2004.

Shah, Raksha. 'The Valiant Jain Patriot Virchand Raghvji Gandhi'. *Jainsamaj Ahimsa Foundation*. https://www.jainsamaj. org/content. php?url=The_Valiant_Jain_Patriot-Virchand_Raghavji. Accessed 21 October 2020.

Zimmer, Heinrich. *Philosophies of India*. Edited by Joseph Campbell. London: Routledge and Kegan Paul Ltd, 1952.

Subramania Bharati

Bharati, S. Vijaya. *Subramania Bharati: Personality and Poetry*. New Delhi: Munshiram Manoharlal, 1975.

Bharati, S. Vijaya, ed. *C. Subramania Bharati's Poems*. 2013. https:// subramaniabharati.com/wp-content/uploads/2013/02/ blog-7-attachment.pdf. Accessed 21 October 2020.

'Bharati, Subramania'. *All Poetry.* https://allpoetry.com/classics/alpha/Subramania%20Bharati.

Bharati, Subramania. *Chariots of Fire: Bharathi's Poetry and Prose.* Translated by Usha Rajagopalan. New Delhi: Hachette India, 2012. Accessed 21 October 2020.

Mahadevan, P. *Subramania Bharati, Patriot and Poet: A Memoir.* Madras: Atri Publishers, 1957.

Nandakumar, Prema. *Bharati.* New Delhi: Sahitya Akademi, 1978. 'When I Think Of My People Broken Down'. *Journal of South Asian Literature,* Volume 12, No. 1 (Fall–Winter 1976).

Jotirao Phule and Savitribai Phule

Dhara, Lalitha, ed. *Kavya Phule, Savitri Jotirao Phule.* Mumbai: Women Development Cell, Dr. Ambedkar College of Commerce and Economics, 2012.

Gavaskar, Mahesh. 'Phule's Critique of Brahmin Power'. In *Untouchable, Dalits in Modern India*Michael, edited by S.M. Michael. Boulder: Lynne Rienner Publishers, 1999.

Guha, Ramachandra. *Makers of Modern India.* New Delhi: Penguin Books India, 2012.

Keer, Dhananjay. *Mahatma Jotirao Phooley: Father of the Indian Social Revolution.* Mumbai: Popular Prakashan, 1974.

Mani, Braj Ranjan and Pamela Sardar, eds. *A Forgotten Liberator: The Life and Struggle of Savitribai Phule.*New Delhi: Mountain Peak, 2008.

O'Hanlon, Rosalind. 'Issues of Widowhood in Colonial Western India'. In *Contesting Power: Resistance and Everyday Social Relations in South Asia,* edited by Douglas E. Haynes and Gyan Prakash. Berkeley: University of California Press, 1992.

O'Hanlon, Rosalind. *Caste, Conflict and Ideology: Mahatma Jotirao Phule and Low Caste Protest in 19th Century Western India* (revised ed.). Cambridge: Cambridge University Press, 2002.

Phule, Savitribai. *Kavya Phule.* Translated by Ujjwala Mhatre and edited by Lalitha Dhara. Mumbai: Dr. Ambedkar College of Commerce and Economics, 2012.

Bal Gangadhar Tilak

Bhagwat, A.K. and G.P. Pradhan. *Lokamanya Tilak: A Biography*. Mumbai: Jaico Publishing House, 2015.

Cashman, Richard I. *The Myth of Lokamanya Tilak and Mass Politics in Maharashtra*. Berkeley: University of California Press, 1975.

Guha, Ramachandra. *Makers of Modern India*. New Delhi: Penguin Books India, 2012.

Inamdar, N.R., ed. *Political Thought and Leadership of Lokmanya Tilak*. New Delhi: Concept Publishing Company, 1983.

Pradhan G.P. *Lokamanya Tilak*. New Delhi: National Book Trust, 1994.

Rao, Anupama. *The Caste Question: Dalits and the Politics of Modern India*. Berkeley: University of California Press, 2009.

Tahmankar, D.V. *Lokamanya Tilak: Father of Indian Unrest and Maker of Modern India*. London: John Murray, 1956.

Tilak, Lokmanya. *Shrimad Bhagwat Geeta: Geeta Rahasya*. New Delhi: Sharda Prakashan, 2014.

Rammohan Roy

Ahluwalia, Shashi and Meenakshi Ahluwalia. *Raja Rammohun Roy and the Indian Renaissance*. New Delhi: Mittal Publications, 1991.

Chandra, Rama Prasad and J.K. Majumdar. *Selections from Official Letters and Documents Relating to the Life of Raja Rammohun Roy*. New Delhi: Anmol Publications, 1987.

Crawford, S. Cromwell. *Ram Mohan Roy: Social, Political, and Religious Reform in 19th Century India*. New York: Paragon House, 1987.

Guha, Ramachandra. *Makers of Modern India*. New Delhi: Penguin Books India, 2012.

Sankhdher, Brijendra Mohan. *Rammohan Roy, the Apostle of Indian Awakening: Some Contemporary Estimates*. New Delhi: Navarang, 1989.

Rabindranath Tagore

Guha, Ramachandra. *Makers of Modern India*. New Delhi: Penguin Books India, 2012.

Dasgupta, Sanjukta and Chinmoy Guha. *Tagore: At Home in the World*. New Delhi: SAGE Publications, 2013.

Tagore, Rabindranath and Albert Einstein, 1930. 'On the Nature of Reality. Albert Einstein in Conversation with Rabindranath Tagore'. https://mast.queensu.ca/~murty/einstein_tagore.pdf. Accessed 26 October 2020.

Tagore, Rabindranath. *Collected Poems and Plays of Rabindranath Tagore*. London: Macmillan Press, 1952.

Tagore, Rabindranath. *A Tagore Reader*. Edited by A. Chakravarty. Boston: Beacon Press, 1961.

Tagore, Rabindranath. *Songs and Poems from Rabindranath Tagore*, London: East-West Publications, 1984.

Tagore, Rabindranath. *The English Writings of Rabindranath Tagore*. Edited by M.K. Ray. New Delhi: Atlantic Publishers, 2007.

Tagore, Rabindranath. *The Essential Tagore*. Edited by F. Alam and R. Chakravarty. Cambridge: Harvard University Press, 2011.

'Gurudev and His Mahatma'. *M.K. Gandhi*. 1941. https://www.mkgandhi. org/short/ev49.htm. Accessed 26 October 2020.

Mohandas Karamchand Gandhi

Chadha, Yogesh. *Gandhi: A Life*. New York: Wiley, 1997.

Fischer, Louis. *The Life of Mahatma Gandhi*. New York: Harper and Row, 1950.

Gandhi, M.K. *An Autobiography or The Story of My Experiments with Truth*. Ahmedabad: Navajivan Publishing House, 1927, 1984.

Gandhi, M.K. *What Jesus Means to Me*. Ahmedabad: Navajivan Publishing House,1959.

Gandhi, M.K. *The Collected Works of Mahatma Gandhi*, 100 Volumes. New Delhi Publications Division, 1994. https://www. gandhiserve.net/.

Gandhi, Rajmohan. *Mohandas: A True Story of a Man, His People and an Empire*. New Delhi: Viking, Penguin Books India, 2006.

Gora. *An Atheist with Gandhi*. Ahmedabad: Navajivan Publishing House, 1951.

Guha, Ramachandra. *Gandhi Before India*. New Delhi: Allan Lane, Penguin Books India, 2013.

Guha, Ramachandra. *Gandhi: The Years That Changed the World, 1914-1948*. New Delhi: Allan Lane, Penguin Books India, 2018.

Hunt, James D. *Gandhi and the Black People of South Africa. Mahatma*

Gandhi's Writings, Philosophy, Audio, Video and Photographs. https://www.mkgandhi.org/articles/jamesdhunt.htm.

Iyer, Raghavan. *The Moral and Political Thought of Mahatma Gandhi*. New Delhi: Oxford University Press, 1986. Accessed 26 October 2020.

Lindley, Mark. *How Gandhi Came to Believe Caste Must be Dismantled by Intermarriage*. Thiruvananthapuram: Centre for Gandhian Studies, University of Kerala, 1997.

Nanda, B.R. *Mahatma Gandhi: A Biography*. New Delhi: Oxford University Press, 1982.

Schouten, Jan Peter. *Jesus as Guru: The Image of Christ Among Hindus and Christians in India*. Translated by Henry and Lucy Jansen. Amsterdam and New York: Rodopi, 2008.

Ram Manohar Lohia

Arumugam, M. *Socialist Thought in India: The Contribution of Ram Manohar Lohia*. New Delhi: Sterling Publishers, 1978.

Chowdhuri, Satyabrata Rai. *Leftism in India: 1917–1947*. London and New Delhi: Palgrave Macmillan, 2008.

Gowda, Chandan. 'Many Lohias? Appropriations of Lohia in Karnataka'. *Economic and Political Weekly*, Volume XLV, No. 40 (2 October 2010).

Kelkar, Indumati. *Dr. Ram Manohar Lohia, His Life and Philosophy*. Published for Samajwadi Sahitya Sansthan. New Delhi: Anamika Publishers and Distributors, 2009.

Mishra, Girish and Braj Kumar Pandey. *Rammanohar Lohia: The Man and his Ism*. New Delhi: Eastern Books, 1992.

Mukul, Akshaya. 'The Great Indian Coalition: What the Mahagathbandan Leaders can Learn from Ram Manohar Lohia'. *Caravan Magazine*, 1 January 2019.

Sarojini Naidu

Baig, Tara Ali. *Sarojini Naidu: Portrait of a Patriot*. New Delhi: Congress Centenary Celebrations Committee, AICC (I), 1985.

Dwivedi, A.N. *Sarojini Naidu and Her Poetry*. Allahabad: Kitab Mahal, 1981.

Gupta, Indra. *India's 50 Most Illustrious Women*. Second edition. New Delhi: Icon Publications, 2004.

King, Bruce. *Modern Indian Poetry in English*. New Delhi: Oxford University Press, 1987.

Mathur, O.P. *The Immortal Bird: Perspectives on Sarojini Naidu*. Edited by K.K. Sharma. Ghaziabad: Vimal Prakashan, 1989.

Mokashi-Punekar, Shanker. 'A Note on Sarojini Naidu'. In *Indian Writing in English*, edited by M.K. Naik. Dharwar: Karnatak, University, 1968.

Naidu, Sarojini. *Sarojini Naidu: Selected Poetry and Prose*. New Delhi: Rupa Publications, 2010.

Naidu, Sarojini. *Speeches and Writings of Sarojini Naidu*. Forgotten Books, 2018.

Naik, M.K. *A History of Indian English Literature*. Dharwar: Karnatak Press, 1982.

Nair, K.R. Ramachandran. *Three Indo-Anglian Poets: Henry Derozio, Toru Dutt, and Sarojini Naidu*. New Delhi: Sterling Publishers, 1987.

Narsimhaiah, C.D. *The Swan and the Eagle*. Shimla: Indian Institute of Advanced Study, 1969.

Rajyalakshmi, P.V. *The Lyric Spring: A Study of the Poetry of Sarojini Naidu*. New Delhi: Abhinav Publications, 1977.

Birsa Munda

Singh, Kumar Suresh. *Birsa Munda and His Movement 1874–1901: A Study of a Millenarian Movement in Chotanagpur*. New Delhi: Oxford University Press, 1983.

Singh, Kumar Suresh. *Birsa Munda (1872–1900)*. New Delhi: National Book Trust, 2002.

Bhimrao Ramji Ambedkar

Das, Bhagwan, ed. *Thus Spoke Ambedkar*, 4 Volumes. Bangalore: Ambedkar Sahitya Prakashana, Ambedkar Memorial Society, 1980.

Keer, Dhananjay. *Dr. Ambedkar: Life and Mission*. Mumbai: Popular Prakashan, 1961.

Kuber, W. N. *Dr. Ambedkar: A Critical Study*. New Delhi: People's Publishing House, 1973.

Mahar, J. Michael, ed. *The Untouchables in Contemporary India*. Jaipur: Rawat Publications, 1998.

Nagaraj, D.R. *The Flaming Feet and Other Essays: The Dalit Movement in India*. Edited by Prithvi Datta Chandra Shobhi. Ranikhet: Permanent Black, 2010.

Pilchik, Terry. *Jai Bhim! Dispatches from a Peaceful Revolution*. Glasgow: Windhorse Publication with Parallax Press, 1988.

Robin, Jeanette. *Dr. Ambedkar and His Movement*. Hyderabad: Dr. Ambedkar Publication Society, 1980.

Zelliot, Eleanor. *Gandhi and Ambedkar: A Study in Leadership*. Tuscon: University of Arizona Press, 1972.

E.V. Ramaswami

Chand, Mool. *The Bahujan and Their Movement*. New Delhi: Bahujan Publication Trust, 1992.

Diehl, Anita. *E.V. Ramaswami Naicker-Periar: A Study of the Influence of a Personality in Contemporary South India*. Sweden: Scandinavian University Books, 1977.

Dirks, Nicholas B. *Castes of Mind: Colonialism and the Making of Modern India*. Princeton, NJ: Princeton University Press, 2001.

Gopalakrishnan, G.P. *Periyar: Father of the Tamil Race*. Chennai: Emerald Publishers, 1991.

Mani, Braj Ranjan. *Debrahmanising History: Dominance and Resistance in Indian Society*. New Delhi: Manohar, 2005.

Omvedt, Gail. *Dalit Visions*. New Delhi: Oscar Publications, 2006.

Saraswathi, S. *Towards Self-Respect*. Chennai: Institute of South Indian Studies, 2004.

Veeramani, K. *Periyar on Women's Rights*. Chennai: Emerald Publishers, 1992.

Veeramani, K. *Collected Works of Periyar E.V.R.* Chennai: The Periyar Self-Respect Propaganda Institution, 2005.

Asghar Ali Engineer

Engineer, Asghar Ali. *The Rights of Women in Islam*. New Dawn Press Group, 2004.

Engineer, Asghar Ali. *A Living Faith: My Quest for Peace, Harmony and Social Change*. New Delhi: Orient Blackswan, 2012.

Institute of Islamic Studies (IIS). *Centre for Study of Society and Secularism.* https://csss-isla.com/institute-of-islamic- studies-iis/. Accessed 26 October 2020.

Sikand, Yoginder. 'Asghar Ali Engineer's Quest for an Islamic Theology of Peace and Religious Pluralism'. *Progressive Dawoodi Bohras.* http:// dawoodi-bohras.com/about_us/people/ engineer/quest/. Accessed 30 October 2020.

Gopi Krishna

Heehs, Peter. *Indian Religions: A Historical Reader of Spiritual Expression and Experience.* New York: New York University Press, 2002.

Krishna, Gopi. *Kundalini: The Evolutionary Energy in Man.* With an Introduction by Frederic Spiegelberg and a psychological commentary by James Hillman. London: Stuart and Watkins, 1970.

Krishna, Gopi. *Kundalini: Path to Higher Consciousness.* New Delhi: Orient Paperbacks, 1976.

Krishna, Gopi. *Living with Kundalini.* Boston: Shambhala Publications, 1993.

Krishna, Gopi. *What Is Cosmic Consciousness?* Connecticut: Bethel Publishers, 2004.

Reichenberg-Ullman, Judyth and Robert Ullman. *Mystics, Masters, Saints, and Sages: Stories of Enlightenment.* Berkeley, Newburyport: Conari Press, 2001.

The Mother of Pondicherry

Collected Works of the Mother, Centenary Edition, 17 Volumes. Puducherry: Sri Aurobindo Ashram, 1978.

Das, Nilima. *Glimpses of the Mother's Life.* Puducherry: Sri Aurobindo Ashram, 1978.

Joshi, Kireet. *Sri Aurobindo and the Mother: Glimpses of Their Experiments, Experiences and Realisations.* New Delhi: The Mother's Institute of Research, in association with Motilal Banarsidass, 1996.

Mother's Agenda (1951–1973), 13 Volumes. English translation. New York: Institute for Evolutionary Research, 1979.

Satprem. *The Mind of the Cells: or Willed Mutation of Our Species.* New York: Institute for Evolutionary Research, 1982.

Satprem. *Mother or The New Species II*. Mysore: Mira Aditi Centre, 2005.

The Mother: A Short Biography. Puducherry: AuroPublications, Sri Aurobindo Society, 2014.

Words of the Mother I, II and III. Puducherry: Sri Aurobindo Ashram, 2004. http://www. collectedworksofsriaurobindo. com. Accessed 26 October 2020.

Jiddu Krishnamurti

Jayakar, Pupul. *J. Krishnamurti: A Biography*. New Delhi: Penguin Books India, 1986.

Krishnamurti, J. *Krishnamurti's Notebook*. London: Gollancz, 1976.

Krishnamurti, J. *The Awakening of Intelligence*. New Delhi: Penguin Books India, 2000.

Krishnamurti, J. *Total Freedom: The Essential Krishnamurti*. Chennai: Krishnamurti Foundation India, 2002.

Lutyens, Mary. *Krishnamurti: The Years of Awakening*. London: John Murray Ltd, 1975; Shambhala Publications, reprint edition, 1997.

Lutyens, Mary. *Krishnamurti: The Years of Fulfilment*. New York: Avon Books, 1983.

Lutyens, Mary. *Life and Death of Krishnamurti*. London: John Murray Ltd, 1990; New Delhi: Srishti Publishers and Distributors, 1999.

Rao, Mukunda. *The Other Side of Belief: Interpreting U.G. Krishnamurti*. New Delhi: Penguin Books India, 2005.

Vas, Luis S.R., ed. *The Mind of J. Krishnamurti*. Mumbai: Jaico Publishing House, 1973.

Vernon, Roland. *Star in the East: Krishnamurti, the Invention of a Messiah*. New Delhi: Penguin Books India, 2002.

U.G. Krishnamurti

Arms, Rodney, ed. *The Mystique of Enlightenment: The Unrational Ideas of a Man Called U.G.* Goa: Dinesh Vaghela, 1982.

Babu, Chandrasekhar. *Stopped in Our Tracks*, Volumes I, II and III. New Delhi: Smriti Books, 2002.

Bhatt, Mahesh. *A Taste of Life: The Last Days of U.G. Krishnamurti*. New Delhi: Penguin Books India, 2009.

Kelker, Shanta. *The Sage and the House Wife*. Bangalore: Sowmya Publishers, 1990.

Brawley, Louis. *Goner: The Final Travels of U.G. Krishnamurti*. Salisbury: Non-Duality Press, 2011

Moorty, Narayana, ed. *Thought is Your Enemy: Conversations with U.G. Krishnamurti*. New Delhi: Smriti Books, 2002.

Newland, Terry, ed. *Mind is a Myth: Disquieting Conversations with the Man called UG*. New Delhi: Dinesh Publications, 1988.

Rao, Mukunda. *The Other Side of Belief: Interpreting U.G. Krishnamurti*. New Delhi: Penguin Books India, 2005.

The Biology of Enlightenment: Early Conversations of U.G. Krishnamurti with Friends after He Came into the Natural State (1967–71). Edited and with an Introduction by Mukunda Rao. Noida: HarperCollins, 2010.

The Penguin U.G. Krishnamurti Reader. Edited with an Introduction by Mukunda Rao. New Delhi: Penguin Books India, 2007.

The Vaswanis

Bhavnani, Nandita. *The Making of Exile: Sindhi Hindus and the Partition of India*. Chennai: Tranquebar Press, 2014.

Rajendran, Abhilash. 'Dada J.P. Vaswani Quotes: A Collection of 100 Quotes of J.P. Vaswani'. *Hindu Blog*. https:// www.hindu-blog. com/2018/11/dada-j-p-vaswani-quotes-collection-of. html. Accessed 11 November 2020.

Sadhu Vaswani Mission Official Website. https:// www.sadhuvaswani. org/. Accessed 2 November 2020.

Vaswani, Dada J.P. *His Life and Teachings*. New Delhi: Sterling Publishers, 2002.

Vaswani, J.P. *Sadhu Vaswani: His Life and Teachings*. New Delhi: Sterling Publishers, 2002.

Vaswani, J.P. *Many Paths: One Goal*. Pune: Gita Publishing House, 2010.

Jesus in India

Alpion, Gezim. *Mother Teresa: Saint or Celebrity?* London: Routledge Press, 2007.

Ascent to the Depth of the Heart: The Spiritual Diary (1948–1973) of Swami Abhishiktananda. New Delhi: ISPCK, 1998.

Baum, Wilhelm and Dietmar W. Winkler. *The Church of the East: A Concise History*. London: Routledge, 2003.

Chawla, Navin. *Mother Teresa: The Authorized Biography*. Rockport: Element Books, 1996.

Clucas, Joan Graff. *Mother Teresa*. New York: Chelsea House Publications, 1988.

Collins, Paul M. *Christian Inculturation in India: Liturgy, Worship, and Society*. Aldershot: Ashgate Publishing Ltd, 2007.

Du Boulay, Shirley. *The Cave of the Heart: The Life of Swami Abhishiktananda*. Maryknoll: Orbis Books, 2005.

Goel, Sita Ram. *Catholic Ashrams: Adopting and Adapting Hindu Dharma*. New Delhi: Voice of India, 1988.

Griffiths, Bede. *Return to the Centre*. London: Fount, 1981.

Griffiths, Bede. *Bede Griffiths: Essential Writings*. Selected with an Introduction by Thomas Matus. New York: Orbis Books, 2004.

Jesudason, Savarirayan. *Ashrams, Ancient and Modern: Their Aims and Ideals*. Vellore: Sri Ramachandra Press, 1937.

Lipner, Julius. *Brahmabandhab Upadhyay: The Life and Thought of a Revolutionary*. New Delhi: Oxford University Press, 1999.

Neill, Stephen. *A History of Christian Missions*. London: Penguin Books India, 1991.

Nikhilananda, Swami. *Life of Sri Ramakrishna*. Mayawati, Uttarakhand: Advaita Ashrama, 2008.

Panikkar, Raimon. *Religion, Philosophy and Culture*. Translated by Robert Vachon. *Polylog: Forum for Intercultural Philosophy*. 2000. http://them. polylog.org/1/fpr-en.htm ISSN 1616-2943. Accessed 5 November 2020.

Pillai, Manu S. *The Courtesan, the Mahatma and the Italian Brahmin*. New Delhi: Westland Publications, 2019.

Raj, Anthony Savari. *A New Hermeneutic of Reality: Raimon Panikkar's Cosmotheandric Vision*. Peter Lang Publishing, 1998.

Rai, Raghu and Navin Chawla. *Faith and Compassion: The Life and Work of Mother Teresa*. Rockport: Element Books, 1996.

Robinson, Bob. *Christians Meeting Hindus: An Analysis and Theological Critique of the Hindu–Christian Encounter in India*. Eugene: Regnum Studies in Mission. OCMS, 2004.

Schouten, Jan Peter. *Jesus as Guru: The Image of Christ among Hindus and*

Christians in India. Translated by Henry and Lucy Jansen. Amsterdam: Rodopi, 2008.

Sebba, Anne. *Mother Teresa: Beyond the Image*. New York: Doubleday, 1997.

Shourie, Arun. *Missionaries in India: Continuities, Changes, Dilemmas*. New Delhi: Rupa Publications, 2006.

Sruthi, Rani. *The Ashram Movement in India: A Call to Engage in Dialogue with the Modern World*. Bangalore Theological Forum 46, 2014.

Taylor, Richard. *Jesus in Indian Art*. Madras: Christian Literature Society, 1975.

Terricabras, Prof. Josep-Maria. 'Laudatio of Raimon Panikkar Alemany'. Presented during the academic ceremony of Raimon Panikkar's Investiture as Doctor Honoris Causa of the University of Girona. 27 March 2008.

Trapnell, Judson B. *Bede Griffiths: A Life in Dialogue*. SUNY Series in Religious Studies. Albany: SUNY Press, 2001.